# HAWKMAN

## ENDLESS FLIGHT

**HAWKMAN: ENDLESS FLIGHT** Published by DC Comics. Cover and compilation copyright © 2003 DC Comics.
All Rights Reserved. Originally published in single magazine form in HAWKMAN 1-6 and HAWKMAN SECRET
FILES 1. Copyright © 2002 DC Comics. All Rights Reserved. All characters, their distinctive likenesses and related indi-
cia featured in this publication are trademarks of DC Comics. The stories, characters, and incidents featured in this publication are entirely fictional. DC Comics does not read or accept unsolicited submissions of ideas, stories, or artwork.

DC Comics, 1700 Broadway, New York, NY 10019
A division of Warner Bros. - An AOL Time Warner Company
Printed in Canada. First Printing.
ISBN: 1-56389-952-3
Cover illustration by Andrew Robinson.

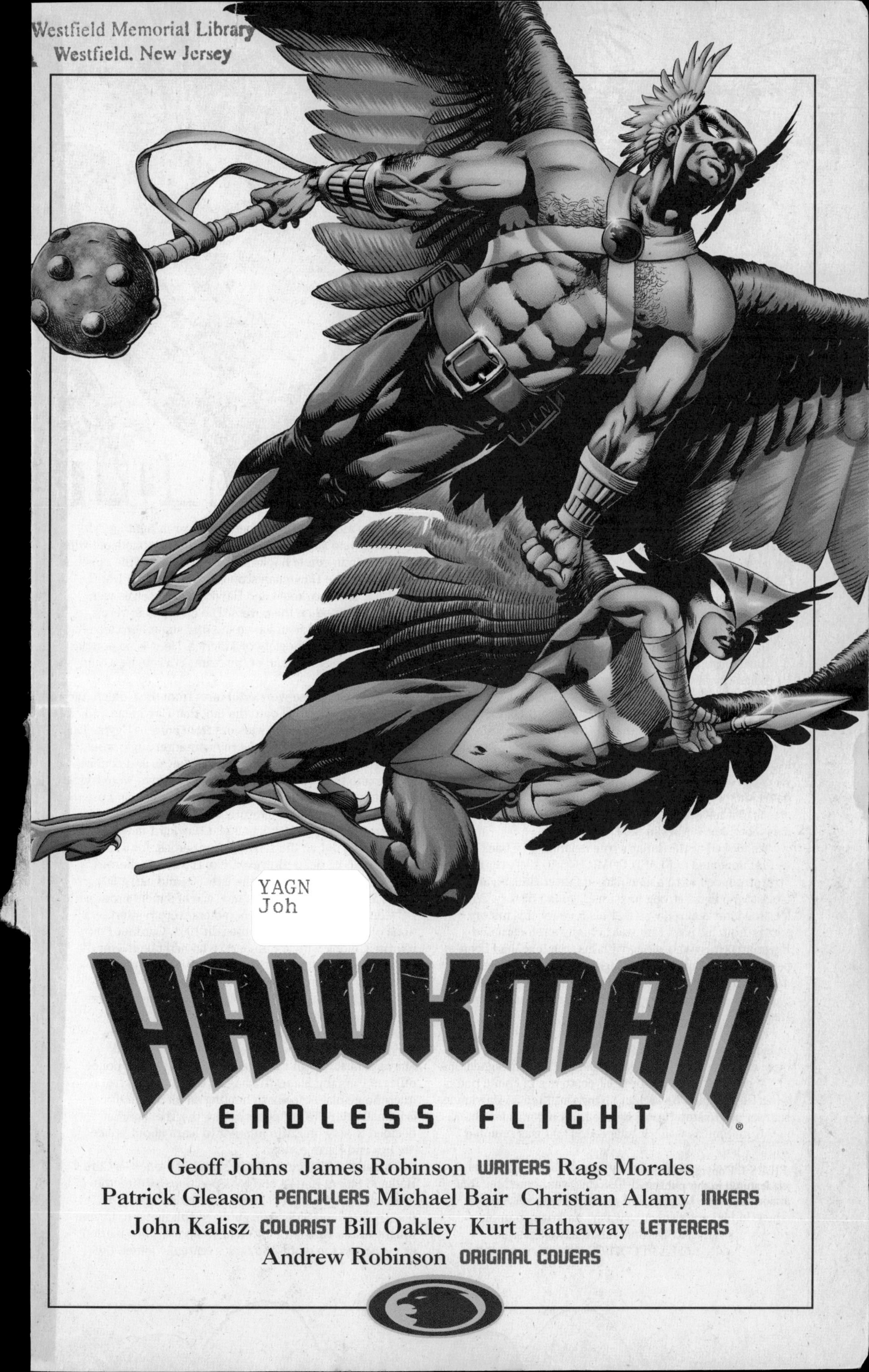



# HAWKMAN

## ENDLESS FLIGHT®

Geoff Johns James Robinson WRITERS Rags Morales
Patrick Gleason PENCILLERS Michael Bair Christian Alamy INKERS
John Kalisz COLORIST Bill Oakley Kurt Hathaway LETTERERS
Andrew Robinson ORIGINAL COVERS

# INTRODUCTION

The road to true love is a long one, full of pain, frustration, and fear. It's a shared bond that is constantly challenged, and in Hawkman's case, often severed. Beneath the weapons, cut knuckles, and brute force — at the root of it all — Hawkman is struggling to travel down this road to love.

Is love worth the trip?

Hawkman believes it is.

Hawkgirl doesn't.

When David Goyer and I began planning the reintroduction of Hawkman, it was daunting. Here was a character that had been around since 1940. Since then, there have been several different incarnations of Hawkman, different "fictional lives" if you will, over the decades. All of them had their highs and lows, and all of them had something we wanted to capture and put into the mix. So we sat down and began to make a list of the best elements, the pieces that make Hawkman into one of the greatest, and most complex, heroes in the DC Universe.

We looked at Hawkman's true beginning — back when he first appeared in FLASH COMICS #1 in 1940. Gardner Fox introduced us to a man named Carter Hall, an archaeologist who had a strong love for Egyptian history. What Mr. Hall later realized was that his love for this history sprang from his past. Hall was actually a reincarnated Egyptian prince who, along with his true love, had been betrayed and murdered by a high priest named Hath-Set. And in this lifetime, his true love had also been reborn as Shiera Sanders, and his enemy, Hath-Set, as Dr. Anton Hastor.

Hall had obtained a strange antigravity material he called Nth metal, and he used it to create a belt and harness, enabling him to fly. (Artist Dennis Nevil designed one of the greatest and most original costumes in comic books when he designed Hawkman.) Now, outfitted as Hawkman, Hall set out to stop Hastor before he could murder Shiera in this lifetime as well. He succeeded and was reunited with his true love.

Hawkman was often brutal against his enemies, as many heroes were in the 1940s. This was something that appealed to us. After all, he was from a place long ago where killing one's enemies wasn't as frowned upon — comparatively, a savage time full of savage people.

Eventually, in FLASH COMICS #24, Shiera took the identity of Hawkgirl and joined her lover in fighting evil. Hawkman and Hawkgirl became the first husband-and-wife partnership in comic books and are still one of the most prominent. The Hawkman strip ran for years in FLASH COMICS, and Hawkman and Hawkgirl themselves were often spotlighted on the covers. The characters were a success, and Hawkman joined the first super-hero team in history, the Justice Society of America. He was so popular that he became chairman of the team — a role he would keep for decades.

As we read these wonderful tales from the Golden Age of comics, we grabbed onto the fact that Hawkman and Hawkgirl were originally warriors from ancient Egypt. This was fascinating to us, and the reincarnation angle would be perfect for both reintroducing the Hawks and connecting them to their roots. It was exactly what we were trying to do: take all the previous "lives" of Hawkman and use the best aspects from each interpretation.

The Golden Age Hawkman and Hawkgirl faded, as most heroes did, in the 1950s. Super-heroes, for a time, appeared to be dead. However, like Hawkman, heroes never stay dead forever. In the late '50s and early '60s, Julius Schwartz ushered in a new age of super-heroes with DC Comics. Many of these characters were reinterpretations of DC's Golden Age heroes. In 1961, Gardner Fox returned, along with Joe Kubert (who had taken over the Golden Age Hawkman strip years earlier), to bring Hawkman to a new generation of readers.

THE BRAVE AND THE BOLD #34 featured the first appearance of Katar Hol and Shayera Thal, the new Hawkman and Hawkgirl. This time around, however, they were more science-fiction oriented. Katar and Shayera, husband and wife, were extraterrestrial police officers from the planet Thanagar. They traveled from their home planet to Earth hunting an intergalactic criminal. After the criminal's arrest, the Thanagarians decided to stay on Earth in order to learn about police tactics and Earth history.

Katar and Shayera adopted secret identities — Carter Hall and Shiera Hall — and took positions as directors of a museum in Midway City. Like their Golden Age counterparts, Carter and Shiera also utilized Nth metal to fly and fought with a variety of different weapons. They battled crime across the globe and both eventually joined the

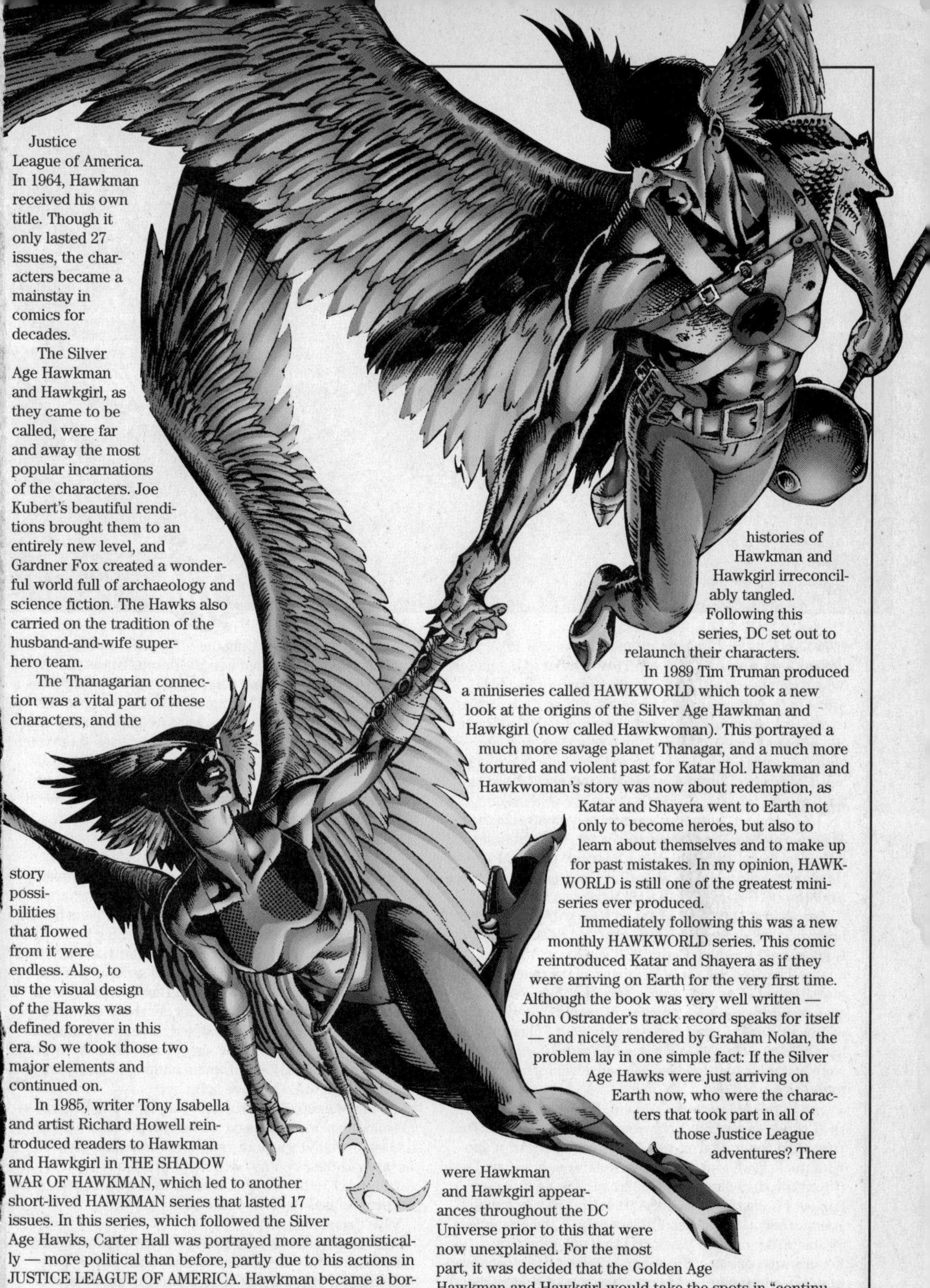

Justice League of America. In 1964, Hawkman received his own title. Though it only lasted 27 issues, the characters became a mainstay in comics for decades.

The Silver Age Hawkman and Hawkgirl, as they came to be called, were far and away the most popular incarnations of the characters. Joe Kubert's beautiful renditions brought them to an entirely new level, and Gardner Fox created a wonderful world full of archaeology and science fiction. The Hawks also carried on the tradition of the husband-and-wife superhero team.

The Thanagarian connection was a vital part of these characters, and the story possibilities that flowed from it were endless. Also, to us the visual design of the Hawks was defined forever in this era. So we took those two major elements and continued on.

In 1985, writer Tony Isabella and artist Richard Howell reintroduced readers to Hawkman and Hawkgirl in THE SHADOW WAR OF HAWKMAN, which led to another short-lived HAWKMAN series that lasted 17 issues. In this series, which followed the Silver Age Hawks, Carter Hall was portrayed more antagonistically — more political than before, partly due to his actions in JUSTICE LEAGUE OF AMERICA. Hawkman became a borderline fascist, as characterized by fellow JLA member Green Arrow, a Carter Hall that had a hard time relating to people, that others were skeptical of. We took this element and moved on.

In the same year as THE SHADOW WAR, the face of DC Comics changed forever with the release of the 12-issue maxiseries CRISIS ON INFINITE EARTHS. Created to simplify the DC Universe, CRISIS unfortunately also left the histories of Hawkman and Hawkgirl irreconcilably tangled. Following this series, DC set out to relaunch their characters.

In 1989 Tim Truman produced a miniseries called HAWKWORLD which took a new look at the origins of the Silver Age Hawkman and Hawkgirl (now called Hawkwoman). This portrayed a much more savage planet Thanagar, and a much more tortured and violent past for Katar Hol. Hawkman and Hawkwoman's story was now about redemption, as Katar and Shayera went to Earth not only to become heroes, but also to learn about themselves and to make up for past mistakes. In my opinion, HAWKWORLD is still one of the greatest miniseries ever produced.

Immediately following this was a new monthly HAWKWORLD series. This comic reintroduced Katar and Shayera as if they were arriving on Earth for the very first time. Although the book was very well written — John Ostrander's track record speaks for itself — and nicely rendered by Graham Nolan, the problem lay in one simple fact: If the Silver Age Hawks were just arriving on Earth now, who were the characters that took part in all of those Justice League adventures? There were Hawkman and Hawkgirl appearances throughout the DC Universe prior to this that were now unexplained. For the most part, it was decided that the Golden Age Hawkman and Hawkgirl would take the spots in "continuity" that the Silver Age Hawks once held. It was now said that they left the Justice Society to help train the League. Although this seemed to work, readers were really being told that the greatest Hawkman run in history never happened — and there were still a few holes in the history. All tough to swallow, even with the sugar of a wonderful HAWKWORLD series that lasted for 32 issues.

When HAWKWORLD began to lag, it was rebooted as

HAWKMAN by Ostrander and Jan Duursema in 1993. This time around, however, Shayera Thal was out of the picture. Now a simple cop in Detroit, Katar Hol continued his prowl in the skies above Chicago. Searching for a way to revive Hawkman further, Ostrander eventually had Katar Hol possessed by a mythical Hawk-being and then merged with the Golden Age Hawkman and Hawkgirl into one new Hawkman. The Golden Age Hawkgirl was killed in the process.

Unfortunately, this scenario was very confusing to explain to readers, and eventually it was thought best to retire Hawkman for awhile. The "merged" mythical Hawkman ventured to another dimension and disappeared from the DC Universe. HAWKMAN lasted 33 issues.

Looking at HAWKWORLD and HAWKMAN, David and I both really enjoyed Ostrander's idea that the original Golden Age Hawkman Carter Hall and his wife Shiera were not reincarnated just once, but many, many times, lifetime after lifetime — as was their enemy, Hath-Set. Ostrander also introduced several Egyptian elements that we gravitated towards. And it was apparent to us that Thanagar would have to play a big role in whoever Hawkman was. There were just too many good stories and adventures in the future to leave it out.

All of this led us to the present. For seven years the DCU had been without a Hawkman. Though Shayera Thal was still a cop in Detroit, she hadn't been seen in years. With the help of co-writer James Robinson, however, David Goyer introduced a new Hawkgirl into the new Justice Society of America series, JSA. Hawkgirl was a troubled young woman named Kendra Saunders — the grandniece of Shiera, the original Hawkgirl. Although reluctant, Kendra was convinced by her grandfather, the great adventurer Speed Saunders, to take on the role of Hawkgirl and train with the JSA.

In truth, David and James had planted the seeds for the return of Hawkman. Kendra Saunders was the next reincarnation of Shiera, the Golden Age Hawkgirl. In JSA #22, David and I began to reveal the updated origins of Hawkman. Without violating any continuity that was still intact, we did our best to weave the elements we pulled together into a new look at Hawkman.

In ancient Egypt, during the reign of Ramses II, a Thanagarian ship crashed into the desert. It was discovered by Prince Khufu and Chay-Ara. Aboard the ship was a strange material called Nth metal, which gave them the ability to float on air as if they were weightless. However, the High Priest of Hath-Set cut the lovers' lives short when he killed them with a dagger forged from the Nth metal.

For some unknown reasons — mystical, or perhaps having to do with the strange properties of the Nth metal — Khufu and Chay-Ara were reborn, again and again, destined to meet one another and fall in love.

Today, Kendra Saunders has the soul of Chay-Ara inside her, but no memories of her past lives. However, when she is summoned to Thanagar to help return their champion, Hawkman, to them, Kendra rediscovers her past connections to the Hawkman legacy. Reaching into a mystic portal, Kendra brings the original Carter Hall back from the dimension he was pulled into, now separated from Katar Hol, who gave his life so that Carter could return.

After returning to Earth, Carter, aware of all of his past lives, tells Kendra they are destined to be lovers. Kendra asks him, "Do you know how creepy that sounds?" Without her past memories, Kendra wants nothing to do with a man attempting to force his love upon her.

So to sum up, Hawkman and Hawkgirl utilize a material from the planet Thanagar called Nth metal to fly. They are reincarnated warriors, reborn lifetime after lifetime because of their contact with this Nth metal, destined to fall in love... until now. For the first time in centuries, one of them refuses the love of the other.

It's that simple.

And that leads us to this series of HAWKMAN, beautifully rendered by the next great Hawkman artists, Rags Morales and Michael Bair — as powerful and elegant as Kubert, with their own sense of style and force.

Like love, Hawkman is a character that will never die. So here's to a long life for HAKWMAN and to finding your way down the road to true love.

Thanks for reading.

— Geoff Johns
November 12, 2002

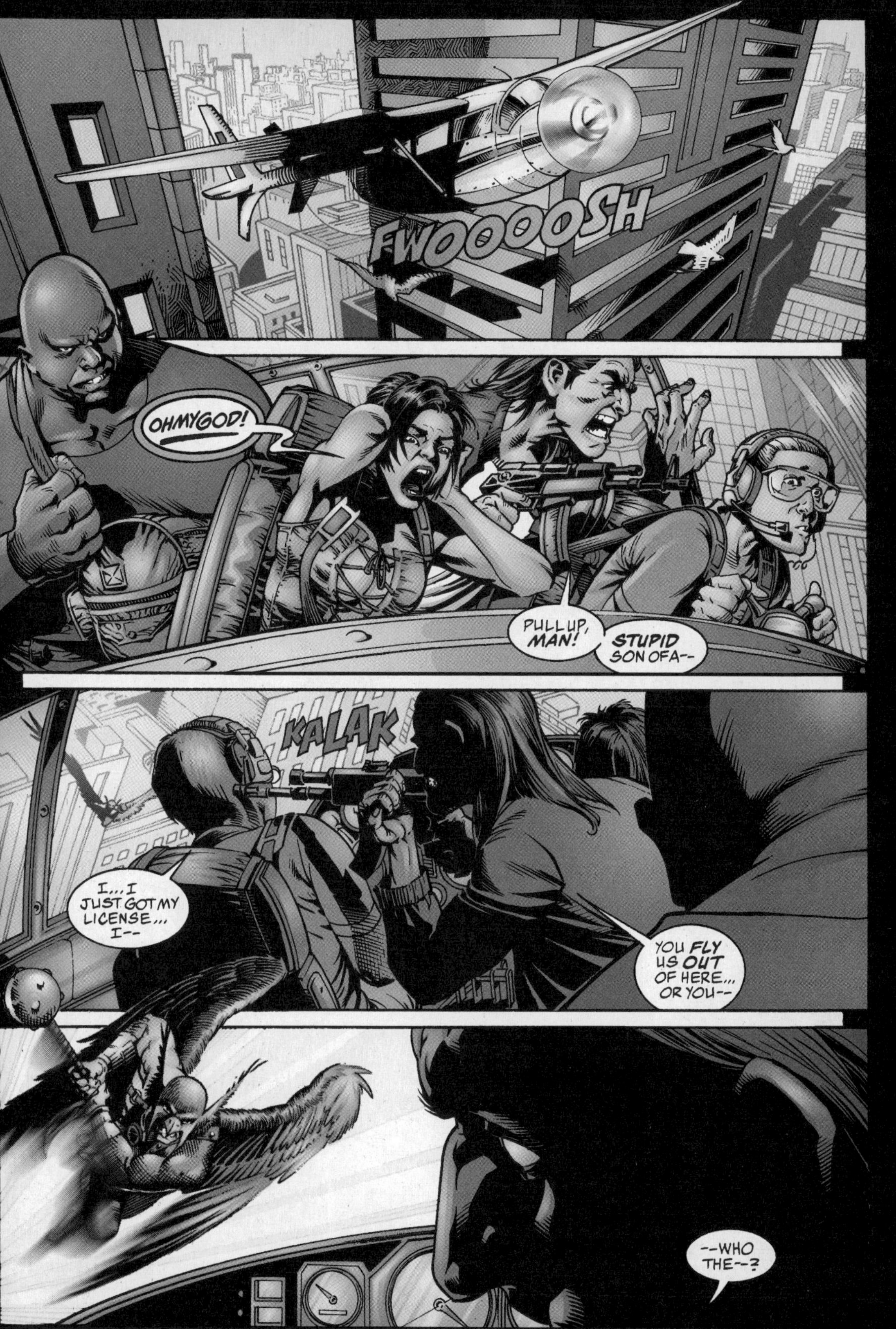
FWOOOOSH
OHMYGOD!
PULL UP, MAN!
STUPID SON OFA--
KALAK
I... I JUST GOT MY LICENSE... I--
YOU FLY US OUT OF HERE... OR YOU--
--WHO THE--?

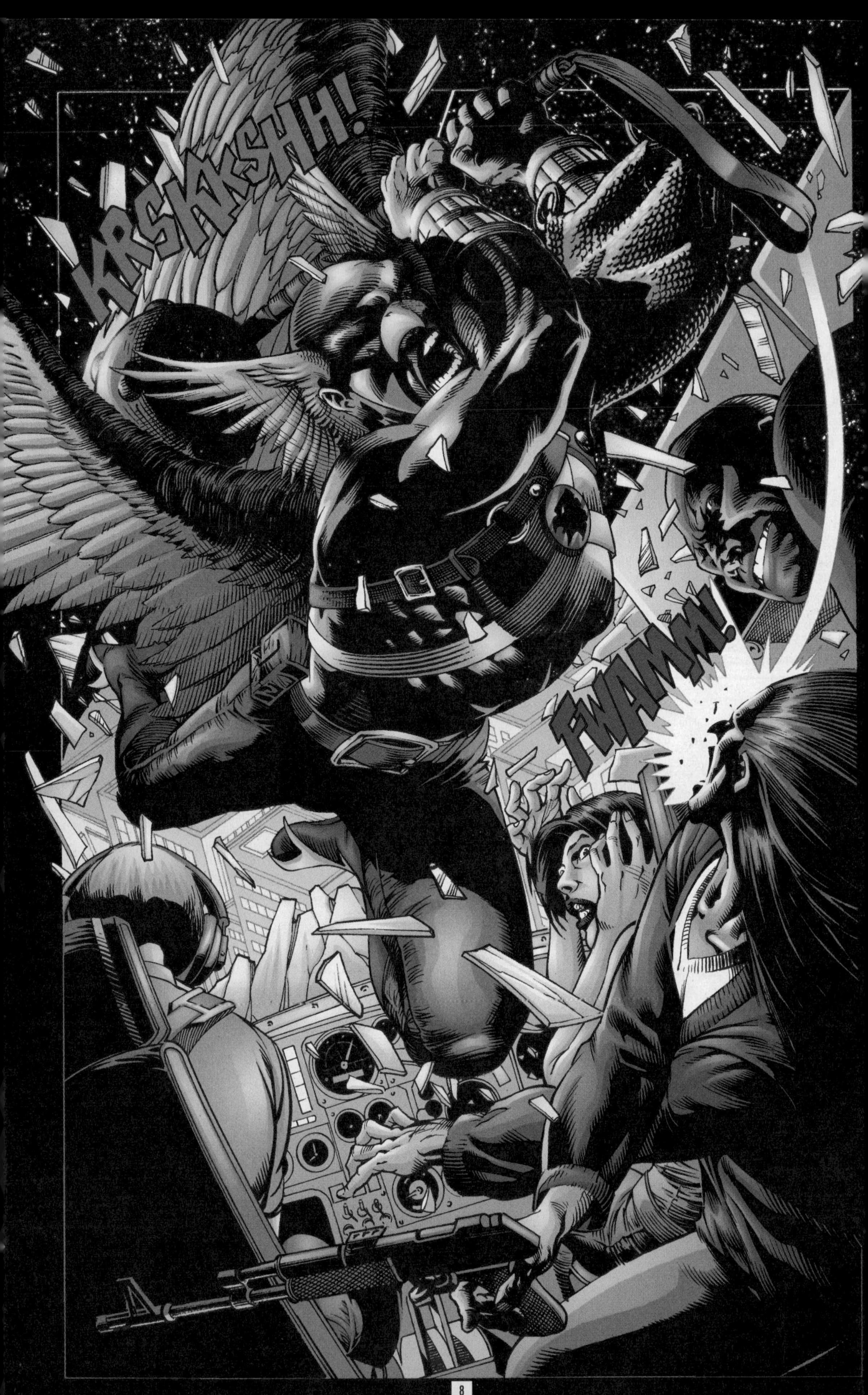
KRSKKSHH!
FWAMM!

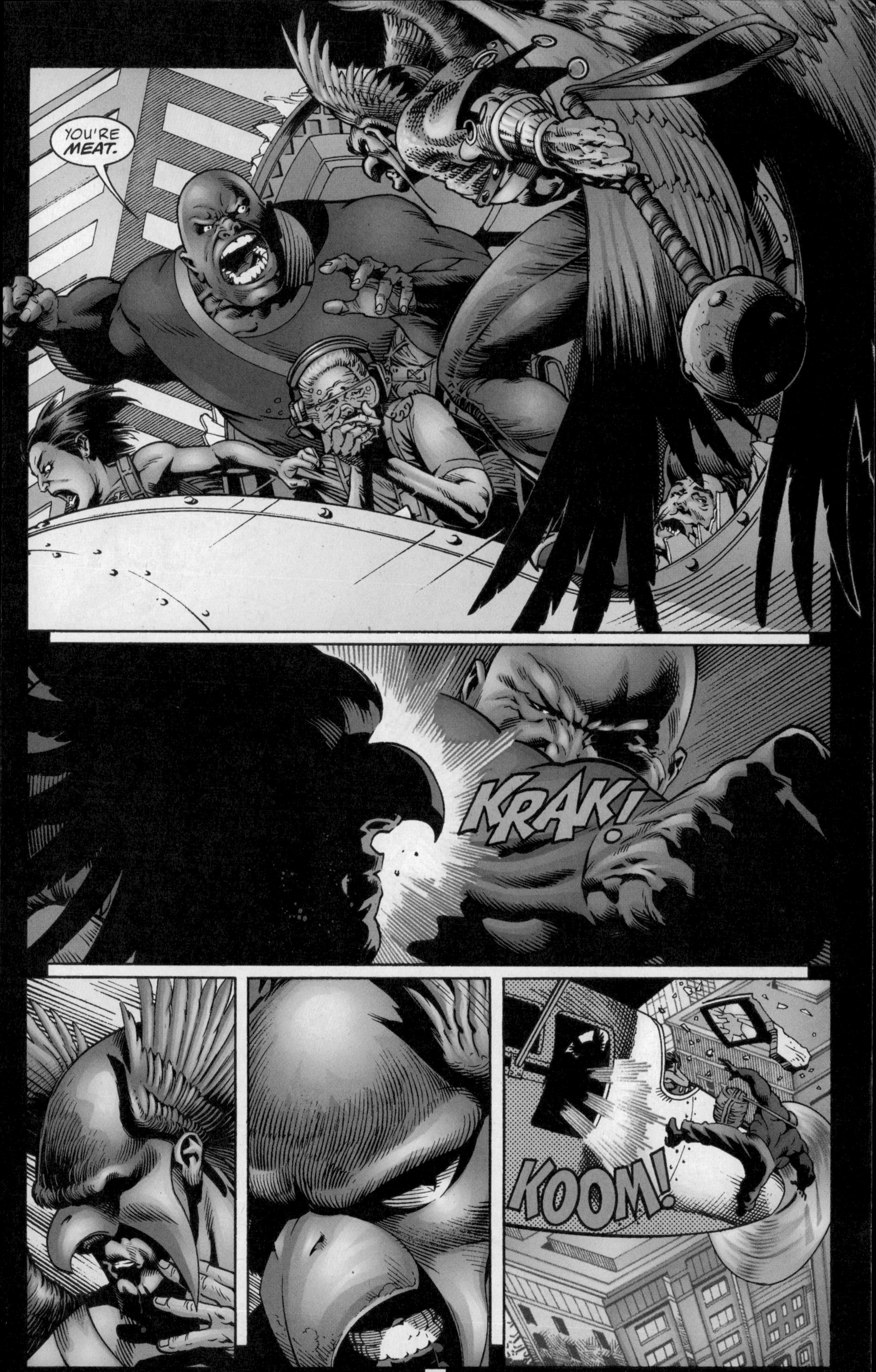
YOU'RE MEAT.
KRAK!
KOOM!

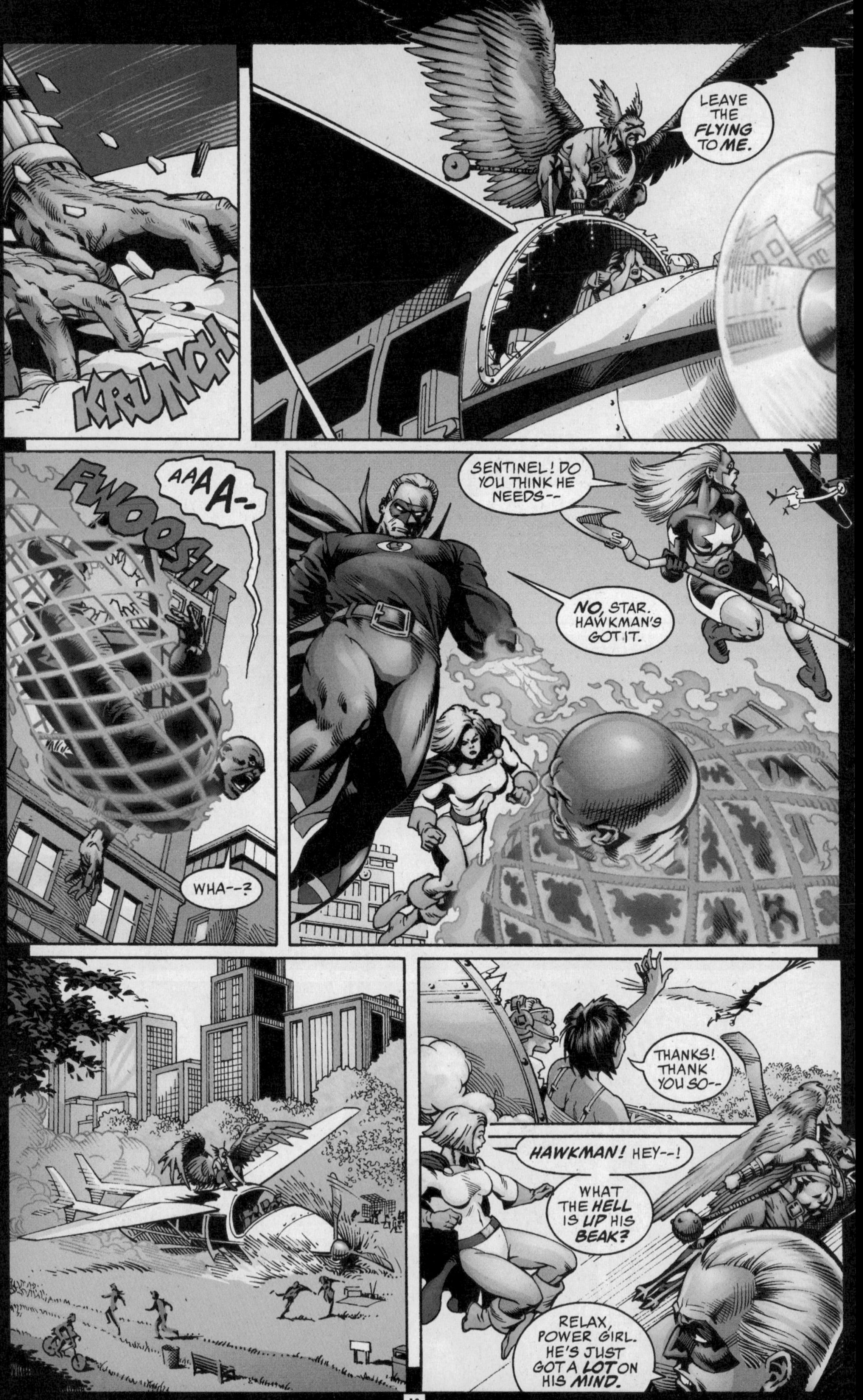
KRUNCH
LEAVE THE FLYING TO ME.
FWOOSH
AAAA--
WHA--?
SENTINEL! DO YOU THINK HE NEEDS--
NO, STAR. HAWKMAN'S GOT IT.
THANKS! THANK YOU SO--
HAWKMAN! HEY--!
WHAT THE HELL IS UP HIS BEAK?
RELAX, POWER GIRL. HE'S JUST GOT A LOT ON HIS MIND.

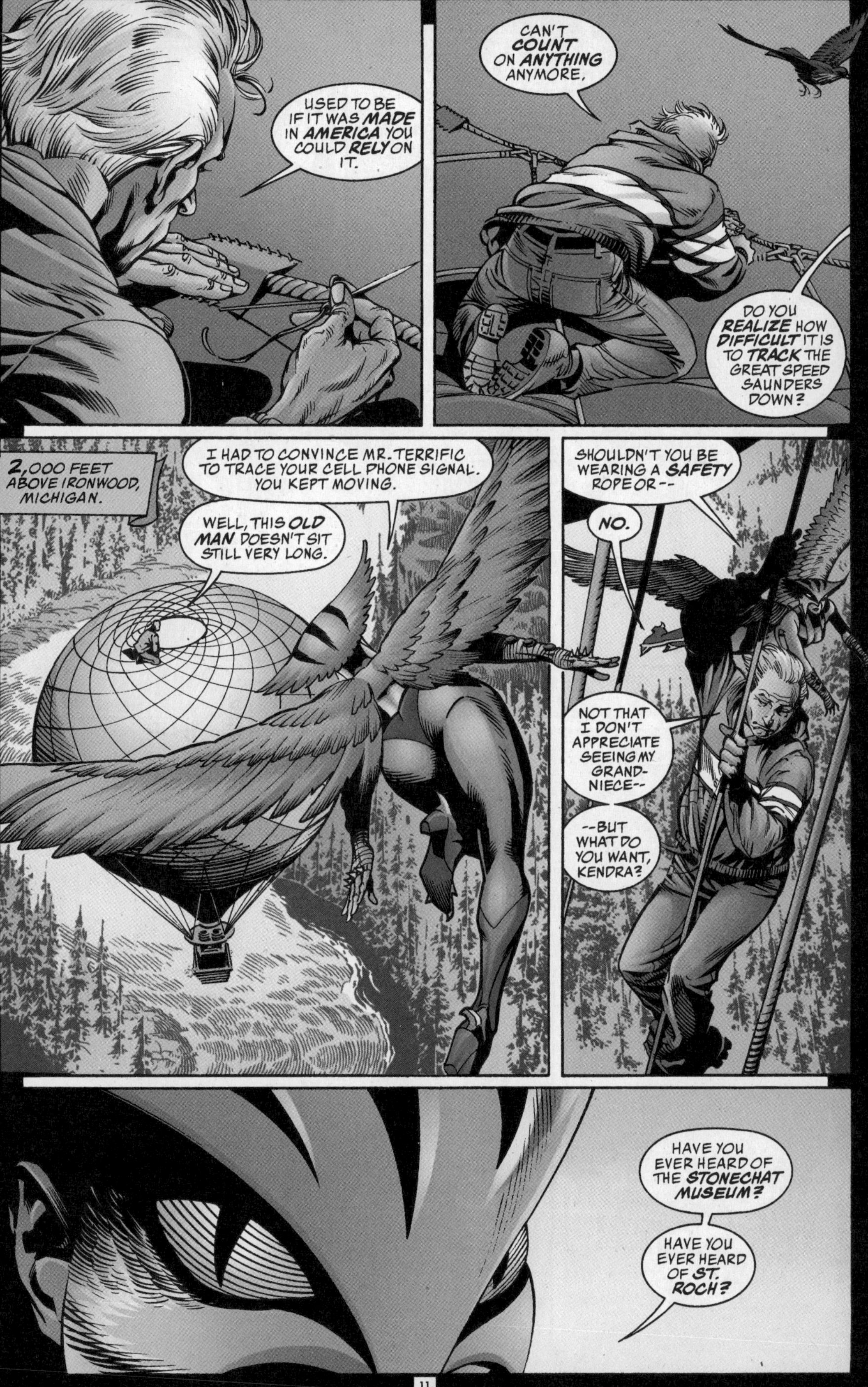
USED TO BE IF IT WAS MADE IN AMERICA YOU COULD RELY ON IT.
CAN'T COUNT ON ANYTHING ANYMORE.
DO YOU REALIZE HOW DIFFICULT IT IS TO TRACK THE GREAT SPEED SAUNDERS DOWN?
2,000 FEET ABOVE IRONWOOD, MICHIGAN.
I HAD TO CONVINCE MR. TERRIFIC TO TRACE YOUR CELL PHONE SIGNAL. YOU KEPT MOVING.
WELL, THIS OLD MAN DOESN'T SIT STILL VERY LONG.
SHOULDN'T YOU BE WEARING A SAFETY ROPE OR--
NO.
NOT THAT I DON'T APPRECIATE SEEING MY GRAND-NIECE--
--BUT WHAT DO YOU WANT, KENDRA?
HAVE YOU EVER HEARD OF THE STONECHAT MUSEUM?
HAVE YOU EVER HEARD OF ST. ROCH?

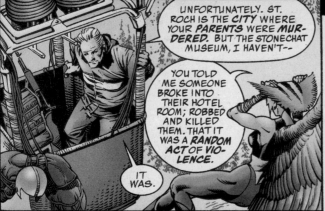

UNFORTUNATELY. ST. ROCH IS THE *CITY* WHERE YOUR *PARENTS* WERE *MURDERED.* BUT THE STONECHAT MUSEUM, I HAVEN'T--

YOU TOLD ME SOMEONE BROKE INTO THEIR HOTEL ROOM; ROBBED AND KILLED THEM. THAT IT WAS A *RANDOM ACT OF VIOLENCE.*

IT WAS.

NO.

I DON'T THINK SO.

WHAT ARE YOU TALKING ABOUT?

YOU KEPT THE *TRUTH* FROM ME *BEFORE,* SPEED. THAT I'VE LIVED... MANY LIVES. AS AN *EGYPTIAN PRINCESS.* SHIERA SAUNDERS, THE *ORIGINAL* HAWKGIRL.

I *NEED* TO *KNOW* IF THERE'S ANYTHING YOU *HAVEN'T* TOLD ME ABOUT MY PARENTS' DEATH.

YOU KNOW AS MUCH AS I DO, KENDRA. NOW WHAT HAVE YOU FOUND THAT--

GOOD ENOUGH.

NICE SEEING YOU, UNCLE SPEED.

WAIT. YOU SHOULD BRING CARTER IN ON THIS. HE CAN HELP Y--

NO.

I DON'T *WANT* HIS HELP. *PROMISE* ME YOU WON'T CONTACT HAWKMAN.

... I WON'T.

HELLO, CARTER?

I REMEMBER...

I REMEMBER THE *FIRST* TIME I CAME HERE.

*YEARS* AGO. WITH SHIERA. MY *WIFE*.

I MISS HER.

THE SUN IS SETTING BUT IT'S STILL SO *HOT. HUMID.*

A CITY LIKE THIS,...SO MOIST EVERY MOVEMENT IS LABORED... LIFE HERE SHOULD GO SLOW. AND YET...

...THERE'S SUCH A *TENSION* IN THE AIR. ELECTRIC.

IT'S A CITY CULTURALLY AND POLITICALLY *DIVIDED*. THEY SAY *NOTHING* CAN GET DONE HERE UNLESS IT'S DONE *DIRTY*.

VOTE **YES!** ON PROPOSITION 1

THE LAST U.S. PRESIDENTIAL RACE WAS AN ANOMALY. ALMOST *TOO CLOSE* TO CALL.

IT'S LIKE THAT *EVERY* ELECTION HERE.

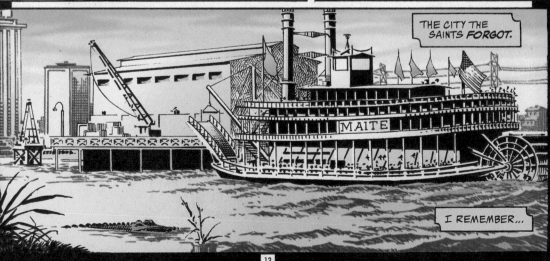

THE CITY THE SAINTS *FORGOT*.

I REMEMBER...

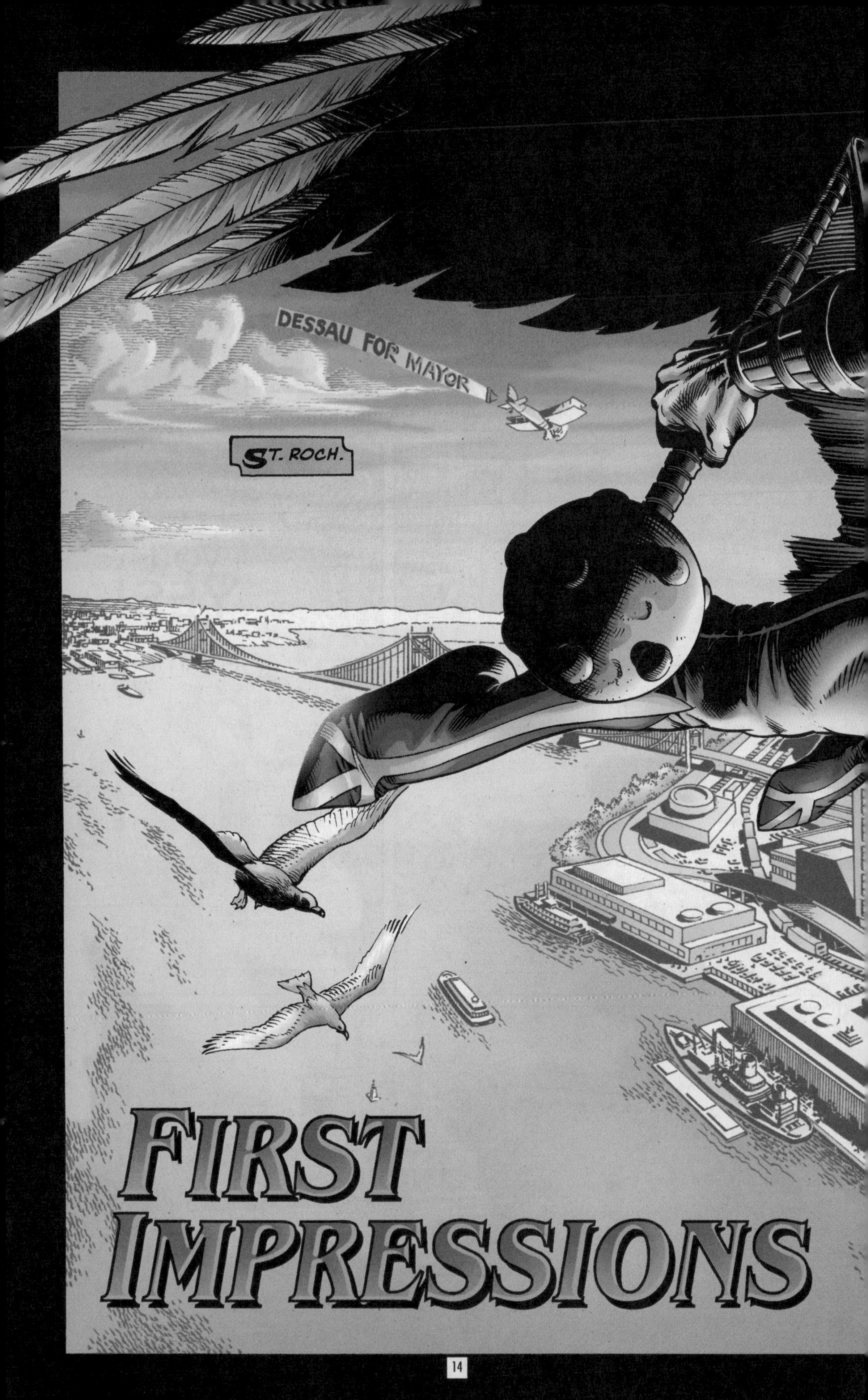
DESSAU FOR MAYOR
ST. ROCH.
FIRST IMPRESSIONS

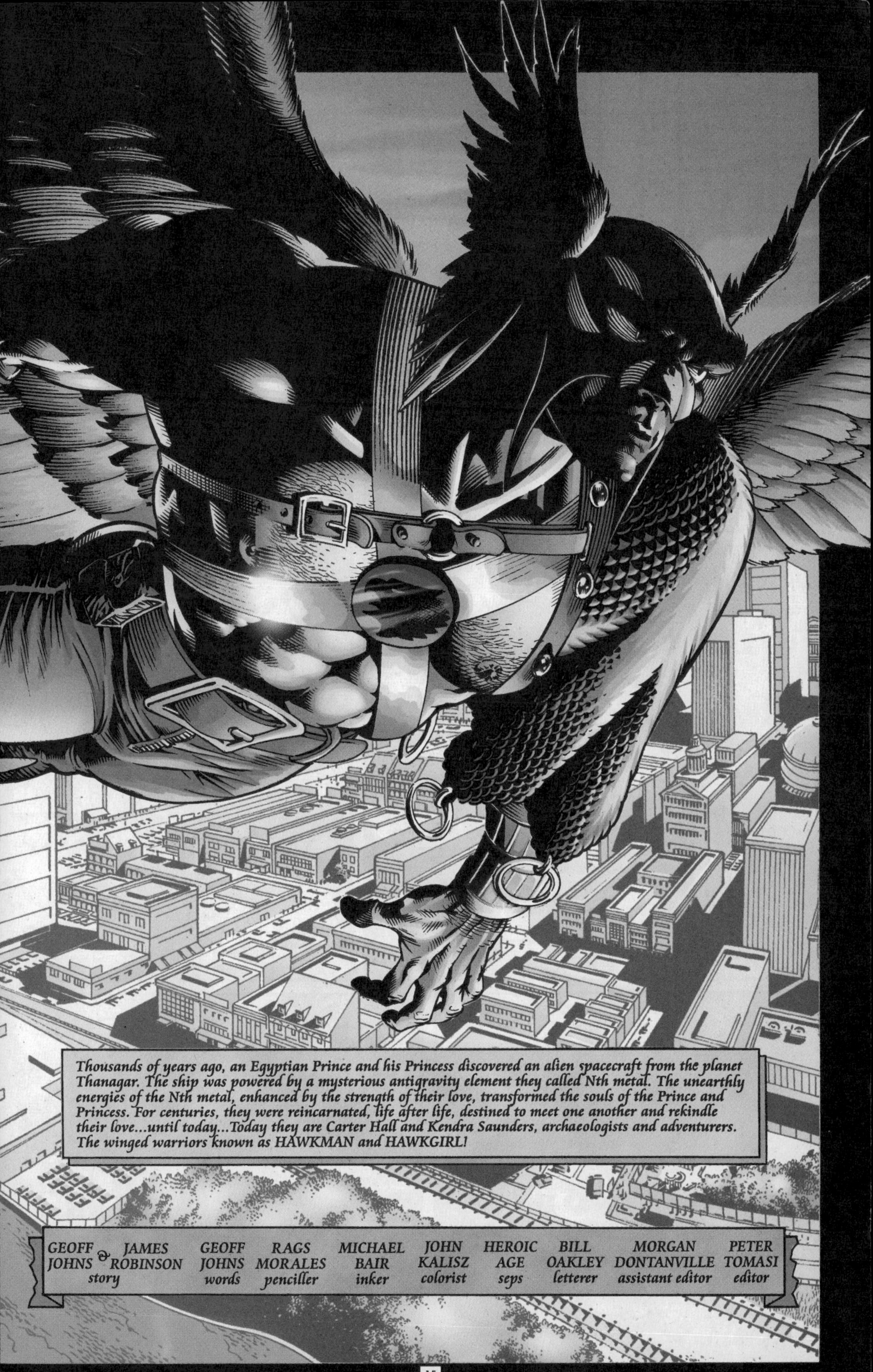
Thousands of years ago, an Egyptian Prince and his Princess discovered an alien spacecraft from the planet Thanagar. The ship was powered by a mysterious antigravity element they called Nth metal. The unearthly energies of the Nth metal, enhanced by the strength of their love, transformed the souls of the Prince and Princess. For centuries, they were reincarnated, life after life, destined to meet one another and rekindle their love...until today...Today they are Carter Hall and Kendra Saunders, archaeologists and adventurers. The winged warriors known as HAWKMAN and HAWKGIRL!
GEOFF JOHNS & JAMES ROBINSON story
GEOFF JOHNS words
RAGS MORALES penciller
MICHAEL BAIR inker
JOHN KALISZ colorist
HEROIC AGE seps
BILL OAKLEY letterer
MORGAN DONTANVILLE assistant editor
PETER TOMASI editor

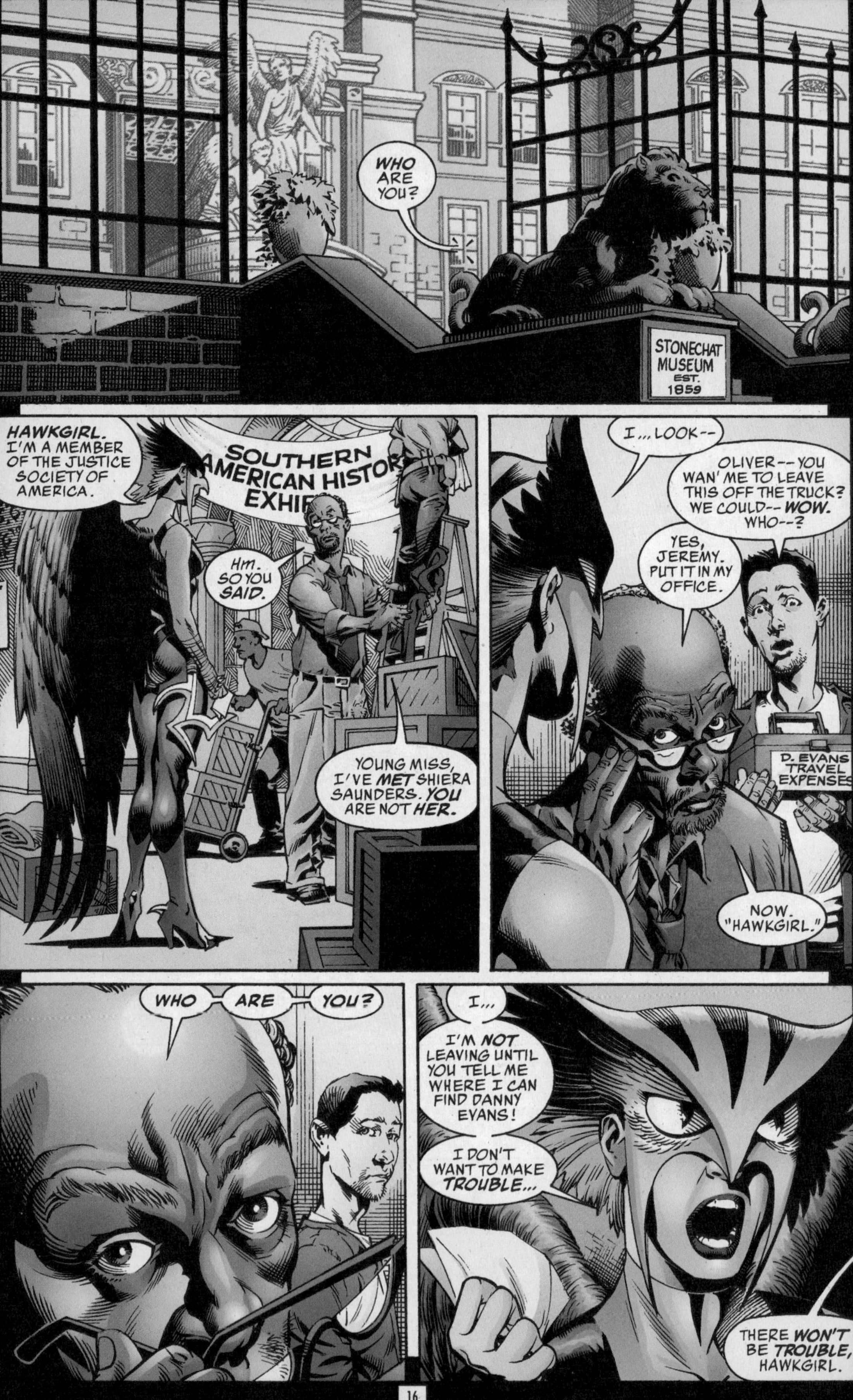
WHO ARE YOU?
STONECHAT MUSEUM EST. 1859
HAWKGIRL. I'M A MEMBER OF THE JUSTICE SOCIETY OF AMERICA.
SOUTHERN AMERICAN HISTOR EXHIB
HM. SO YOU SAID.
YOUNG MISS, I'VE MET SHIERA SAUNDERS. YOU ARE NOT HER.
I... LOOK--
OLIVER--YOU WAN' ME TO LEAVE THIS OFF THE TRUCK? WE COULD-- WOW. WHO--?
YES, JEREMY. PUT IT IN MY OFFICE.
D. EVANS TRAVEL EXPENSES
NOW. "HAWKGIRL."
WHO ARE YOU?
I...
I'M NOT LEAVING UNTIL YOU TELL ME WHERE I CAN FIND DANNY EVANS!
I DON'T WANT TO MAKE TROUBLE...
THERE WON'T BE TROUBLE, HAWKGIRL.

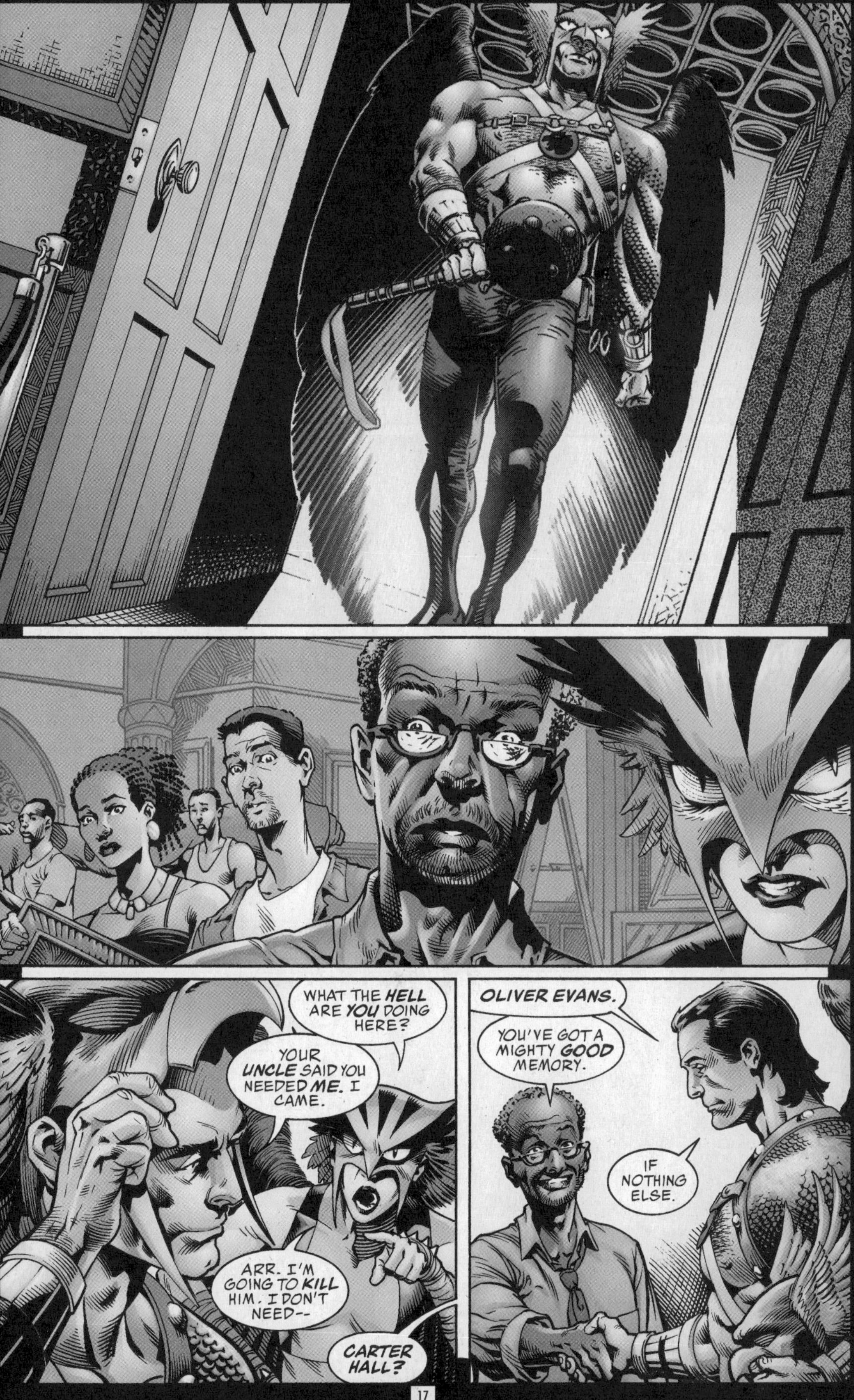
WHAT THE HELL ARE YOU DOING HERE?
YOUR UNCLE SAID YOU NEEDED ME. I CAME.
ARR. I'M GOING TO KILL HIM. I DON'T NEED--
CARTER HALL?
OLIVER EVANS.
YOU'VE GOT A MIGHTY GOOD MEMORY.
IF NOTHING ELSE.

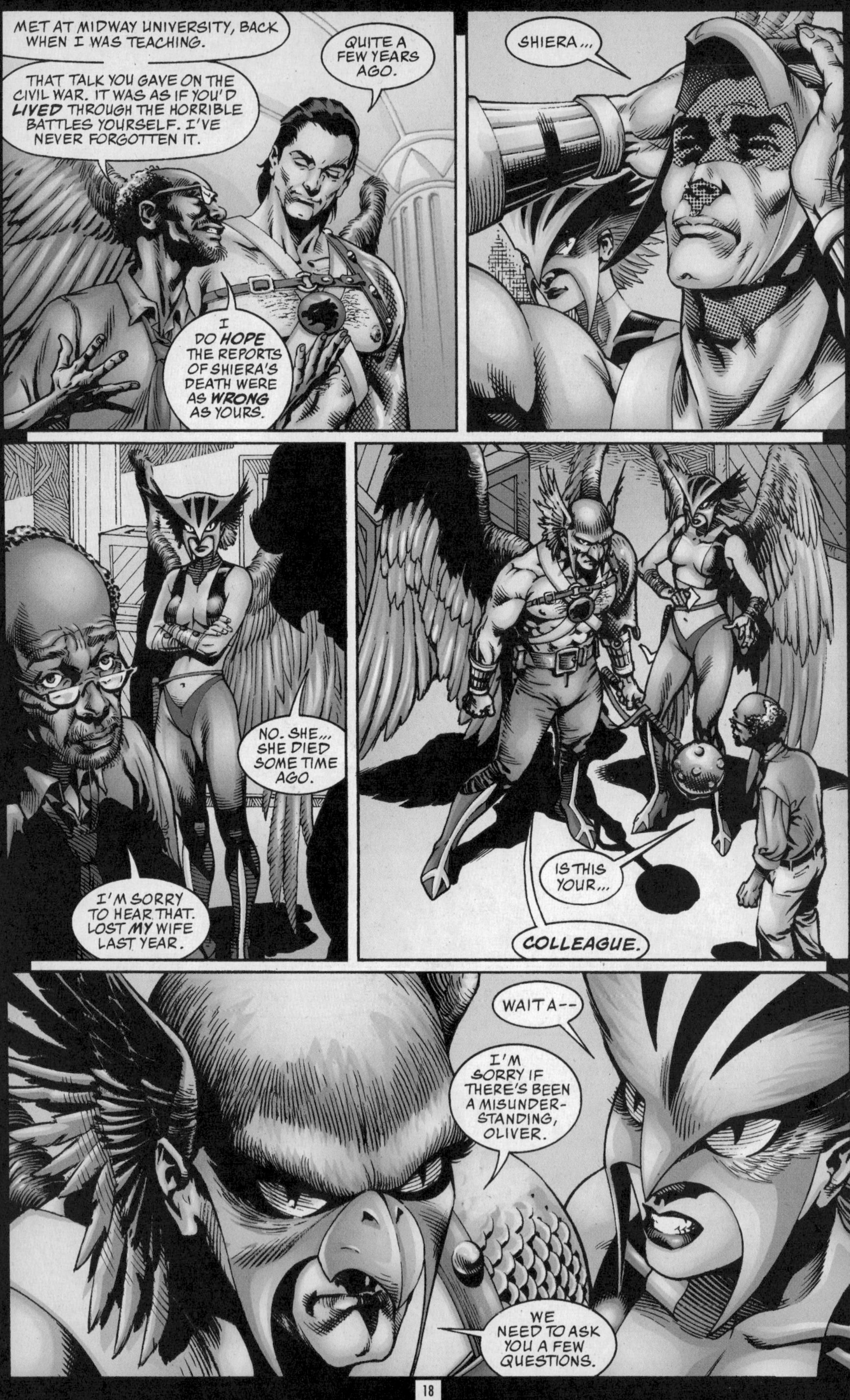
MET AT MIDWAY UNIVERSITY, BACK WHEN I WAS TEACHING.
THAT TALK YOU GAVE ON THE CIVIL WAR. IT WAS AS IF YOU'D LIVED THROUGH THE HORRIBLE BATTLES YOURSELF. I'VE NEVER FORGOTTEN IT.
QUITE A FEW YEARS AGO.
I DO HOPE THE REPORTS OF SHIERA'S DEATH WERE AS WRONG AS YOURS.
SHIERA...
NO. SHE... SHE DIED SOME TIME AGO.
I'M SORRY TO HEAR THAT. LOST MY WIFE LAST YEAR.
IS THIS YOUR...
COLLEAGUE.
WAIT A--
I'M SORRY IF THERE'S BEEN A MISUNDERSTANDING, OLIVER.
WE NEED TO ASK YOU A FEW QUESTIONS.

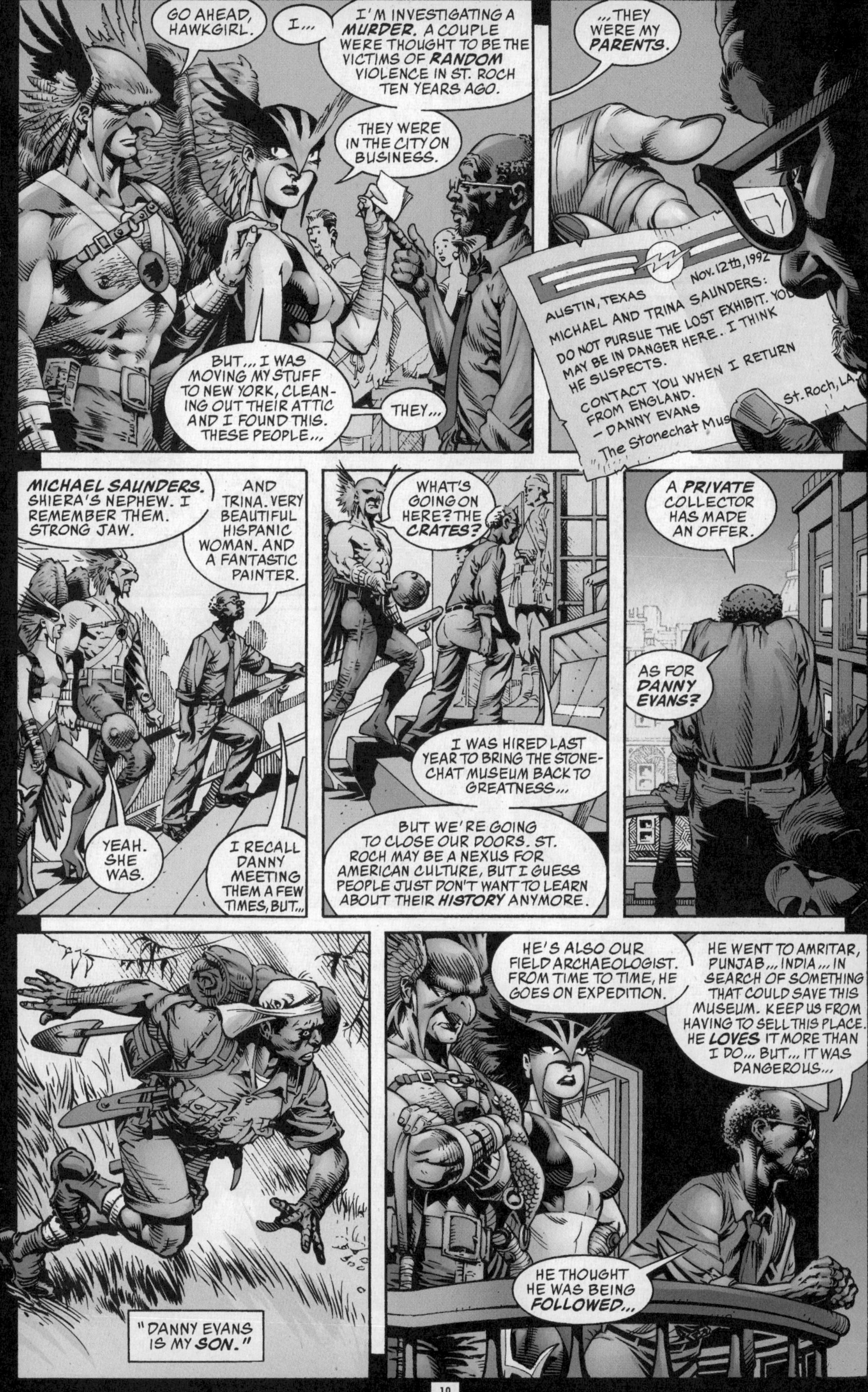
GO AHEAD, HAWKGIRL.
I...
I'M INVESTIGATING A MURDER. A COUPLE WERE THOUGHT TO BE THE VICTIMS OF RANDOM VIOLENCE IN ST. ROCH TEN YEARS AGO.
THEY WERE IN THE CITY ON BUSINESS.
BUT... I WAS MOVING MY STUFF TO NEW YORK, CLEANING OUT THEIR ATTIC AND I FOUND THIS. THESE PEOPLE...
THEY...
...THEY WERE MY PARENTS.
Nov. 12th, 1992
AUSTIN, TEXAS
MICHAEL AND TRINA SAUNDERS:
DO NOT PURSUE THE LOST EXHIBIT. YO
MAY BE IN DANGER HERE. I THINK
HE SUSPECTS.
CONTACT YOU WHEN I RETURN
FROM ENGLAND.
- DANNY EVANS
St. Roch, LA
The Stonechat Mus
MICHAEL SAUNDERS. SHIERA'S NEPHEW. I REMEMBER THEM. STRONG JAW.
AND TRINA. VERY BEAUTIFUL HISPANIC WOMAN. AND A FANTASTIC PAINTER.
YEAH. SHE WAS.
I RECALL DANNY MEETING THEM A FEW TIMES, BUT...
WHAT'S GOING ON HERE? THE CRATES?
I WAS HIRED LAST YEAR TO BRING THE STONECHAT MUSEUM BACK TO GREATNESS...
BUT WE'RE GOING TO CLOSE OUR DOORS. ST. ROCH MAY BE A NEXUS FOR AMERICAN CULTURE, BUT I GUESS PEOPLE JUST DON'T WANT TO LEARN ABOUT THEIR HISTORY ANYMORE.
A PRIVATE COLLECTOR HAS MADE AN OFFER.
AS FOR DANNY EVANS?
"DANNY EVANS IS MY SON."
HE'S ALSO OUR FIELD ARCHAEOLOGIST. FROM TIME TO TIME, HE GOES ON EXPEDITION.
HE WENT TO AMRITAR, PUNJAB... INDIA... IN SEARCH OF SOMETHING THAT COULD SAVE THIS MUSEUM. KEEP US FROM HAVING TO SELL THIS PLACE. HE LOVES IT MORE THAN I DO... BUT... IT WAS DANGEROUS...
HE THOUGHT HE WAS BEING FOLLOWED...

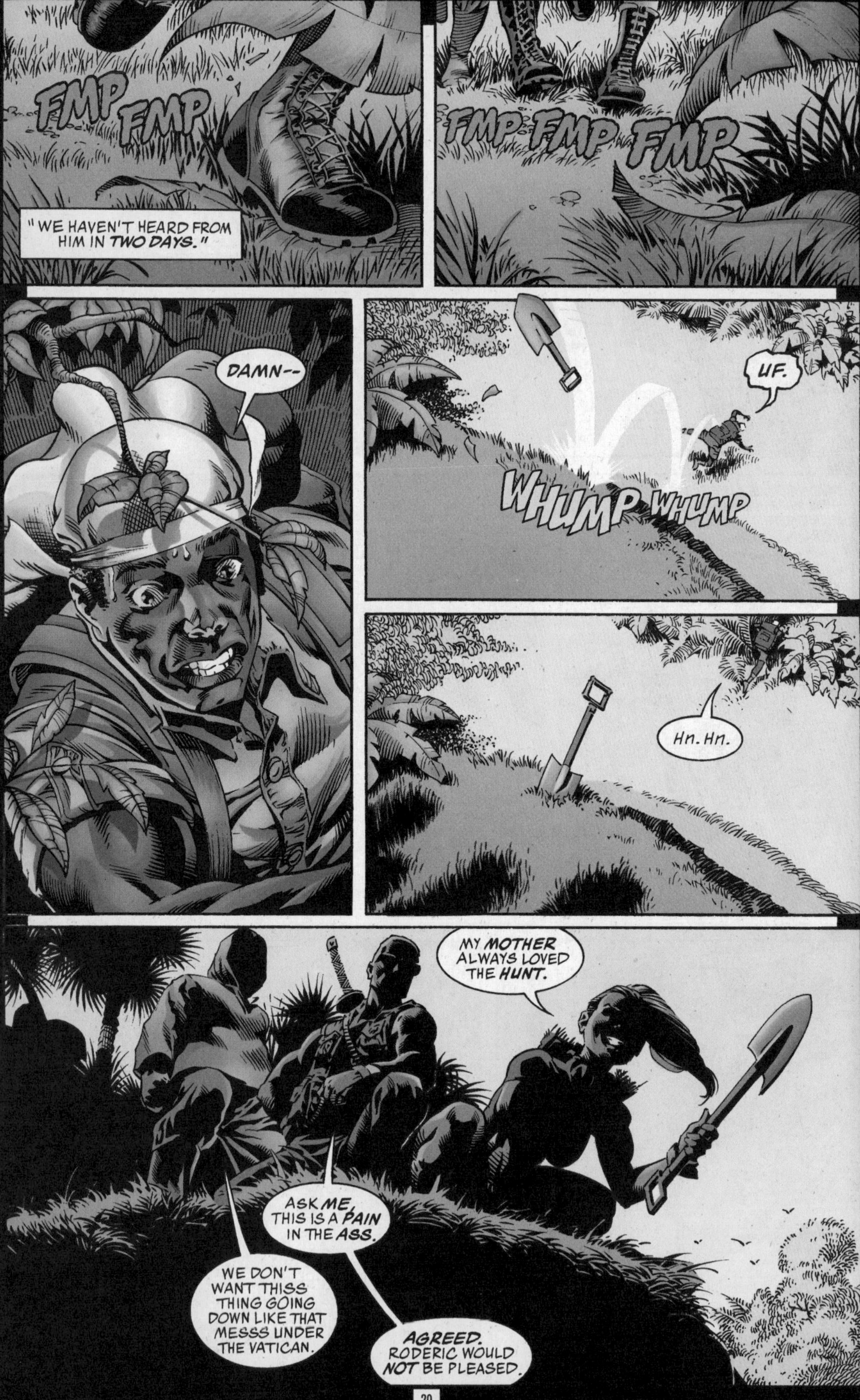
FMP FMP
"WE HAVEN'T HEARD FROM HIM IN TWO DAYS."
FMP FMP FMP
DAMN--
UF.
WHUMP WHUMP
Hn. Hn.
MY MOTHER ALWAYS LOVED THE HUNT.
ASK ME, THIS IS A PAIN IN THE ASS.
WE DON'T WANT THISS THING GOING DOWN LIKE THAT MESSS UNDER THE VATICAN.
AGREED. RODERIC WOULD NOT BE PLEASED.

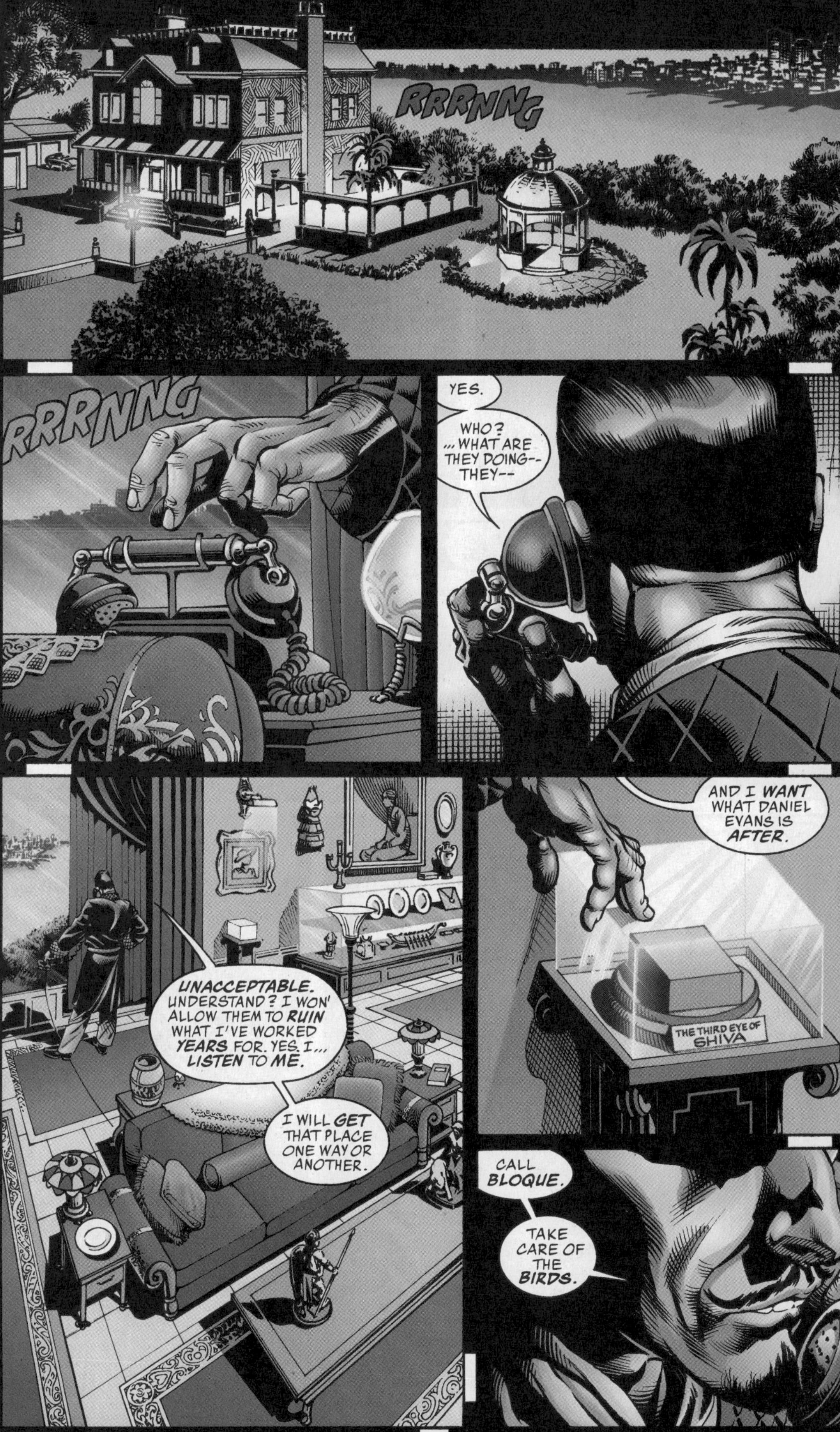
RRRNNG
RRRNNG
YES.
WHO? ...WHAT ARE THEY DOING-- THEY--
UNACCEPTABLE. UNDERSTAND? I WON' ALLOW THEM TO RUIN WHAT I'VE WORKED YEARS FOR. YES. I... LISTEN TO ME.
I WILL GET THAT PLACE ONE WAY OR ANOTHER.
AND I WANT WHAT DANIEL EVANS IS AFTER.
THE THIRD EYE OF SHIVA
CALL BLOQUE.
TAKE CARE OF THE BIRDS.

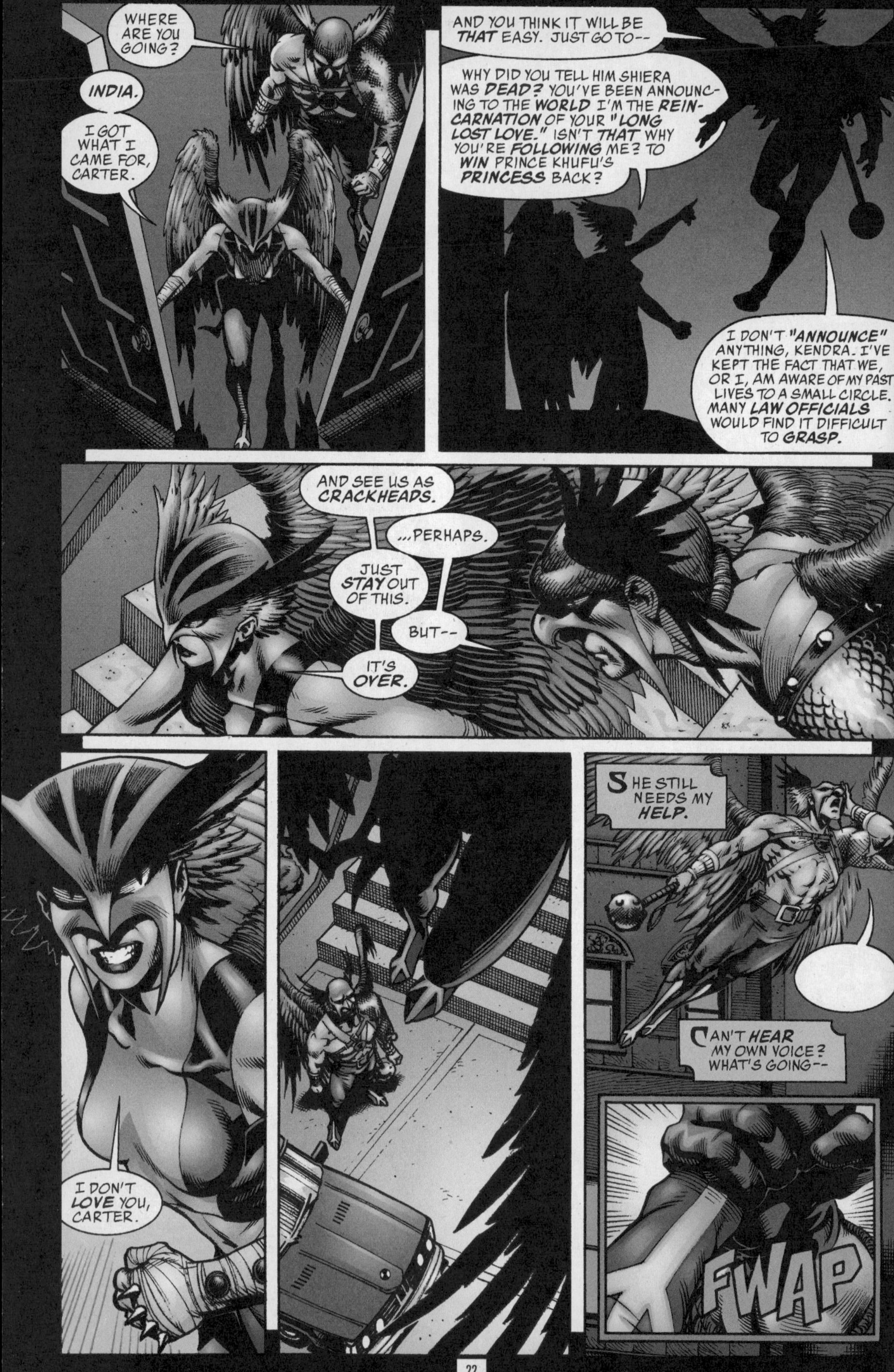
WHERE ARE YOU GOING?
INDIA.
I GOT WHAT I CAME FOR, CARTER.
AND YOU THINK IT WILL BE THAT EASY. JUST GO TO--
WHY DID YOU TELL HIM SHIERA WAS DEAD? YOU'VE BEEN ANNOUNCING TO THE WORLD I'M THE REINCARNATION OF YOUR "LONG LOST LOVE." ISN'T THAT WHY YOU'RE FOLLOWING ME? TO WIN PRINCE KHUFU'S PRINCESS BACK?
I DON'T "ANNOUNCE" ANYTHING, KENDRA. I'VE KEPT THE FACT THAT WE, OR I, AM AWARE OF MY PAST LIVES TO A SMALL CIRCLE. MANY LAW OFFICIALS WOULD FIND IT DIFFICULT TO GRASP.
AND SEE US AS CRACKHEADS.
...PERHAPS.
JUST STAY OUT OF THIS.
BUT--
IT'S OVER.
I DON'T LOVE YOU, CARTER.
SHE STILL NEEDS MY HELP.
CAN'T HEAR MY OWN VOICE? WHAT'S GOING--
FWAP

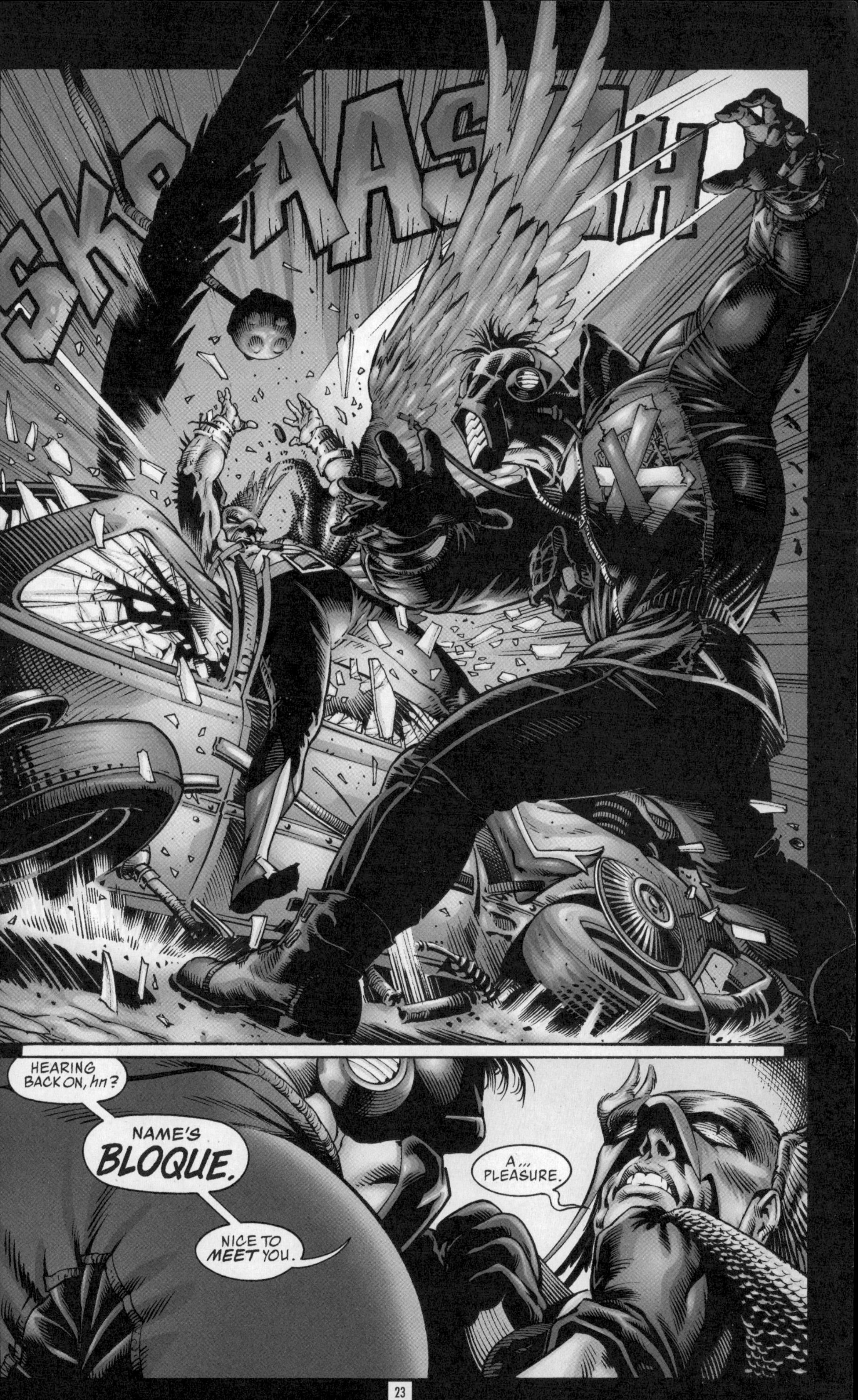
SKRAASHH
HEARING BACK ON, hn?
NAME'S BLOQUE.
NICE TO MEET YOU.
A... PLEASURE.

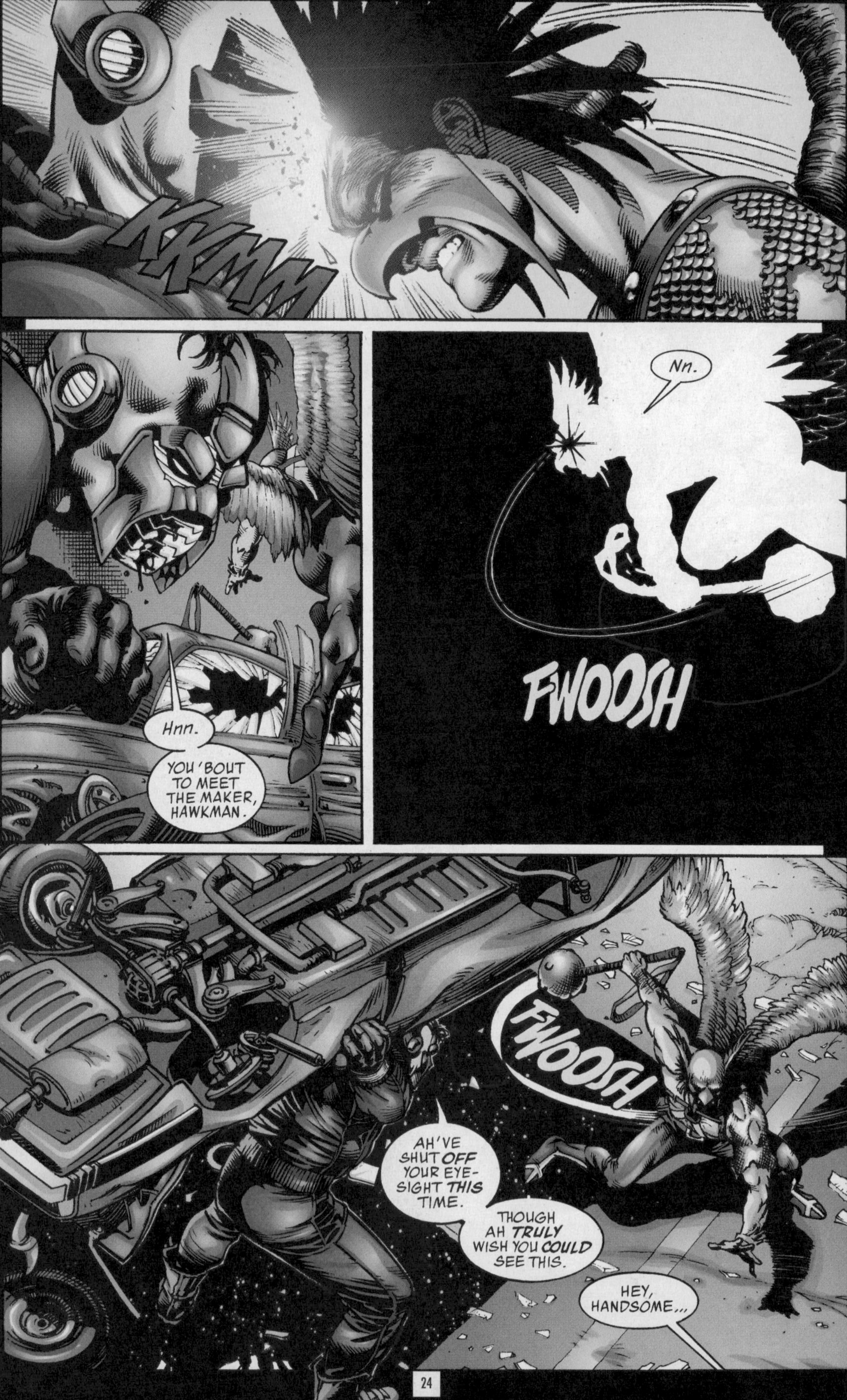
KKMMM
Hnn.
YOU 'BOUT TO MEET THE MAKER, HAWKMAN.
Nn.
FWOOSH
FWOOSH
AH'VE SHUT OFF YOUR EYE-SIGHT THIS TIME.
THOUGH AH TRULY WISH YOU COULD SEE THIS.
HEY, HANDSOME...

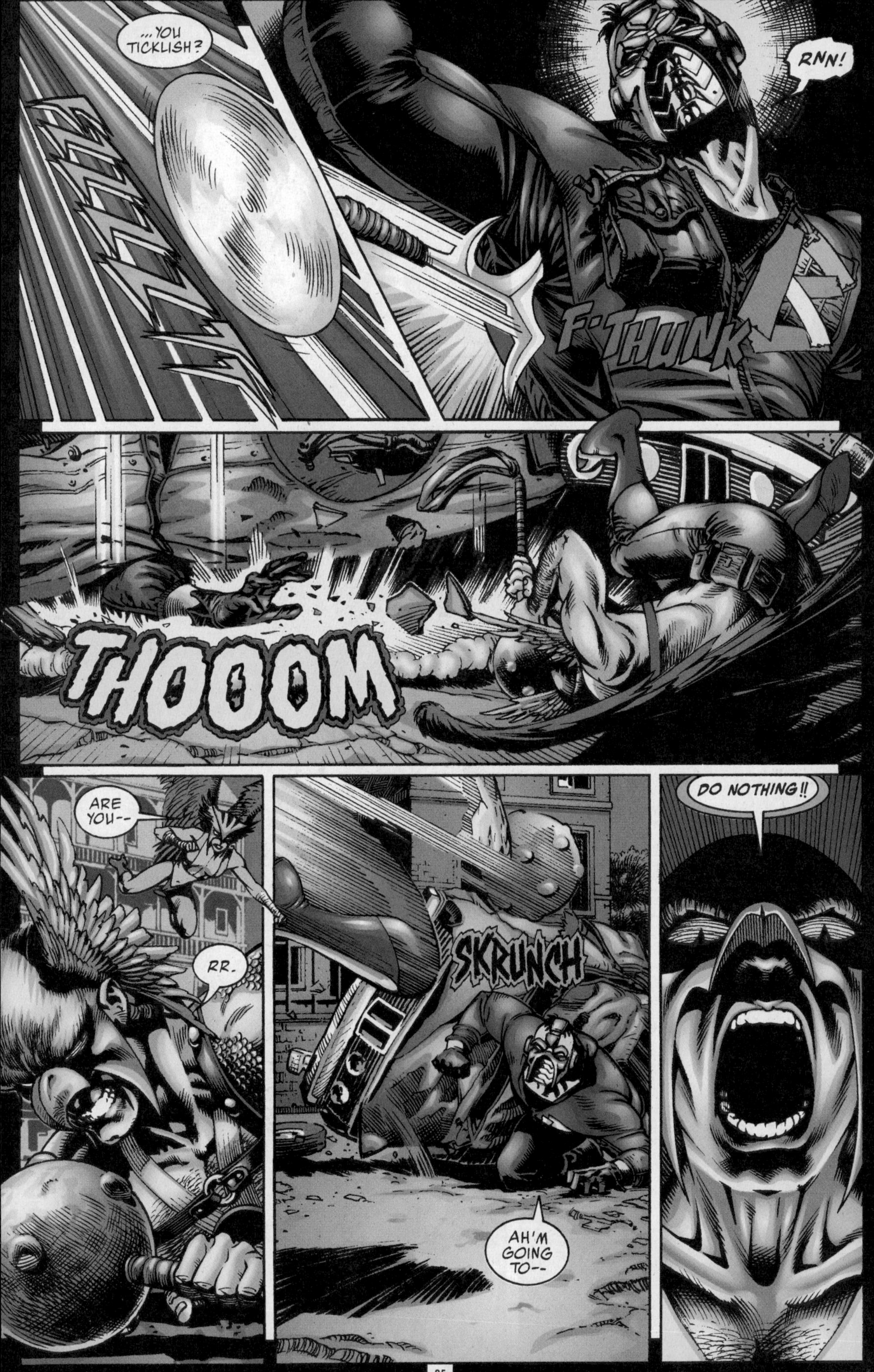
...YOU TICKLISH?
RNN!
F-THUNK
THOOOM
ARE YOU--
RR.
SKRUNCH
AH'M GOING TO--
DO NOTHING!!

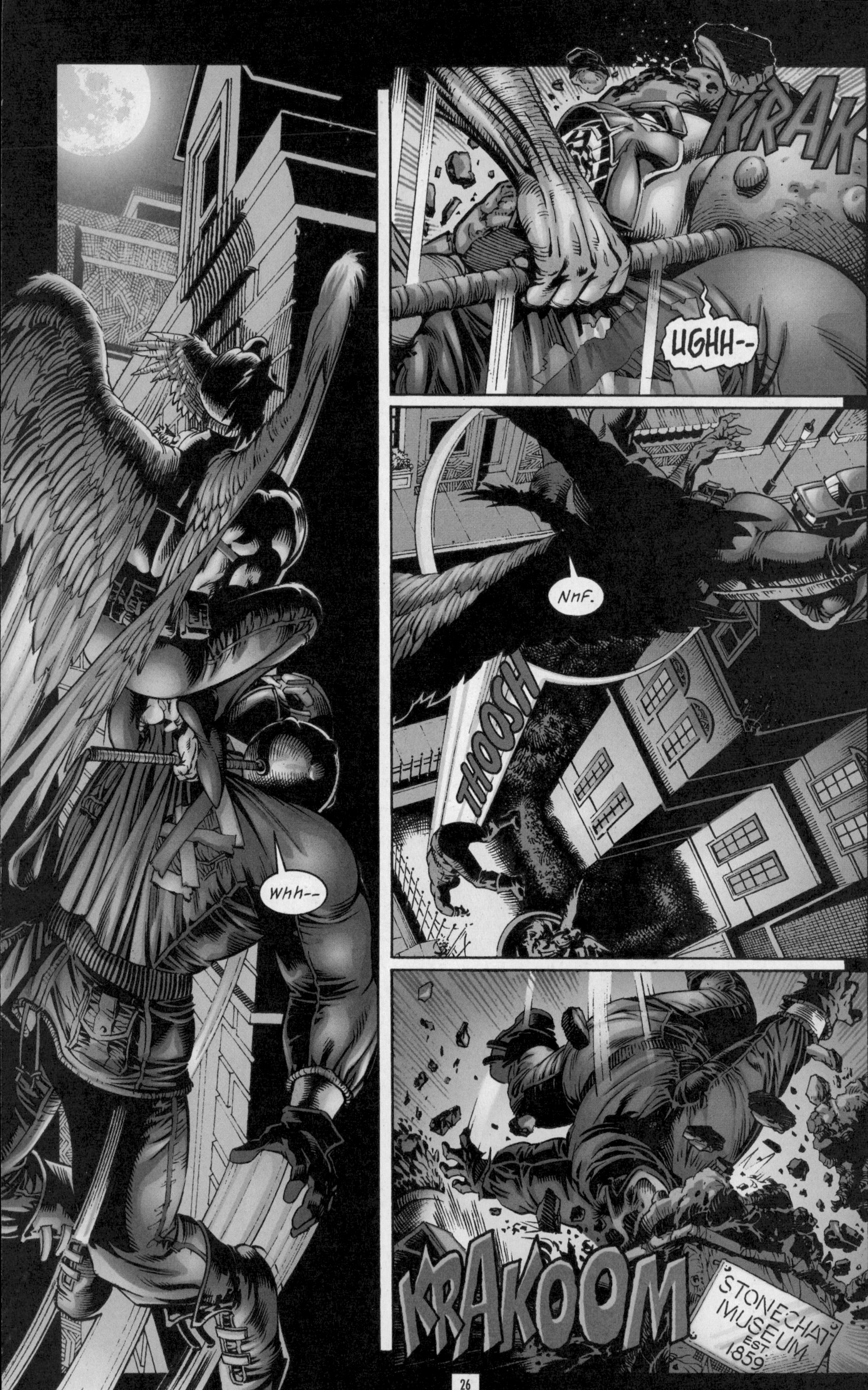
Whh--
KRAK
UGHH--
Nnf.
THOOSH
KRAKOOM
STONECHAT MUSEUM EST. 1859

SORRY ABOUT THE *STATUE.*

IT'S ALL RIGHT. I'M JUST GLAD YOU TWO DIDN'T GET INJURED.

THE POLICE CHIEF WANTS TO MEET YOU WHEN YOU GET BACK. THANK YOU FOR FINALLY CATCHING THE MOST WANTED HIT MAN IN ST. ROCH.

WHY HE WAS AFTER YOU WE DON'--

WE'LL FIND OUT. AND WE'LL CONTACT YOU *SOON,* OLIVER.

GOOD LUCK. AND THANKS.

YOU DON'T LIKE *POLICE?* BARELY SAID A *WORD.*

NOT REALLY, NO. I HAVE A... HISTORY...

HOW DID YOU DO THAT?

DO WHAT?

*LIFT* THAT GUY, BLOQUE. THE COPS SAID HE WEIGHED OVER A *TON.*

THE N*th* METAL WE HAVE IN OUR WING HARNESSES. IT NEGATES THE EFFECTS OF GRAVITY ON US. GIVES US THE *GIFT* OF FLIGHT... AND WE CAN CARRY TWENTY TIMES WHAT WE NORMALLY COULD.

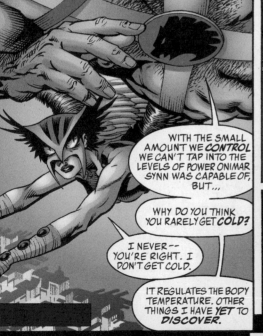

WITH THE SMALL AMOUNT WE *CONTROL* WE CAN'T TAP INTO THE LEVELS OF POWER ONIMAR SYNN WAS CAPABLE OF, BUT...

WHY DO YOU THINK YOU RARELY GET *COLD?*

I NEVER-- YOU'RE RIGHT. I DON'T GET COLD.

IT REGULATES THE BODY TEMPERATURE. OTHER THINGS I HAVE *YET* TO *DISCOVER.*

THINGS WE CAN *DIS-COVER* TOGETHER.

CARTER, I--

*NOT* AS *LOVERS,* KENDRA. YOU HAVE THE *POTENTIAL* TO BE A *GREAT* HERO. LET ME *HELP* YOU, *TEACH* YOU.

LET'S DO THIS...GO TO INDIA ...AS *PARTNERS.*

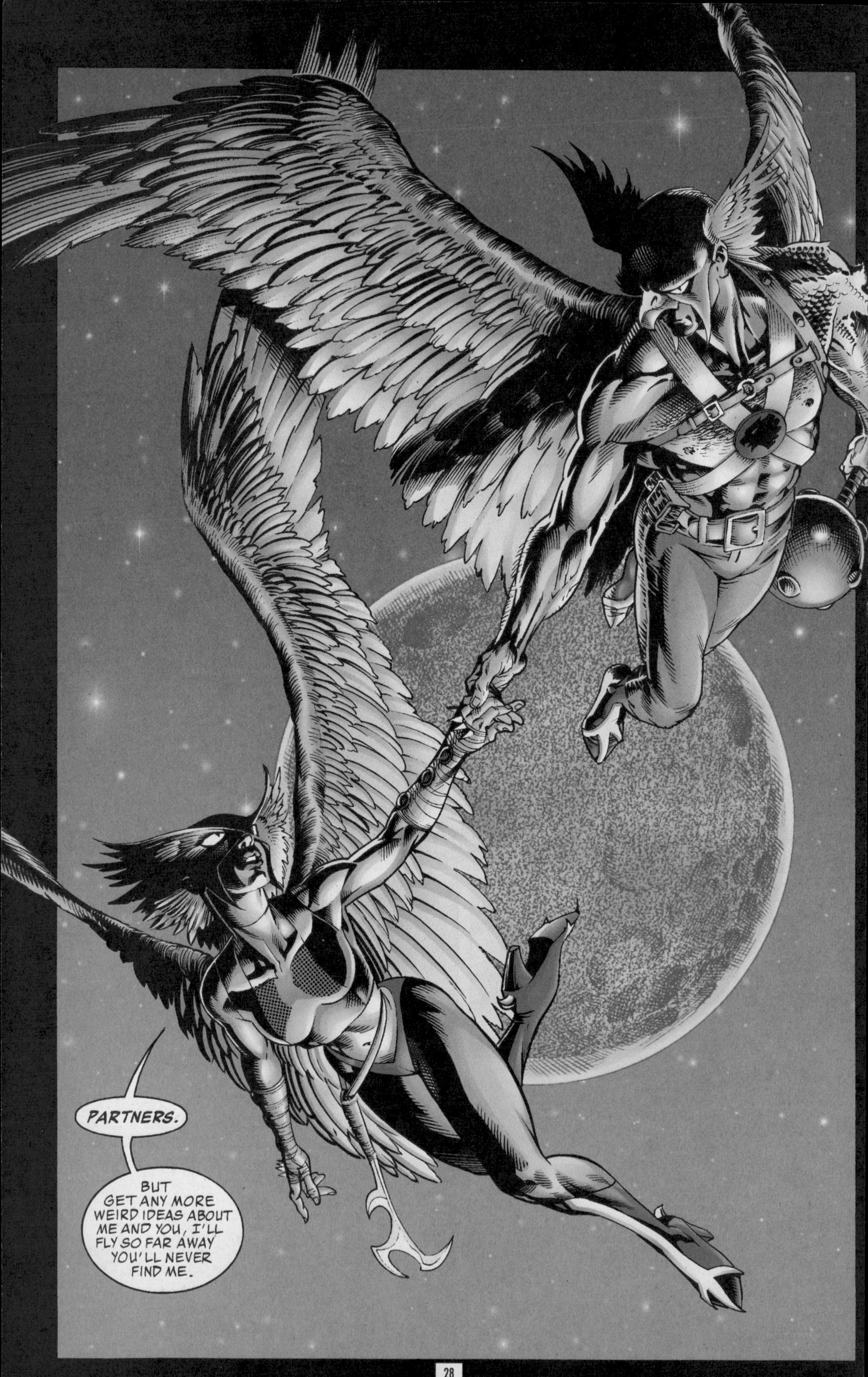
PARTNERS.
BUT GET ANY MORE WEIRD IDEAS ABOUT ME AND YOU, I'LL FLY SO FAR AWAY YOU'LL NEVER FIND ME.

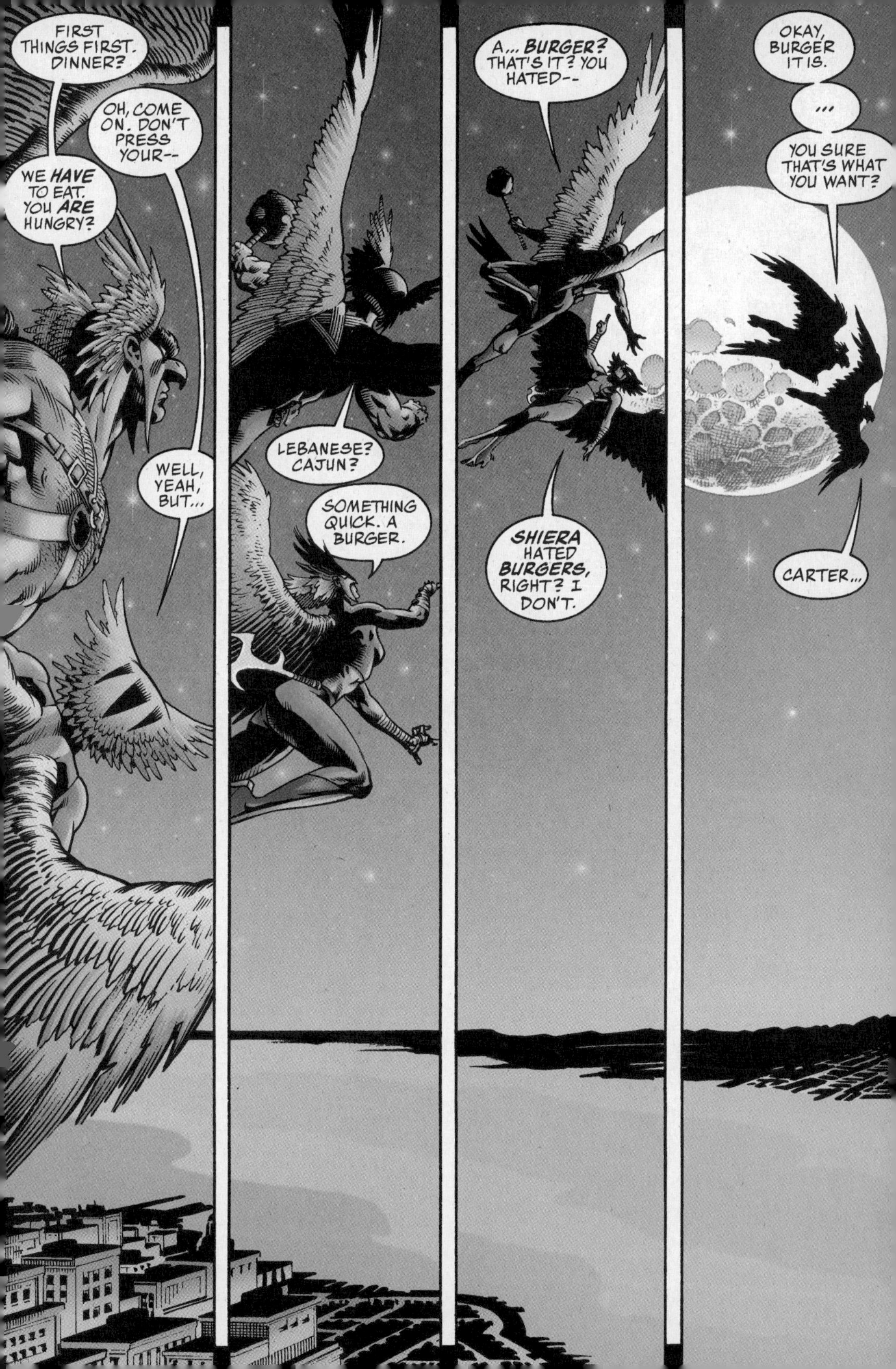
FIRST THINGS FIRST. DINNER?
OH, COME ON. DON'T PRESS YOUR--
WE HAVE TO EAT. YOU ARE HUNGRY?
WELL, YEAH, BUT...
LEBANESE? CAJUN?
SOMETHING QUICK. A BURGER.
A... BURGER? THAT'S IT? YOU HATED--
SHIERA HATED BURGERS, RIGHT? I DON'T.
OKAY, BURGER IT IS.
...
YOU SURE THAT'S WHAT YOU WANT?
CARTER...

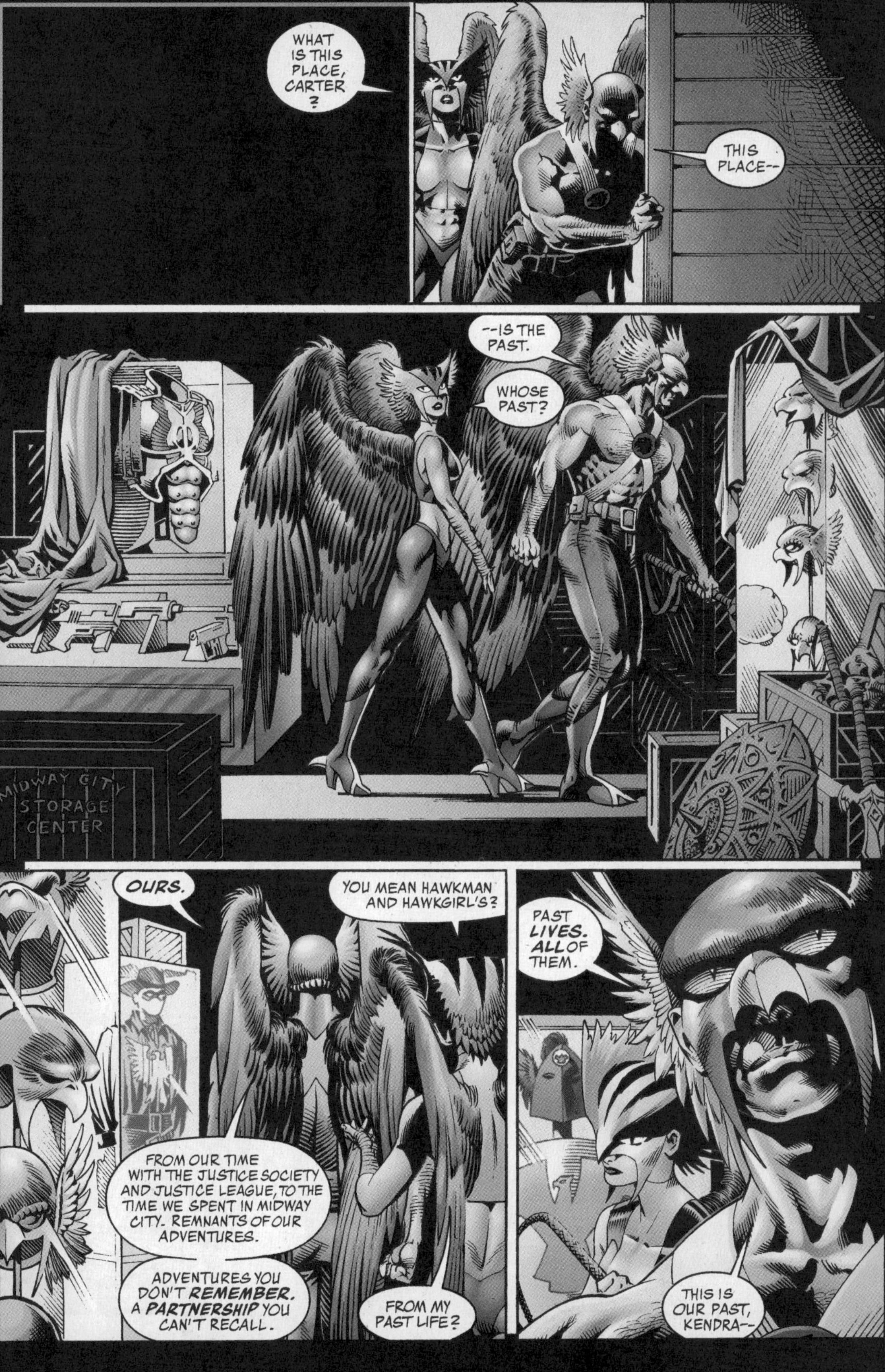

WHAT IS THIS PLACE, CARTER?
THIS PLACE--
--IS THE PAST.
WHOSE PAST?
MIDWAY CITY STORAGE CENTER
OURS.
YOU MEAN HAWKMAN AND HAWKGIRL'S?
FROM OUR TIME WITH THE JUSTICE SOCIETY AND JUSTICE LEAGUE, TO THE TIME WE SPENT IN MIDWAY CITY. REMNANTS OF OUR ADVENTURES.
ADVENTURES YOU DON'T **REMEMBER.** A **PARTNERSHIP** YOU CAN'T RECALL.
FROM MY PAST LIFE?
PAST **LIVES. ALL** OF THEM.
THIS IS OUR PAST, KENDRA--

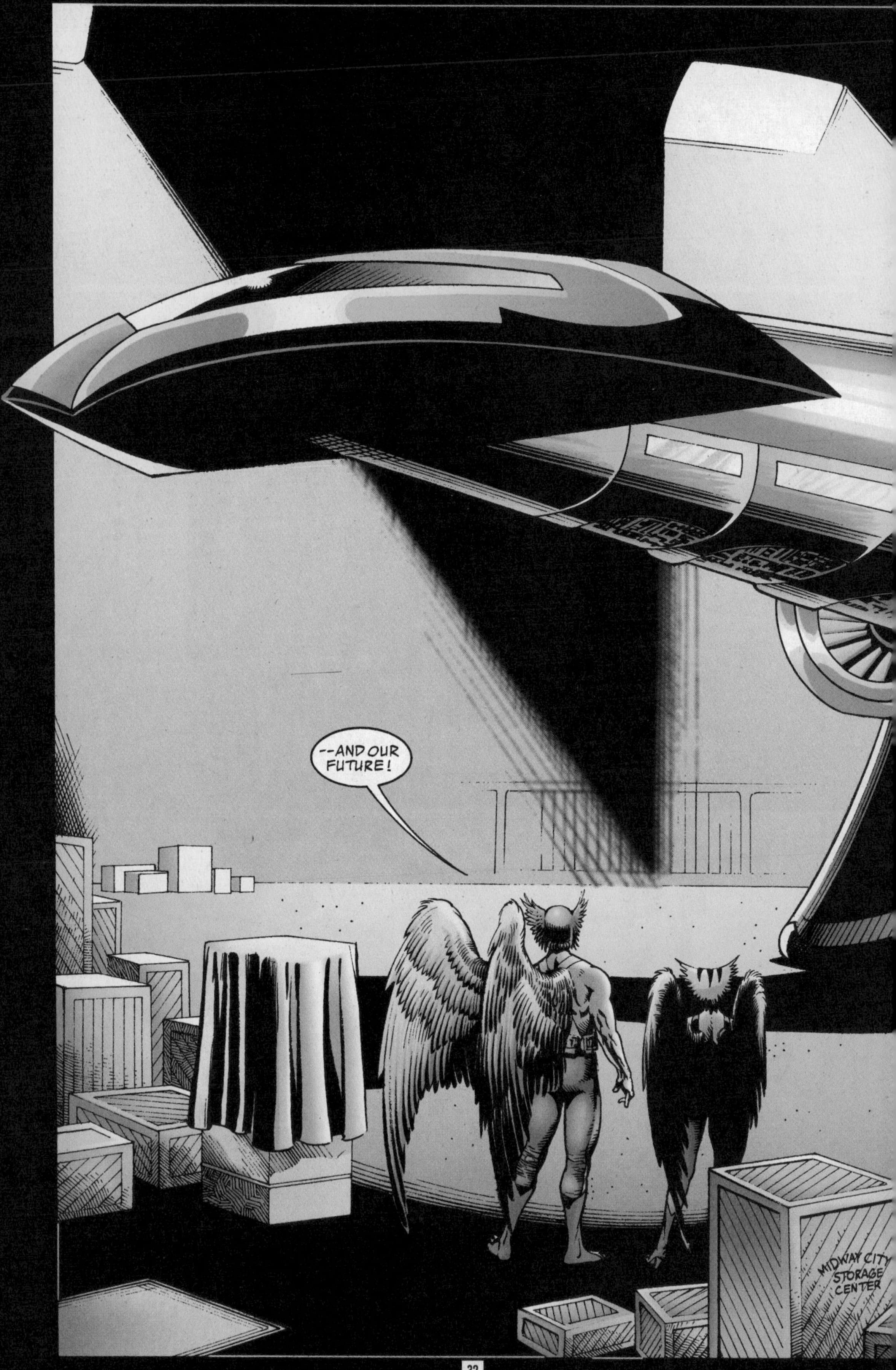
--AND OUR FUTURE!
MIDWAY CITY STORAGE CENTER

Thousands of years ago, an Egyptian Prince and his Princess discovered an alien spacecraft from the planet Thanagar. The ship was powered by a mysterious antigravity element they called Nth metal. The unearthly energies of the Nth metal, enhanced by the strength of their love, transformed the souls of the Prince and Princess. For centuries, they were reincarnated, life after life, destined to meet one another and rekindle their love...until today...Today they are Carter Hall and Kendra Saunders, archaeologists and adventurers. The winged warriors known as HAWKMAN and HAWKGIRL!

# Into the Sky

| JOHNS & ROBINSON | JOHNS | MORALES | BAIR | OAKLEY | KALISZ | HEROIC AGE | DONTANVILLE | TOMASI |
|---|---|---|---|---|---|---|---|---|
| story | words | penciller | inker | letterer | colorist | separations | assistant editor | editor |

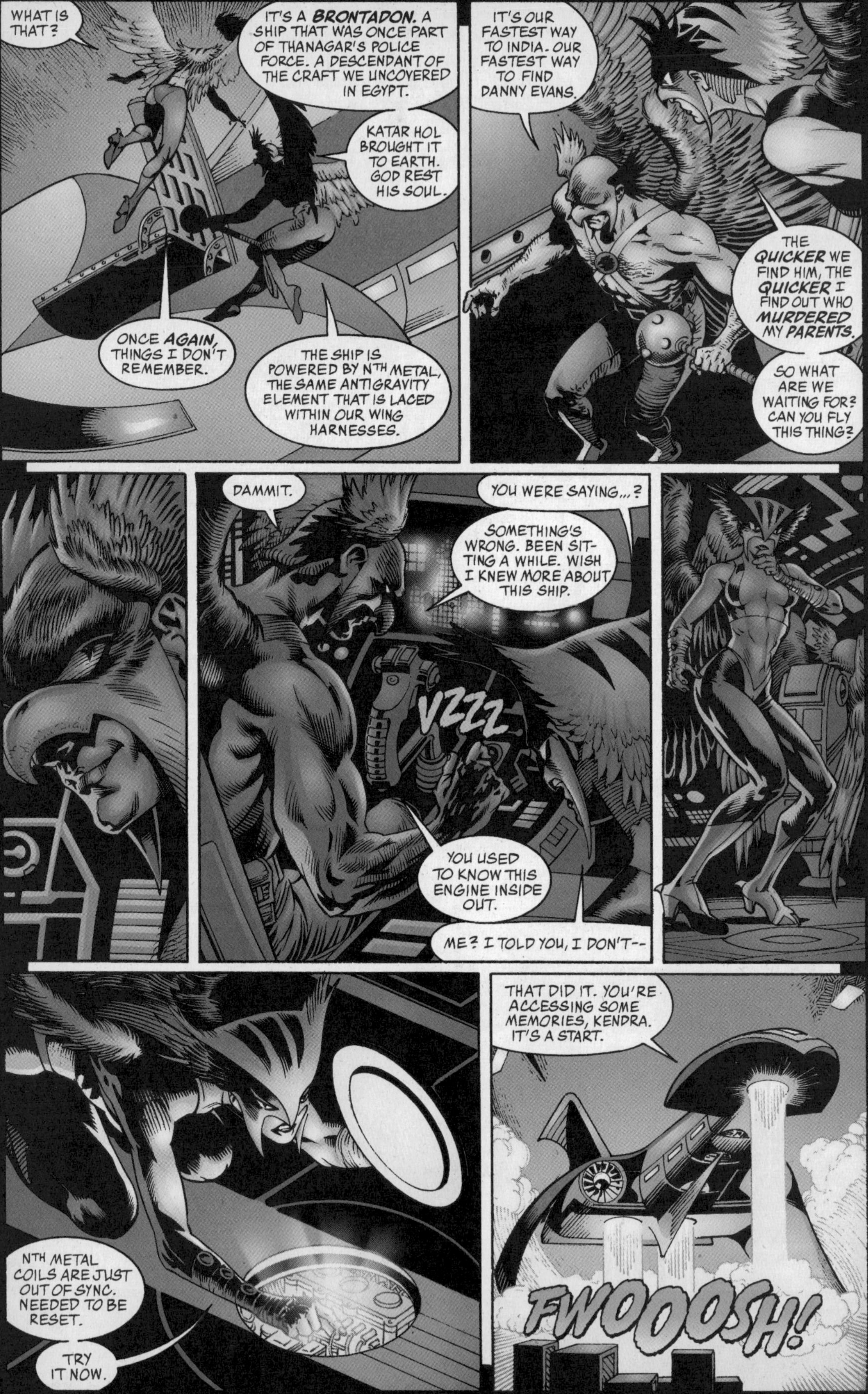
WHAT IS THAT?
IT'S A BRONTADON. A SHIP THAT WAS ONCE PART OF THANAGAR'S POLICE FORCE. A DESCENDANT OF THE CRAFT WE UNCOVERED IN EGYPT.
KATAR HOL BROUGHT IT TO EARTH. GOD REST HIS SOUL.
ONCE AGAIN, THINGS I DON'T REMEMBER.
THE SHIP IS POWERED BY Nth METAL, THE SAME ANTIGRAVITY ELEMENT THAT IS LACED WITHIN OUR WING HARNESSES.
IT'S OUR FASTEST WAY TO INDIA. OUR FASTEST WAY TO FIND DANNY EVANS.
THE QUICKER WE FIND HIM, THE QUICKER I FIND OUT WHO MURDERED MY PARENTS.
SO WHAT ARE WE WAITING FOR? CAN YOU FLY THIS THING?
DAMMIT.
YOU WERE SAYING...?
SOMETHING'S WRONG. BEEN SITTING A WHILE. WISH I KNEW MORE ABOUT THIS SHIP.
VZZZ
YOU USED TO KNOW THIS ENGINE INSIDE OUT.
ME? I TOLD YOU, I DON'T--
Nth METAL COILS ARE JUST OUT OF SYNC. NEEDED TO BE RESET.
TRY IT NOW.
THAT DID IT. YOU'RE ACCESSING SOME MEMORIES, KENDRA. IT'S A START.
FWOOOSH!

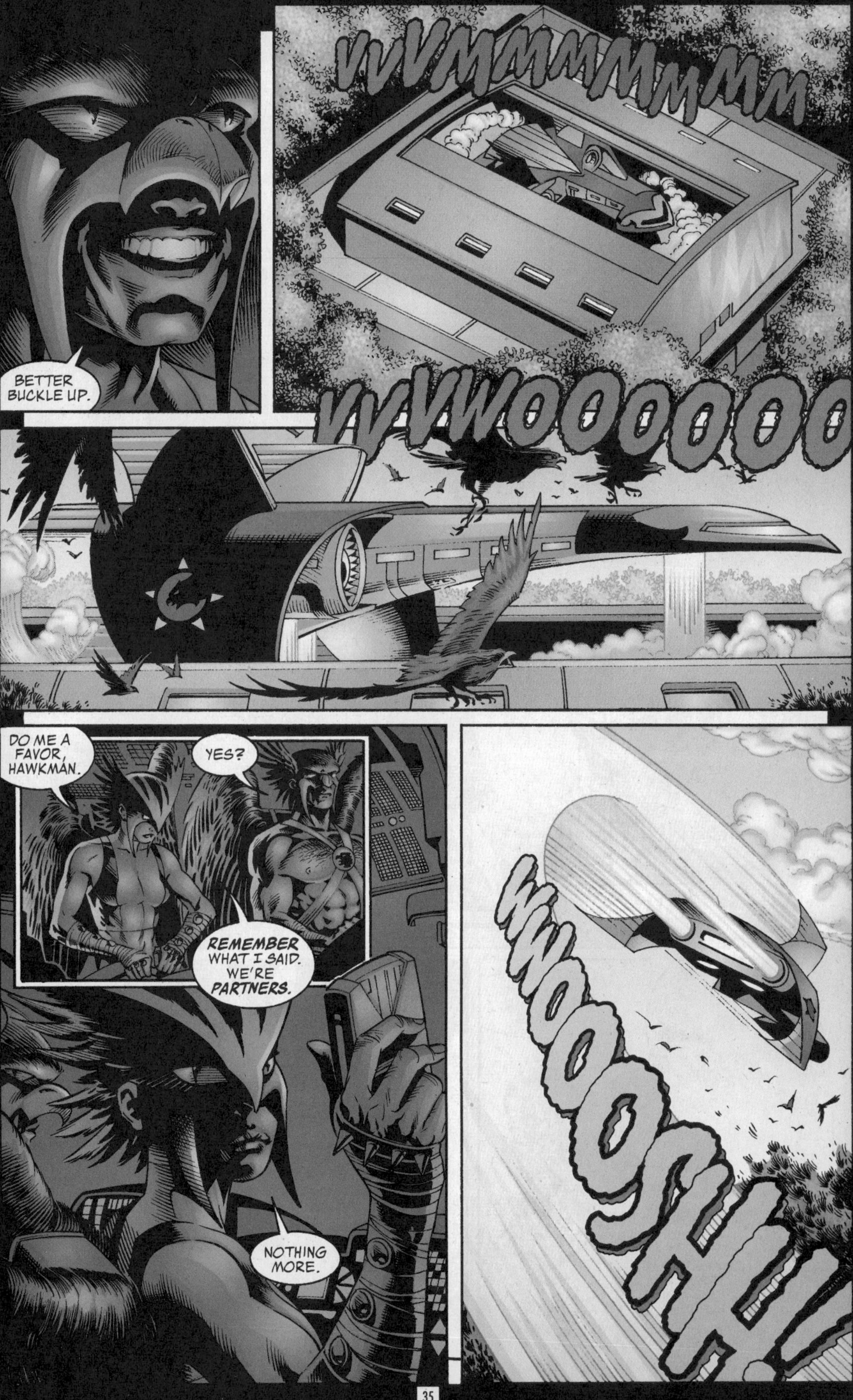
BETTER BUCKLE UP.
VVVMMMMMMMMMM
VVVWOOOOOOOO
DO ME A FAVOR, HAWKMAN.
YES?
REMEMBER WHAT I SAID. WE'RE PARTNERS.
NOTHING MORE.
WWOOOOSH!!

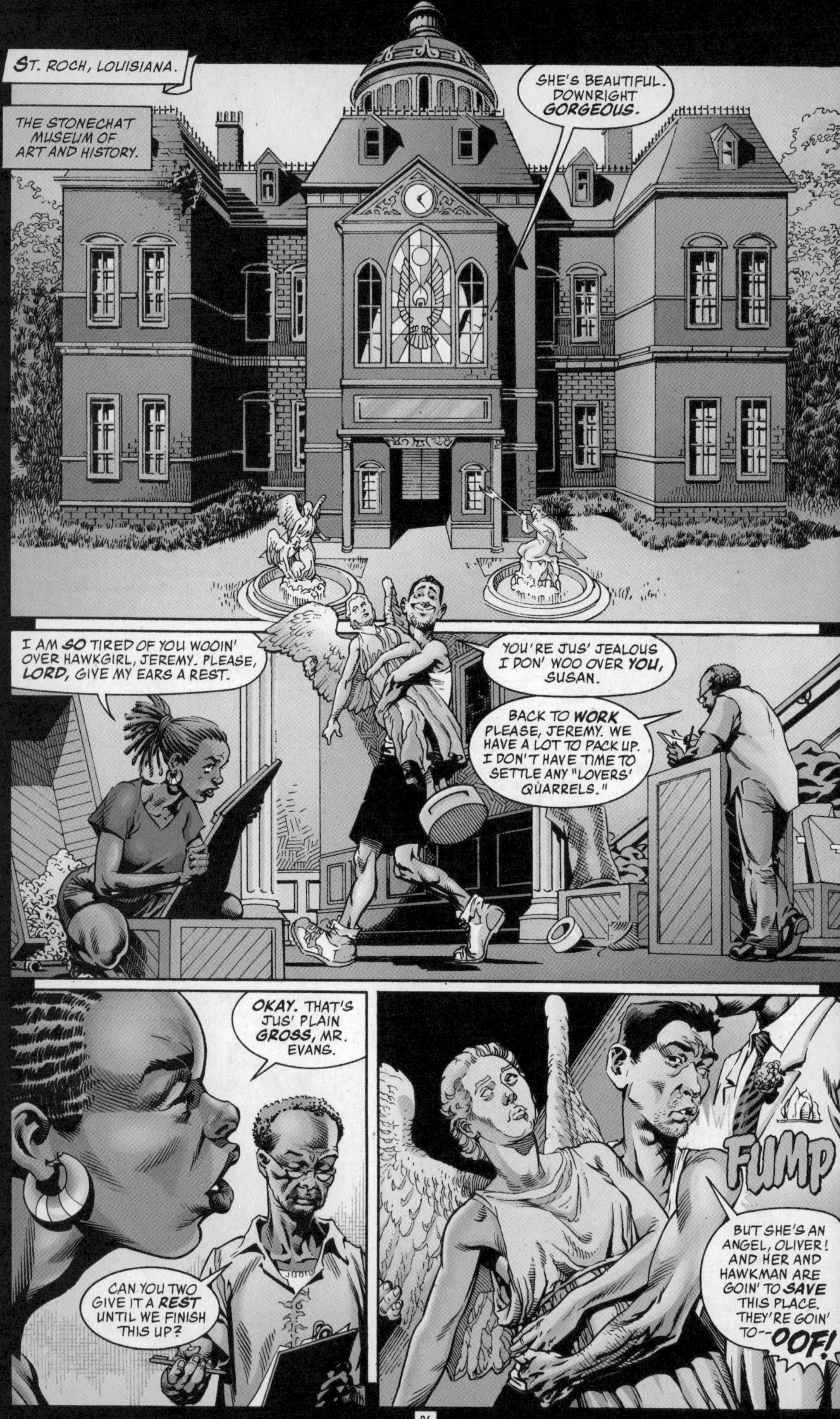
ST. ROCH, LOUISIANA.
THE STONECHAT MUSEUM OF ART AND HISTORY.
SHE'S BEAUTIFUL. DOWNRIGHT GORGEOUS.
I AM SO TIRED OF YOU WOOIN' OVER HAWKGIRL, JEREMY. PLEASE, LORD, GIVE MY EARS A REST.
YOU'RE JUS' JEALOUS I DON' WOO OVER YOU, SUSAN.
BACK TO WORK PLEASE, JEREMY. WE HAVE A LOT TO PACK UP. I DON'T HAVE TIME TO SETTLE ANY "LOVERS' QUARRELS."
OKAY. THAT'S JUS' PLAIN GROSS, MR. EVANS.
CAN YOU TWO GIVE IT A REST UNTIL WE FINISH THIS UP?
FUMP
BUT SHE'S AN ANGEL, OLIVER! AND HER AND HAWKMAN ARE GOIN' TO SAVE THIS PLACE. THEY'RE GOIN' TO--OOF!

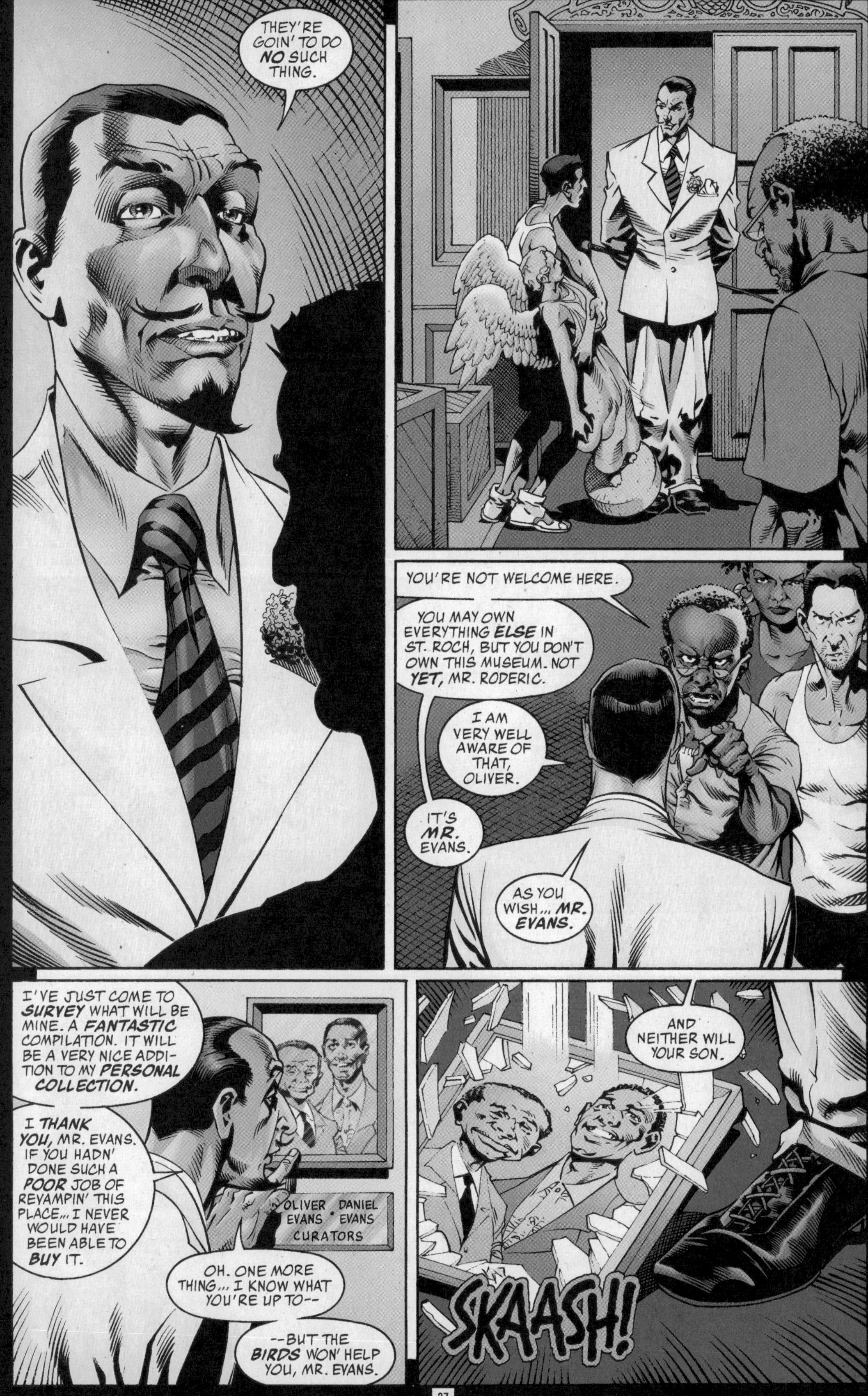
THEY'RE GOIN' TO DO NO SUCH THING.
YOU'RE NOT WELCOME HERE.
YOU MAY OWN EVERYTHING ELSE IN ST. ROCH, BUT YOU DON'T OWN THIS MUSEUM. NOT YET, MR. RODERIC.
I AM VERY WELL AWARE OF THAT, OLIVER.
IT'S MR. EVANS.
AS YOU WISH... MR. EVANS.
I'VE JUST COME TO SURVEY WHAT WILL BE MINE. A FANTASTIC COMPILATION. IT WILL BE A VERY NICE ADDITION TO MY PERSONAL COLLECTION.
I THANK YOU, MR. EVANS. IF YOU HADN' DONE SUCH A POOR JOB OF REVAMPIN' THIS PLACE... I NEVER WOULD HAVE BEEN ABLE TO BUY IT.
OLIVER EVANS • DANIEL EVANS
CURATORS
OH. ONE MORE THING... I KNOW WHAT YOU'RE UP TO--
--BUT THE BIRDS WON' HELP YOU, MR. EVANS.
AND NEITHER WILL YOUR SON.
SKAASH!

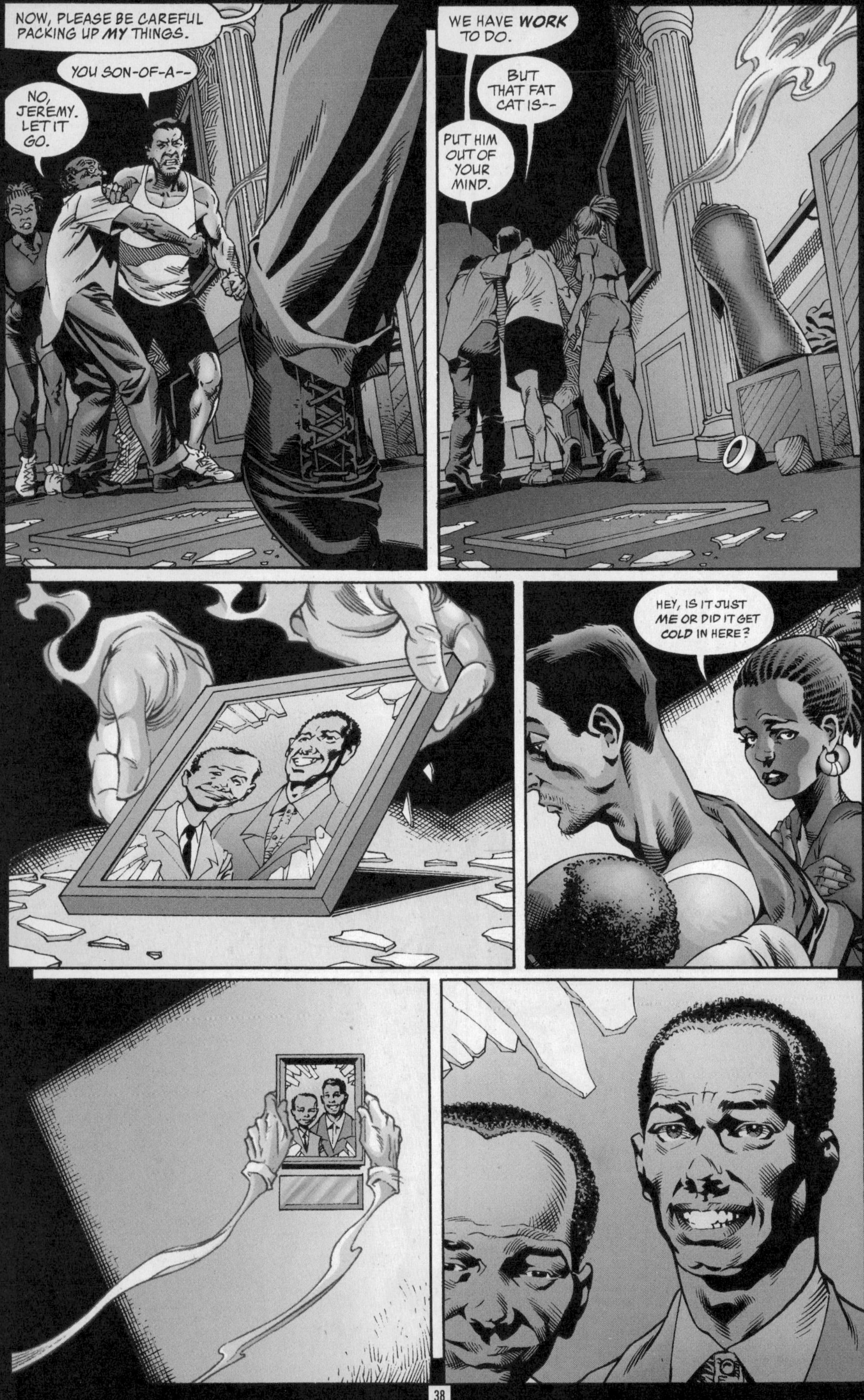
NOW, PLEASE BE CAREFUL PACKING UP MY THINGS.
YOU SON-OF-A--
NO, JEREMY. LET IT GO.
WE HAVE WORK TO DO.
BUT THAT FAT CAT IS--
PUT HIM OUT OF YOUR MIND.
HEY, IS IT JUST ME OR DID IT GET COLD IN HERE?

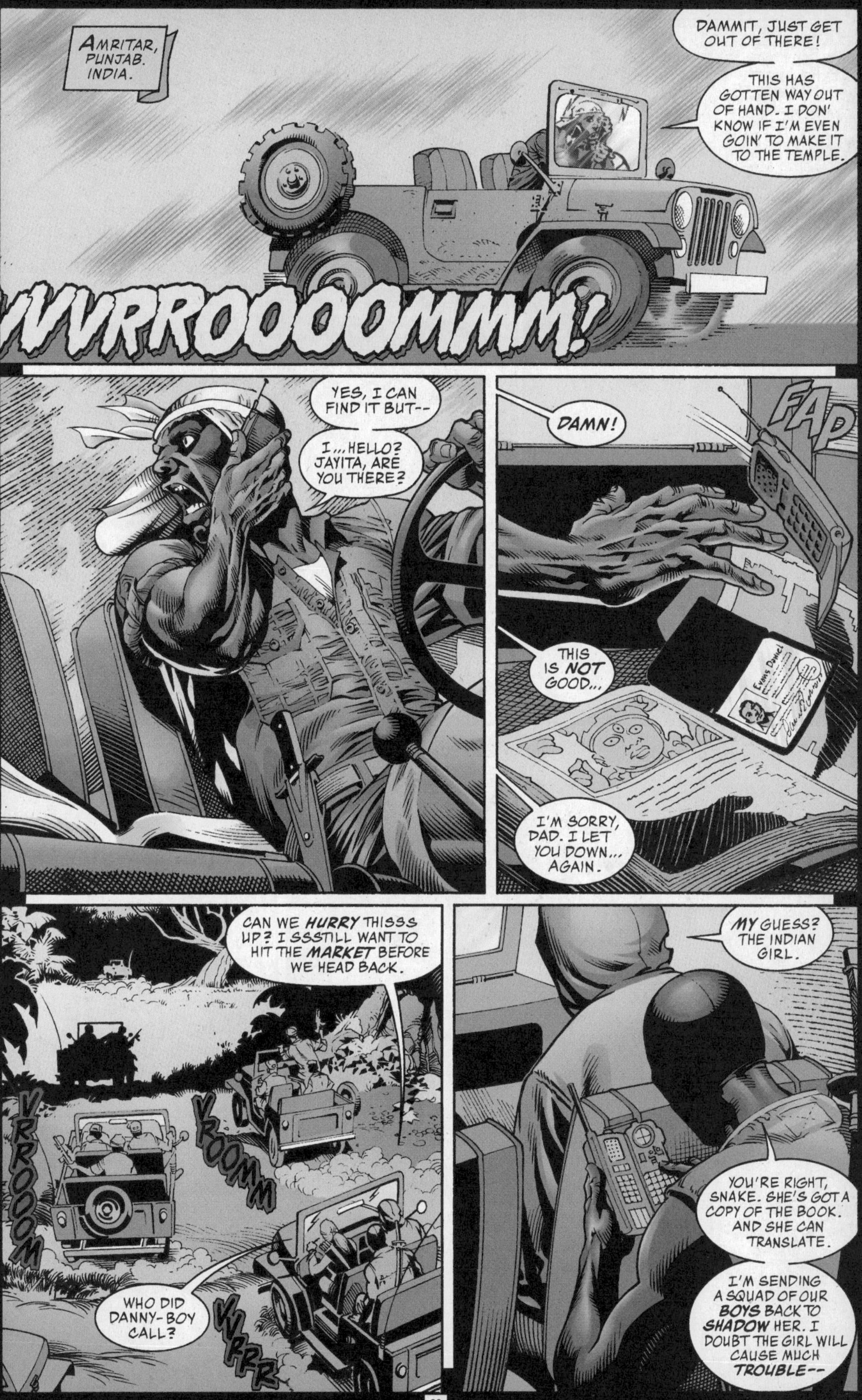
AMRITAR, PUNJAB. INDIA.
DAMMIT, JUST GET OUT OF THERE!
THIS HAS GOTTEN WAY OUT OF HAND. I DON' KNOW IF I'M EVEN GOIN' TO MAKE IT TO THE TEMPLE.
VVRROOOOMMMM!
YES, I CAN FIND IT BUT--
I...HELLO? JAYITA, ARE YOU THERE?
FAP
DAMN!
THIS IS NOT GOOD...
I'M SORRY, DAD. I LET YOU DOWN... AGAIN.
CAN WE HURRY THISSS UP? I SSSTILL WANT TO HIT THE MARKET BEFORE WE HEAD BACK.
VRROOOOM
VROOMM
WHO DID DANNY-BOY CALL?
VVRRR
MY GUESS? THE INDIAN GIRL.
YOU'RE RIGHT, SNAKE. SHE'S GOT A COPY OF THE BOOK. AND SHE CAN TRANSLATE.
I'M SENDING A SQUAD OF OUR BOYS BACK TO SHADOW HER. I DOUBT THE GIRL WILL CAUSE MUCH TROUBLE--

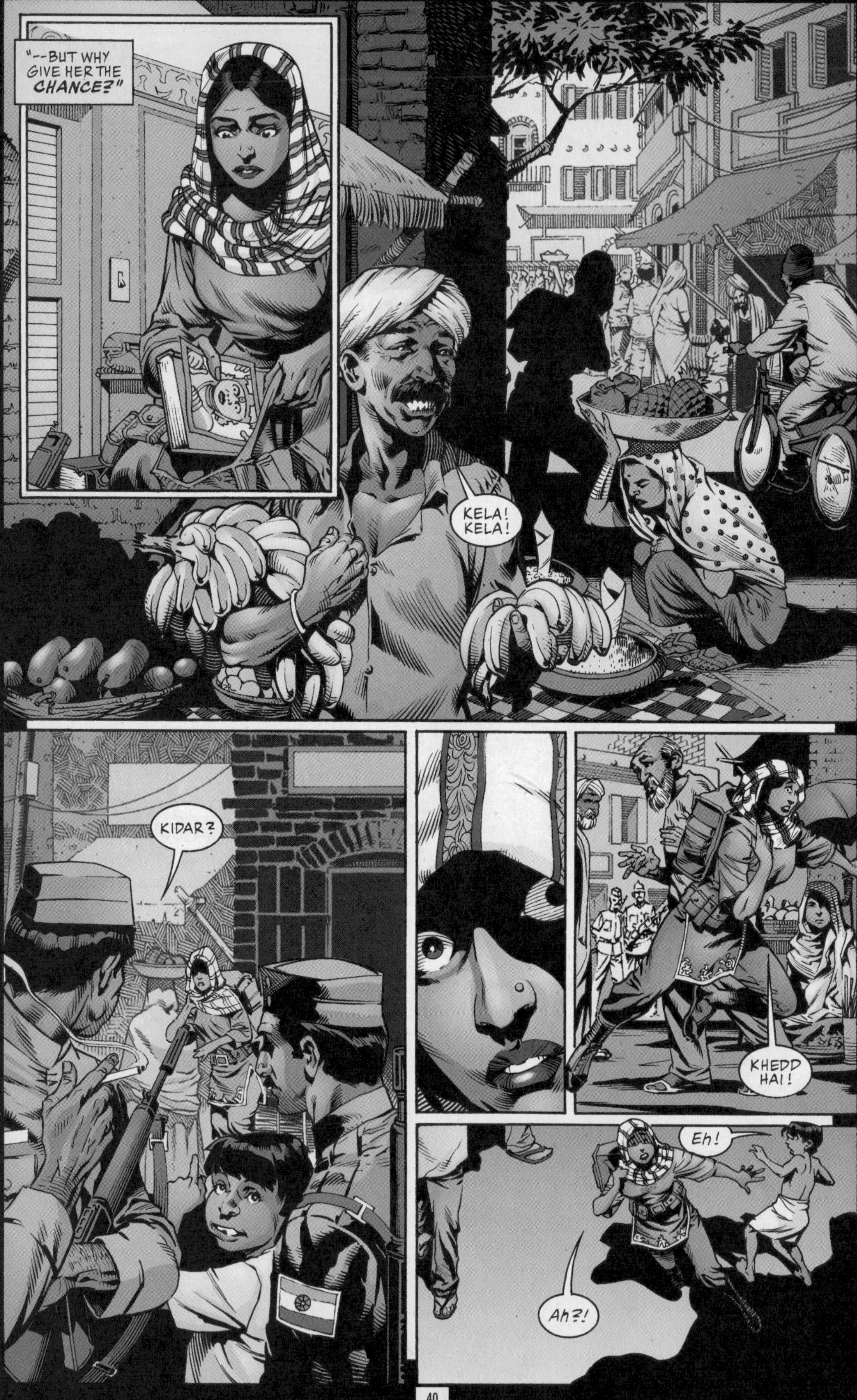
"--BUT WHY GIVE HER THE CHANCE?"
KELA! KELA!
KIDAR?
KHEDD HAI!
Eh!
Ah?!

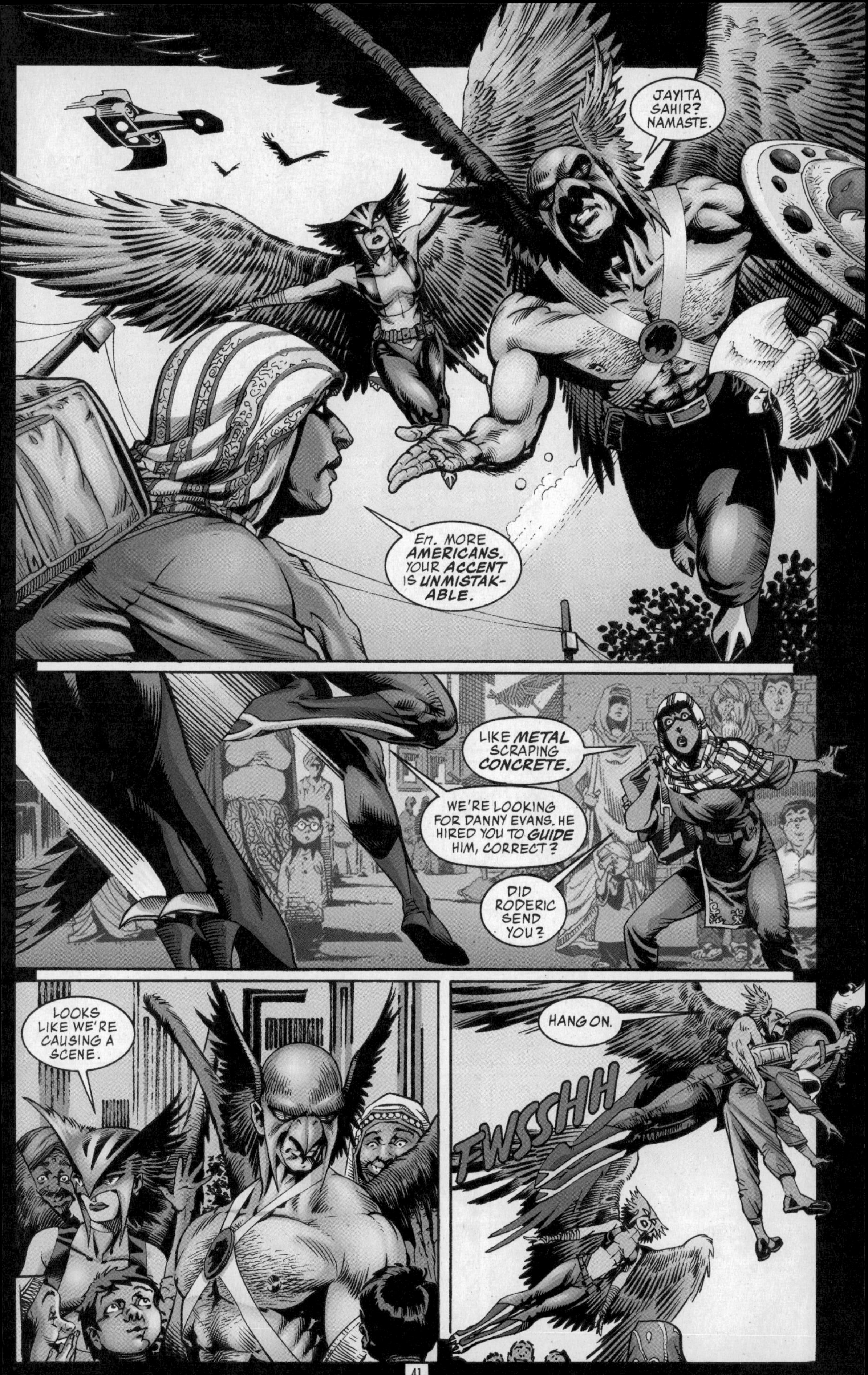
JAYITA SAHIR? NAMASTE.
En. MORE AMERICANS. YOUR ACCENT IS UNMISTAKABLE.
LIKE METAL SCRAPING CONCRETE.
WE'RE LOOKING FOR DANNY EVANS. HE HIRED YOU TO GUIDE HIM, CORRECT?
DID RODERIC SEND YOU?
LOOKS LIKE WE'RE CAUSING A SCENE.
HANG ON.
FWSSHH

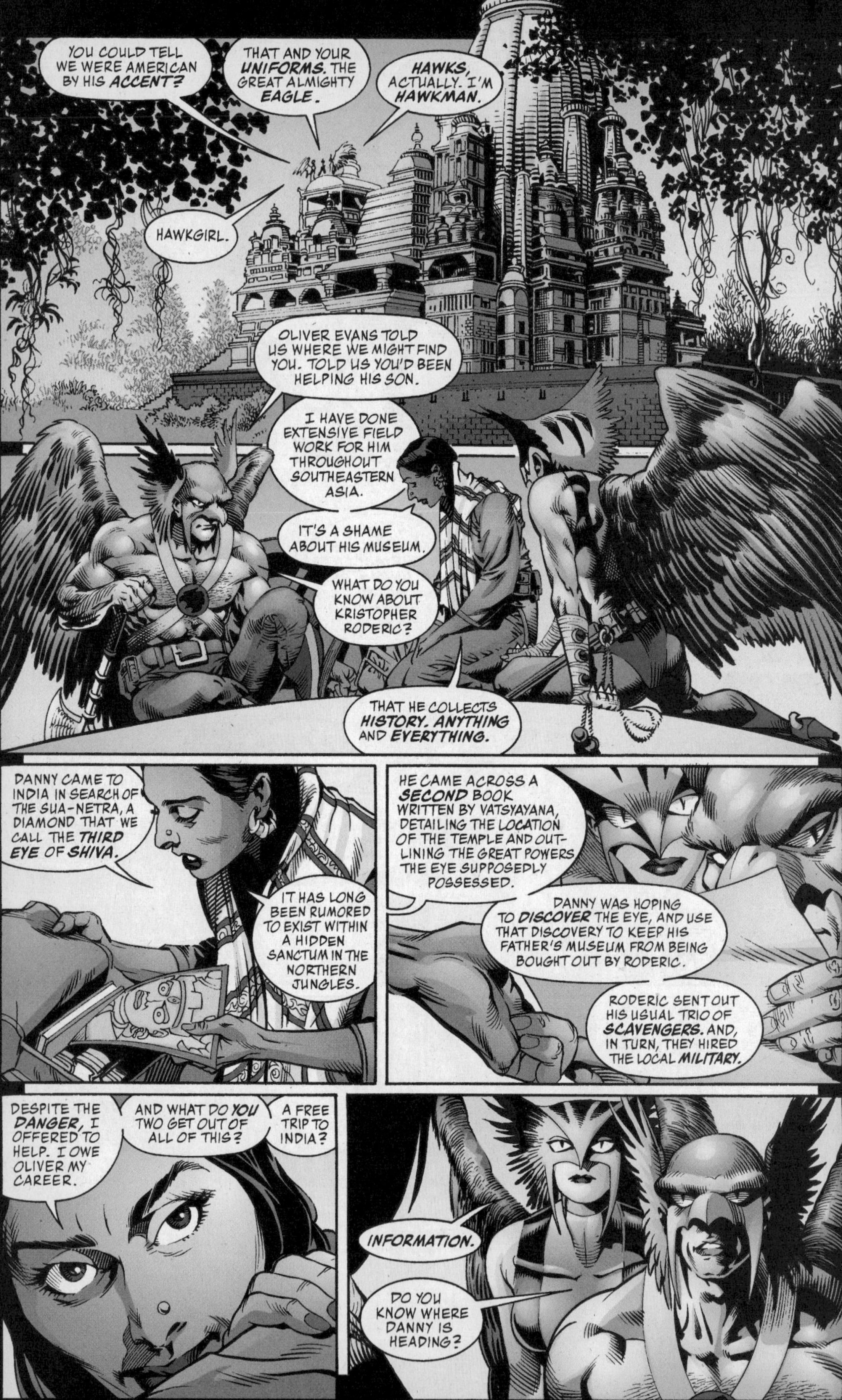

YOU COULD TELL WE WERE AMERICAN BY HIS ACCENT?
THAT AND YOUR UNIFORMS. THE GREAT ALMIGHTY EAGLE.
HAWKS, ACTUALLY. I'M HAWKMAN.
HAWKGIRL.
OLIVER EVANS TOLD US WHERE WE MIGHT FIND YOU. TOLD US YOU'D BEEN HELPING HIS SON.
I HAVE DONE EXTENSIVE FIELD WORK FOR HIM THROUGHOUT SOUTHEASTERN ASIA.
IT'S A SHAME ABOUT HIS MUSEUM.
WHAT DO YOU KNOW ABOUT KRISTOPHER RODERIC?
THAT HE COLLECTS HISTORY. ANYTHING AND EVERYTHING.
DANNY CAME TO INDIA IN SEARCH OF THE SUA-NETRA, A DIAMOND THAT WE CALL THE THIRD EYE OF SHIVA.
IT HAS LONG BEEN RUMORED TO EXIST WITHIN A HIDDEN SANCTUM IN THE NORTHERN JUNGLES.
HE CAME ACROSS A SECOND BOOK WRITTEN BY VATSYAYANA, DETAILING THE LOCATION OF THE TEMPLE AND OUT-LINING THE GREAT POWERS THE EYE SUPPOSEDLY POSSESSED.
DANNY WAS HOPING TO DISCOVER THE EYE, AND USE THAT DISCOVERY TO KEEP HIS FATHER'S MUSEUM FROM BEING BOUGHT OUT BY RODERIC.
RODERIC SENT OUT HIS USUAL TRIO OF SCAVENGERS. AND, IN TURN, THEY HIRED THE LOCAL MILITARY.
DESPITE THE DANGER, I OFFERED TO HELP. I OWE OLIVER MY CAREER.
AND WHAT DO YOU TWO GET OUT OF ALL OF THIS?
A FREE TRIP TO INDIA?
INFORMATION.
DO YOU KNOW WHERE DANNY IS HEADING?

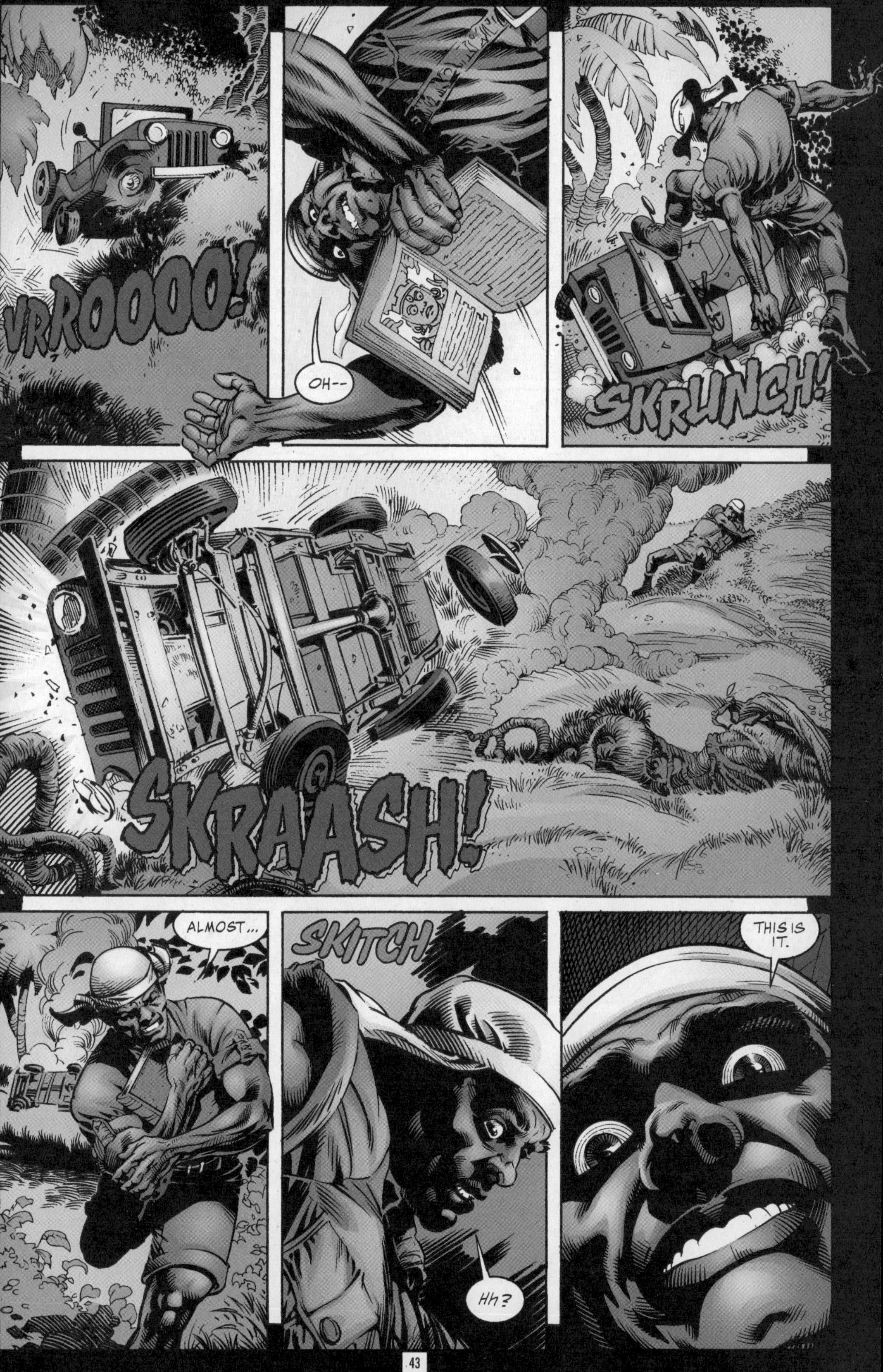

VRROOOO!
OH--
SKRUNCH!
SKRAASH!
ALMOST...
SKITCH
Hh?
THIS IS IT.

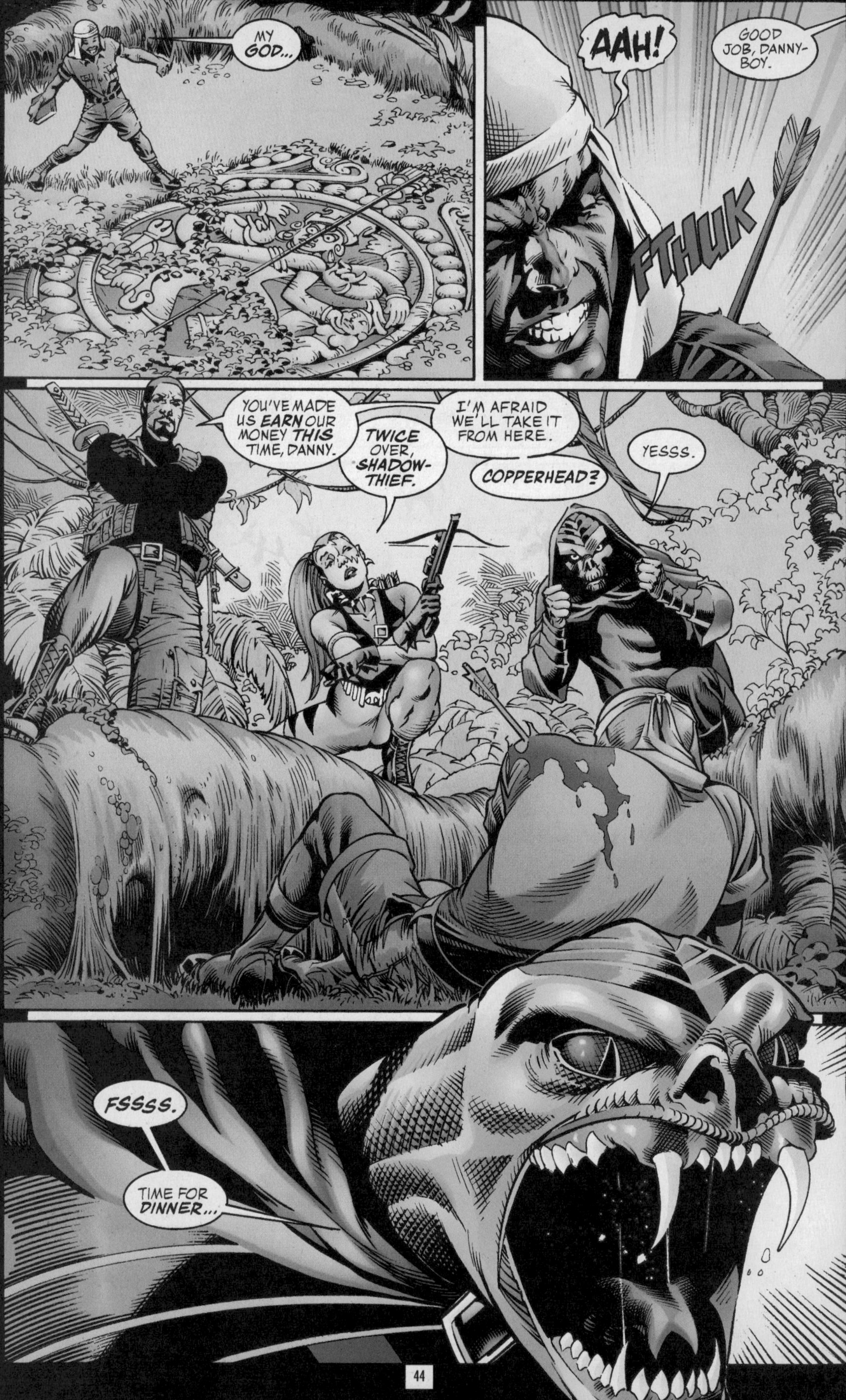
MY GOD...
AAH!
GOOD JOB, DANNY-BOY.
FTHUK
YOU'VE MADE US EARN OUR MONEY THIS TIME, DANNY.
TWICE OVER, SHADOW-THIEF.
I'M AFRAID WE'LL TAKE IT FROM HERE.
COPPERHEAD?
YESSS.
FSSSS.
TIME FOR DINNER...

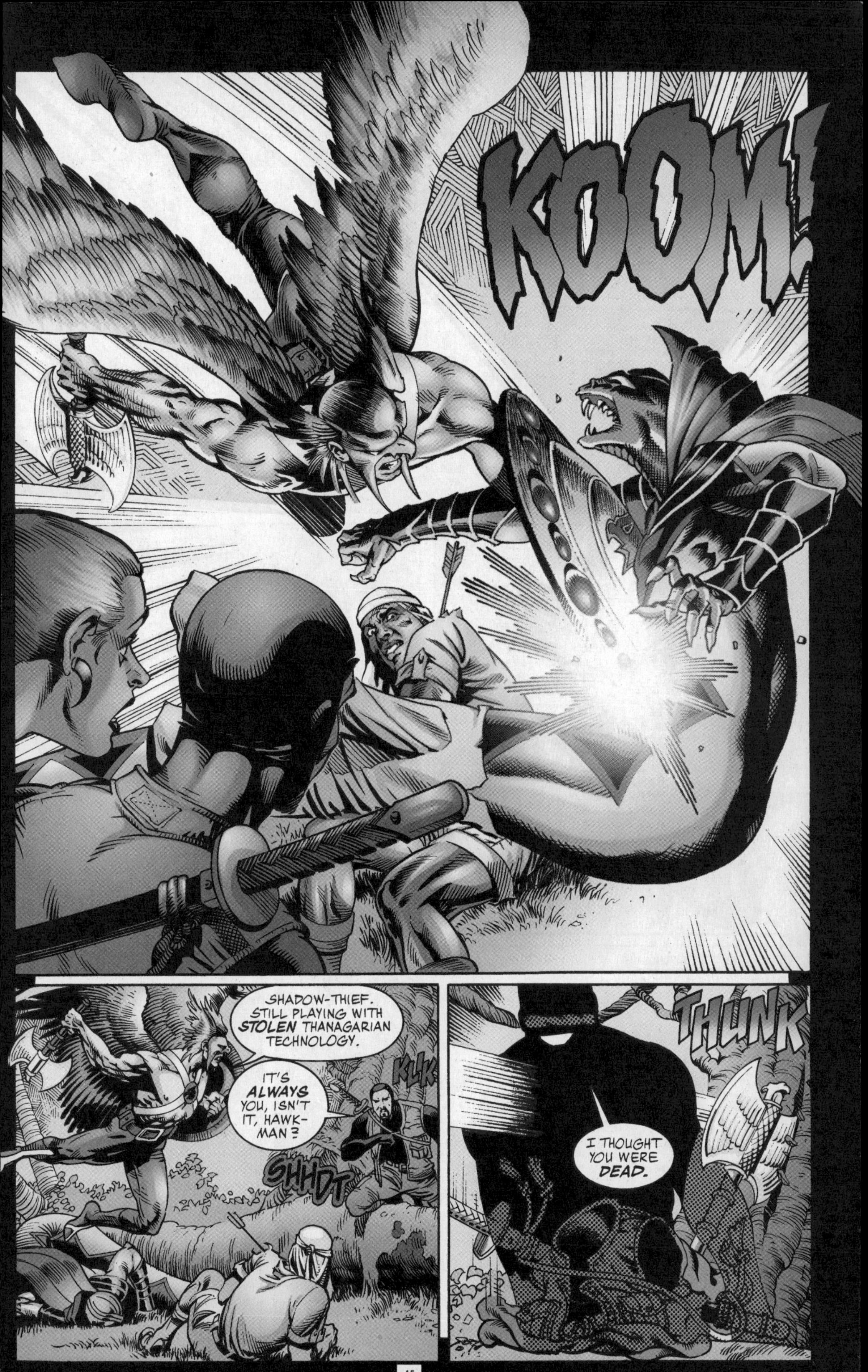
KOOM!
SHADOW-THIEF. STILL PLAYING WITH STOLEN THANAGARIAN TECHNOLOGY.
IT'S ALWAYS YOU, ISN'T IT, HAWK-MAN?
KLIK
SHHDT
THUNK
I THOUGHT YOU WERE DEAD.

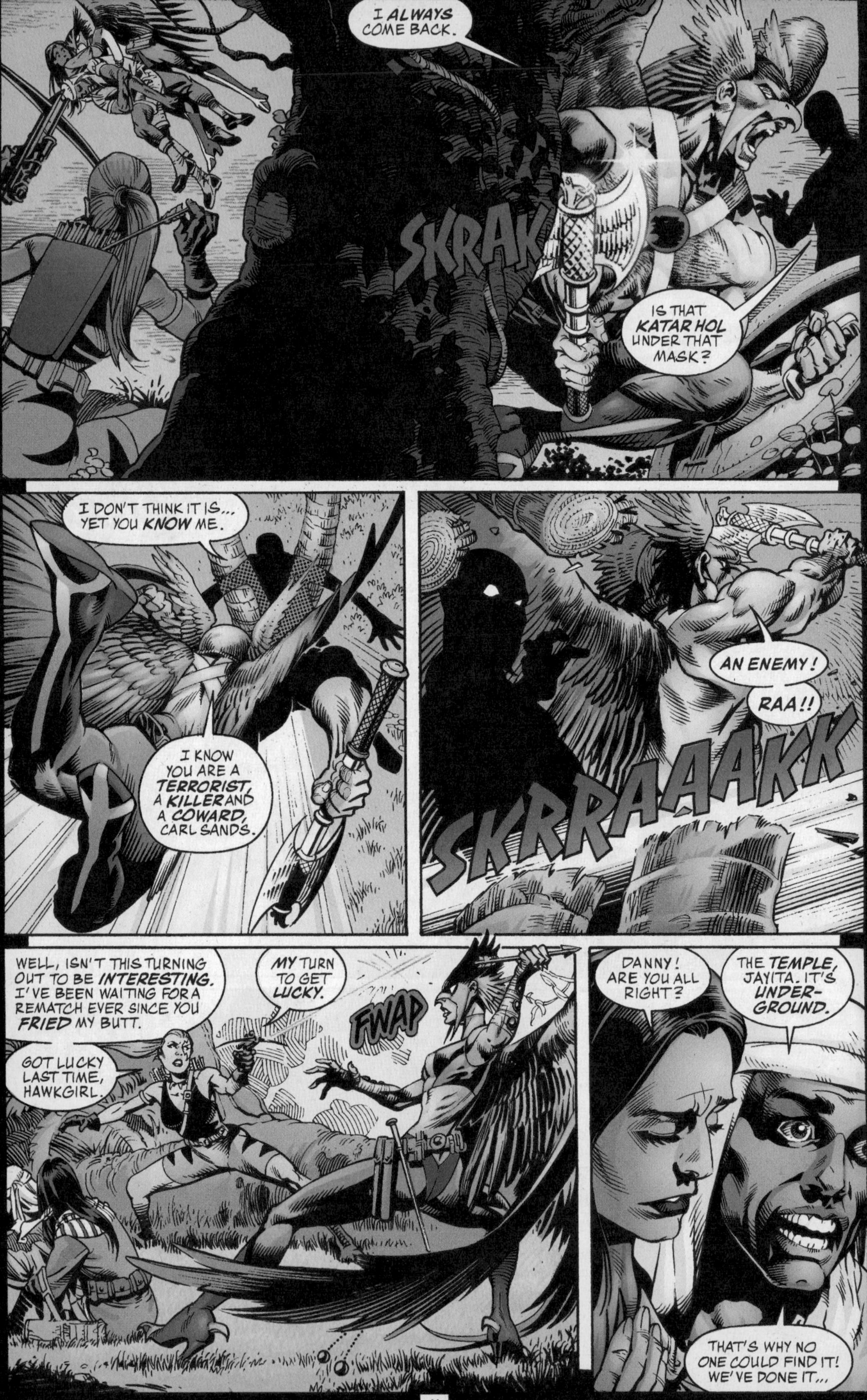
I ALWAYS COME BACK.
SKRAK
IS THAT KATAR HOL UNDER THAT MASK?
I DON'T THINK IT IS... YET YOU KNOW ME.
I KNOW YOU ARE A TERRORIST, A KILLER AND A COWARD, CARL SANDS.
AN ENEMY!
RAA!!
SKRRAAAKK
WELL, ISN'T THIS TURNING OUT TO BE INTERESTING. I'VE BEEN WAITING FOR A REMATCH EVER SINCE YOU FRIED MY BUTT.
GOT LUCKY LAST TIME, HAWKGIRL.
MY TURN TO GET LUCKY.
FWAP
DANNY! ARE YOU ALL RIGHT?
THE TEMPLE, JAYITA. IT'S UNDER-GROUND.
THAT'S WHY NO ONE COULD FIND IT! WE'VE DONE IT...

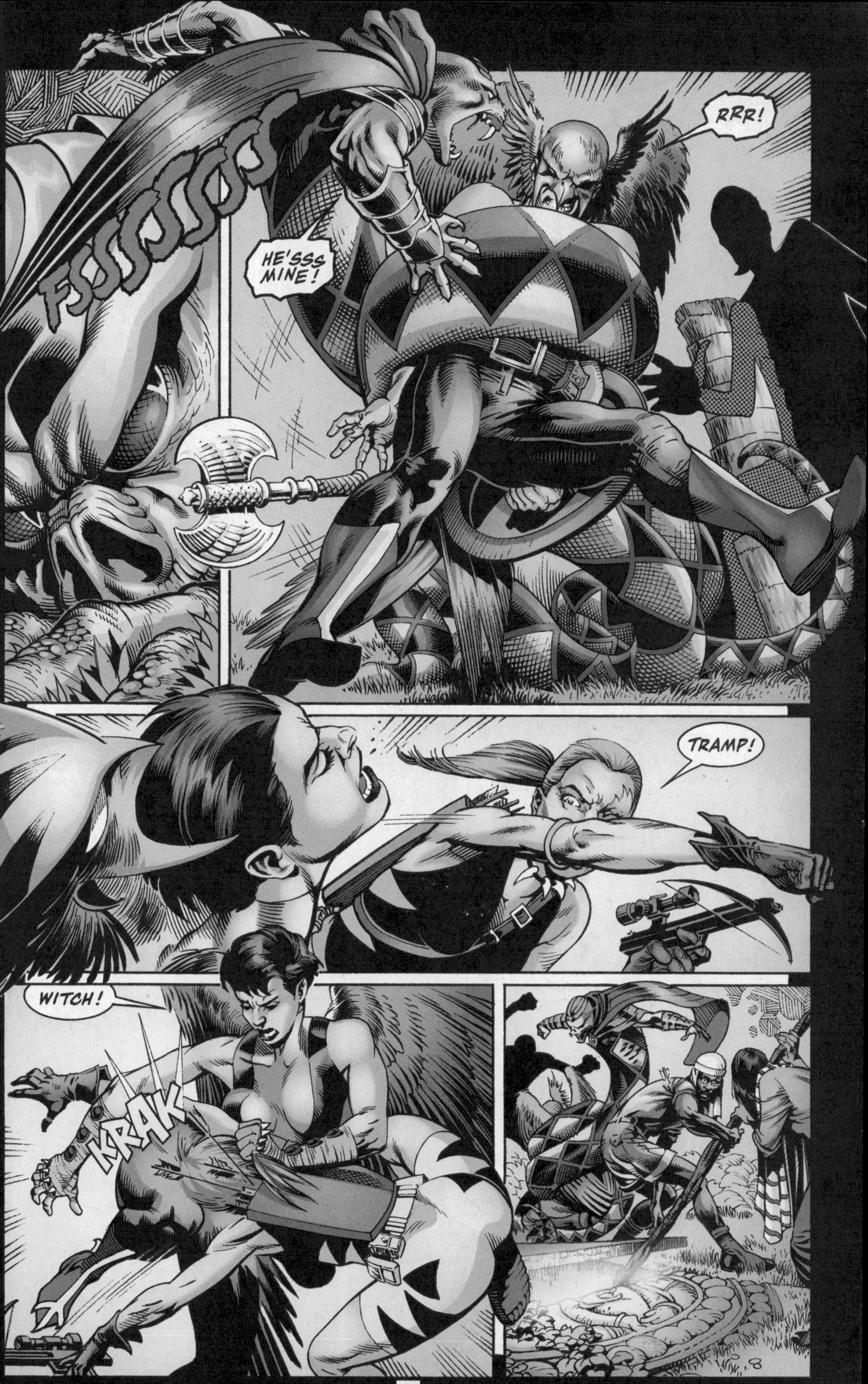
RRR!
FSSSSSSSS
HE'SSS MINE!
TRAMP!
WITCH!
KRAK

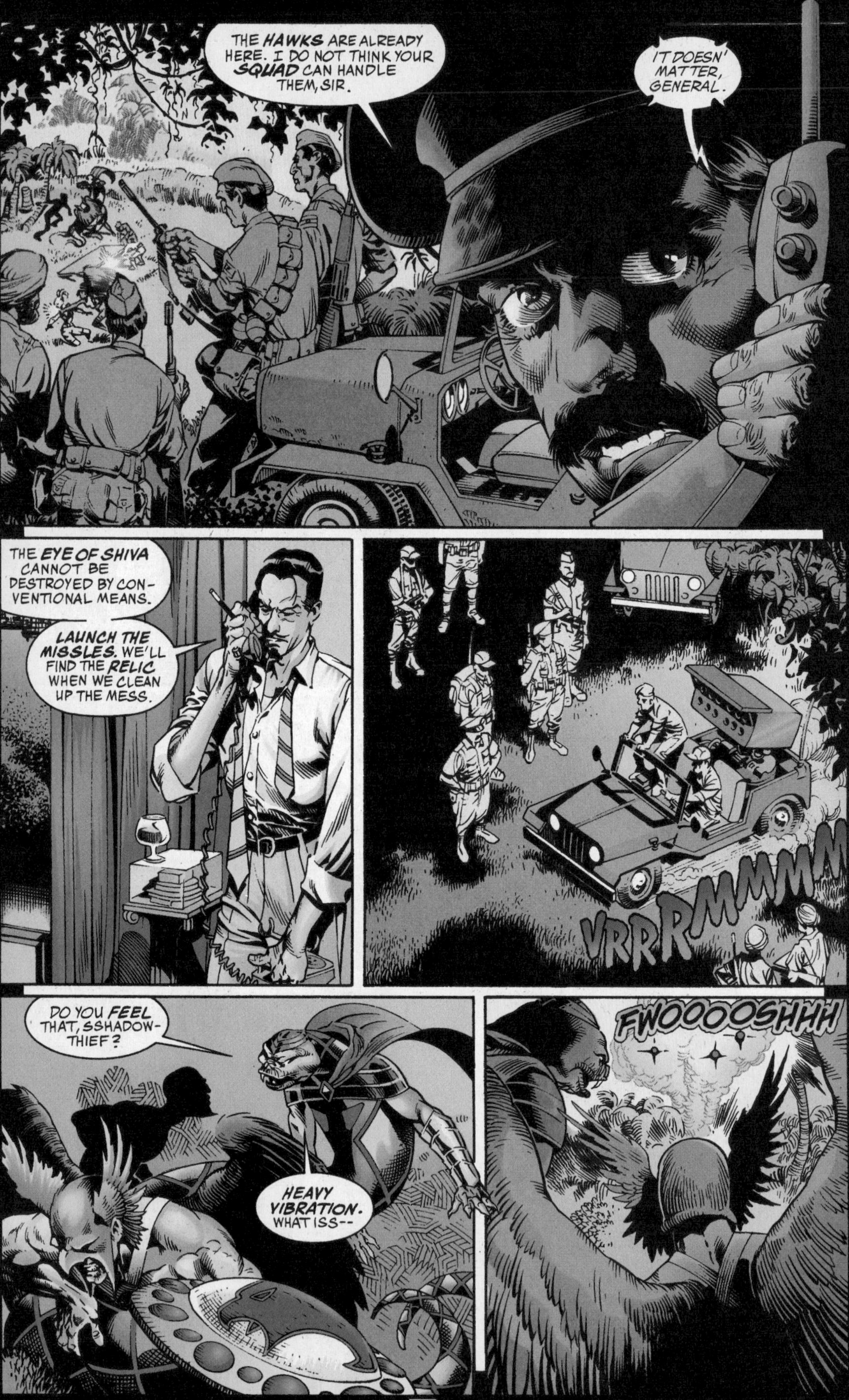
THE HAWKS ARE ALREADY HERE. I DO NOT THINK YOUR SQUAD CAN HANDLE THEM, SIR.
IT DOESN' MATTER, GENERAL.
THE EYE OF SHIVA CANNOT BE DESTROYED BY CONVENTIONAL MEANS.
LAUNCH THE MISSLES. WE'LL FIND THE RELIC WHEN WE CLEAN UP THE MESS.
VRRRMMMMM
DO YOU FEEL THAT, SSHADOW-THIEF?
HEAVY VIBRATION. WHAT ISS--
FWOOOOSHHH

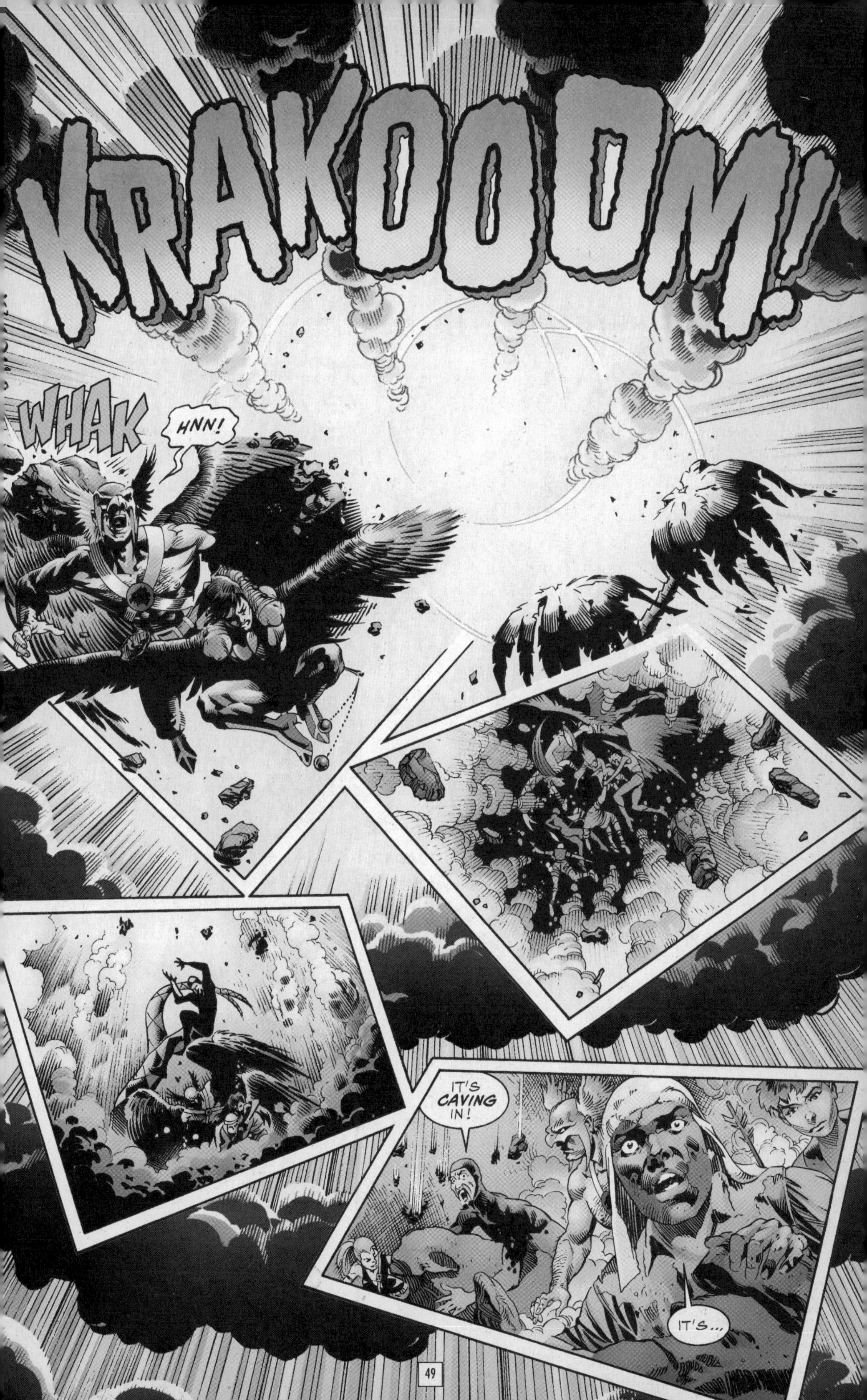
KRAKOOOM!
WHAK
HNN!
IT'S CAVING IN!
IT'S...

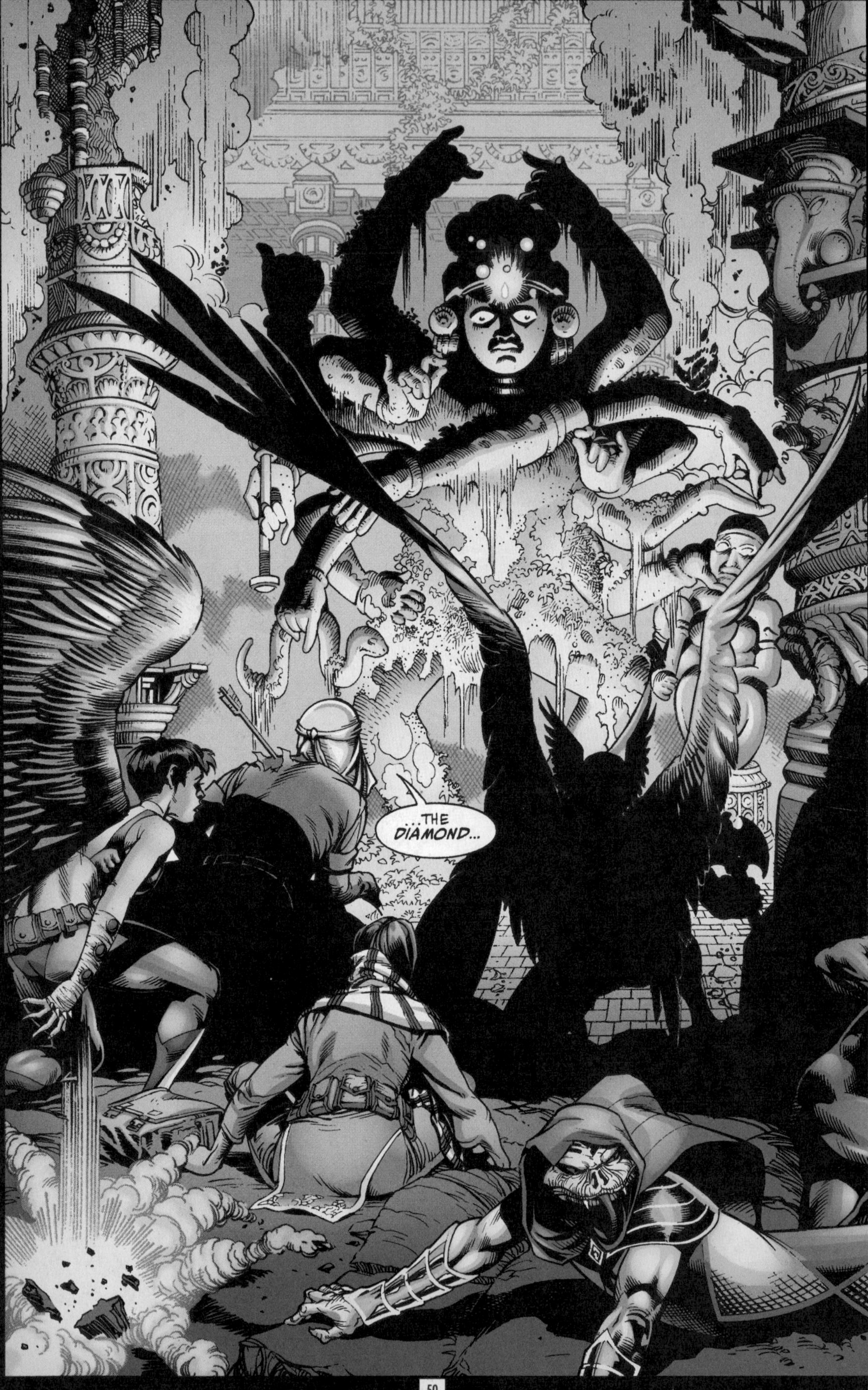
...THE DIAMOND...

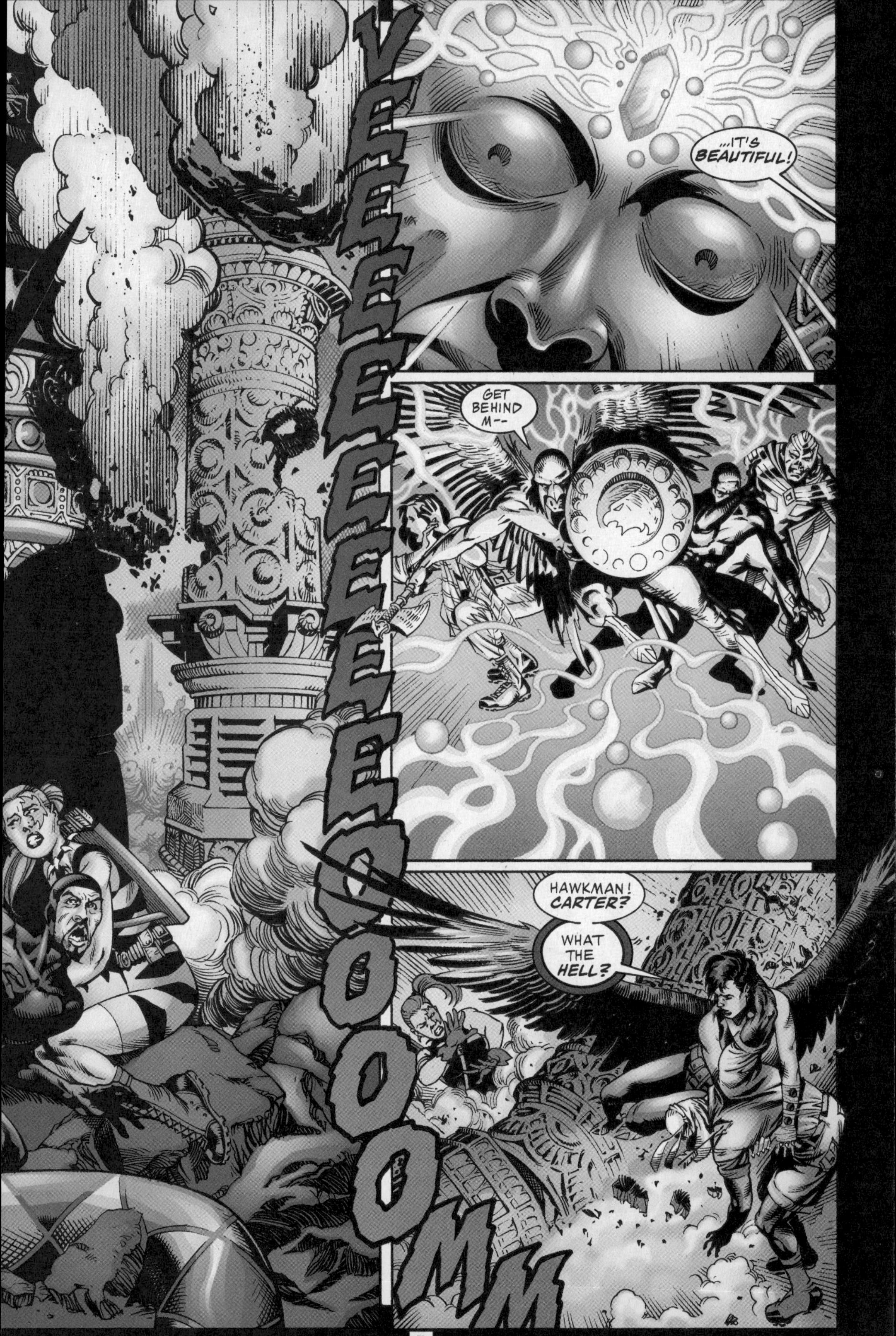
VEEEEEEEEEEEOOOOOOMM
...IT'S BEAUTIFUL!
GET BEHIND M--
HAWKMAN! CARTER?
WHAT THE HELL?

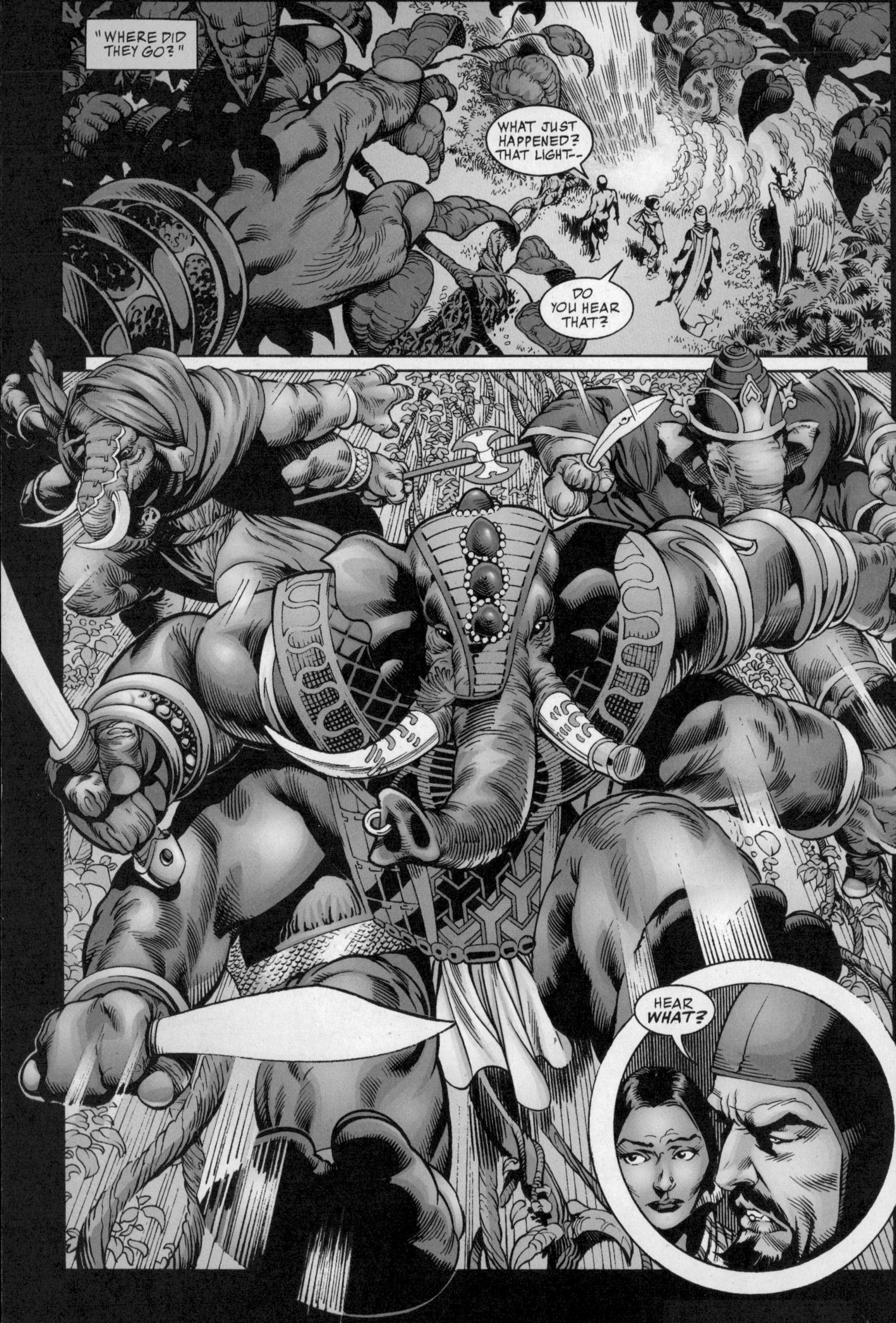
"WHERE DID THEY GO?"
WHAT JUST HAPPENED? THAT LIGHT--
DO YOU HEAR THAT?
HEAR WHAT?

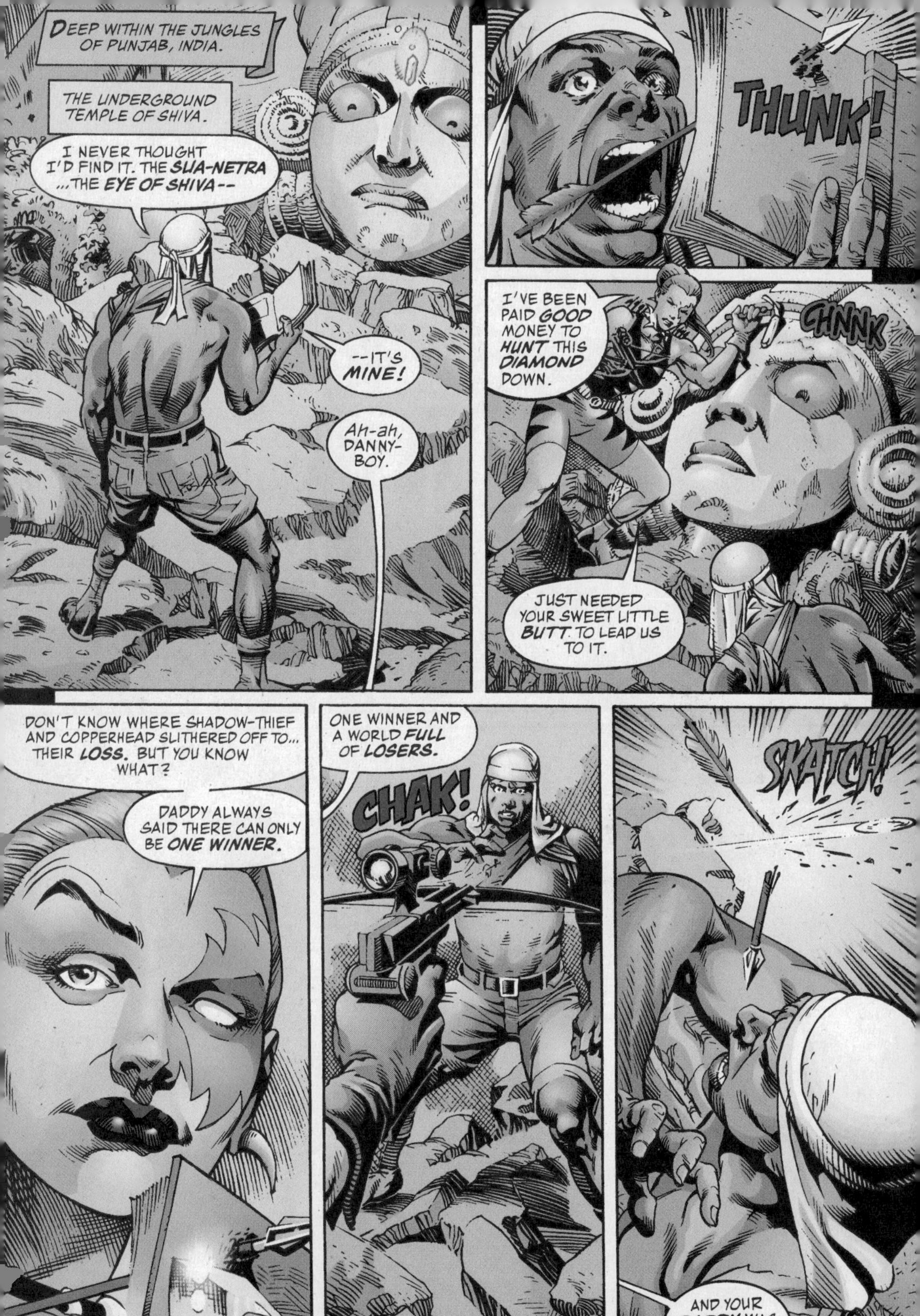
DEEP WITHIN THE JUNGLES OF PUNJAB, INDIA.
THE UNDERGROUND TEMPLE OF SHIVA.
I NEVER THOUGHT I'D FIND IT. THE SUA-NETRA ...THE EYE OF SHIVA--
--IT'S MINE!
Ah-ah, DANNY-BOY.
THUNK!
I'VE BEEN PAID GOOD MONEY TO HUNT THIS DIAMOND DOWN.
CHNNK
JUST NEEDED YOUR SWEET LITTLE BUTT TO LEAD US TO IT.
DON'T KNOW WHERE SHADOW-THIEF AND COPPERHEAD SLITHERED OFF TO... THEIR LOSS. BUT YOU KNOW WHAT?
DADDY ALWAYS SAID THERE CAN ONLY BE ONE WINNER.
ONE WINNER AND A WORLD FULL OF LOSERS.
CHAK!
SKATCH!
AND YOUR DADDY WAS A LOSER, TIGRESS.

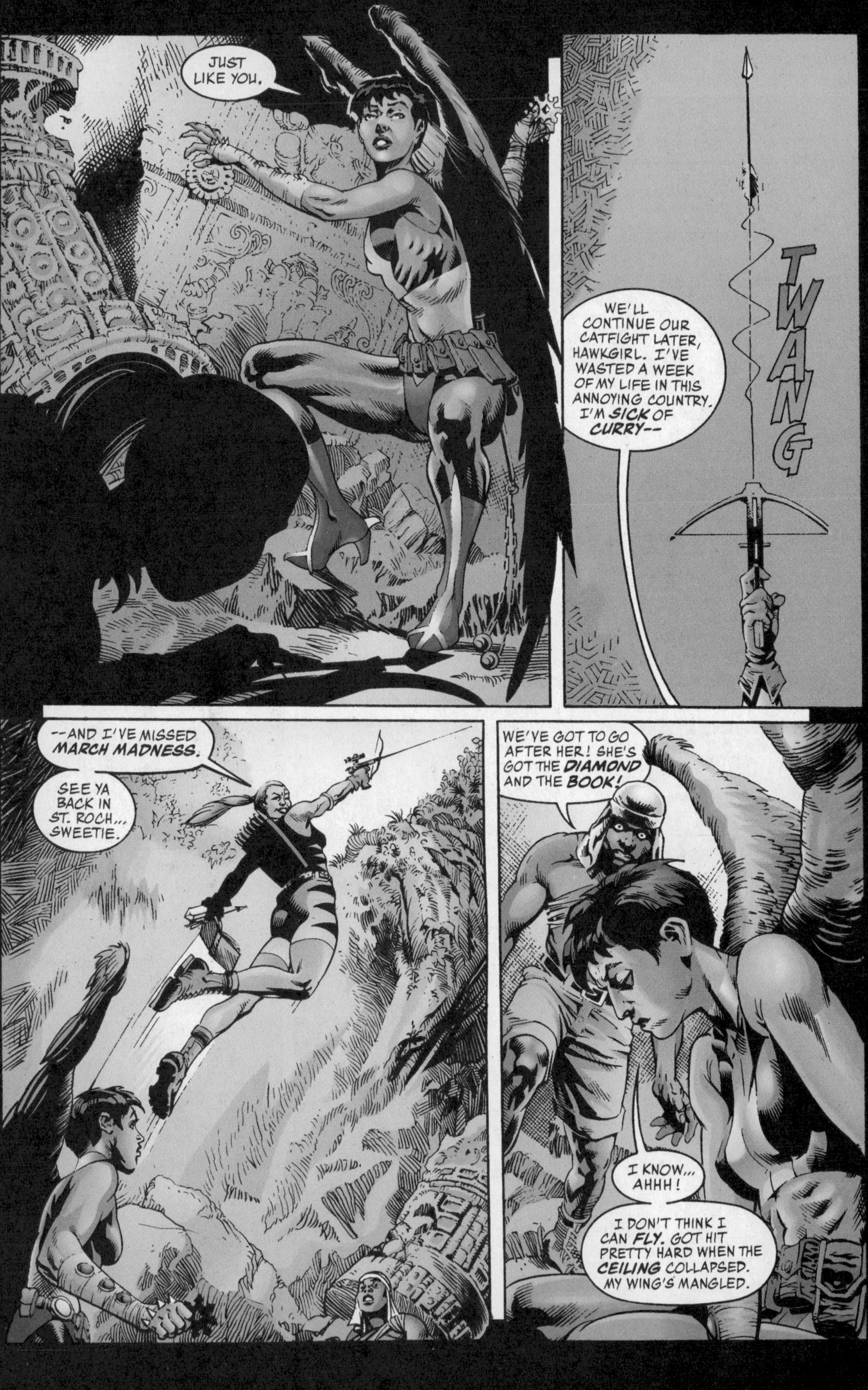
JUST LIKE YOU.
WE'LL CONTINUE OUR CATFIGHT LATER, HAWKGIRL. I'VE WASTED A WEEK OF MY LIFE IN THIS ANNOYING COUNTRY. I'M SICK OF CURRY--
TWANG
--AND I'VE MISSED MARCH MADNESS.
SEE YA BACK IN ST. ROCH... SWEETIE.
WE'VE GOT TO GO AFTER HER! SHE'S GOT THE DIAMOND AND THE BOOK!
I KNOW... AHHH!
I DON'T THINK I CAN FLY. GOT HIT PRETTY HARD WHEN THE CEILING COLLAPSED. MY WING'S MANGLED.

MY **FATHER** SENT YOU AND HAWKMAN, RIGHT? DIDN'T THINK I COULD HANDLE THIS.

WHERE DID... uh... **HAWKMAN** AND THE OTHERS GO? THERE WAS A **FLASH** OF LIGHT AND THEN--

SKRACH

JAYITA PARTIALLY TRANSLATED THE BOOK... SAID THIS TEMPLE IS A DOORWAY TO THE **BATTLELANDS.** THE WORLD OF GANESHA, SON OF SHIVA.

WE WEREN'T SUPPOSED TO **DISTURB** THE **TEMPLE.** DAMMIT, I JUST WANTED THE **DIAMOND.** WITHOUT IT, MY FATHER'S MUSEUM IS LOST--

--AND THAT DEVIL **RODERIC** GETS IT ALL.

WHEN THE **EXPLOSION** ERUPTED, IT MUST HAVE TRIGGERED A KIND OF **SAFETY** MECHANISM. POSSIBLY OPENING THE DOORWAY TO THE BATTLELANDS.

SO HOW DO WE OPEN IT BACK UP?

AND WHO THE HELL **CAUSED** THAT EXPLOSION?

KLAK KLAK

THAT WOULD BE US, AMERICAN.

OH, DAMN.

YOU **BETTER** BE WORTH THIS, DANNY.

WHAT ARE YOU--?

NORMALLY THIS WOULD NOT FALL UNDER THE MILITARY'S JURISDICTION.

BUT WE HAVE BEEN PAID VERY WELL TO KILL YOU.

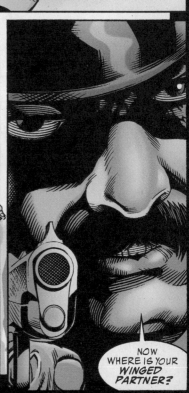

NOW WHERE IS YOUR **WINGED PARTNER?**

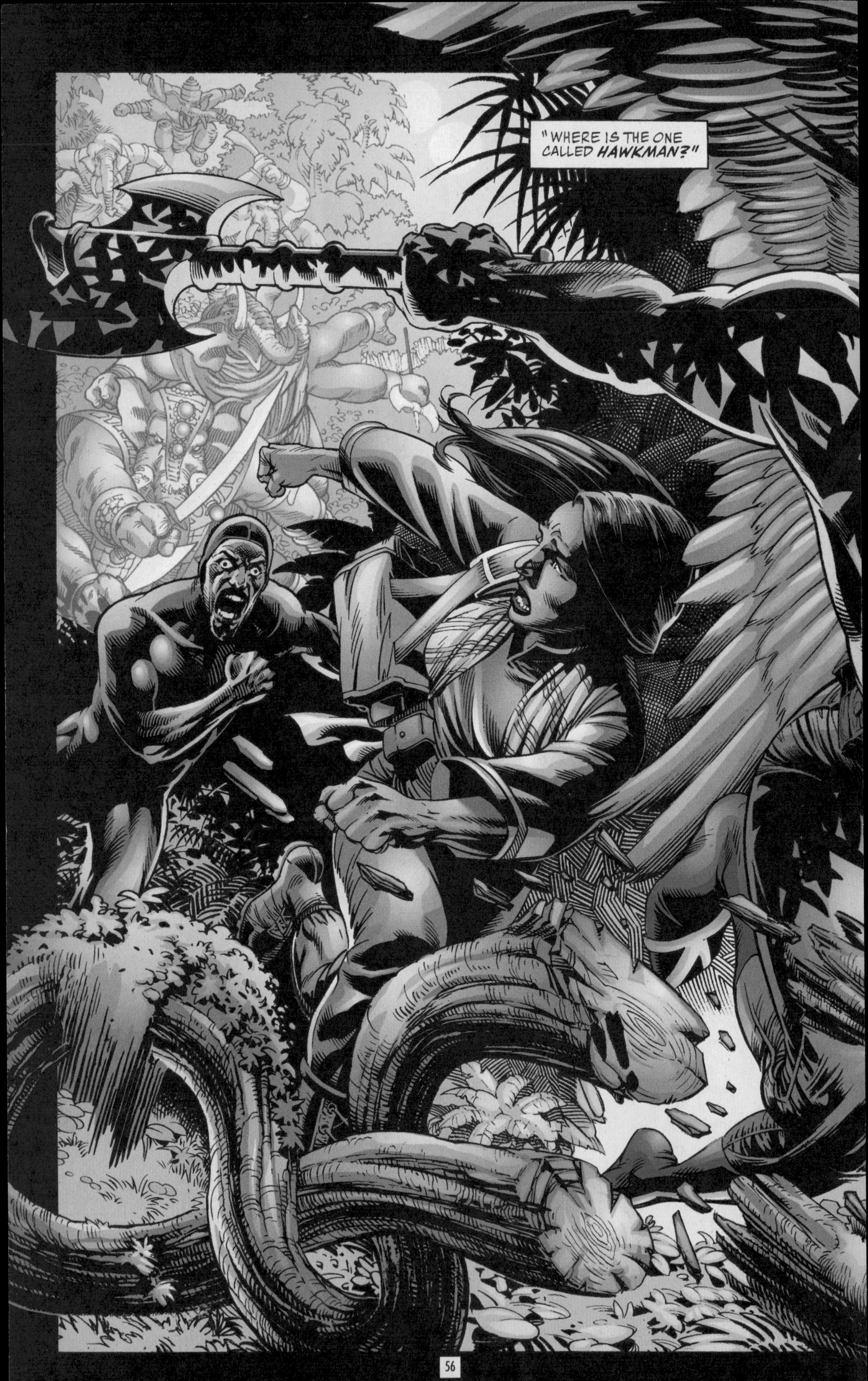
"WHERE IS THE ONE CALLED HAWKMAN?"

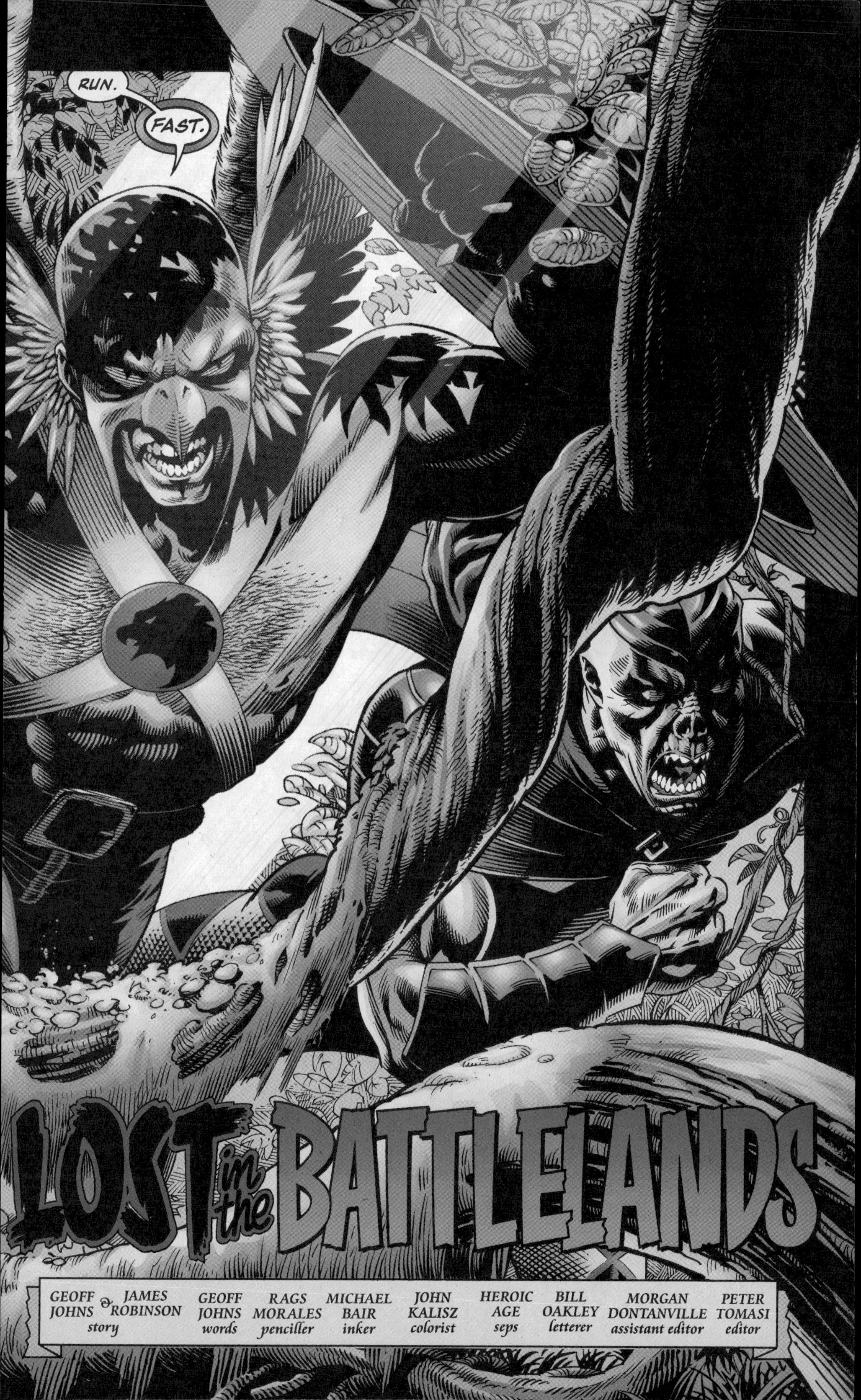

RUN.
FAST.
LOST in the BATTLELANDS
GEOFF JOHNS & JAMES ROBINSON story
GEOFF JOHNS words
RAGS MORALES penciller
MICHAEL BAIR inker
JOHN KALISZ colorist
HEROIC AGE seps
BILL OAKLEY letterer
MORGAN DONTANVILLE assistant editor
PETER TOMASI editor

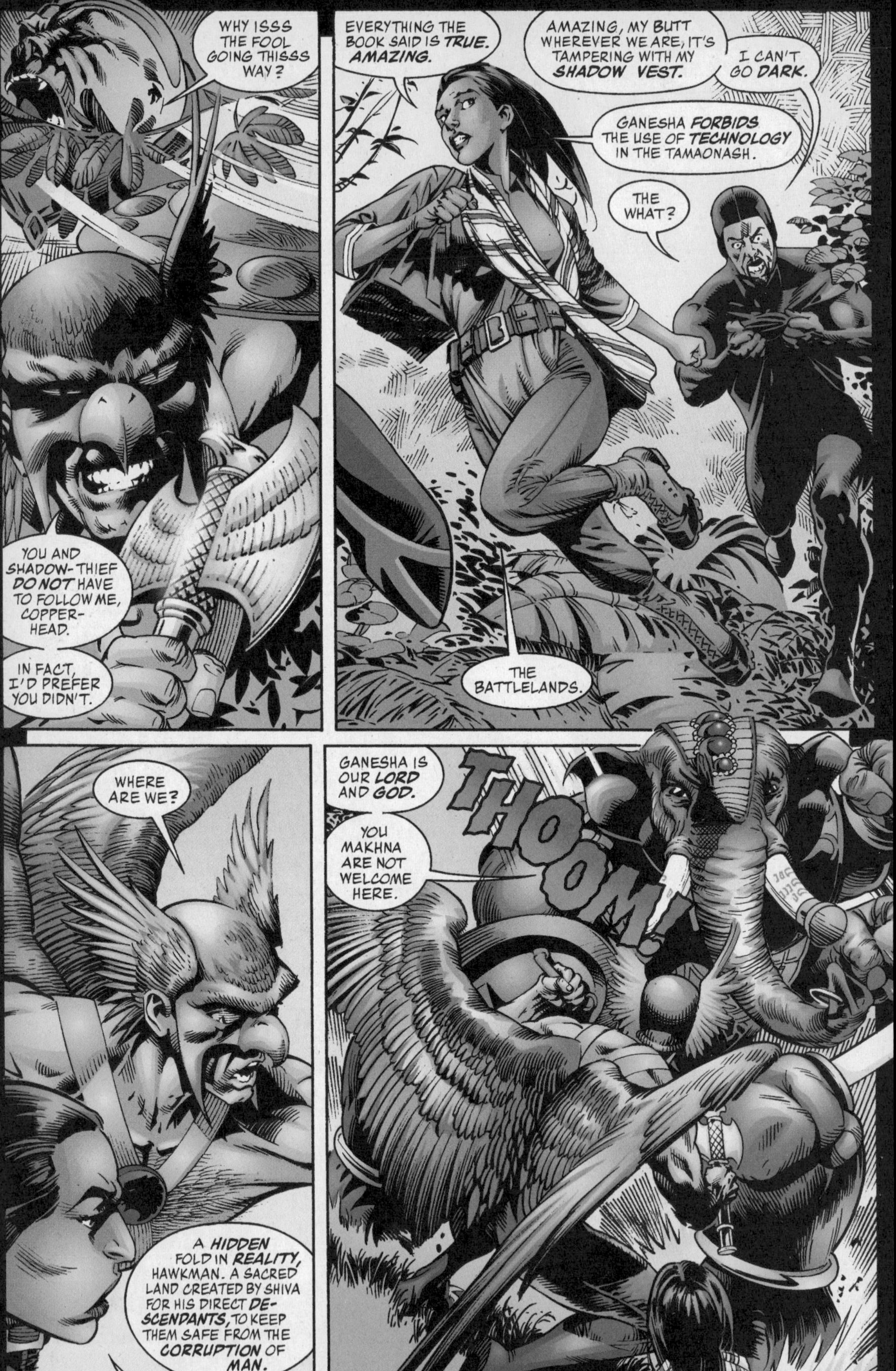
WHY ISSS THE FOOL GOING THISSS WAY?
YOU AND SHADOW-THIEF DO NOT HAVE TO FOLLOW ME, COPPER-HEAD.
IN FACT, I'D PREFER YOU DIDN'T.
EVERYTHING THE BOOK SAID IS TRUE. AMAZING.
AMAZING, MY BUTT WHEREVER WE ARE, IT'S TAMPERING WITH MY SHADOW VEST.
I CAN'T GO DARK.
GANESHA FORBIDS THE USE OF TECHNOLOGY IN THE TAMAONASH.
THE WHAT?
THE BATTLELANDS.
WHERE ARE WE?
A HIDDEN FOLD IN REALITY, HAWKMAN. A SACRED LAND CREATED BY SHIVA FOR HIS DIRECT DE-SCENDANTS, TO KEEP THEM SAFE FROM THE CORRUPTION OF MAN.
THE WORLD OF GANESHA.
GANESHA IS OUR LORD AND GOD.
YOU MAKHNA ARE NOT WELCOME HERE.
THOOOM!

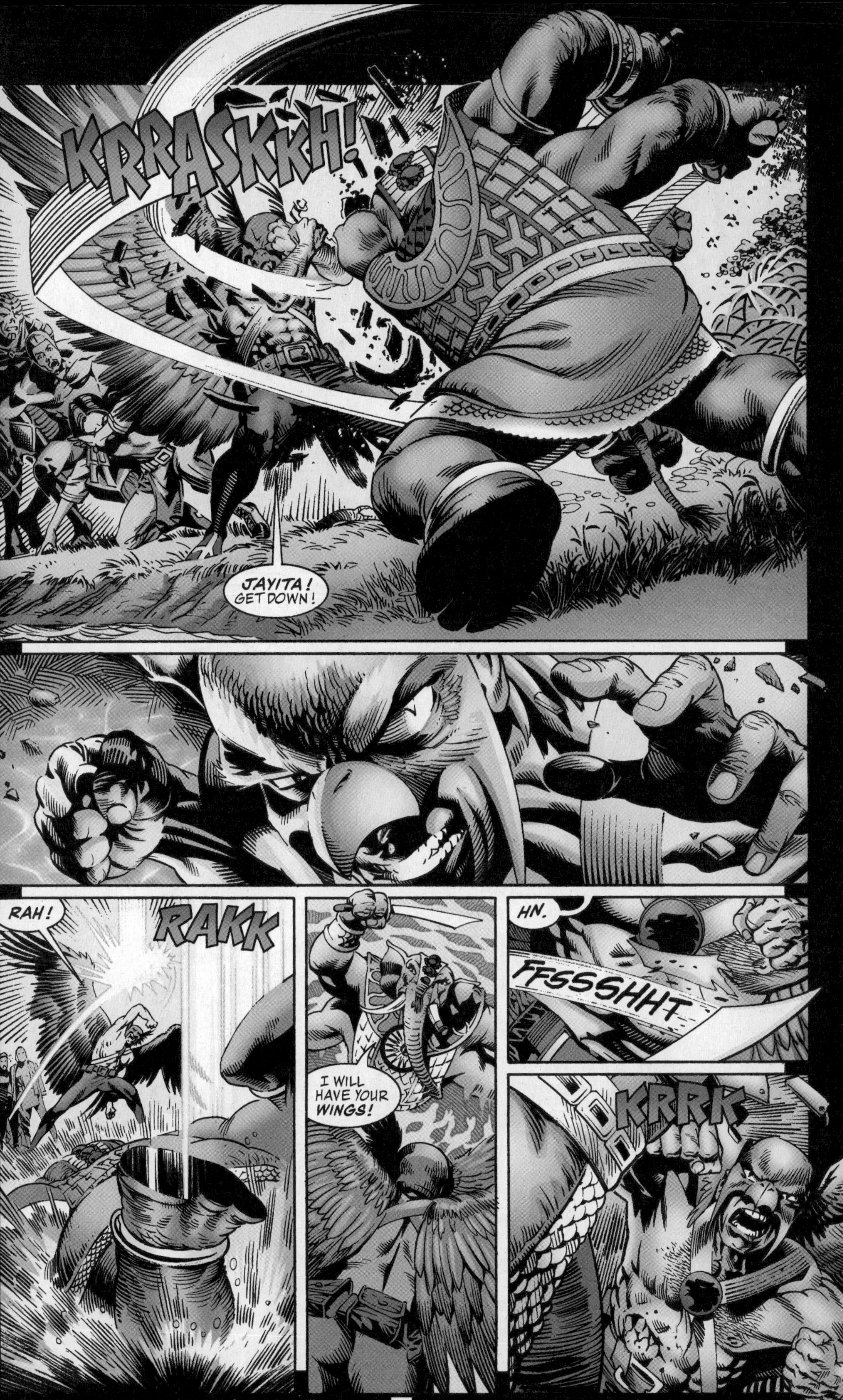
KRRASKKH!
JAYITA! GET DOWN!
RAH!
RAKK
I WILL HAVE YOUR WINGS!
HN.
FFSSSHHT
KRRK

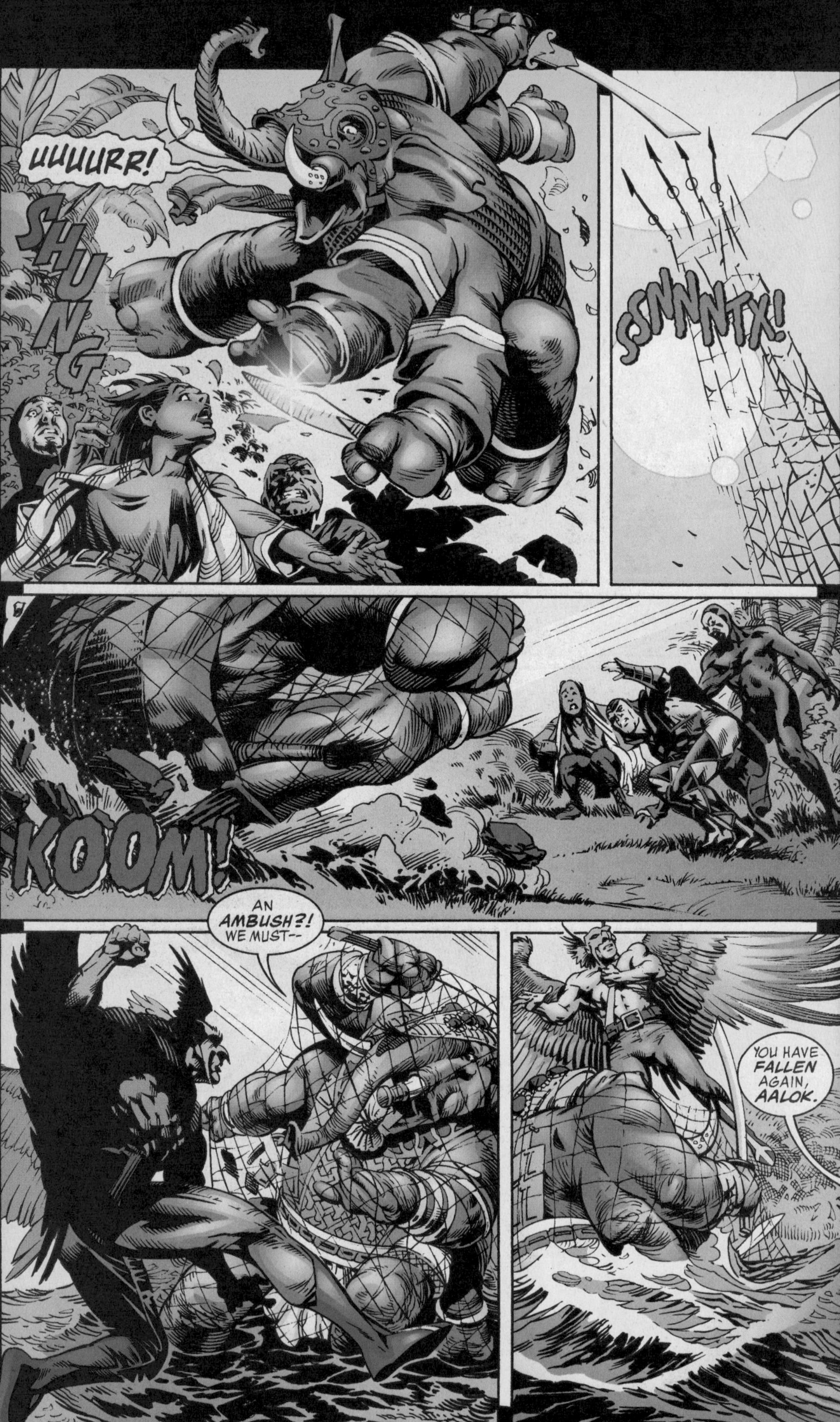
UUUURR!
SHUNG
SSNNNTX!
KOOM!
AN AMBUSH?! WE MUST--
YOU HAVE FALLEN AGAIN, AALOK.

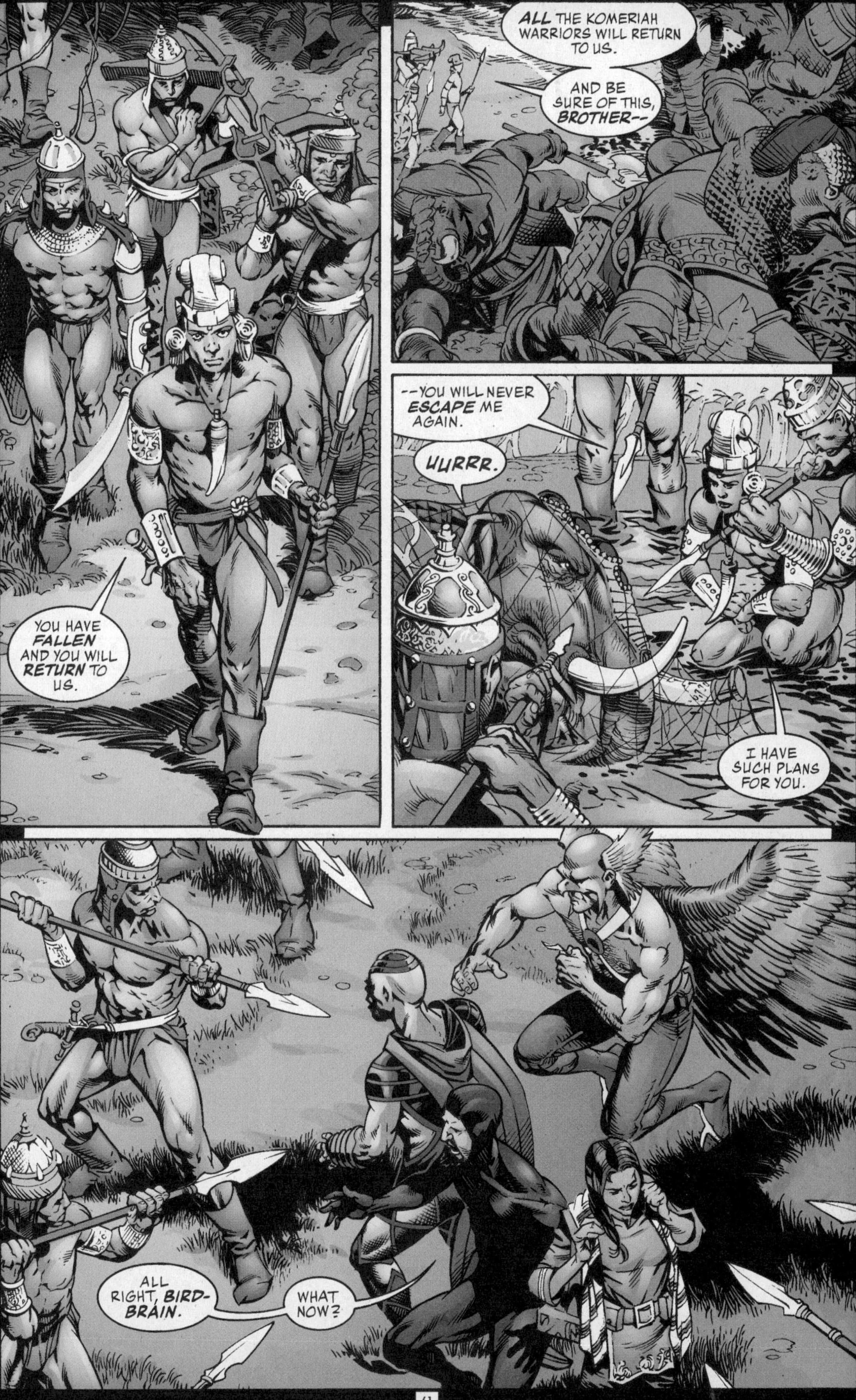
YOU HAVE FALLEN AND YOU WILL RETURN TO US.
ALL THE KOMERIAH WARRIORS WILL RETURN TO US.
AND BE SURE OF THIS, BROTHER--
--YOU WILL NEVER ESCAPE ME AGAIN.
UURRR.
I HAVE SUCH PLANS FOR YOU.
ALL RIGHT, BIRD-BRAIN.
WHAT NOW?

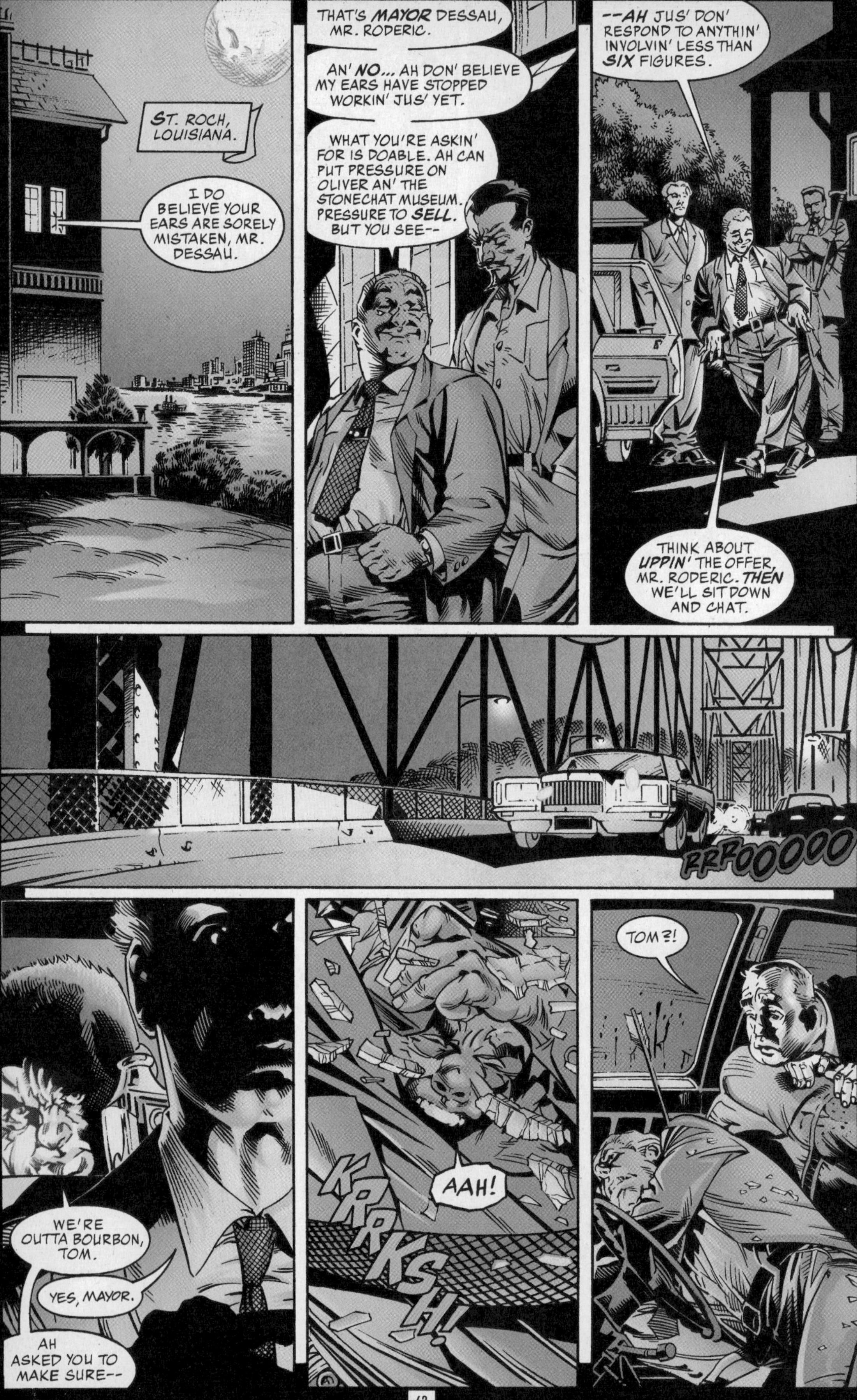
ST. ROCH, LOUISIANA.
I DO BELIEVE YOUR EARS ARE SORELY MISTAKEN, MR. DESSAU.
THAT'S MAYOR DESSAU, MR. RODERIC.
AN' NO... AH DON' BELIEVE MY EARS HAVE STOPPED WORKIN' JUS' YET.
WHAT YOU'RE ASKIN' FOR IS DOABLE. AH CAN PUT PRESSURE ON OLIVER AN' THE STONECHAT MUSEUM. PRESSURE TO SELL. BUT YOU SEE--
--AH JUS' DON' RESPOND TO ANYTHIN' INVOLVIN' LESS THAN SIX FIGURES.
THINK ABOUT UPPIN' THE OFFER, MR. RODERIC. THEN WE'LL SIT DOWN AND CHAT.
RRROOOOOO
WE'RE OUTTA BOURBON, TOM.
YES, MAYOR.
AH ASKED YOU TO MAKE SURE--
AAH!
KRRKSH!
TOM?!

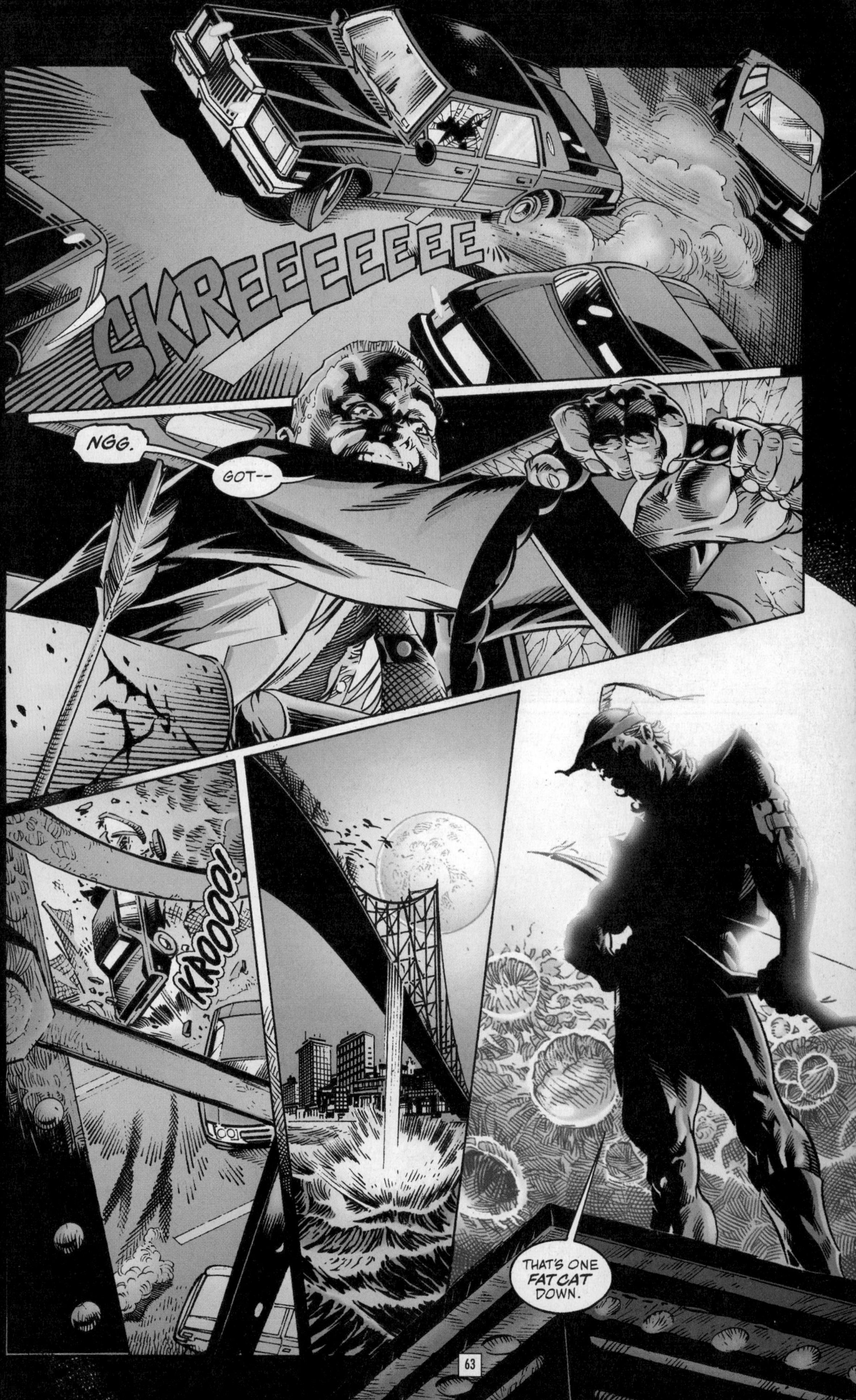
SKREEEEEEEE
NGG.
GOT--
KROOOO!
THAT'S ONE
FAT CAT
DOWN.

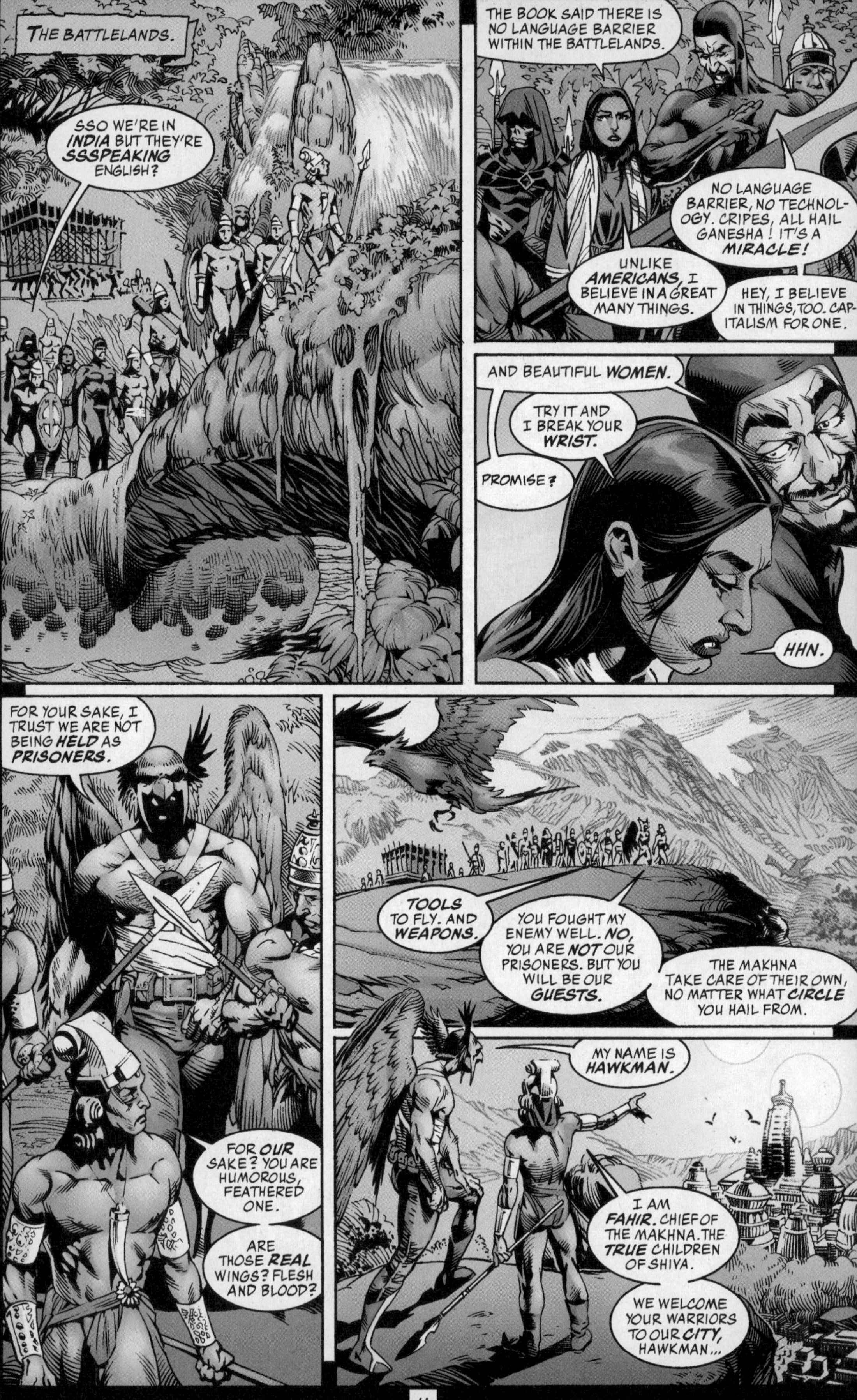
THE BATTLELANDS.
SSO WE'RE IN INDIA BUT THEY'RE SSSPEAKING ENGLISH?
THE BOOK SAID THERE IS NO LANGUAGE BARRIER WITHIN THE BATTLELANDS.
NO LANGUAGE BARRIER, NO TECHNOLOGY. CRIPES, ALL HAIL GANESHA! IT'S A MIRACLE!
UNLIKE AMERICANS, I BELIEVE IN A GREAT MANY THINGS.
HEY, I BELIEVE IN THINGS, TOO. CAPITALISM FOR ONE.
AND BEAUTIFUL WOMEN.
TRY IT AND I BREAK YOUR WRIST.
PROMISE?
HHN.
FOR YOUR SAKE, I TRUST WE ARE NOT BEING HELD AS PRISONERS.
FOR OUR SAKE? YOU ARE HUMOROUS, FEATHERED ONE.
ARE THOSE REAL WINGS? FLESH AND BLOOD?
TOOLS TO FLY. AND WEAPONS.
YOU FOUGHT MY ENEMY WELL. NO, YOU ARE NOT OUR PRISONERS. BUT YOU WILL BE OUR GUESTS.
THE MAKHNA TAKE CARE OF THEIR OWN, NO MATTER WHAT CIRCLE YOU HAIL FROM.
MY NAME IS HAWKMAN.
I AM FAHIR. CHIEF OF THE MAKHNA. THE TRUE CHILDREN OF SHIVA.
WE WELCOME YOUR WARRIORS TO OUR CITY, HAWKMAN...

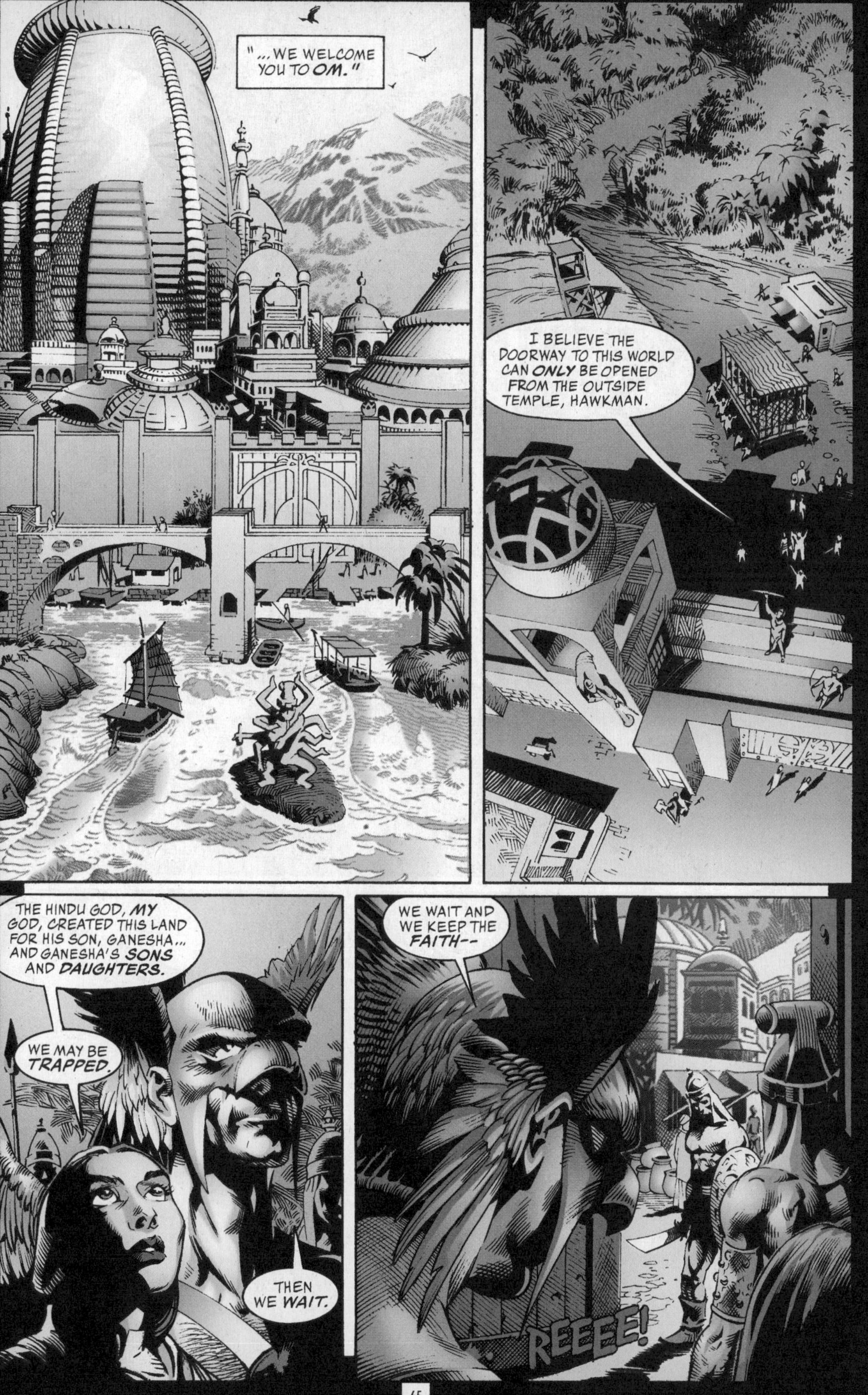
"...WE WELCOME YOU TO OM."
I BELIEVE THE DOORWAY TO THIS WORLD CAN ONLY BE OPENED FROM THE OUTSIDE TEMPLE, HAWKMAN.
THE HINDU GOD, MY GOD, CREATED THIS LAND FOR HIS SON, GANESHA... AND GANESHA'S SONS AND DAUGHTERS.
WE MAY BE TRAPPED.
THEN WE WAIT.
WE WAIT AND WE KEEP THE FAITH--
REEEE!

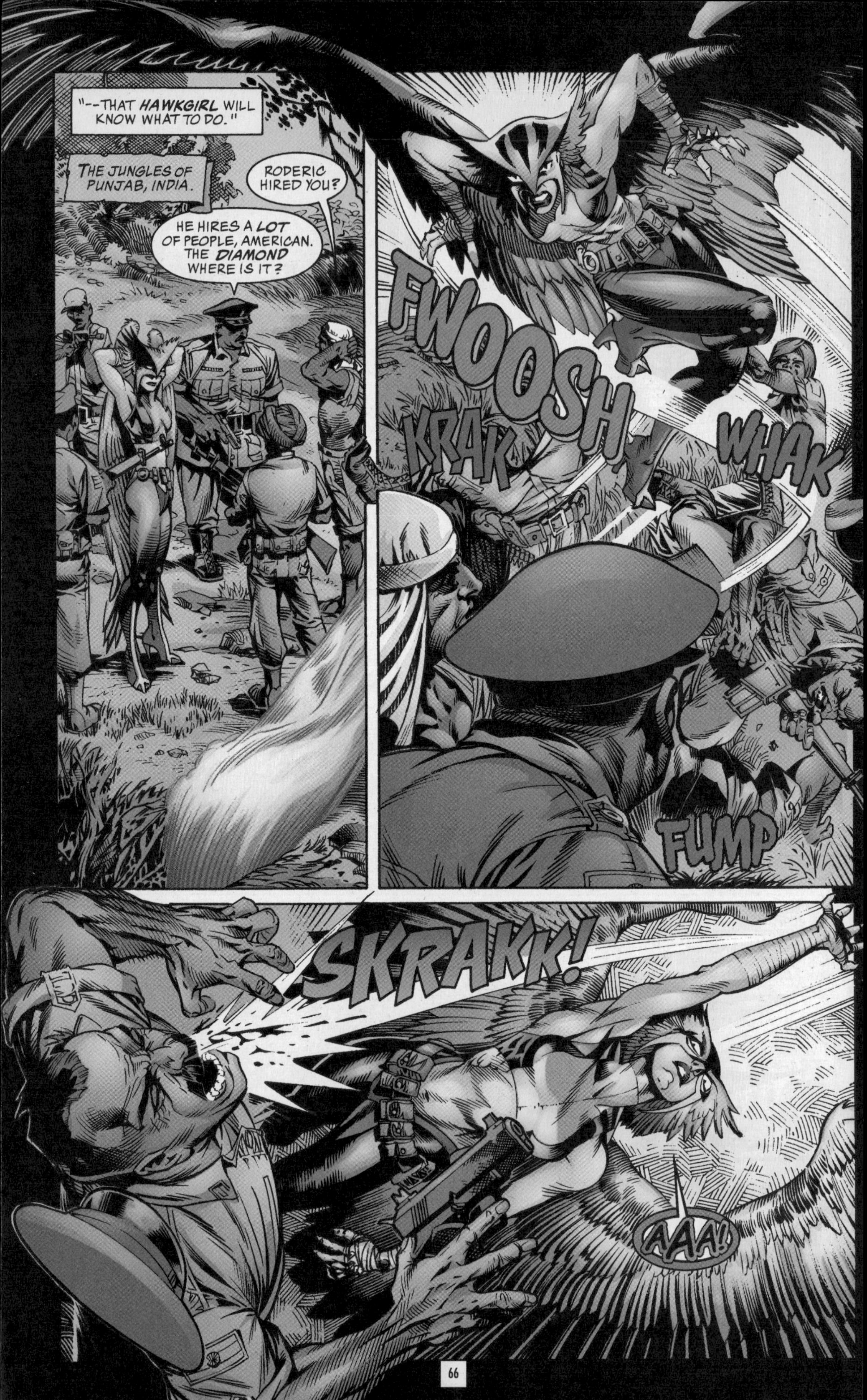

"--THAT HAWKGIRL WILL KNOW WHAT TO DO."
THE JUNGLES OF PUNJAB, INDIA.
RODERIC HIRED YOU?
HE HIRES A LOT OF PEOPLE, AMERICAN. THE DIAMOND WHERE IS IT?
FWOOSH
KRAK
WHAK
FUMP
SKRAKK!
AAA!

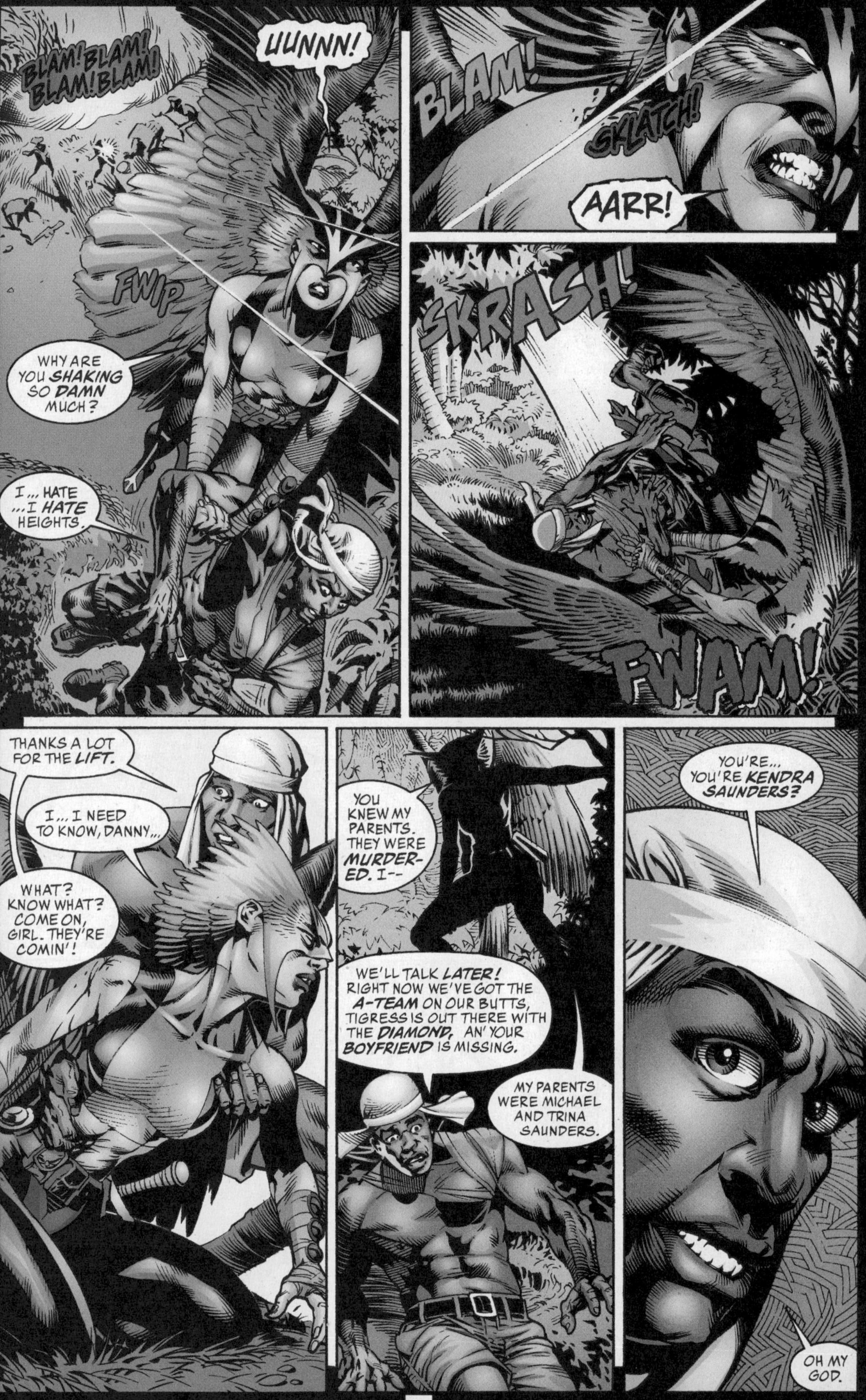
BLAM! BLAM! BLAM! BLAM!
UUNNN!
FWIP
WHY ARE YOU SHAKING SO DAMN MUCH?
I... HATE ...I HATE HEIGHTS.
BLAM!
SKLATCH!
AARR!
SKRASH!
FWAM!
THANKS A LOT FOR THE LIFT.
I... I NEED TO KNOW, DANNY...
WHAT? KNOW WHAT? COME ON, GIRL. THEY'RE COMIN'!
YOU KNEW MY PARENTS. THEY WERE MURDER-ED. I--
WE'LL TALK LATER! RIGHT NOW WE'VE GOT THE A-TEAM ON OUR BUTTS, TIGRESS IS OUT THERE WITH THE DIAMOND, AN' YOUR BOYFRIEND IS MISSING.
MY PARENTS WERE MICHAEL AND TRINA SAUNDERS.
YOU'RE... YOU'RE KENDRA SAUNDERS?
OH MY GOD.

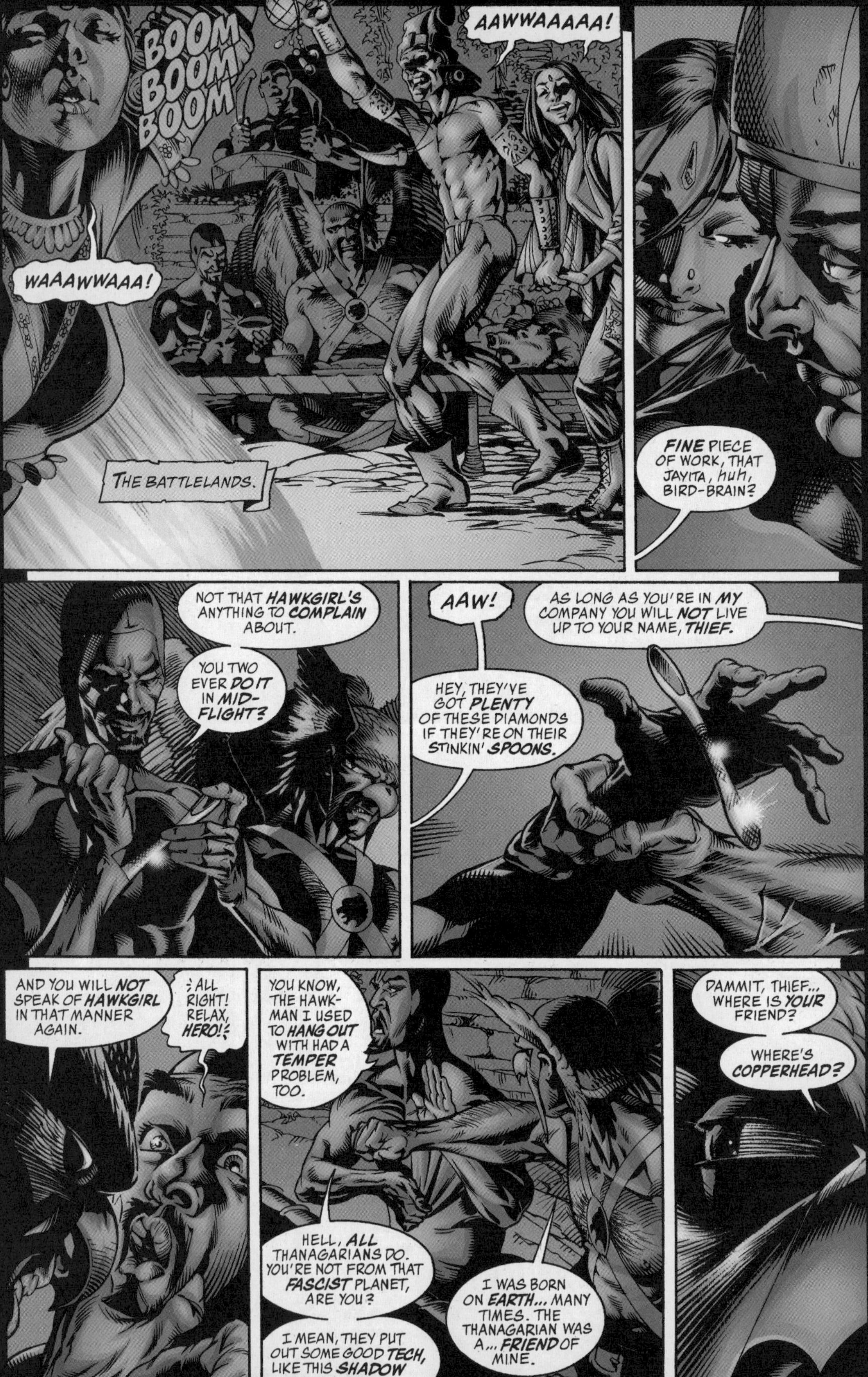
BOOM BOOM BOOM
AAWWAAAAA!
WAAAWWAAA!
THE BATTLELANDS.
FINE PIECE OF WORK, THAT JAYITA, huh, BIRD-BRAIN?
NOT THAT HAWKGIRL'S ANYTHING TO COMPLAIN ABOUT.
YOU TWO EVER DO IT IN MID-FLIGHT?
AAW!
AS LONG AS YOU'RE IN MY COMPANY YOU WILL NOT LIVE UP TO YOUR NAME, THIEF.
HEY, THEY'VE GOT PLENTY OF THESE DIAMONDS IF THEY'RE ON THEIR STINKIN' SPOONS.
AND YOU WILL NOT SPEAK OF HAWKGIRL IN THAT MANNER AGAIN.
ALL RIGHT! RELAX, HERO!
YOU KNOW, THE HAWK-MAN I USED TO HANG OUT WITH HAD A TEMPER PROBLEM, TOO.
HELL, ALL THANAGARIANS DO. YOU'RE NOT FROM THAT FASCIST PLANET, ARE YOU?
I MEAN, THEY PUT OUT SOME GOOD TECH, LIKE THIS SHADOW VEST, BUT--
I WAS BORN ON EARTH... MANY TIMES. THE THANAGARIAN WAS A... FRIEND OF MINE.
DAMMIT, THIEF... WHERE IS YOUR FRIEND?
WHERE'S COPPERHEAD?

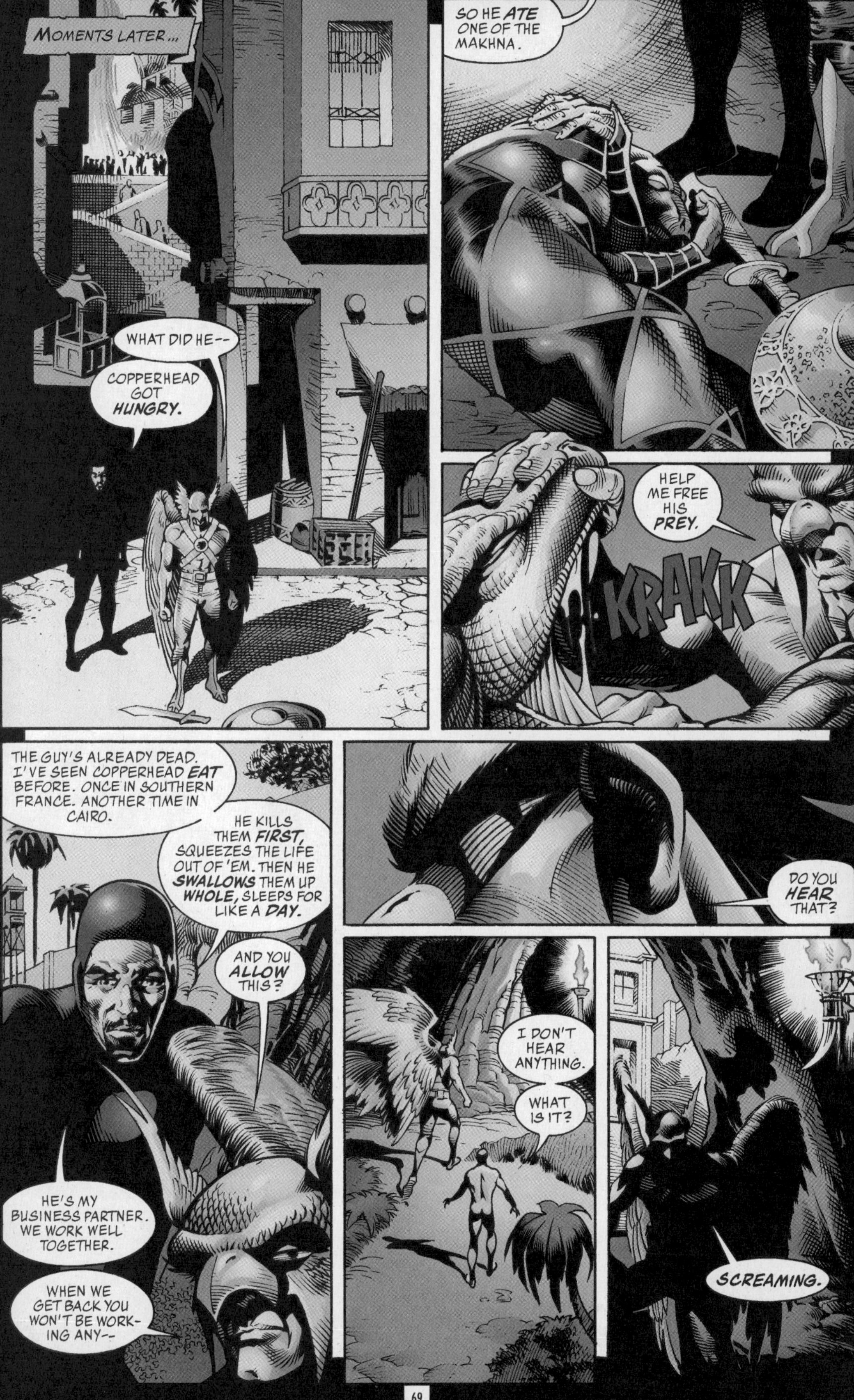
MOMENTS LATER...
WHAT DID HE--
COPPERHEAD GOT HUNGRY.
SO HE ATE ONE OF THE MAKHNA.
HELP ME FREE HIS PREY.
KRAKK
THE GUY'S ALREADY DEAD. I'VE SEEN COPPERHEAD EAT BEFORE. ONCE IN SOUTHERN FRANCE. ANOTHER TIME IN CAIRO.
HE KILLS THEM FIRST, SQUEEZES THE LIFE OUT OF 'EM. THEN HE SWALLOWS THEM UP WHOLE, SLEEPS FOR LIKE A DAY.
AND YOU ALLOW THIS?
HE'S MY BUSINESS PARTNER. WE WORK WELL TOGETHER.
WHEN WE GET BACK YOU WON'T BE WORKING ANY--
DO YOU HEAR THAT?
I DON'T HEAR ANYTHING.
WHAT IS IT?
SCREAMING.

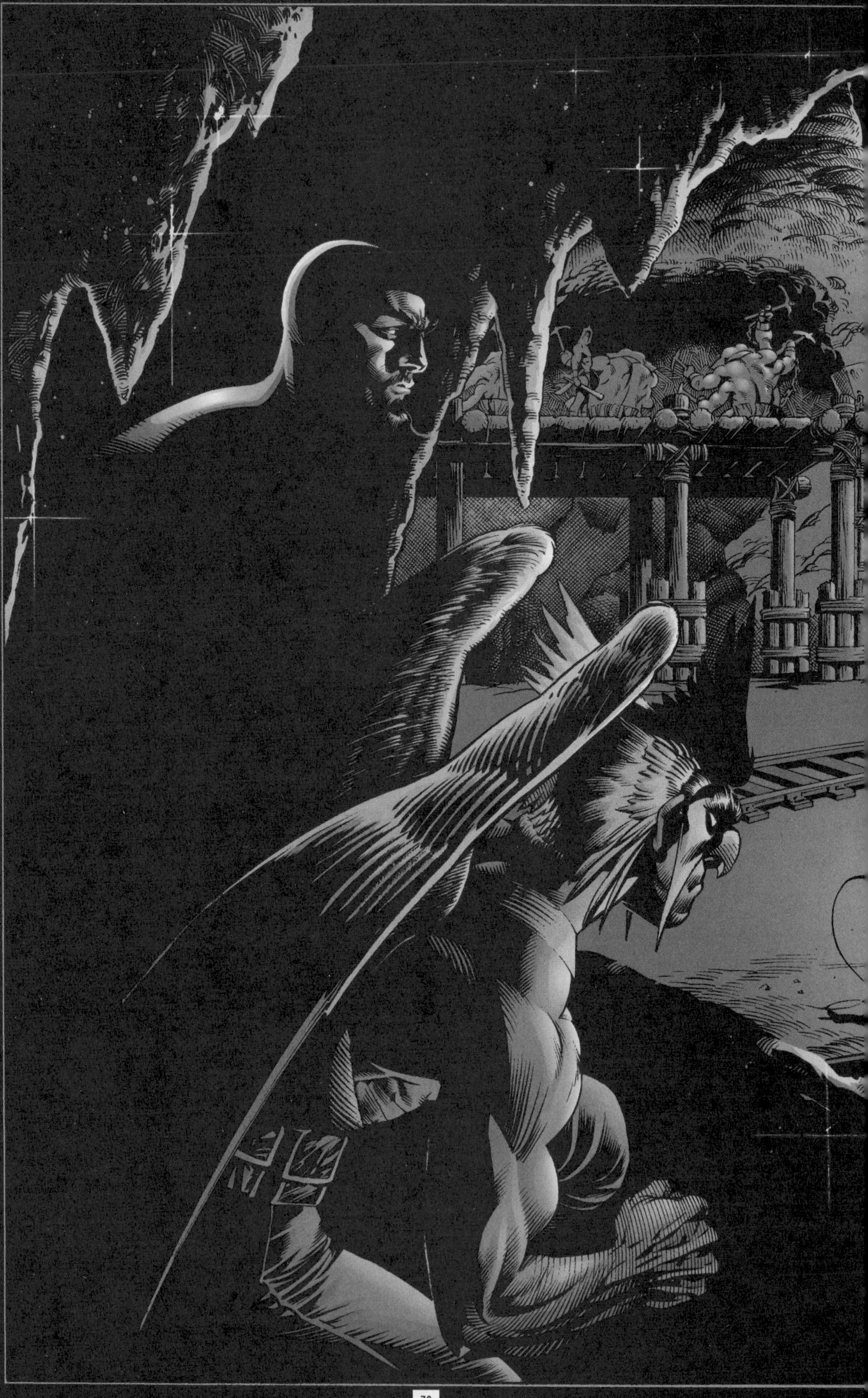

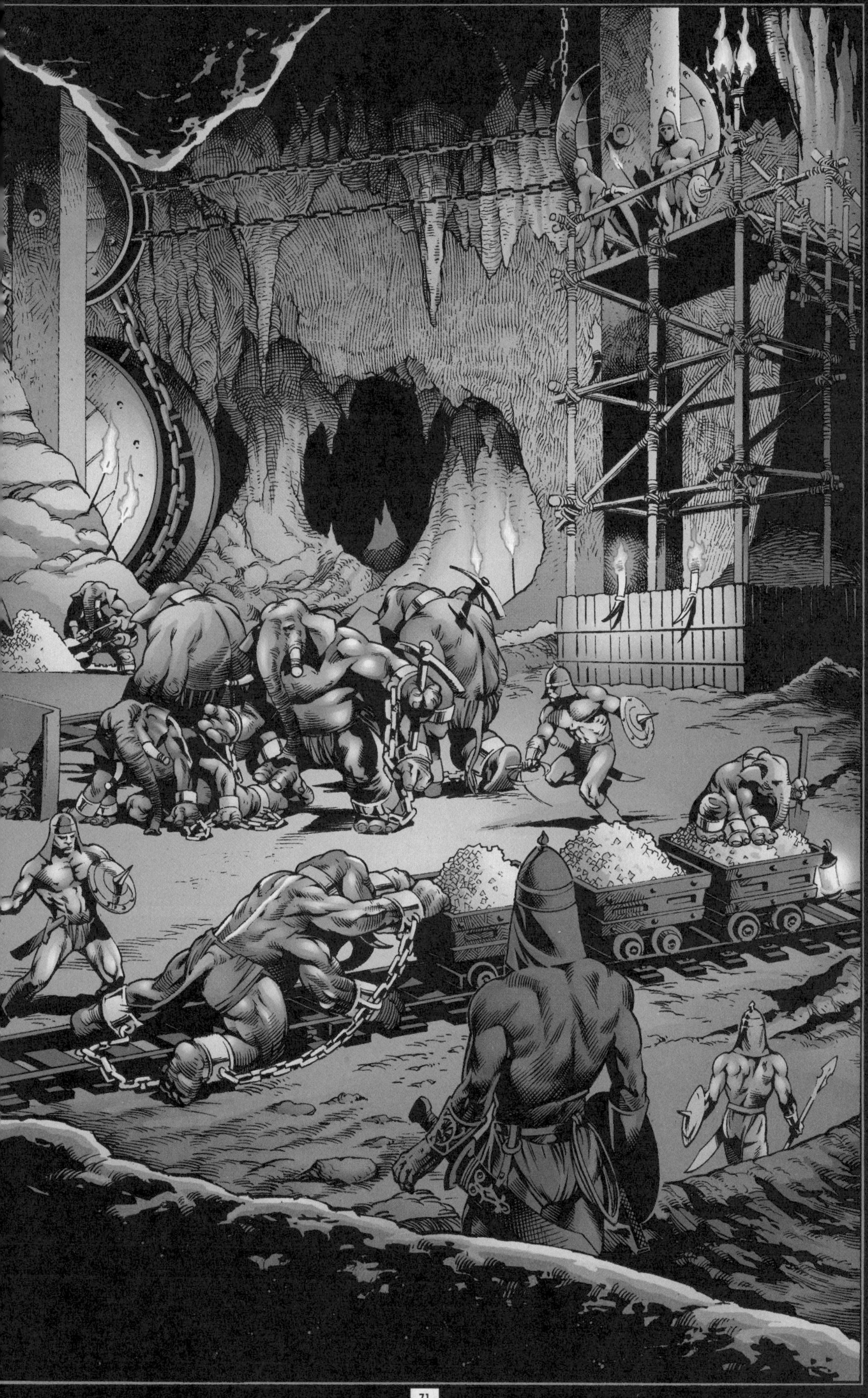

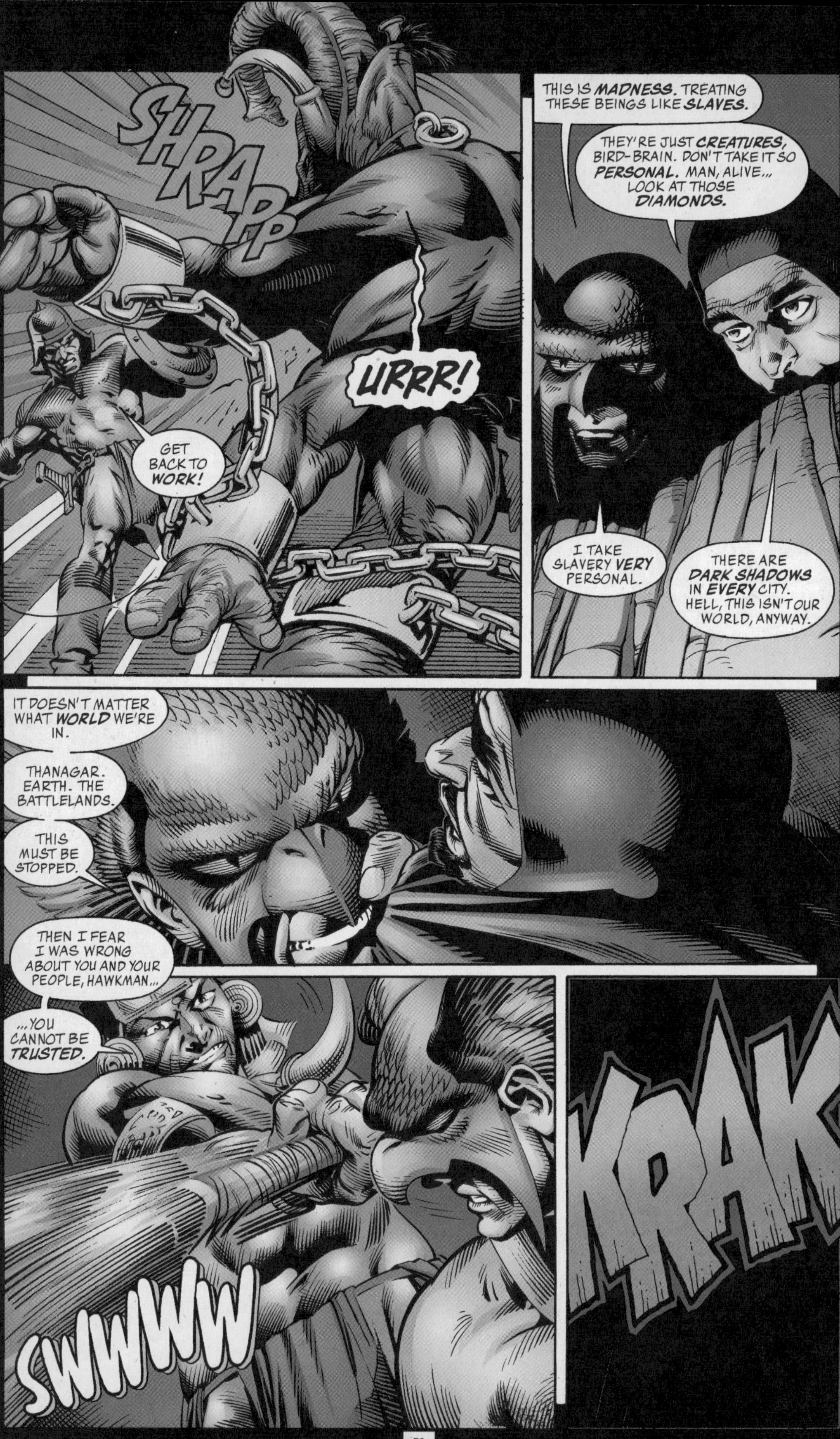

SHRAPP
URRR!
GET BACK TO WORK!
THIS IS MADNESS. TREATING THESE BEINGS LIKE SLAVES.
THEY'RE JUST CREATURES, BIRD-BRAIN. DON'T TAKE IT SO PERSONAL. MAN, ALIVE... LOOK AT THOSE DIAMONDS.
I TAKE SLAVERY VERY PERSONAL.
THERE ARE DARK SHADOWS IN EVERY CITY. HELL, THIS ISN'T OUR WORLD, ANYWAY.
IT DOESN'T MATTER WHAT WORLD WE'RE IN.
THANAGAR. EARTH. THE BATTLELANDS.
THIS MUST BE STOPPED.
THEN I FEAR I WAS WRONG ABOUT YOU AND YOUR PEOPLE, HAWKMAN...
...YOU CANNOT BE TRUSTED.
SWWWW
KRAK

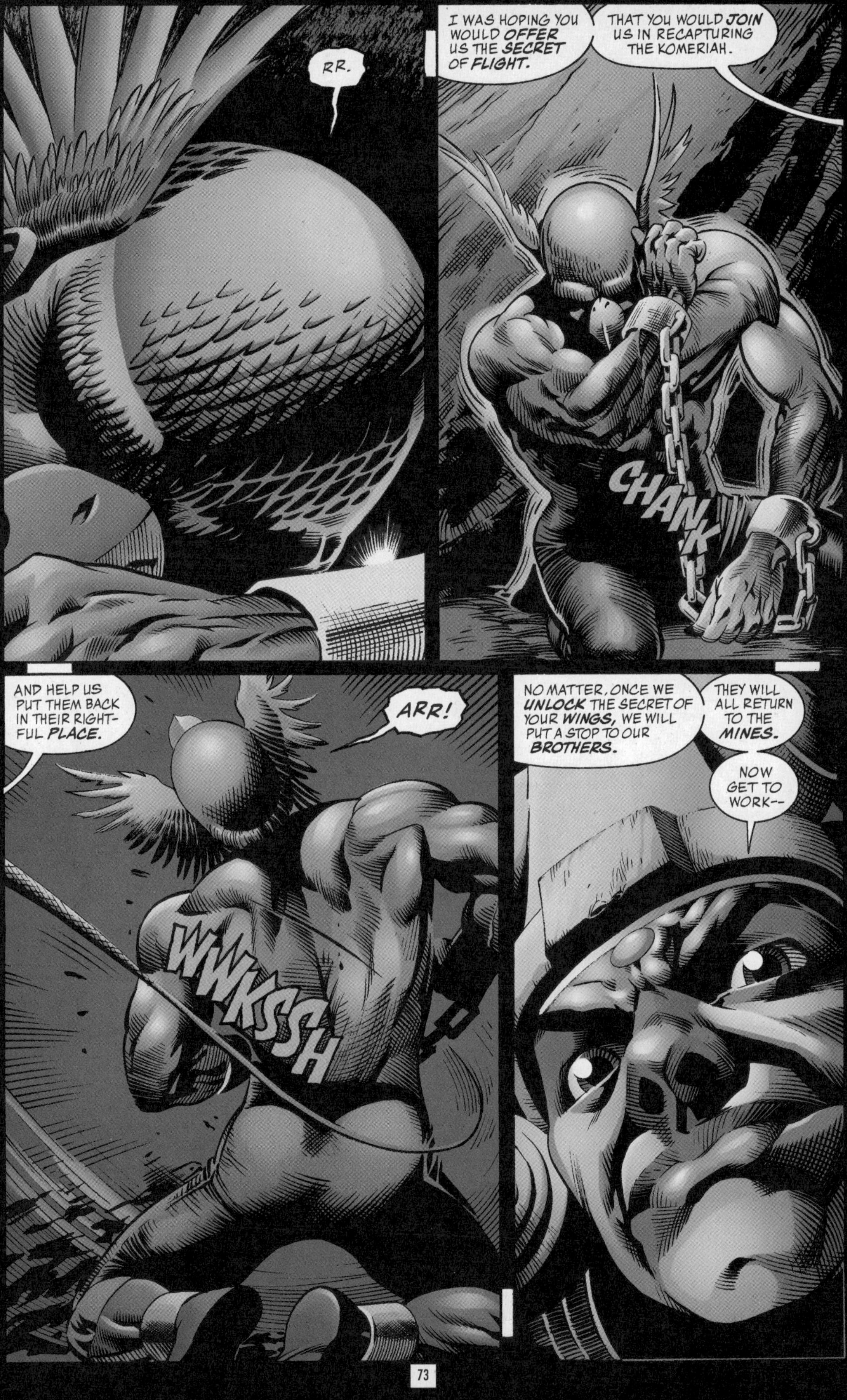
RR.
I WAS HOPING YOU WOULD OFFER US THE SECRET OF FLIGHT.
THAT YOU WOULD JOIN US IN RECAPTURING THE KOMERIAH.
CHANK
AND HELP US PUT THEM BACK IN THEIR RIGHTFUL PLACE.
ARR!
WWKSSH
NO MATTER, ONCE WE UNLOCK THE SECRET OF YOUR WINGS, WE WILL PUT A STOP TO OUR BROTHERS.
THEY WILL ALL RETURN TO THE MINES.
NOW GET TO WORK--

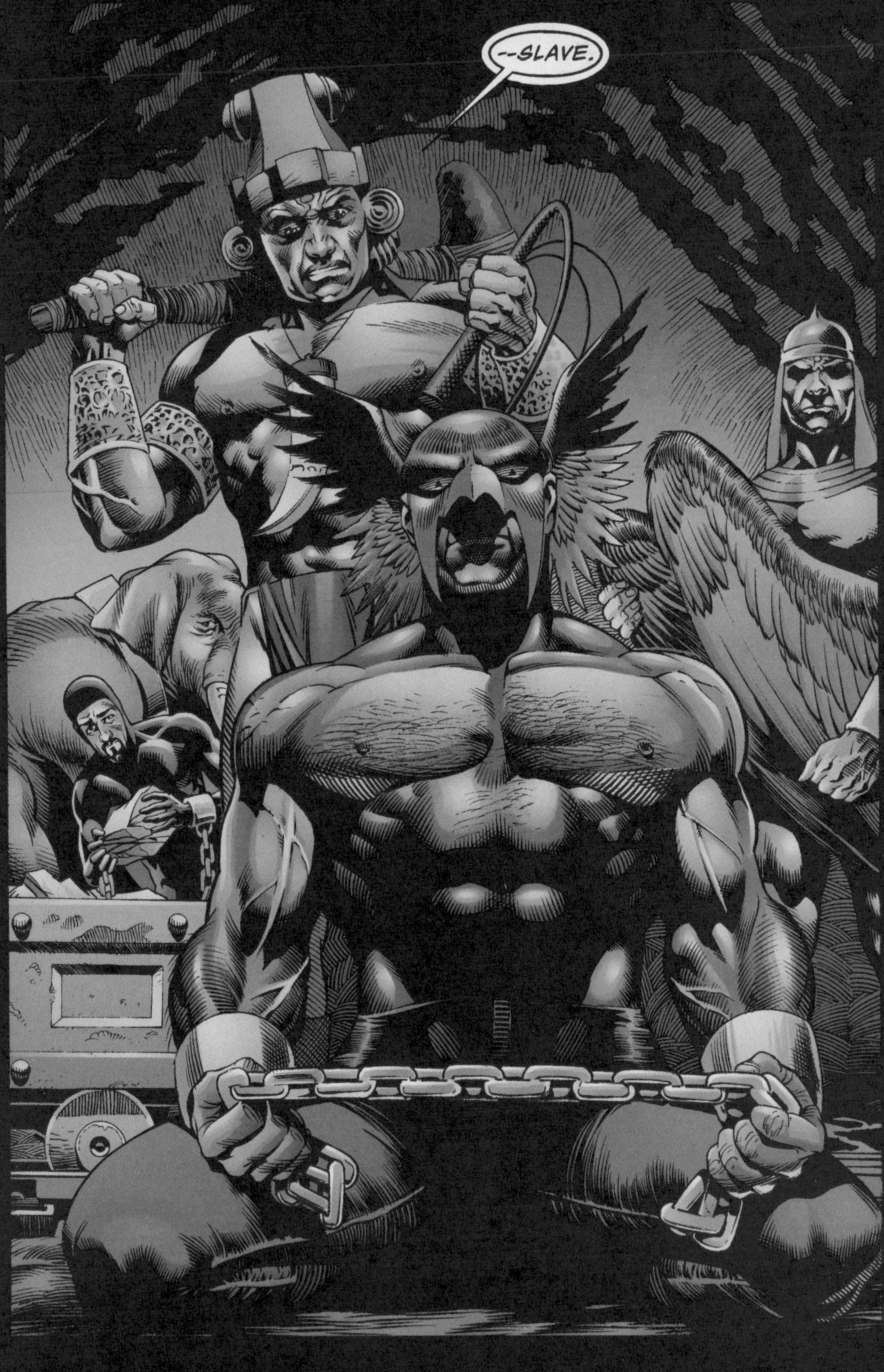
--SLAVE.

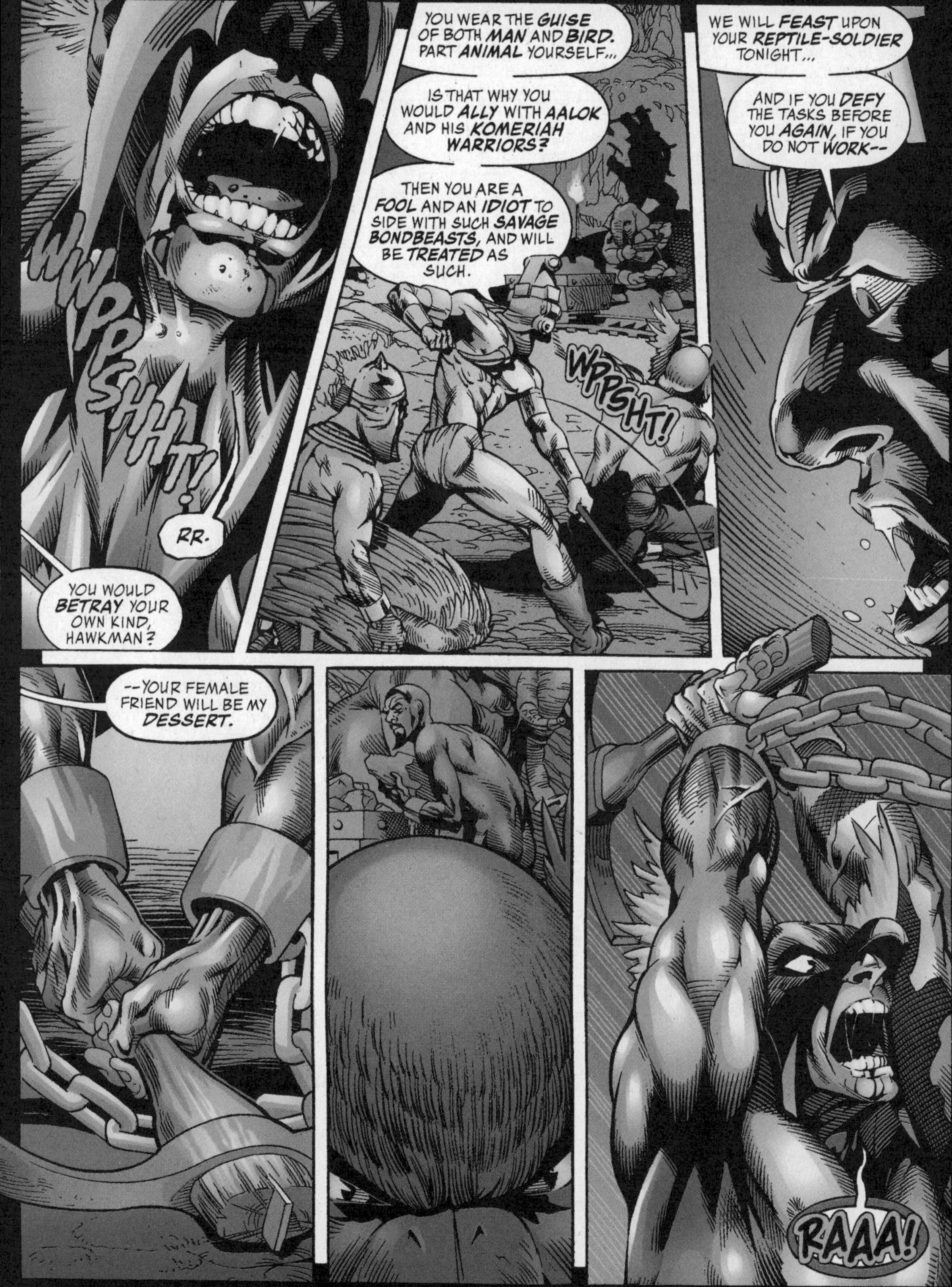
WWPPSHHT!
RR.
YOU WOULD BETRAY YOUR OWN KIND, HAWKMAN?
YOU WEAR THE GUISE OF BOTH MAN AND BIRD. PART ANIMAL YOURSELF...
IS THAT WHY YOU WOULD ALLY WITH AALOK AND HIS KOMERIAH WARRIORS?
THEN YOU ARE A FOOL AND AN IDIOT TO SIDE WITH SUCH SAVAGE BONDBEASTS, AND WILL BE TREATED AS SUCH.
WPPSHT!
WE WILL FEAST UPON YOUR REPTILE-SOLDIER TONIGHT...
AND IF YOU DEFY THE TASKS BEFORE YOU AGAIN, IF YOU DO NOT WORK--
--YOUR FEMALE FRIEND WILL BE MY DESSERT.
RAAA!

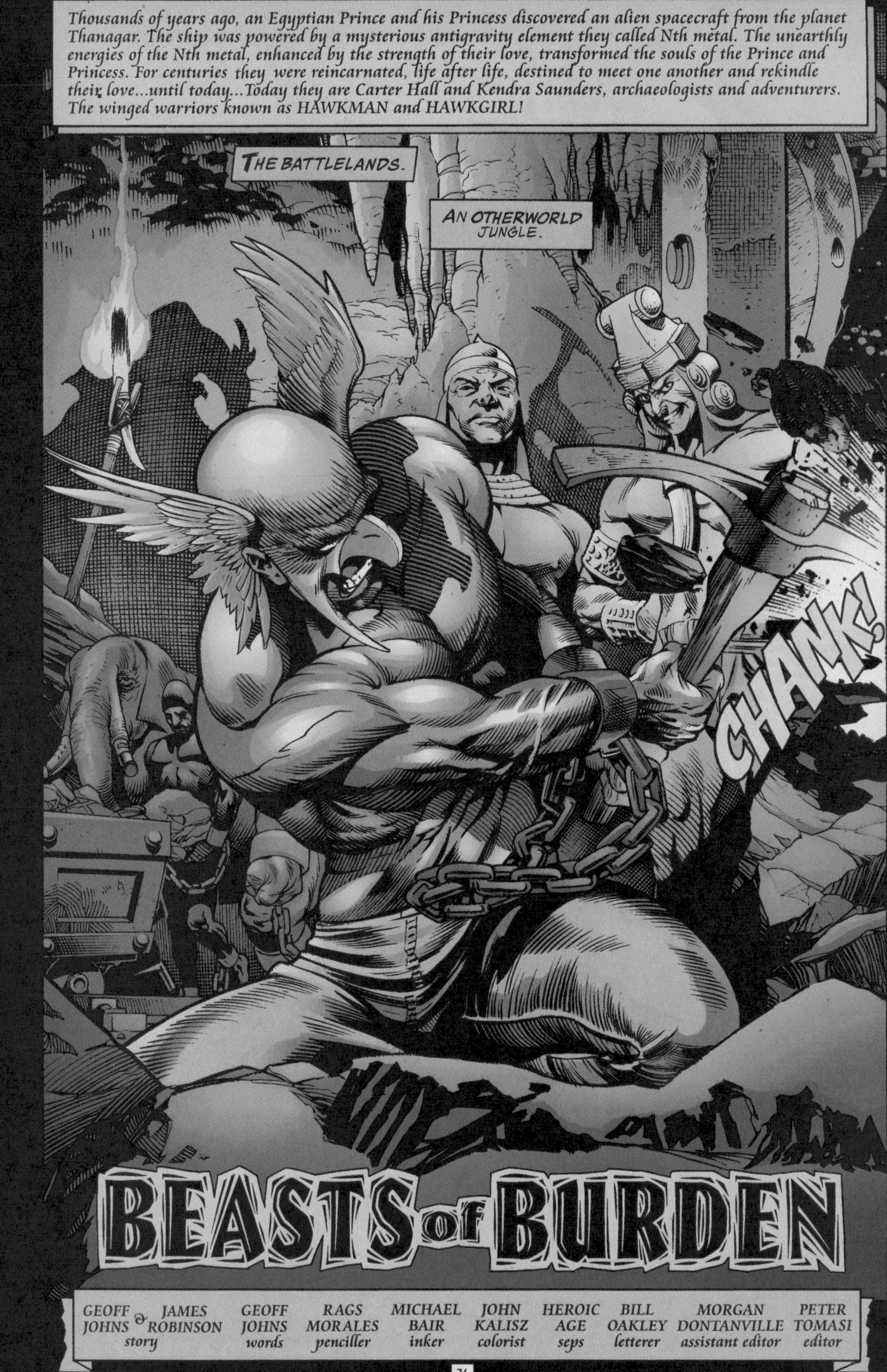

Thousands of years ago, an Egyptian Prince and his Princess discovered an alien spacecraft from the planet Thanagar. The ship was powered by a mysterious antigravity element they called Nth metal. The unearthly energies of the Nth metal, enhanced by the strength of their love, transformed the souls of the Prince and Princess. For centuries they were reincarnated, life after life, destined to meet one another and rekindle their love...until today...Today they are Carter Hall and Kendra Saunders, archaeologists and adventurers. The winged warriors known as HAWKMAN and HAWKGIRL!
THE BATTLELANDS.
AN OTHERWORLD JUNGLE.
CHANK!
BEASTS of BURDEN
GEOFF JOHNS & JAMES ROBINSON story
GEOFF JOHNS words
RAGS MORALES penciller
MICHAEL BAIR inker
JOHN KALISZ colorist
HEROIC AGE seps
BILL OAKLEY letterer
MORGAN DONTANVILLE assistant editor
PETER TOMASI editor

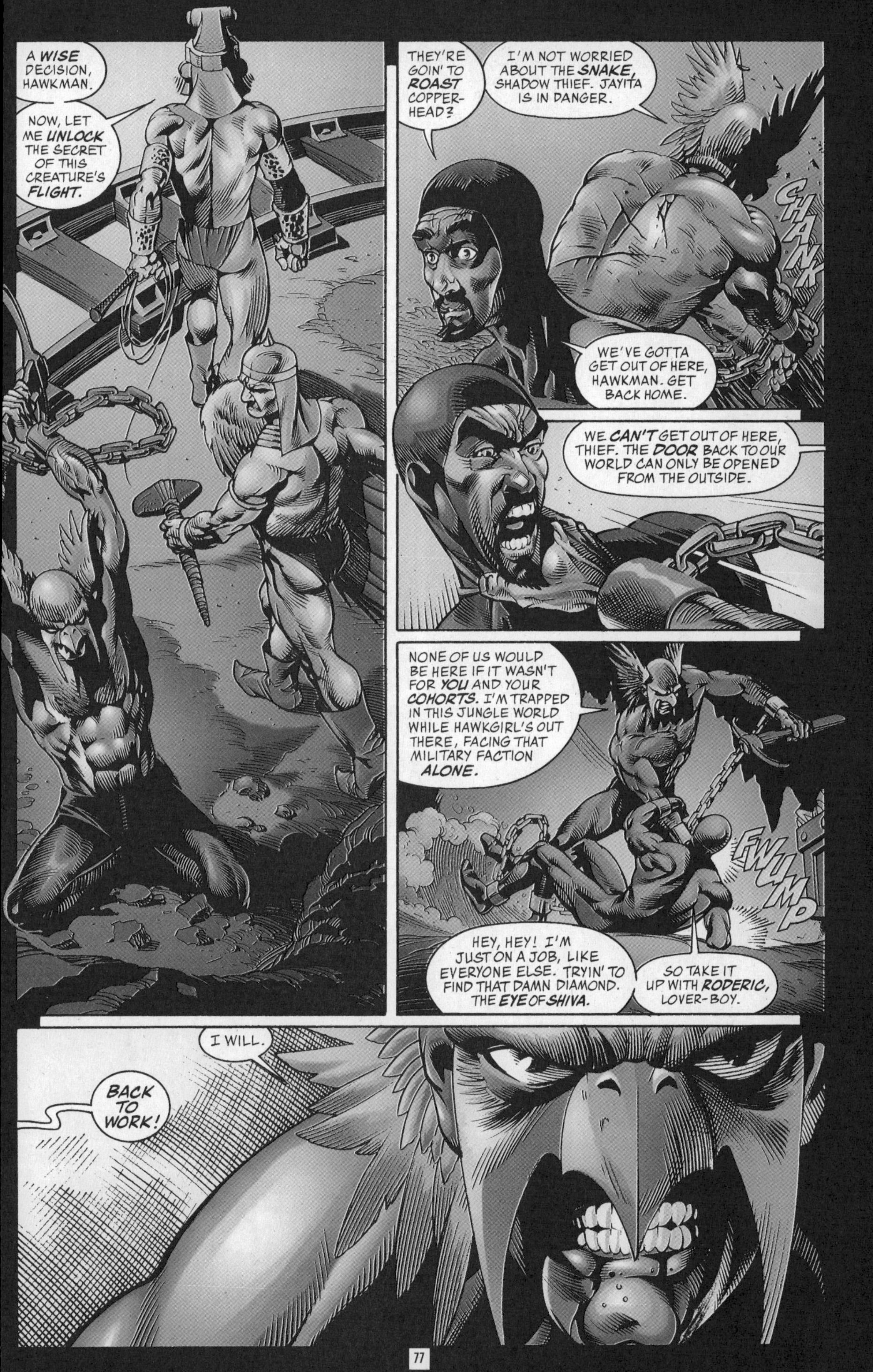
A WISE DECISION, HAWKMAN.
NOW, LET ME UNLOCK THE SECRET OF THIS CREATURE'S FLIGHT.
THEY'RE GOIN' TO ROAST COPPERHEAD?
I'M NOT WORRIED ABOUT THE SNAKE, SHADOW THIEF. JAYITA IS IN DANGER.
CHANK
WE'VE GOTTA GET OUT OF HERE, HAWKMAN. GET BACK HOME.
WE CAN'T GET OUT OF HERE, THIEF. THE DOOR BACK TO OUR WORLD CAN ONLY BE OPENED FROM THE OUTSIDE.
NONE OF US WOULD BE HERE IF IT WASN'T FOR YOU AND YOUR COHORTS. I'M TRAPPED IN THIS JUNGLE WORLD WHILE HAWKGIRL'S OUT THERE, FACING THAT MILITARY FACTION ALONE.
FWUMP
HEY, HEY! I'M JUST ON A JOB, LIKE EVERYONE ELSE. TRYIN' TO FIND THAT DAMN DIAMOND. THE EYE OF SHIVA.
SO TAKE IT UP WITH RODERIC, LOVER-BOY.
I WILL.
BACK TO WORK!

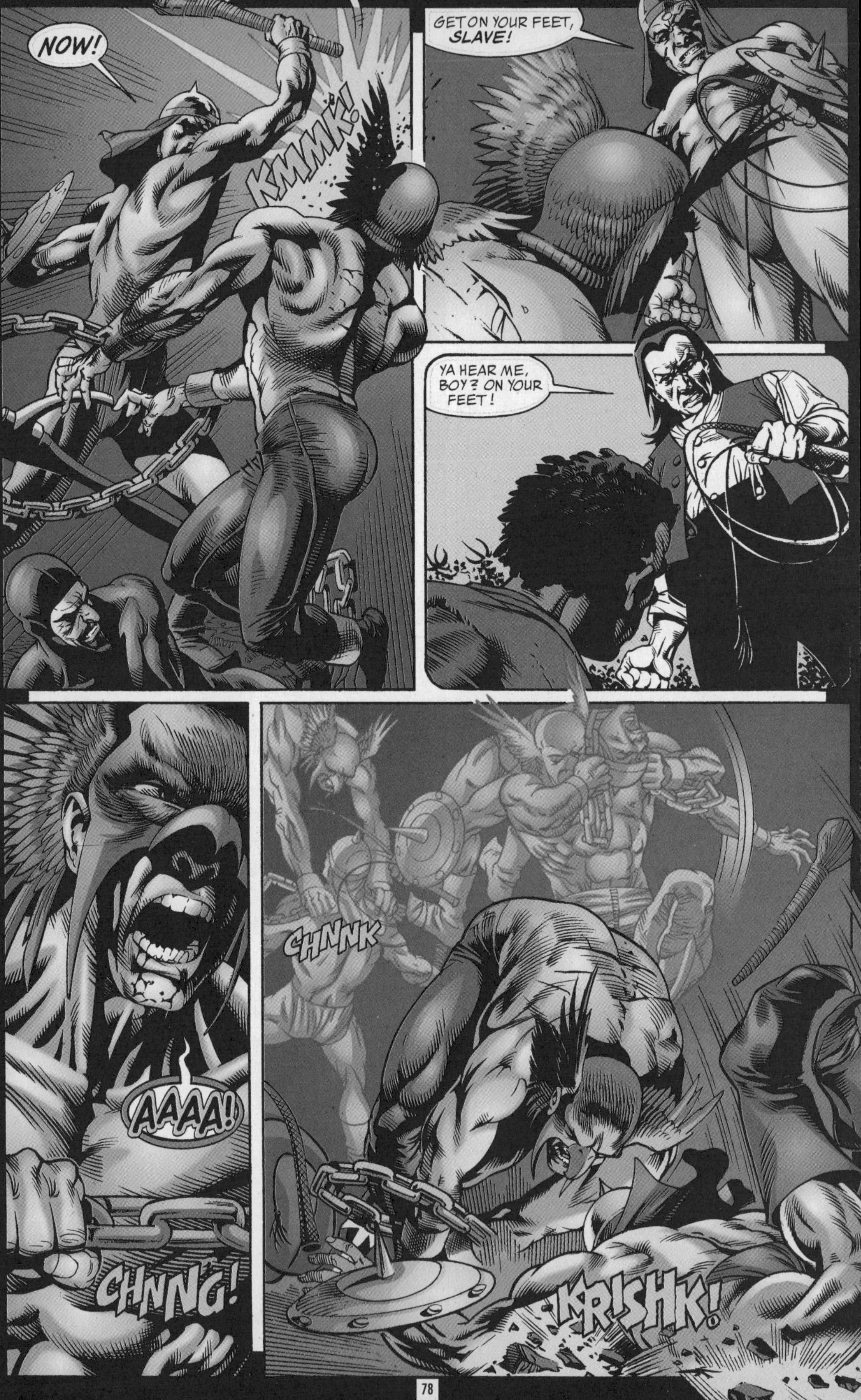
NOW!
KMMK!
GET ON YOUR FEET, SLAVE!
YA HEAR ME, BOY? ON YOUR FEET!
AAAA!
CHNNG!
CHNNK
KRISHK!

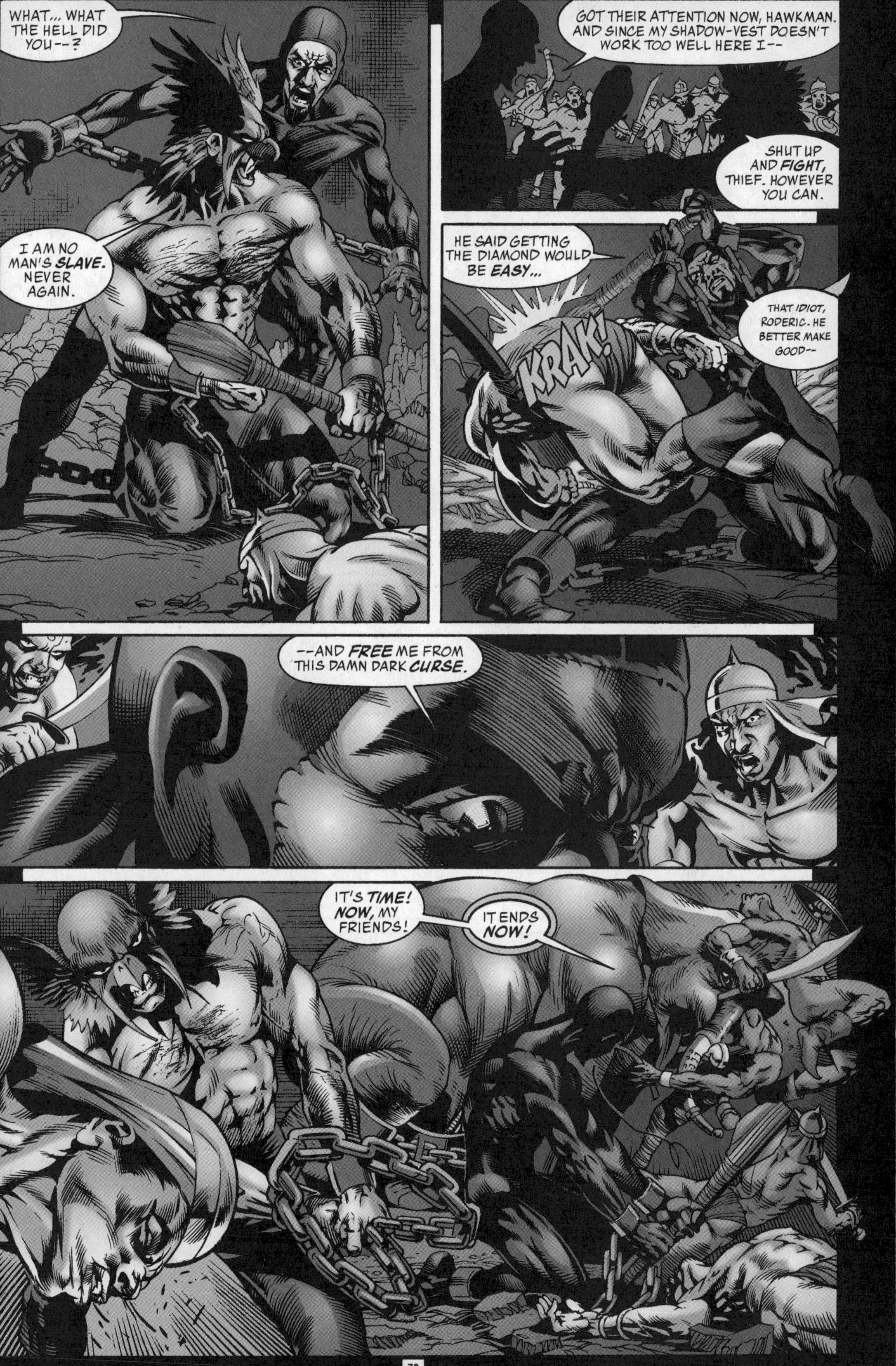
WHAT... WHAT THE HELL DID YOU--?
I AM NO MAN'S SLAVE. NEVER AGAIN.
GOT THEIR ATTENTION NOW, HAWKMAN. AND SINCE MY SHADOW-VEST DOESN'T WORK TOO WELL HERE I--
SHUT UP AND FIGHT, THIEF. HOWEVER YOU CAN.
HE SAID GETTING THE DIAMOND WOULD BE EASY...
KRAK!
THAT IDIOT, RODERIC. HE BETTER MAKE GOOD--
--AND FREE ME FROM THIS DAMN DARK CURSE.
IT'S TIME! NOW, MY FRIENDS!
IT ENDS NOW!

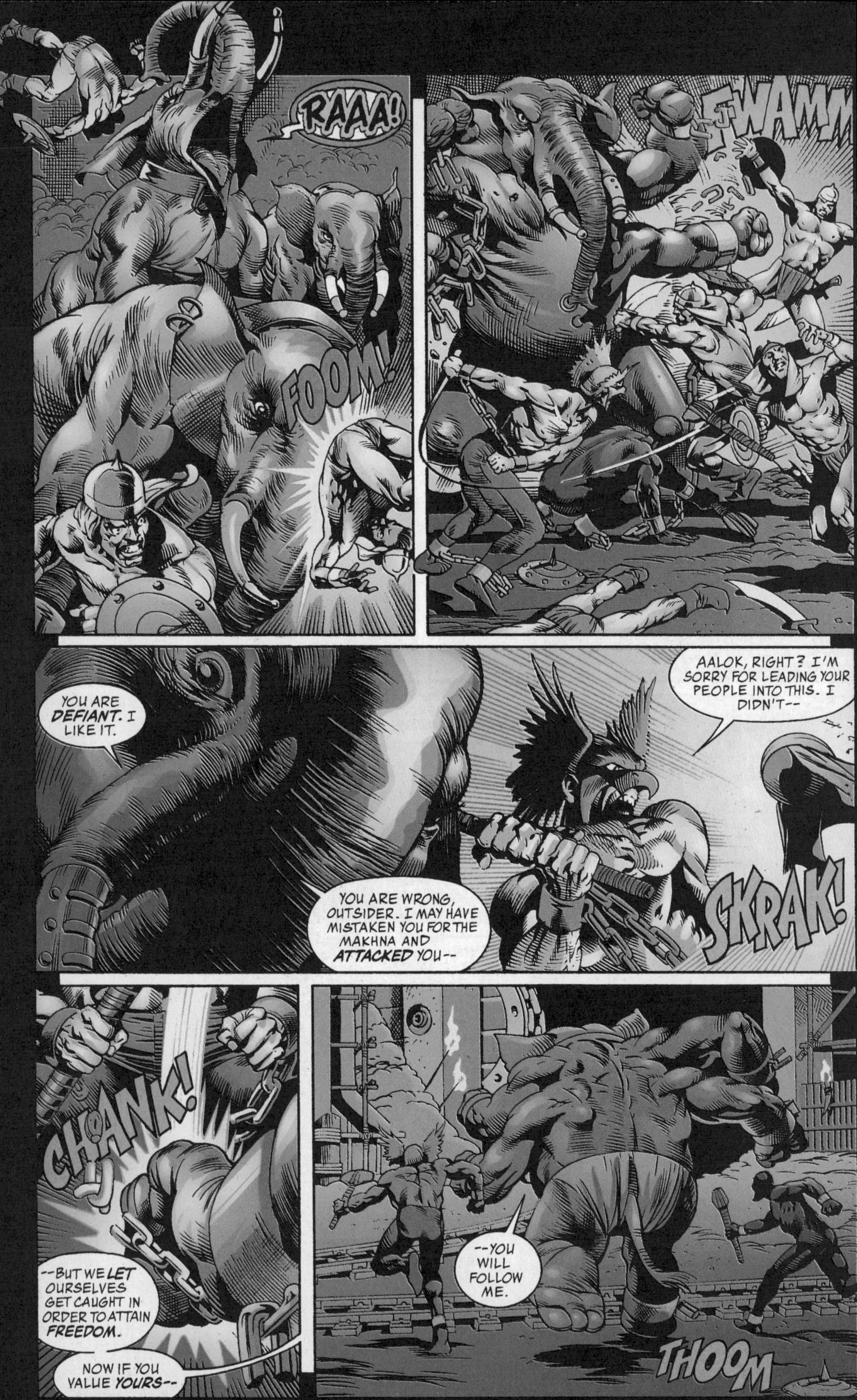
RAAA!
FOOM!
FWAMM
YOU ARE DEFIANT. I LIKE IT.
AALOK, RIGHT? I'M SORRY FOR LEADING YOUR PEOPLE INTO THIS. I DIDN'T--
YOU ARE WRONG, OUTSIDER. I MAY HAVE MISTAKEN YOU FOR THE MAKHNA AND ATTACKED YOU--
SKRAK!
CHANK!
--BUT WE LET OURSELVES GET CAUGHT IN ORDER TO ATTAIN FREEDOM.
NOW IF YOU VALUE YOURS--
--YOU WILL FOLLOW ME.
THOOM

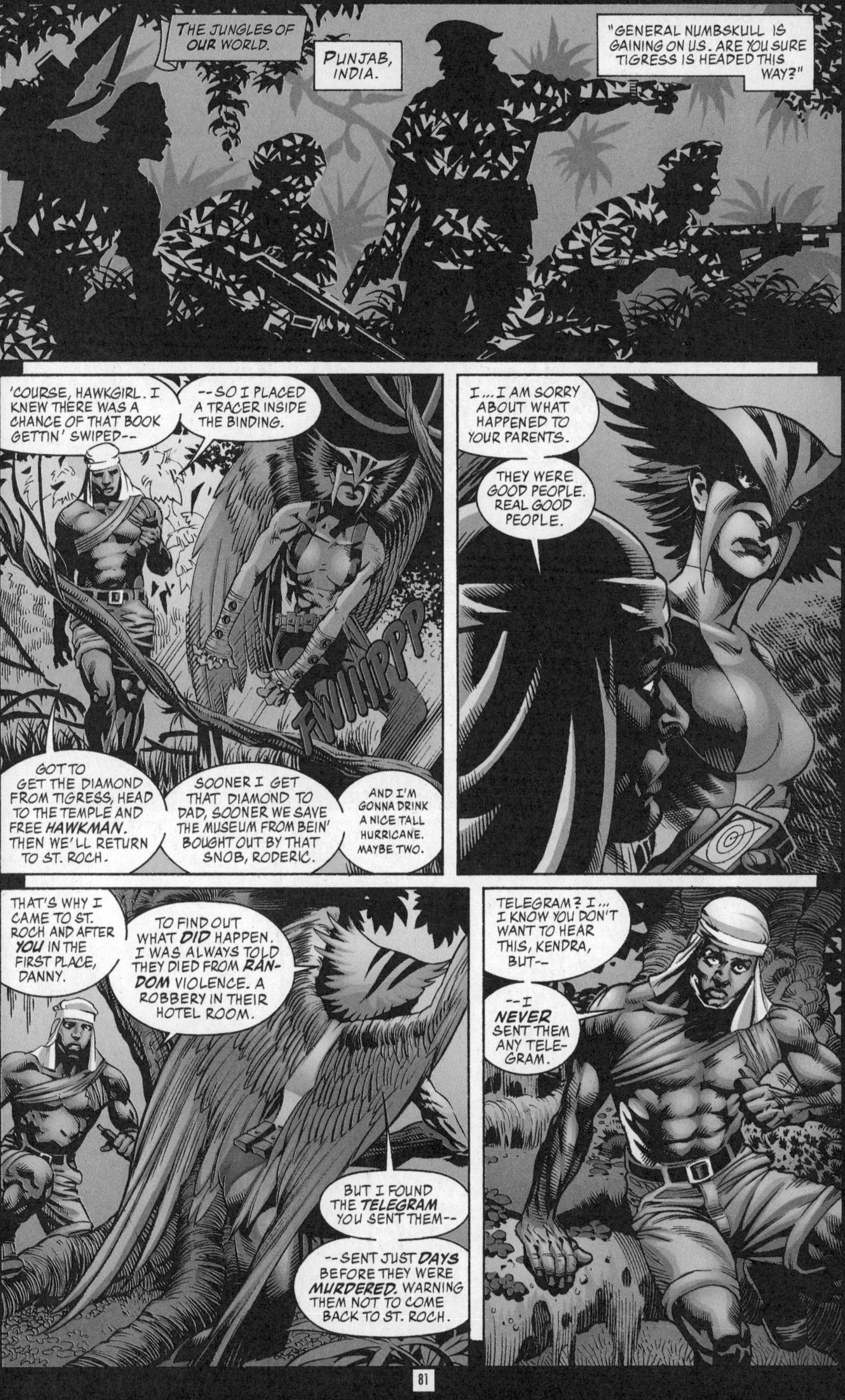

THE JUNGLES OF OUR WORLD.
PUNJAB, INDIA.
"GENERAL NUMBSKULL IS GAINING ON US. ARE YOU SURE TIGRESS IS HEADED THIS WAY?"
'COURSE, HAWKGIRL. I KNEW THERE WAS A CHANCE OF THAT BOOK GETTIN' SWIPED--
--SO I PLACED A TRACER INSIDE THE BINDING.
FWIIIPPP
GOT TO GET THE DIAMOND FROM TIGRESS, HEAD TO THE TEMPLE AND FREE HAWKMAN. THEN WE'LL RETURN TO ST. ROCH.
SOONER I GET THAT DIAMOND TO DAD, SOONER WE SAVE THE MUSEUM FROM BEIN' BOUGHT OUT BY THAT SNOB, RODERIC.
AND I'M GONNA DRINK A NICE TALL HURRICANE. MAYBE TWO.
I... I AM SORRY ABOUT WHAT HAPPENED TO YOUR PARENTS.
THEY WERE GOOD PEOPLE. REAL GOOD PEOPLE.
THAT'S WHY I CAME TO ST. ROCH AND AFTER YOU IN THE FIRST PLACE, DANNY.
TO FIND OUT WHAT DID HAPPEN. I WAS ALWAYS TOLD THEY DIED FROM RANDOM VIOLENCE. A ROBBERY IN THEIR HOTEL ROOM.
BUT I FOUND THE TELEGRAM YOU SENT THEM--
--SENT JUST DAYS BEFORE THEY WERE MURDERED. WARNING THEM NOT TO COME BACK TO ST. ROCH.
TELEGRAM? I... I KNOW YOU DON'T WANT TO HEAR THIS, KENDRA, BUT--
--I NEVER SENT THEM ANY TELEGRAM.

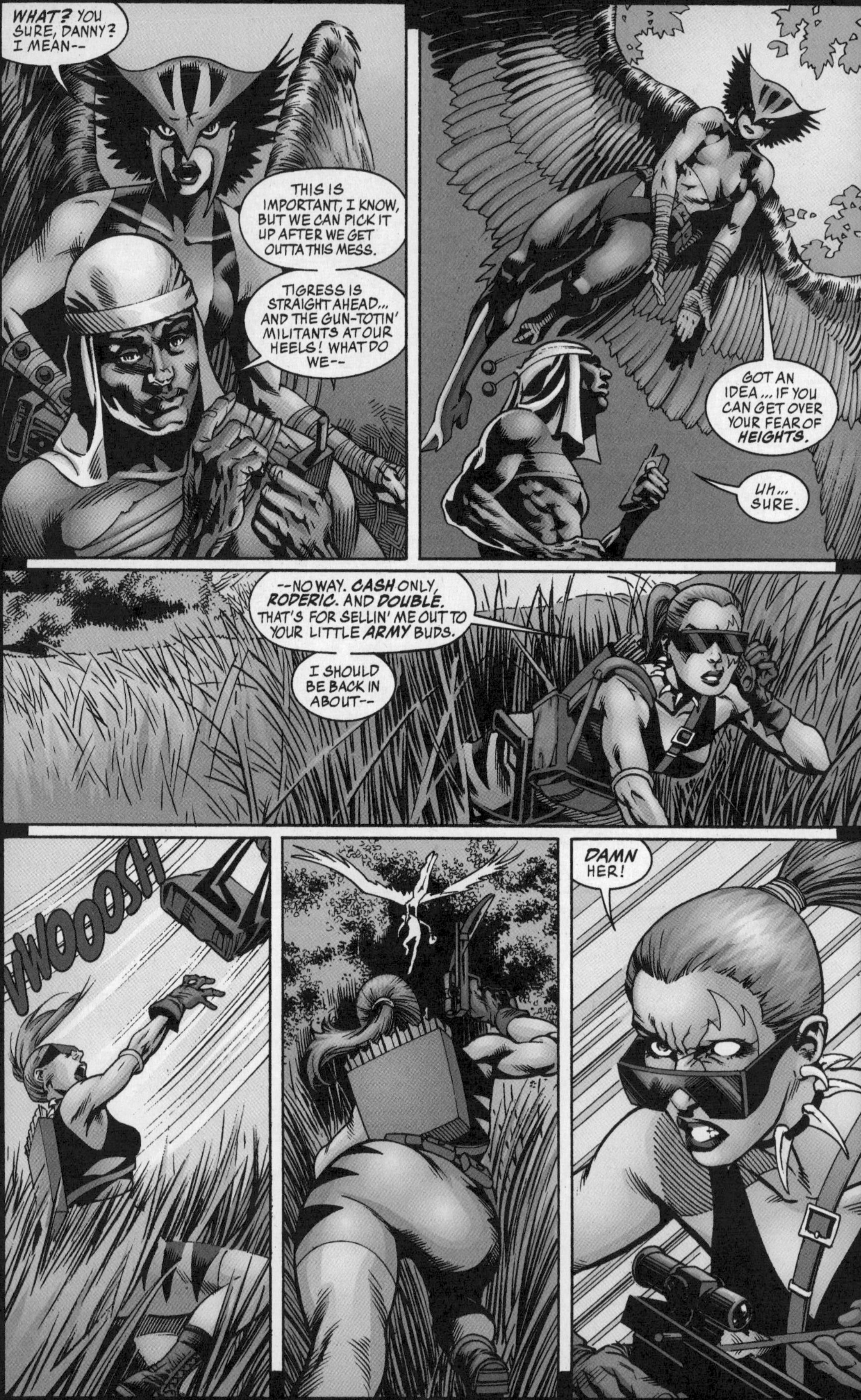
WHAT? YOU SURE, DANNY? I MEAN--
THIS IS IMPORTANT, I KNOW, BUT WE CAN PICK IT UP AFTER WE GET OUTTA THIS MESS.
TIGRESS IS STRAIGHT AHEAD... AND THE GUN-TOTIN' MILITANTS AT OUR HEELS! WHAT DO WE--
GOT AN IDEA... IF YOU CAN GET OVER YOUR FEAR OF HEIGHTS.
UH... SURE.
--NO WAY. CASH ONLY, RODERIC. AND DOUBLE. THAT'S FOR SELLIN' ME OUT TO YOUR LITTLE ARMY BUDS.
I SHOULD BE BACK IN ABOUT--
VWOOOSH
DAMN HER!

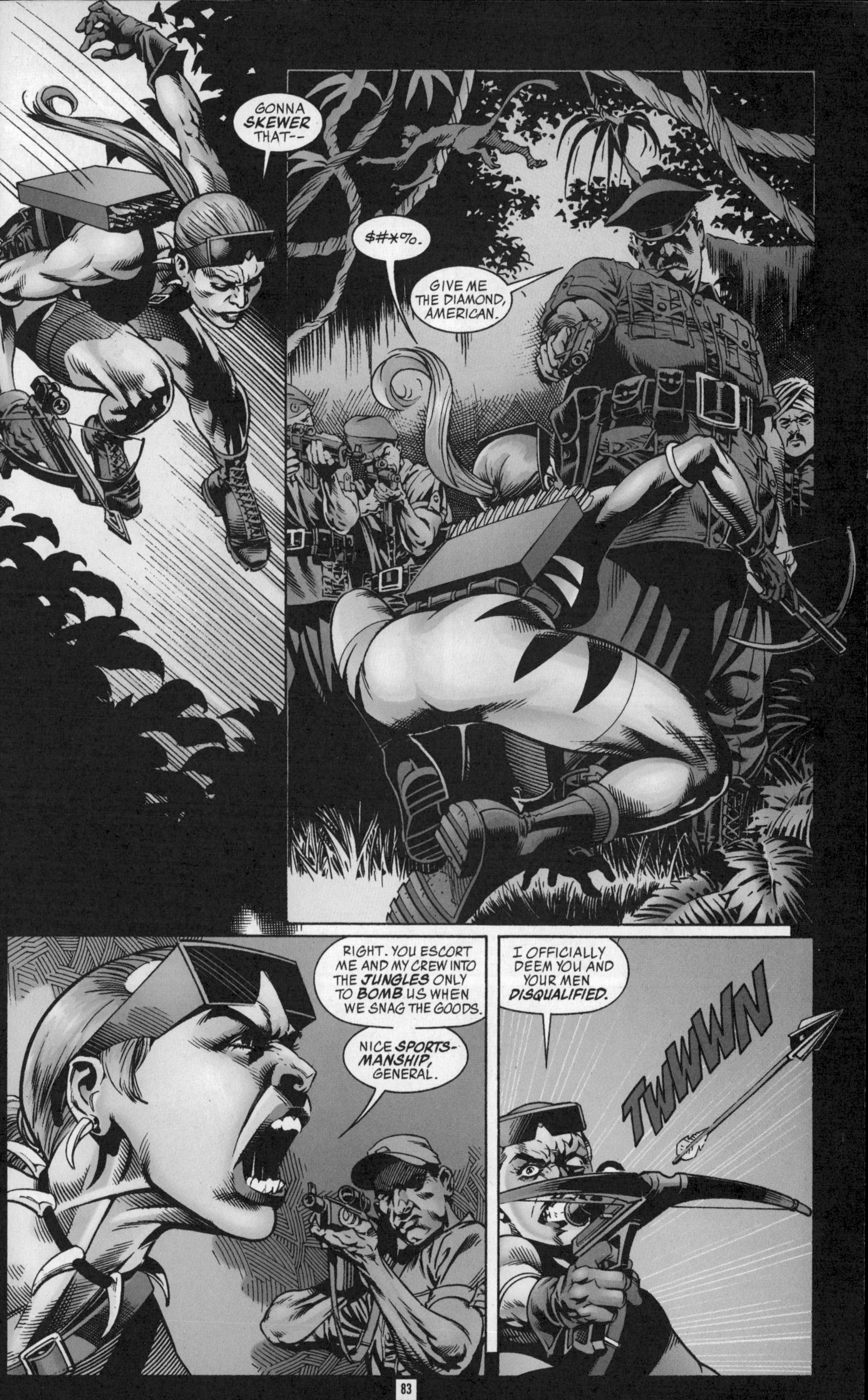
GONNA SKEWER THAT--
$#*%.
GIVE ME THE DIAMOND, AMERICAN.
RIGHT. YOU ESCORT ME AND MY CREW INTO THE JUNGLES ONLY TO BOMB US WHEN WE SNAG THE GOODS.
NICE SPORTS-MANSHIP, GENERAL.
I OFFICIALLY DEEM YOU AND YOUR MEN DISQUALIFIED.
TWWWN

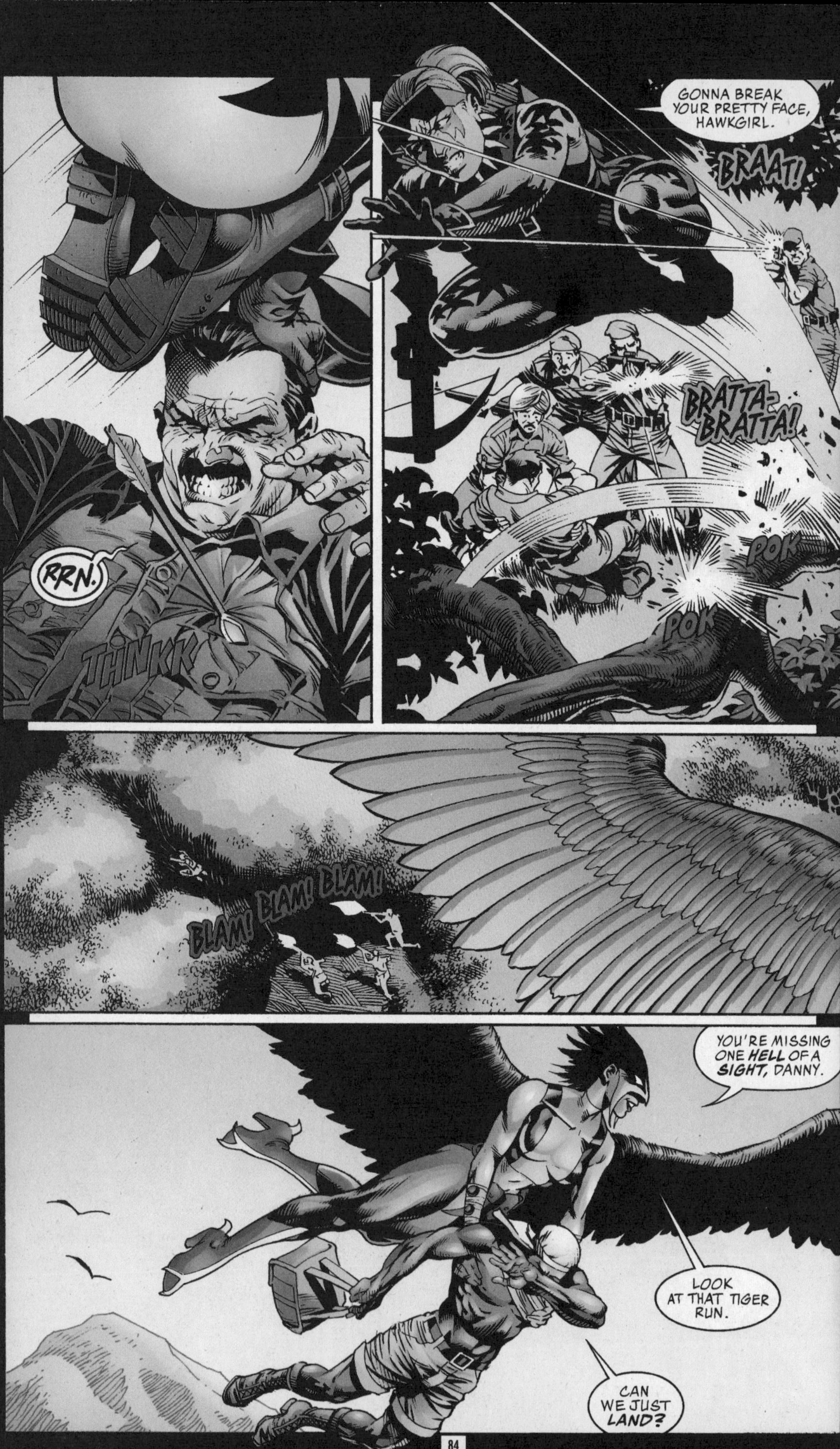
GONNA BREAK YOUR PRETTY FACE, HAWKGIRL.
BRAAT!
BRATTA-BRATTA!
POK
POK
RRN.
THINKK
BLAM! BLAM! BLAM!
YOU'RE MISSING ONE HELL OF A SIGHT, DANNY.
LOOK AT THAT TIGER RUN.
CAN WE JUST LAND?

*THE BATTLELANDS.*

WHAT WERE YOU HOPING TO ACCOMPLISH HERE, AALOK?

THESE MARBLE PILLARS HOLD UP THE GATES TO THE CITY. THE GATES THAT KEEP ME AND MY KOMERIAH BRETHREN OUT.

ALLOWING MYSELF TO GET CAUGHT WAS THE ONLY WAY IN.

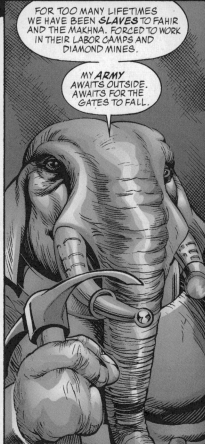

FOR TOO MANY LIFETIMES WE HAVE BEEN *SLAVES* TO FAHIR AND THE MAKHNA. FORCED TO WORK IN THEIR LABOR CAMPS AND DIAMOND MINES.

MY *ARMY* AWAITS OUTSIDE. AWAITS FOR THE GATES TO FALL.

YOU THINK TEARING THESE PILLARS DOWN IS GOING TO BE *EASY*, JUMBO?

CHANK!

JUST NEED TO KNOW WHERE TO *HIT* THEM, THIEF!

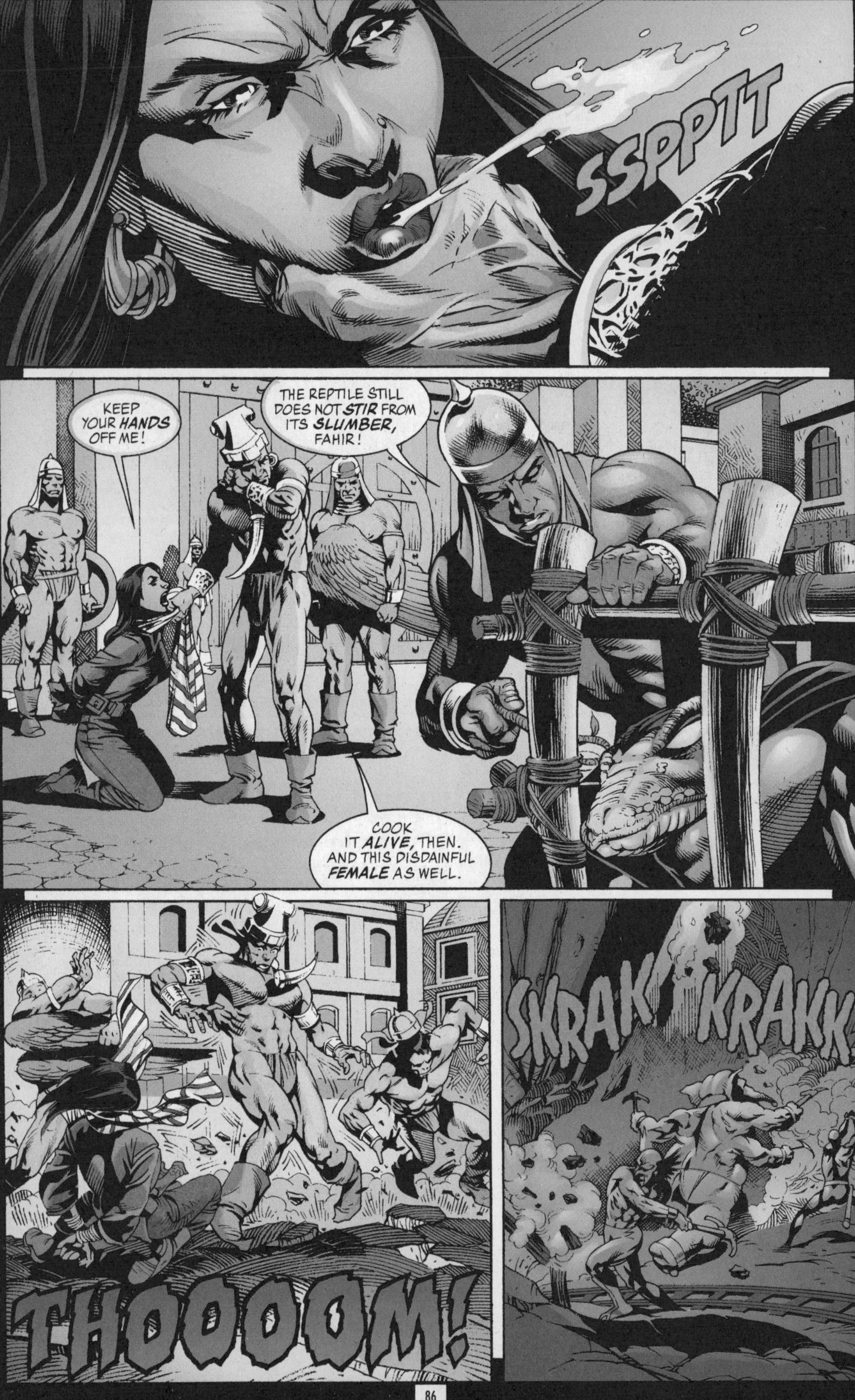
SSPPTT
KEEP YOUR HANDS OFF ME!
THE REPTILE STILL DOES NOT STIR FROM ITS SLUMBER, FAHIR!
COOK IT ALIVE, THEN. AND THIS DISDAINFUL FEMALE AS WELL.
THOOOOM!
SKRAK KRAKK

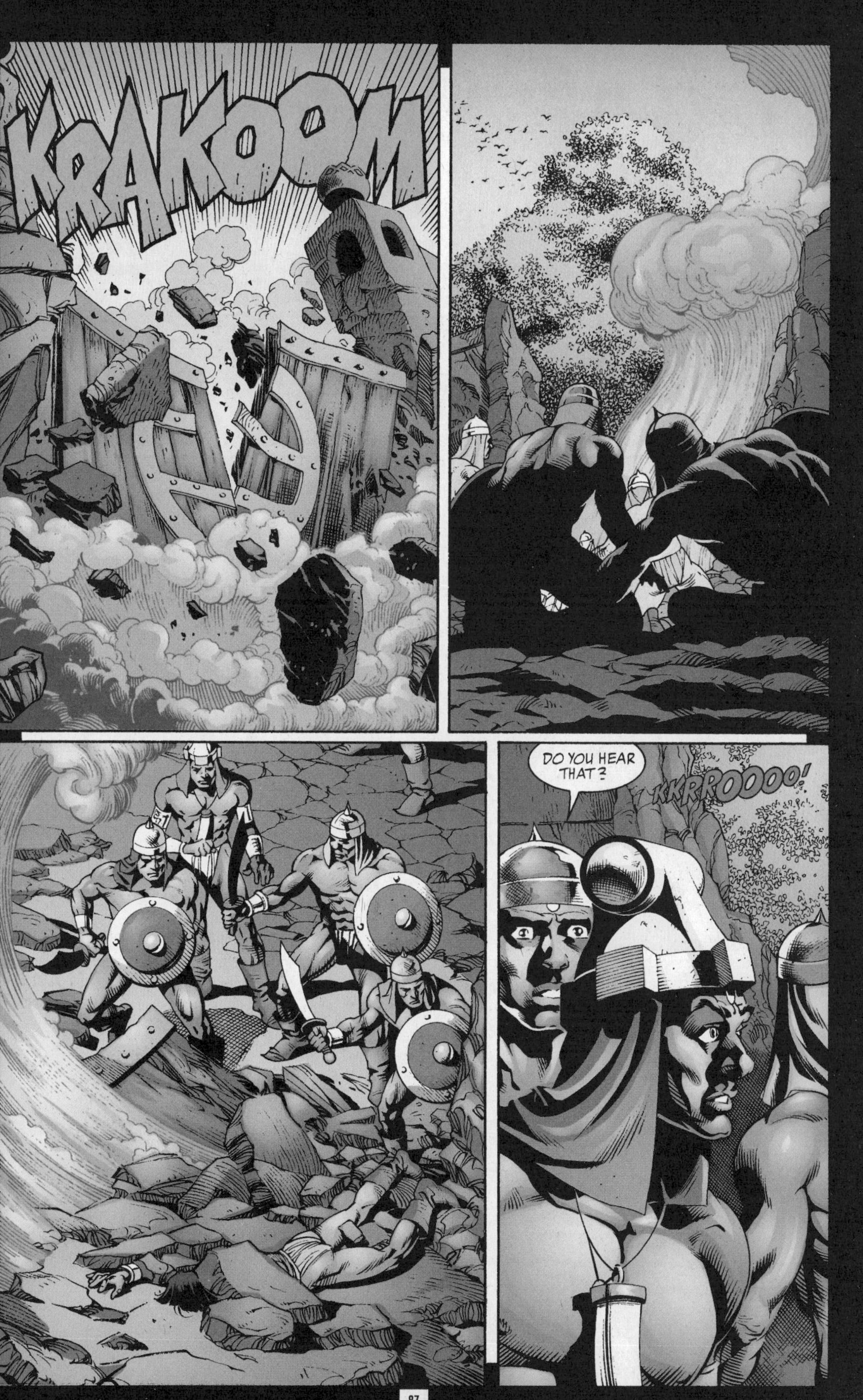
KRAKOOM
DO YOU HEAR THAT?
KKRROOOO!

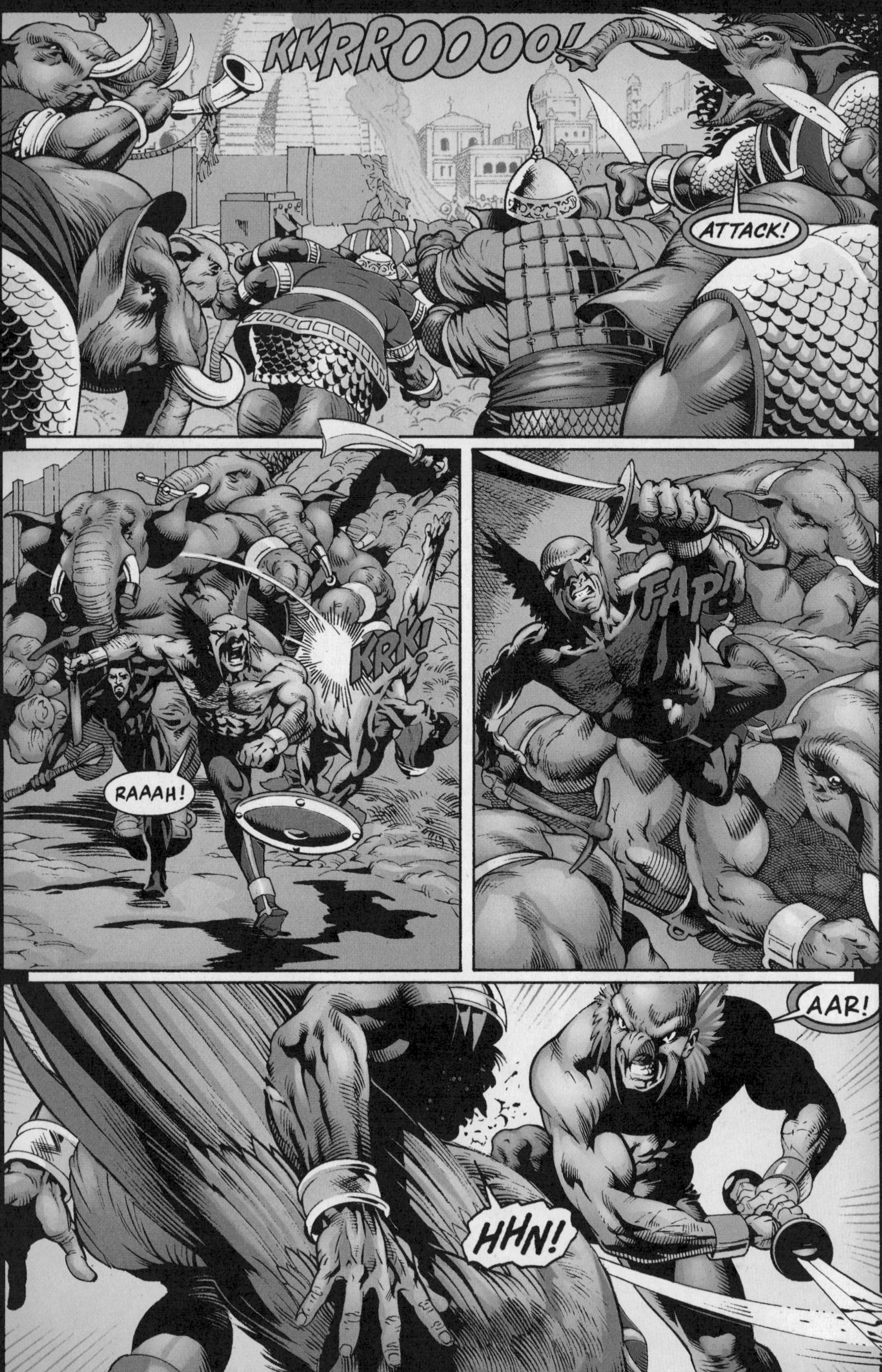
KKRROOOO!
ATTACK!
KRK!
RAAAH!
FAP!
AAR!
HHN!

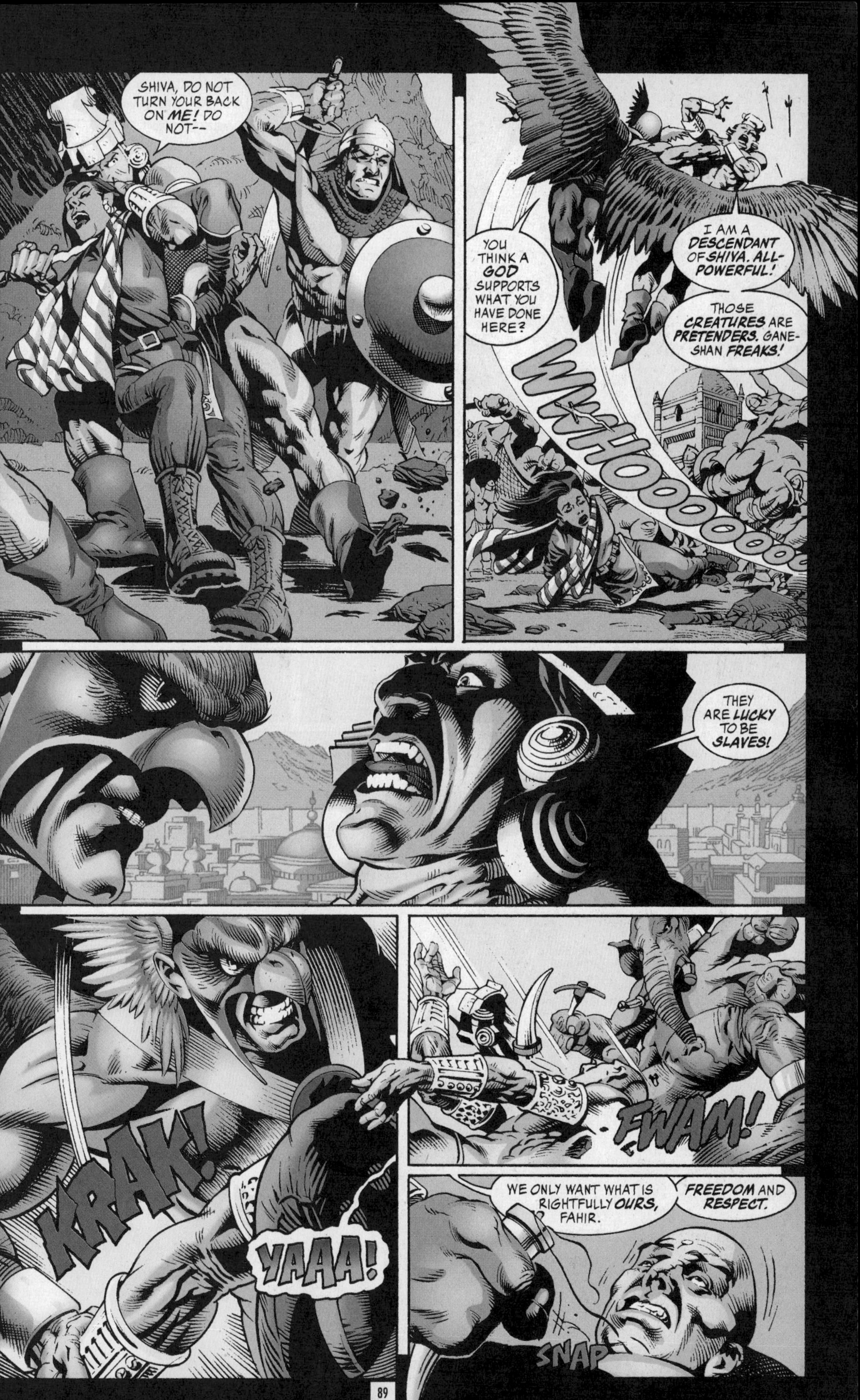

SHIVA, DO NOT TURN YOUR BACK ON ME! DO NOT--
YOU THINK A GOD SUPPORTS WHAT YOU HAVE DONE HERE?
I AM A DESCENDANT OF SHIVA. ALL-POWERFUL!
THOSE CREATURES ARE PRETENDERS. GANE-SHAN FREAKS!
WHHOOOOOOO
THEY ARE LUCKY TO BE SLAVES!
KRAK!
YAAA!
FWAM!
WE ONLY WANT WHAT IS RIGHTFULLY OURS, FAHIR.
FREEDOM AND RESPECT.
SNAP

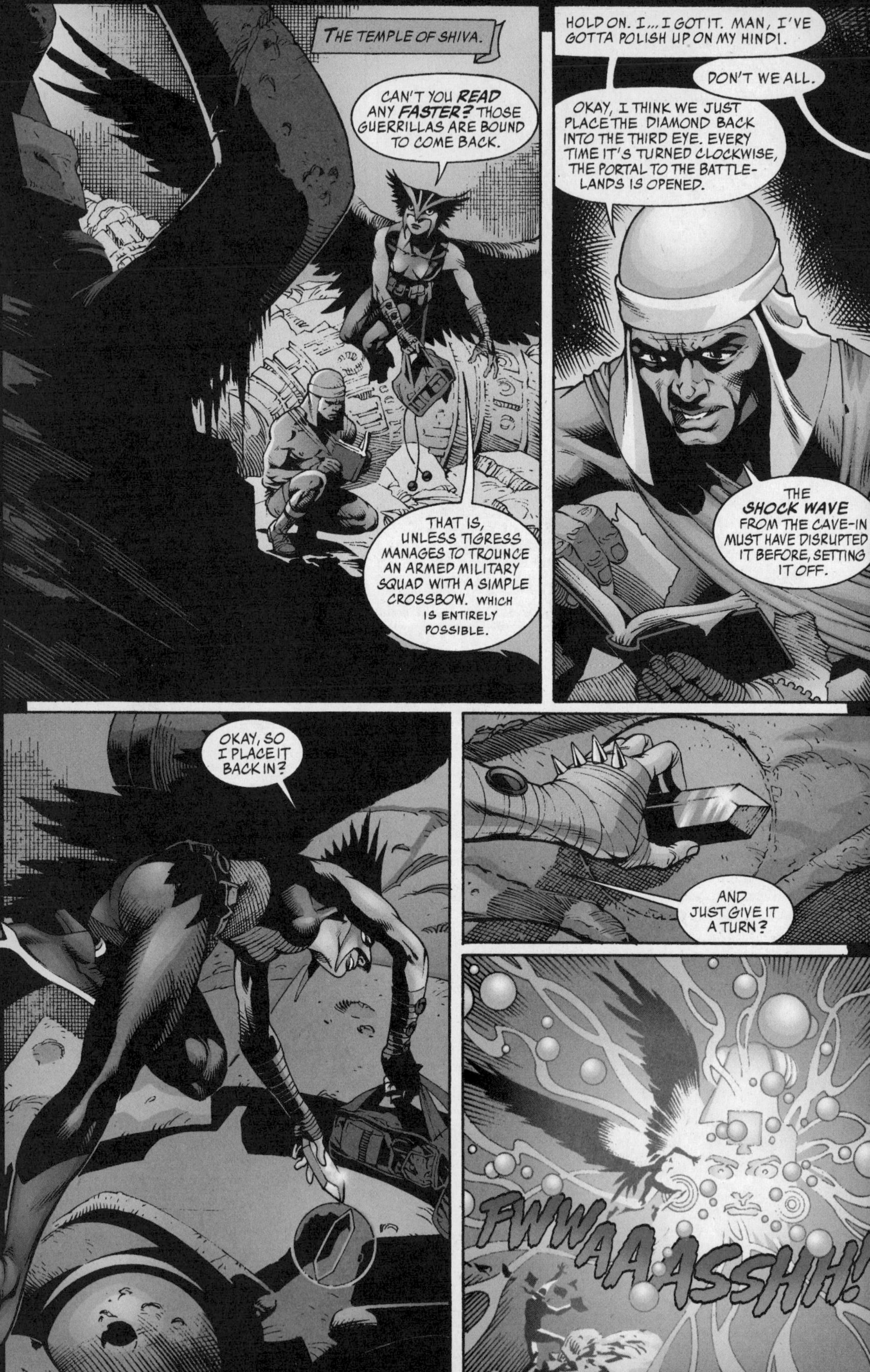
THE TEMPLE OF SHIVA.
CAN'T YOU READ ANY FASTER? THOSE GUERRILLAS ARE BOUND TO COME BACK.
THAT IS, UNLESS TIGRESS MANAGES TO TROUNCE AN ARMED MILITARY SQUAD WITH A SIMPLE CROSSBOW. WHICH IS ENTIRELY POSSIBLE.
HOLD ON. I... I GOT IT. MAN, I'VE GOTTA POLISH UP ON MY HINDI.
DON'T WE ALL.
OKAY, I THINK WE JUST PLACE THE DIAMOND BACK INTO THE THIRD EYE. EVERY TIME IT'S TURNED CLOCKWISE, THE PORTAL TO THE BATTLE-LANDS IS OPENED.
THE SHOCK WAVE FROM THE CAVE-IN MUST HAVE DISRUPTED IT BEFORE, SETTING IT OFF.
OKAY, SO I PLACE IT BACK IN?
AND JUST GIVE IT A TURN?
FWWAAAASSHH!

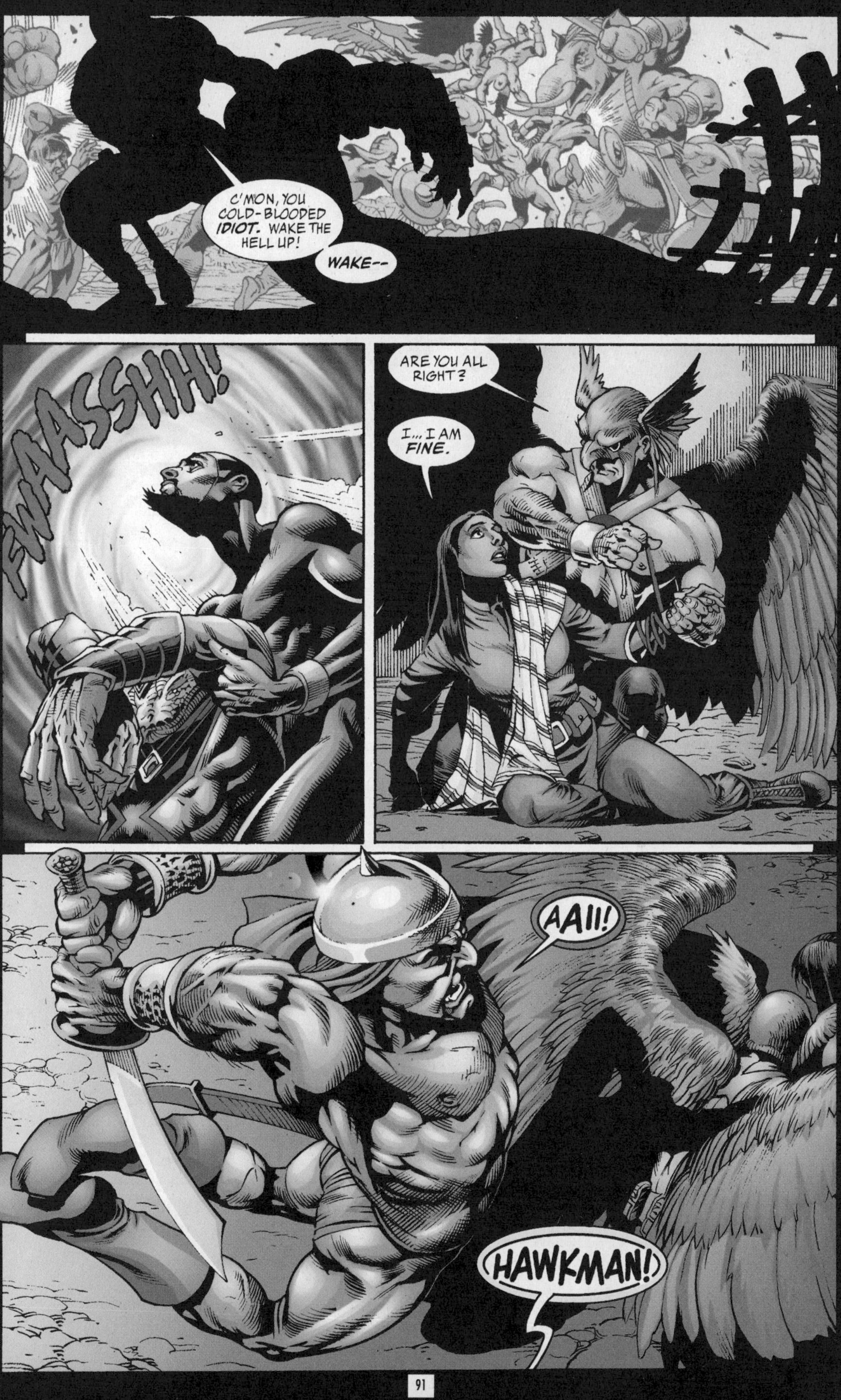
C'MON, YOU COLD-BLOODED IDIOT. WAKE THE HELL UP!
WAKE--
FWAASSHH!
ARE YOU ALL RIGHT?
I... I AM FINE.
AAII!
HAWKMAN!

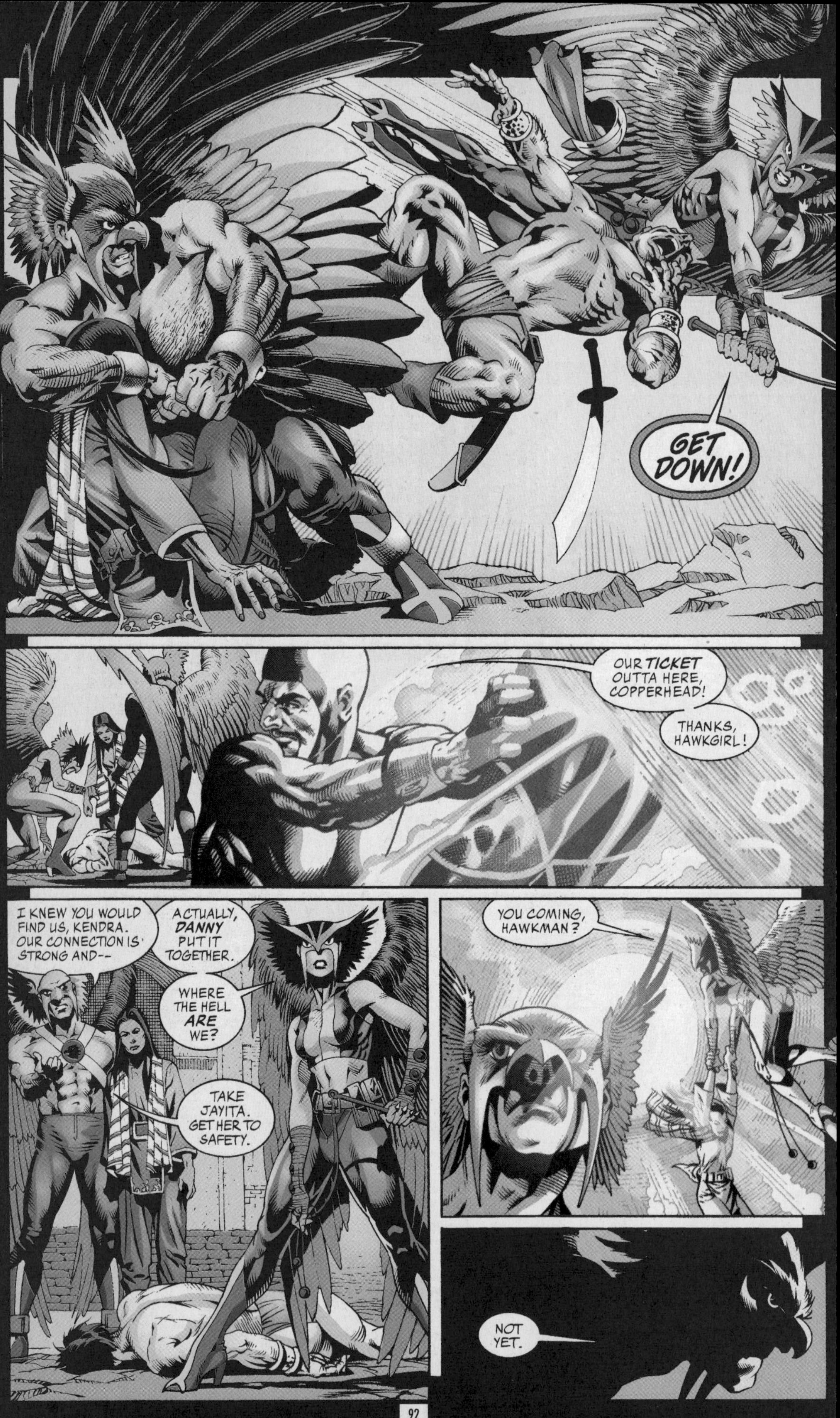
GET DOWN!
OUR TICKET OUTTA HERE, COPPERHEAD!
THANKS, HAWKGIRL!
I KNEW YOU WOULD FIND US, KENDRA. OUR CONNECTION IS STRONG AND--
ACTUALLY, DANNY PUT IT TOGETHER.
WHERE THE HELL ARE WE?
TAKE JAYITA. GET HER TO SAFETY.
YOU COMING, HAWKMAN?
NOT YET.

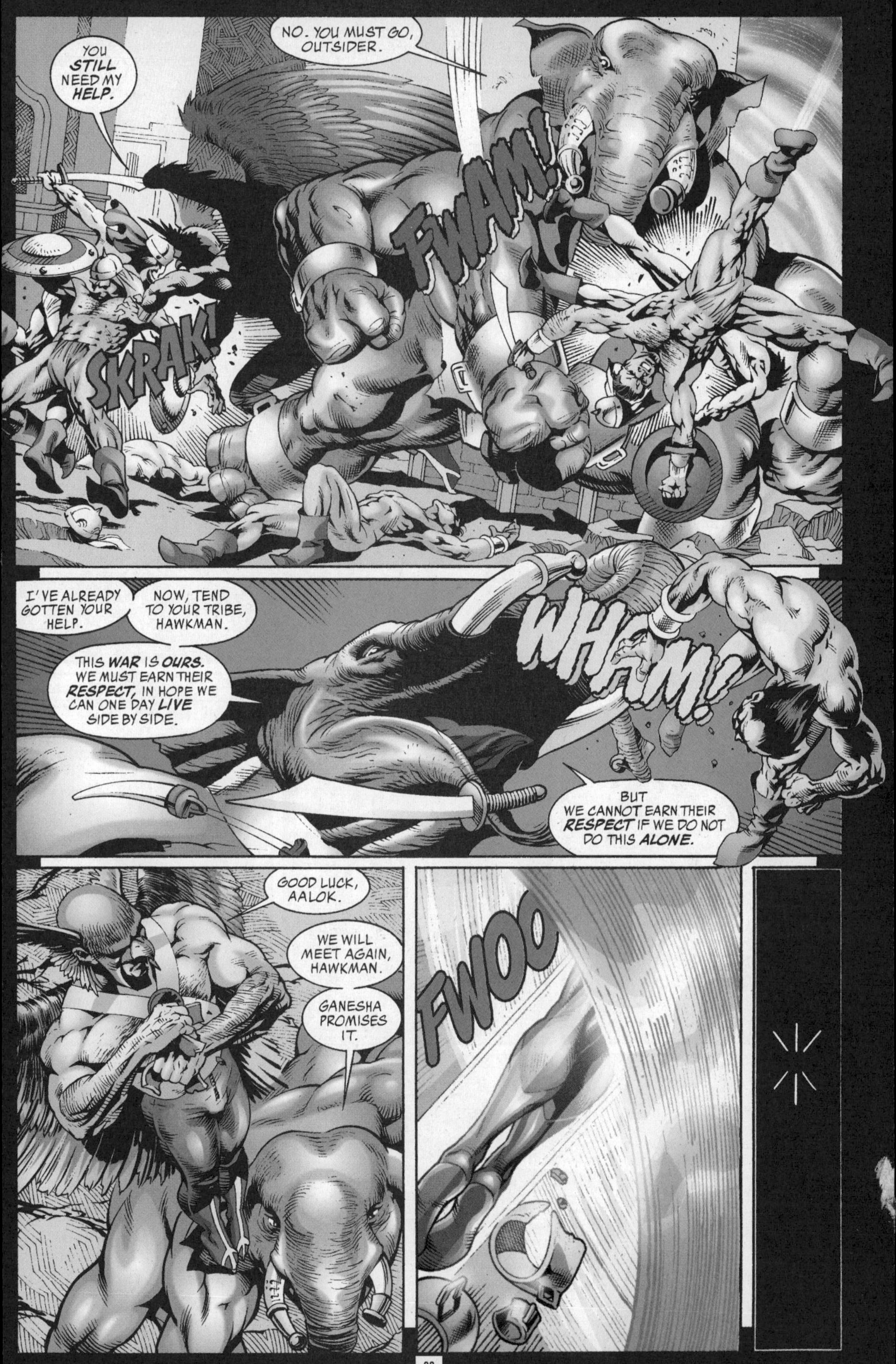
YOU STILL NEED MY HELP.
NO. YOU MUST GO, OUTSIDER.
FWAM!
SKRAK!
I'VE ALREADY GOTTEN YOUR HELP.
NOW, TEND TO YOUR TRIBE, HAWKMAN.
THIS WAR IS OURS. WE MUST EARN THEIR RESPECT, IN HOPE WE CAN ONE DAY LIVE SIDE BY SIDE.
WHAM!
BUT WE CANNOT EARN THEIR RESPECT IF WE DO NOT DO THIS ALONE.
GOOD LUCK, AALOK.
WE WILL MEET AGAIN, HAWKMAN.
GANESHA PROMISES IT.
FWOO

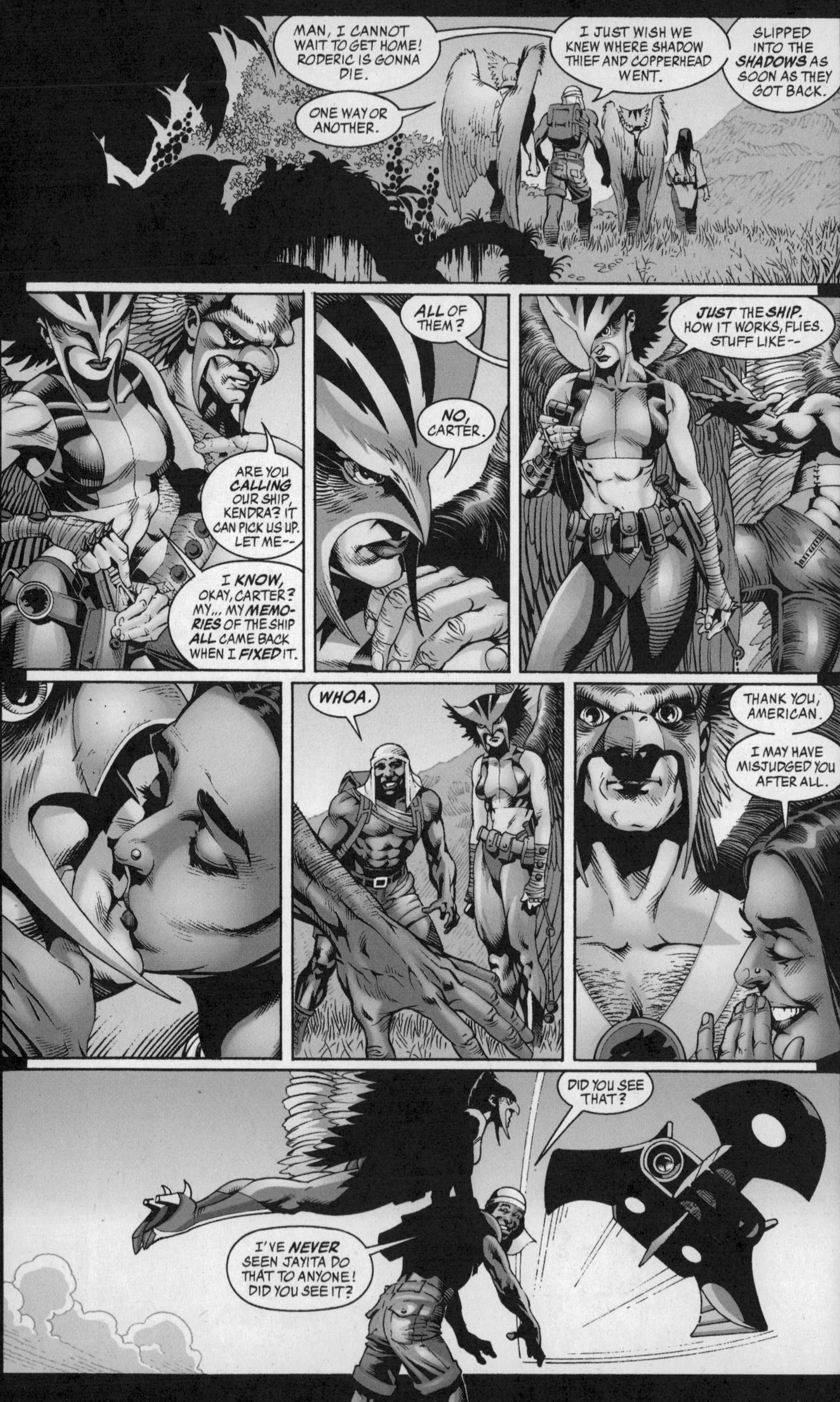

MAN, I CANNOT WAIT TO GET HOME! RODERIC IS GONNA DIE.
ONE WAY OR ANOTHER.
I JUST WISH WE KNEW WHERE SHADOW THIEF AND COPPERHEAD WENT.
SLIPPED INTO THE SHADOWS AS SOON AS THEY GOT BACK.
ARE YOU CALLING OUR SHIP, KENDRA? IT CAN PICK US UP. LET ME--
I KNOW, OKAY, CARTER? MY... MY MEMORIES OF THE SHIP ALL CAME BACK WHEN I FIXED IT.
ALL OF THEM?
NO, CARTER.
JUST THE SHIP. HOW IT WORKS, FLIES. STUFF LIKE--
WHOA.
THANK YOU, AMERICAN.
I MAY HAVE MISJUDGED YOU AFTER ALL.
DID YOU SEE THAT?
I'VE NEVER SEEN JAYITA DO THAT TO ANYONE! DID YOU SEE IT?

# EPILOGUE ONE: KRISTOPHER RODERIC

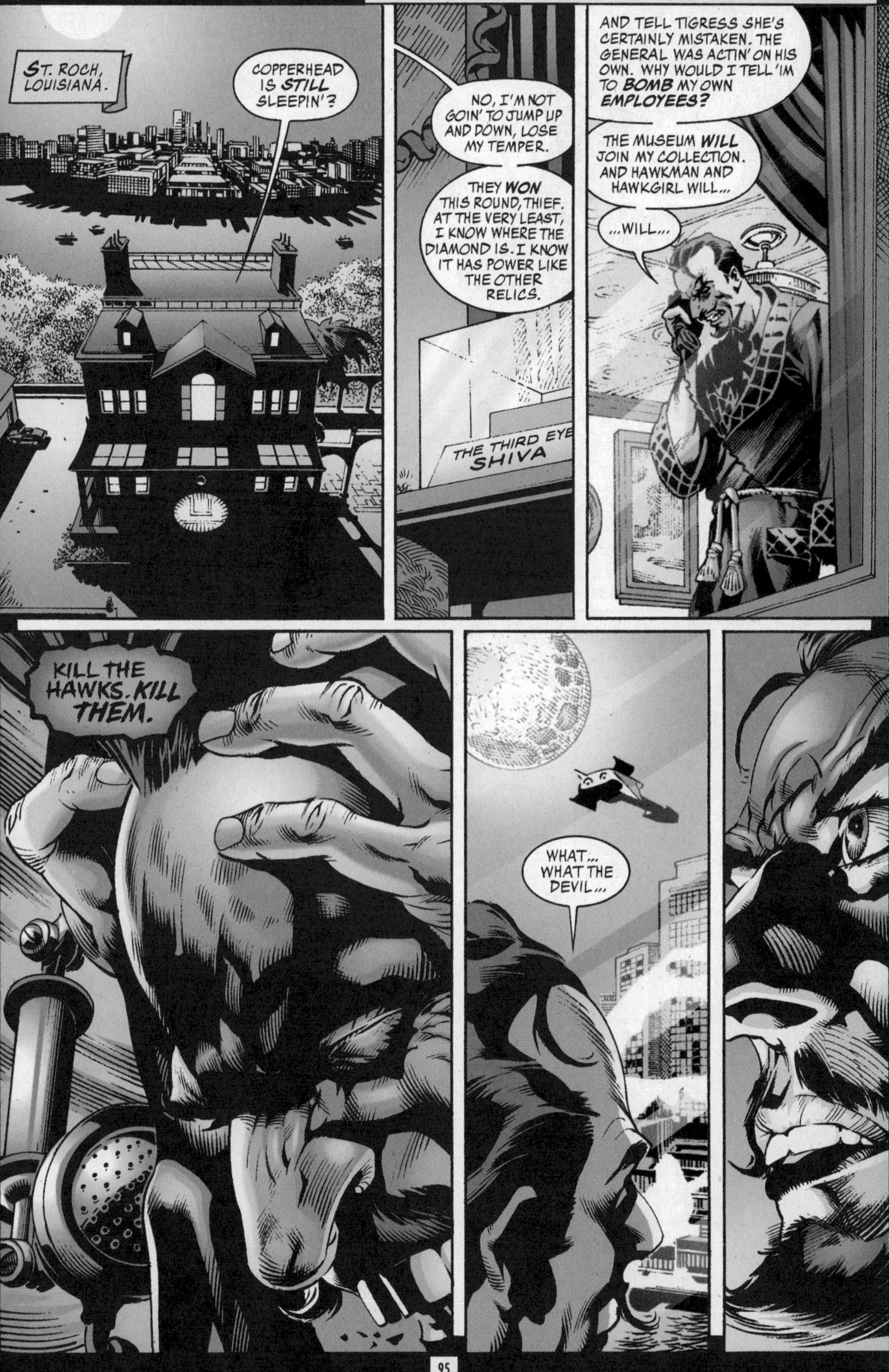

ST. ROCH, LOUISIANA.
COPPERHEAD IS STILL SLEEPIN'?
NO, I'M NOT GOIN' TO JUMP UP AND DOWN, LOSE MY TEMPER.
THEY WON THIS ROUND, THIEF. AT THE VERY LEAST, I KNOW WHERE THE DIAMOND IS. I KNOW IT HAS POWER LIKE THE OTHER RELICS.
THE THIRD EYE SHIVA
AND TELL TIGRESS SHE'S CERTAINLY MISTAKEN. THE GENERAL WAS ACTIN' ON HIS OWN. WHY WOULD I TELL 'IM TO BOMB MY OWN EMPLOYEES?
THE MUSEUM WILL JOIN MY COLLECTION. AND HAWKMAN AND HAWKGIRL WILL...
...WILL...
KILL THE HAWKS. KILL THEM.
WHAT... WHAT THE DEVIL...

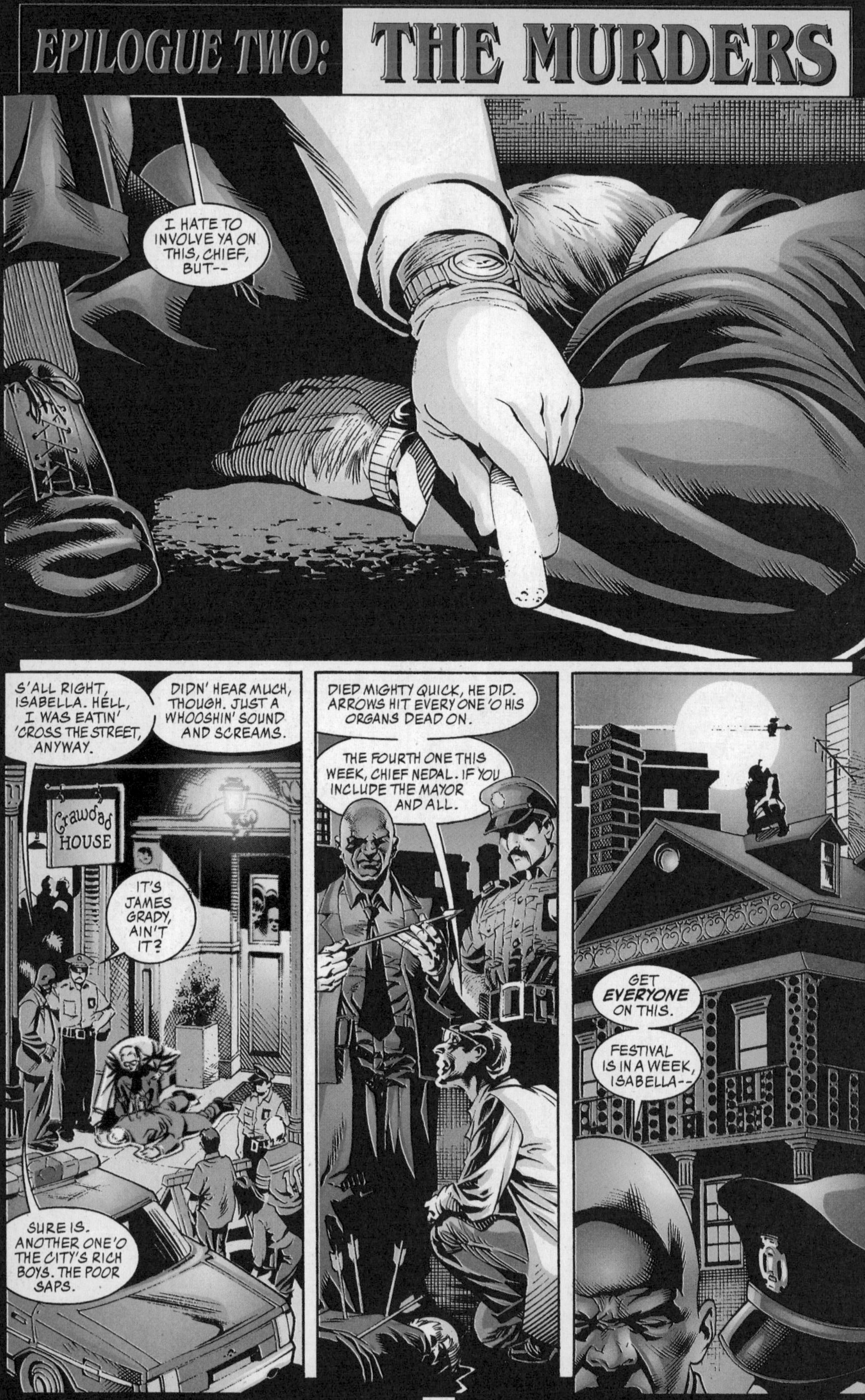
EPILOGUE TWO: THE MURDERS
I HATE TO INVOLVE YA ON THIS, CHIEF, BUT--
S'ALL RIGHT, ISABELLA. HELL, I WAS EATIN' 'CROSS THE STREET, ANYWAY.
DIDN' HEAR MUCH, THOUGH. JUST A WHOOSHIN' SOUND AND SCREAMS.
Crawdad HOUSE
IT'S JAMES GRADY, AIN'T IT?
SURE IS. ANOTHER ONE'O THE CITY'S RICH BOYS. THE POOR SAPS.
DIED MIGHTY QUICK, HE DID. ARROWS HIT EVERY ONE 'O HIS ORGANS DEAD ON.
THE FOURTH ONE THIS WEEK, CHIEF NEDAL. IF YOU INCLUDE THE MAYOR AND ALL.
GET EVERYONE ON THIS.
FESTIVAL IS IN A WEEK, ISABELLA--

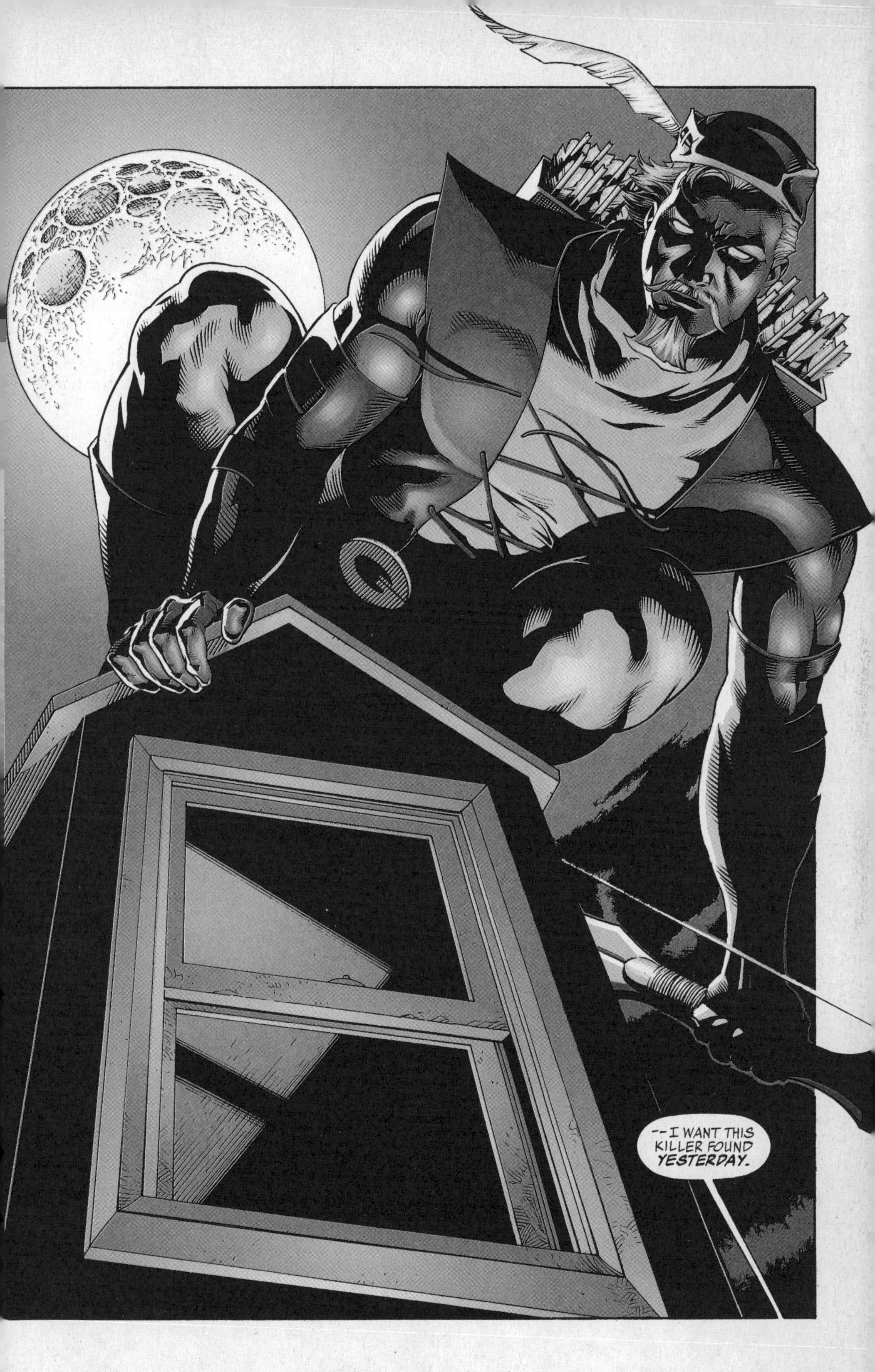
--I WANT THIS KILLER FOUND YESTERDAY.

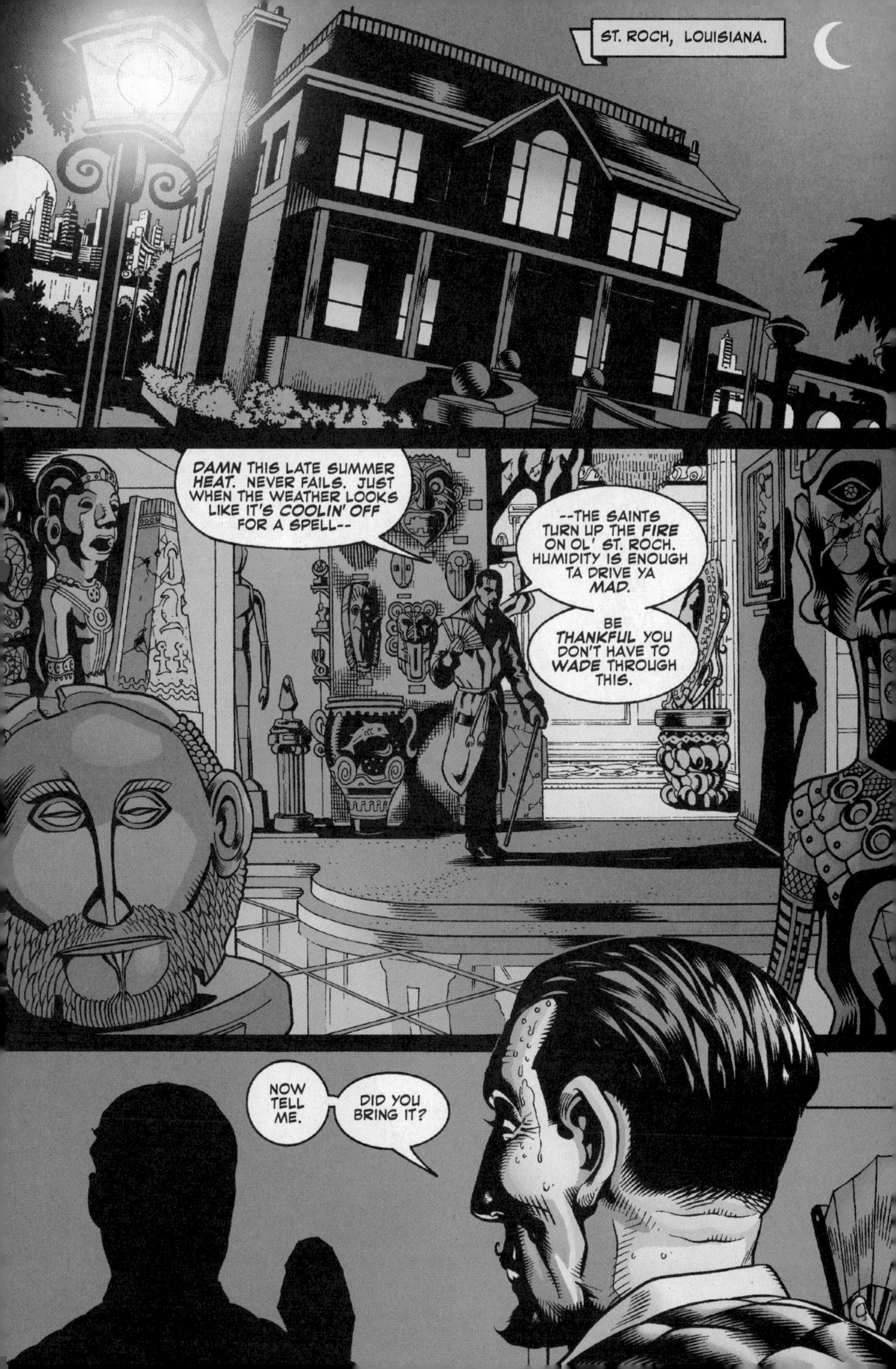
ST. ROCH, LOUISIANA.
DAMN THIS LATE SUMMER HEAT. NEVER FAILS. JUST WHEN THE WEATHER LOOKS LIKE IT'S COOLIN' OFF FOR A SPELL--
--THE SAINTS TURN UP THE FIRE ON OL' ST. ROCH. HUMIDITY IS ENOUGH TA DRIVE YA MAD.
BE THANKFUL YOU DON'T HAVE TO WADE THROUGH THIS.
NOW TELL ME.
DID YOU BRING IT?

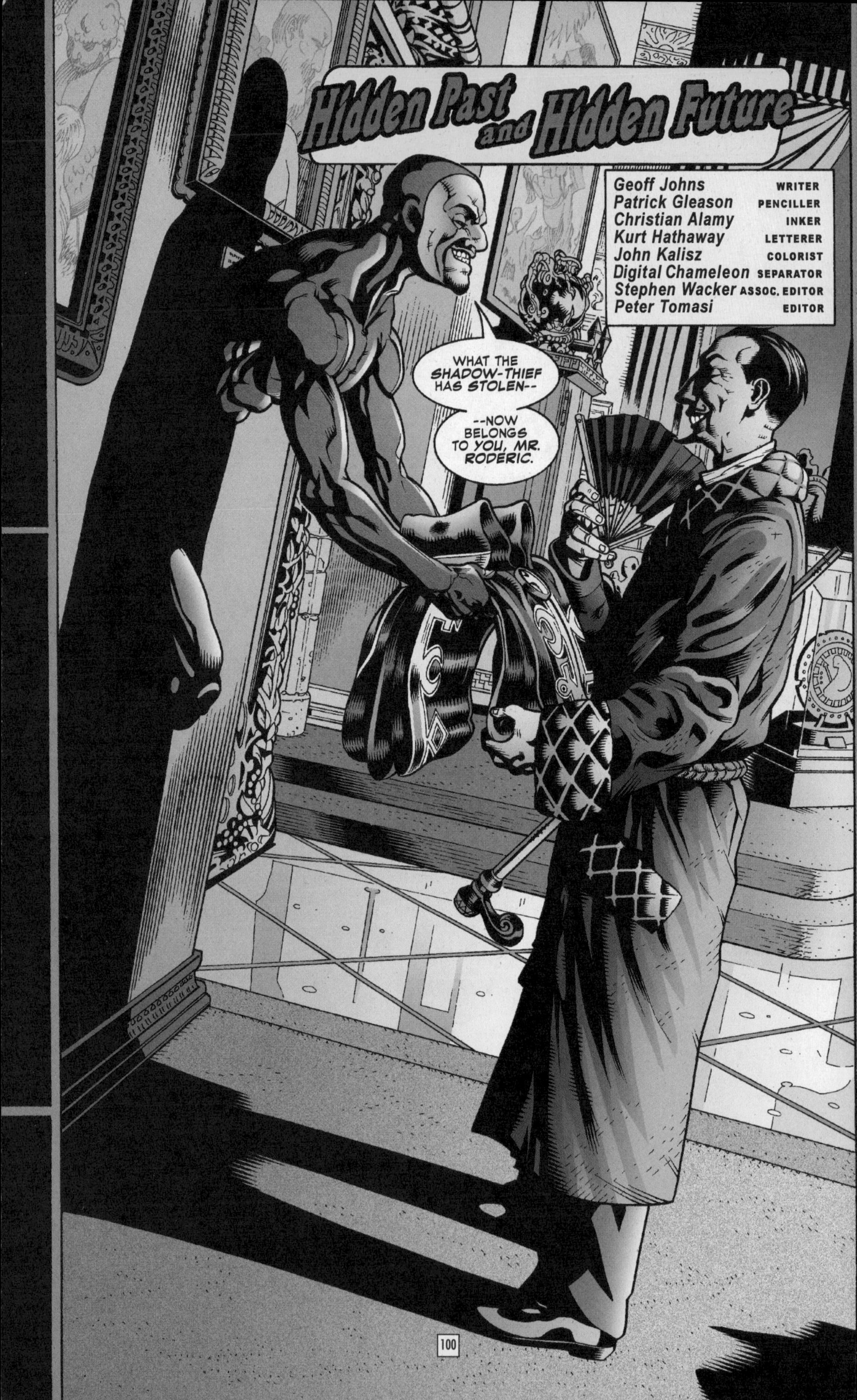

Hidden Past and Hidden Future
Geoff Johns WRITER
Patrick Gleason PENCILLER
Christian Alamy INKER
Kurt Hathaway LETTERER
John Kalisz COLORIST
Digital Chameleon SEPARATOR
Stephen Wacker ASSOC. EDITOR
Peter Tomasi EDITOR
WHAT THE SHADOW-THIEF HAS STOLEN--
--NOW BELONGS TO YOU, MR. RODERIC.

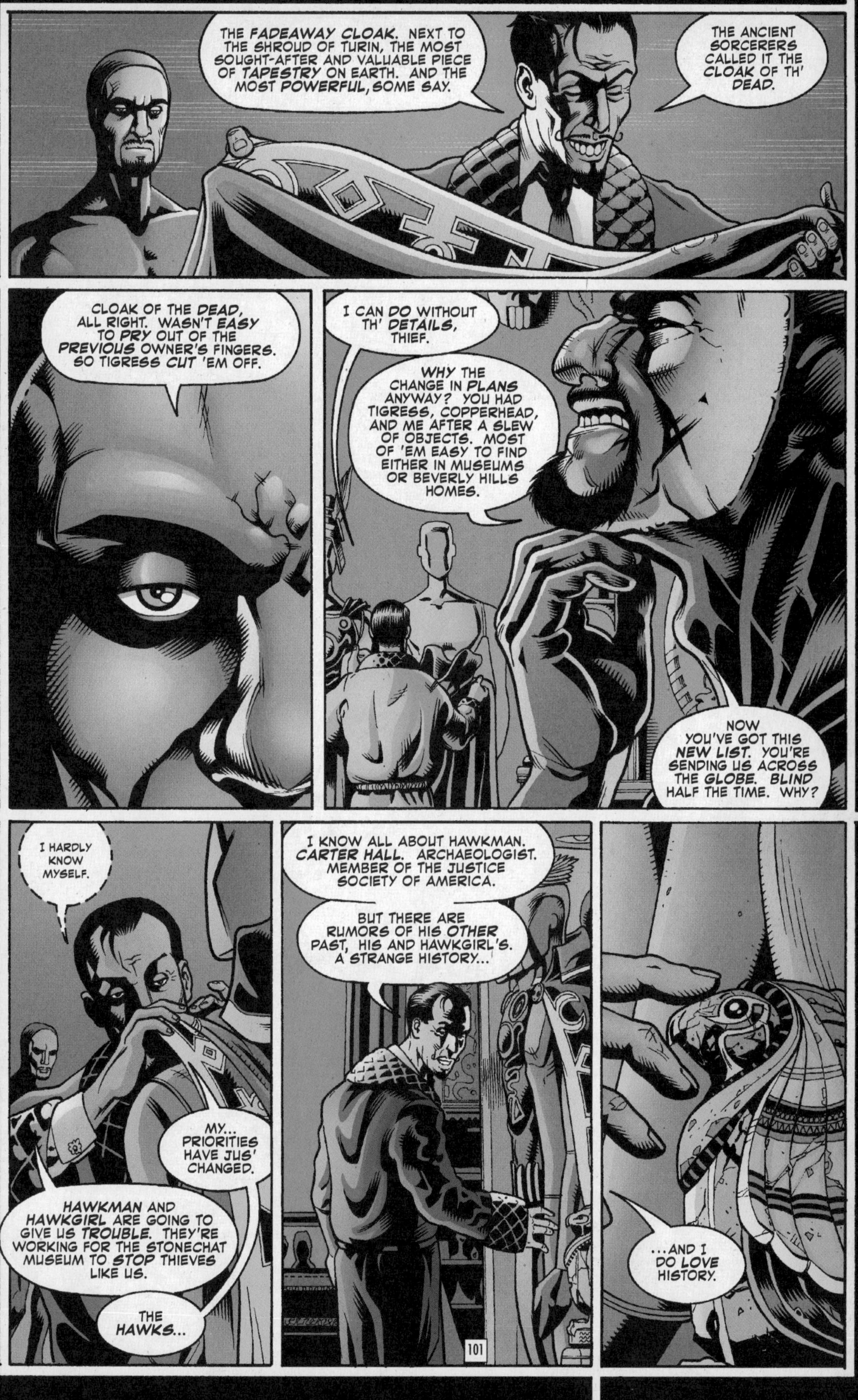
THE FADEAWAY CLOAK. NEXT TO THE SHROUD OF TURIN, THE MOST SOUGHT-AFTER AND VALUABLE PIECE OF TAPESTRY ON EARTH. AND THE MOST POWERFUL, SOME SAY.
THE ANCIENT SORCERERS CALLED IT THE CLOAK OF TH' DEAD.
CLOAK OF THE DEAD, ALL RIGHT. WASN'T EASY TO PRY OUT OF THE PREVIOUS OWNER'S FINGERS. SO TIGRESS CUT 'EM OFF.
I CAN DO WITHOUT TH' DETAILS, THIEF.
WHY THE CHANGE IN PLANS ANYWAY? YOU HAD TIGRESS, COPPERHEAD, AND ME AFTER A SLEW OF OBJECTS. MOST OF 'EM EASY TO FIND EITHER IN MUSEUMS OR BEVERLY HILLS HOMES.
NOW YOU'VE GOT THIS NEW LIST. YOU'RE SENDING US ACROSS THE GLOBE. BLIND HALF THE TIME. WHY?
I HARDLY KNOW MYSELF.
MY... PRIORITIES HAVE JUS' CHANGED.
HAWKMAN AND HAWKGIRL ARE GOING TO GIVE US TROUBLE. THEY'RE WORKING FOR THE STONECHAT MUSEUM TO STOP THIEVES LIKE US.
THE HAWKS...
I KNOW ALL ABOUT HAWKMAN. CARTER HALL. ARCHAEOLOGIST. MEMBER OF THE JUSTICE SOCIETY OF AMERICA.
BUT THERE ARE RUMORS OF HIS OTHER PAST, HIS AND HAWKGIRL'S. A STRANGE HISTORY...
...AND I DO LOVE HISTORY.

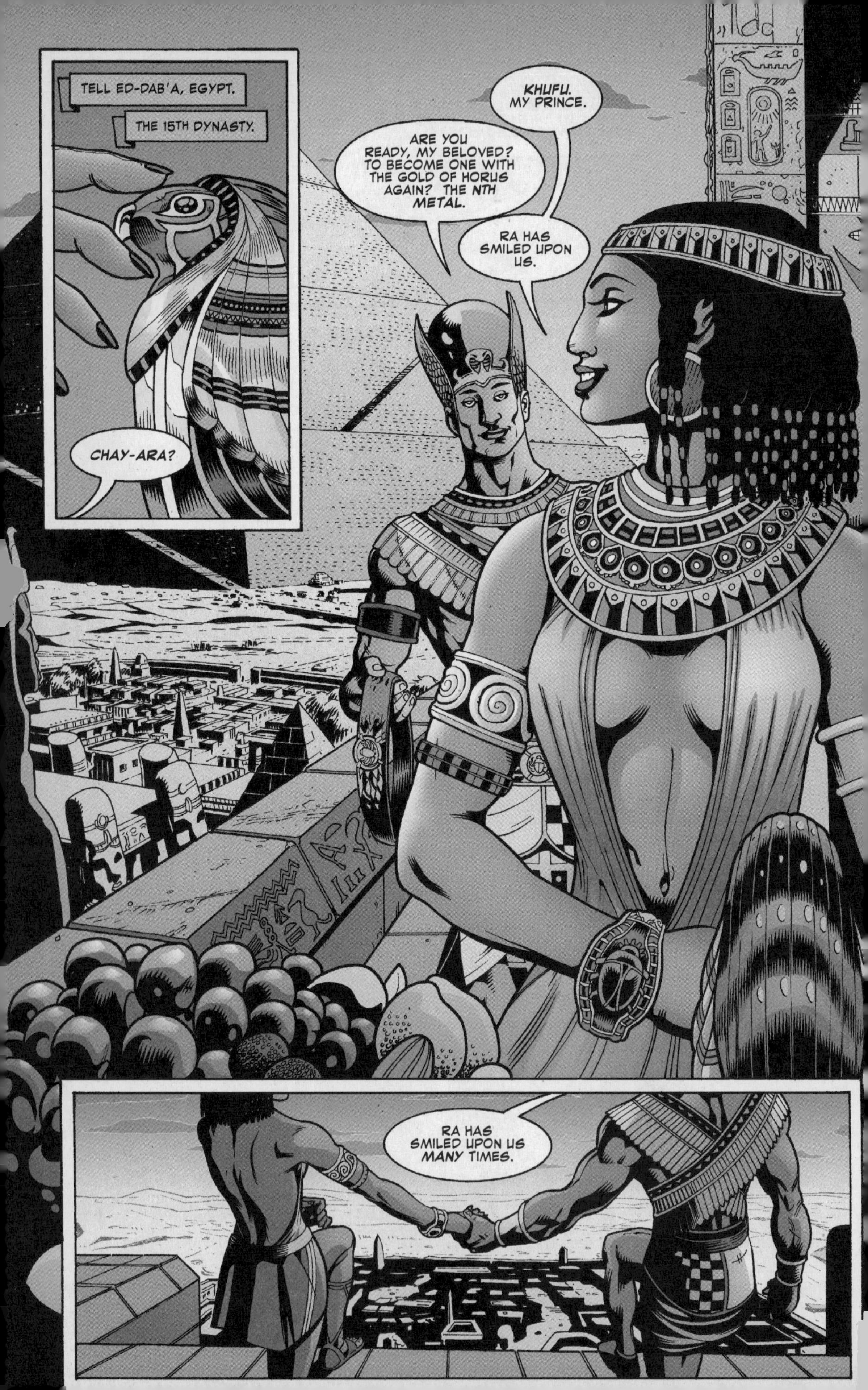
TELL ED-DAB'A, EGYPT.
THE 15TH DYNASTY.
CHAY-ARA?
ARE YOU READY, MY BELOVED? TO BECOME ONE WITH THE GOLD OF HORUS AGAIN? THE NTH METAL.
KHUFU. MY PRINCE.
RA HAS SMILED UPON US.
RA HAS SMILED UPON US MANY TIMES.

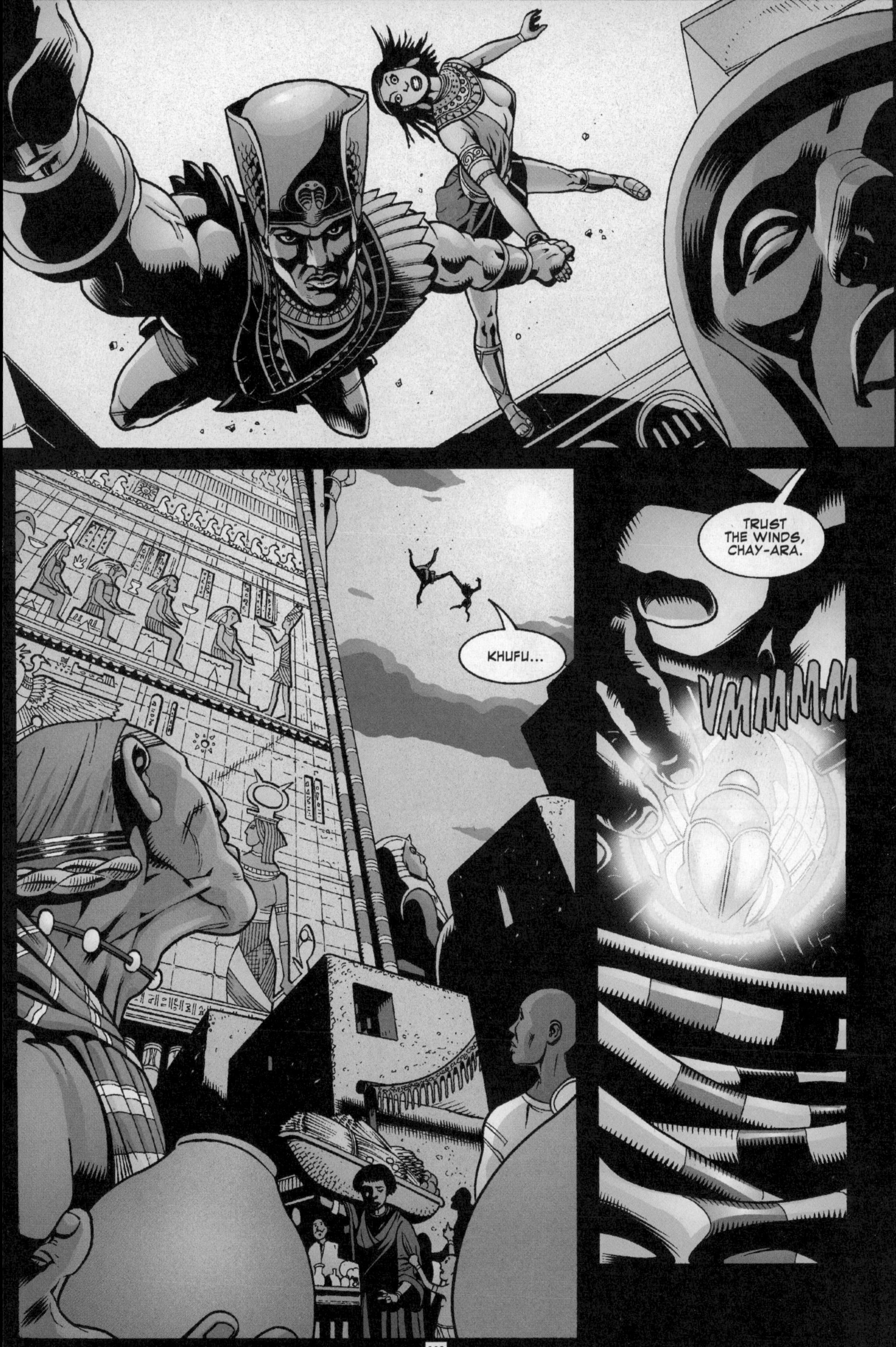
KHUFU...
TRUST THE WINDS, CHAY-ARA.
VMMMM

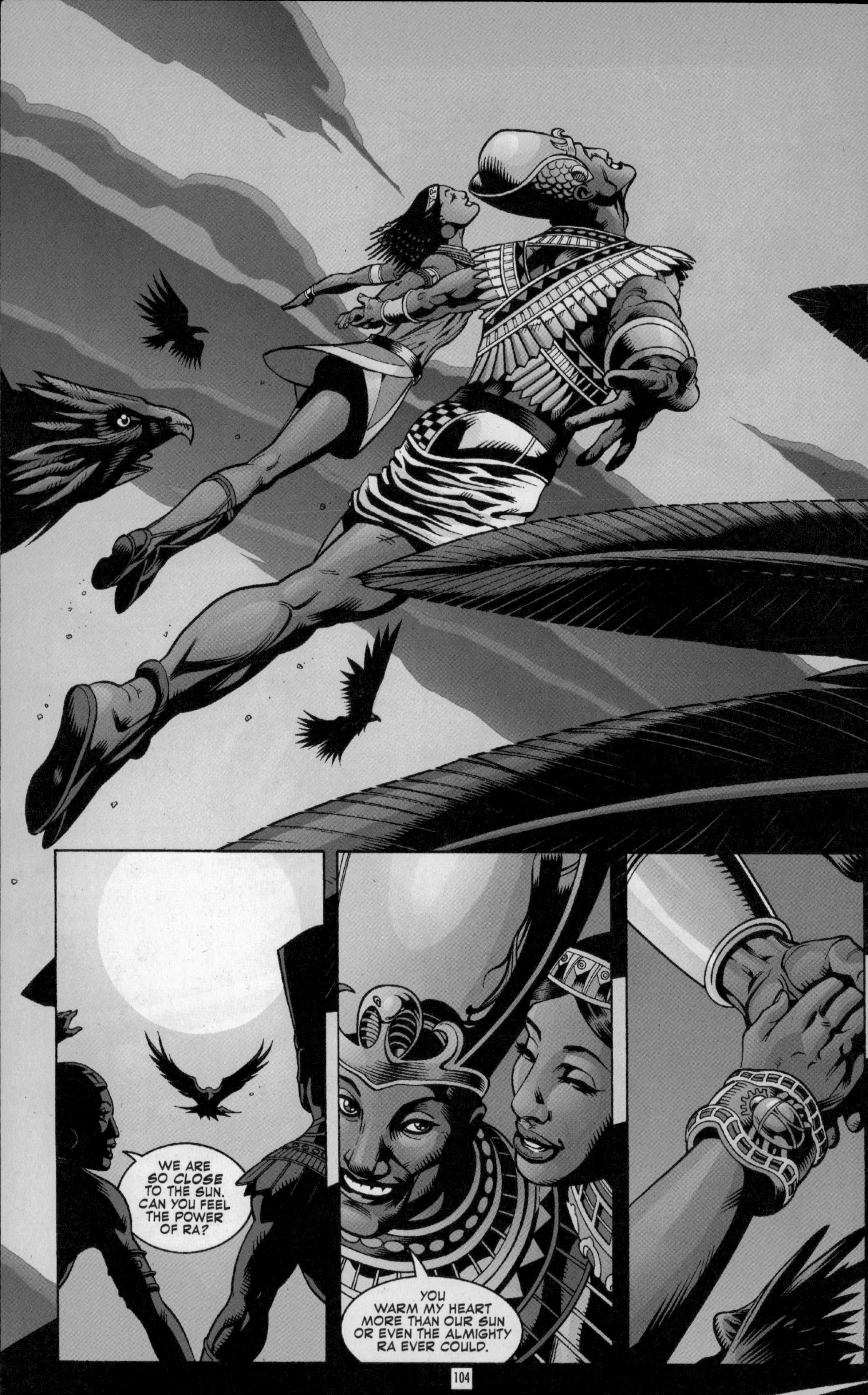
WE ARE SO CLOSE TO THE SUN. CAN YOU FEEL THE POWER OF RA?
YOU WARM MY HEART MORE THAN OUR SUN OR EVEN THE ALMIGHTY RA EVER COULD.

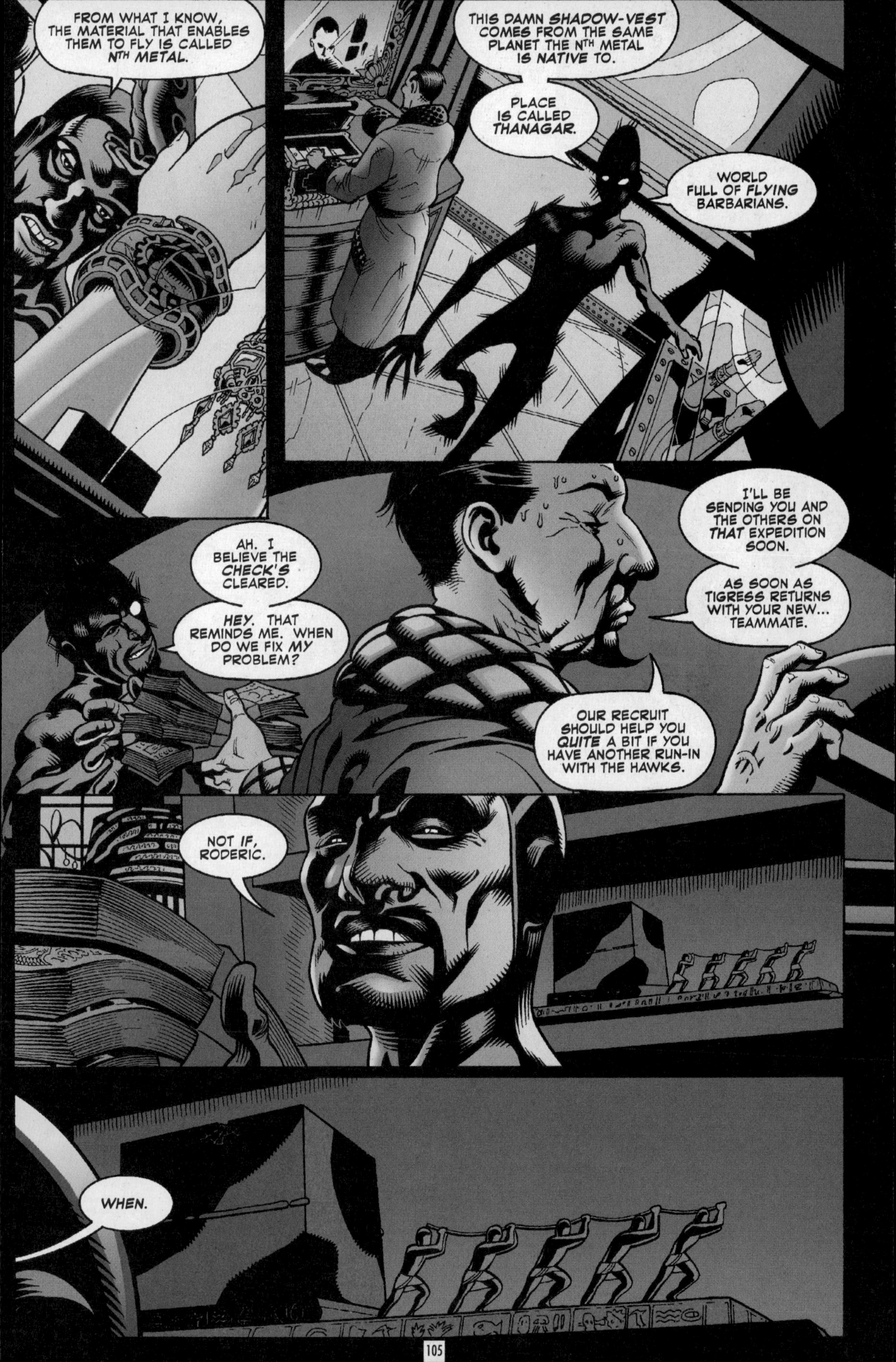
FROM WHAT I KNOW, THE MATERIAL THAT ENABLES THEM TO FLY IS CALLED Nth METAL.
THIS DAMN SHADOW-VEST COMES FROM THE SAME PLANET THE Nth METAL IS NATIVE TO.
PLACE IS CALLED THANAGAR.
WORLD FULL OF FLYING BARBARIANS.
AH. I BELIEVE THE CHECK'S CLEARED.
HEY. THAT REMINDS ME. WHEN DO WE FIX MY PROBLEM?
I'LL BE SENDING YOU AND THE OTHERS ON THAT EXPEDITION SOON.
AS SOON AS TIGRESS RETURNS WITH YOUR NEW... TEAMMATE.
OUR RECRUIT SHOULD HELP YOU QUITE A BIT IF YOU HAVE ANOTHER RUN-IN WITH THE HAWKS.
NOT IF, RODERIC.
WHEN.

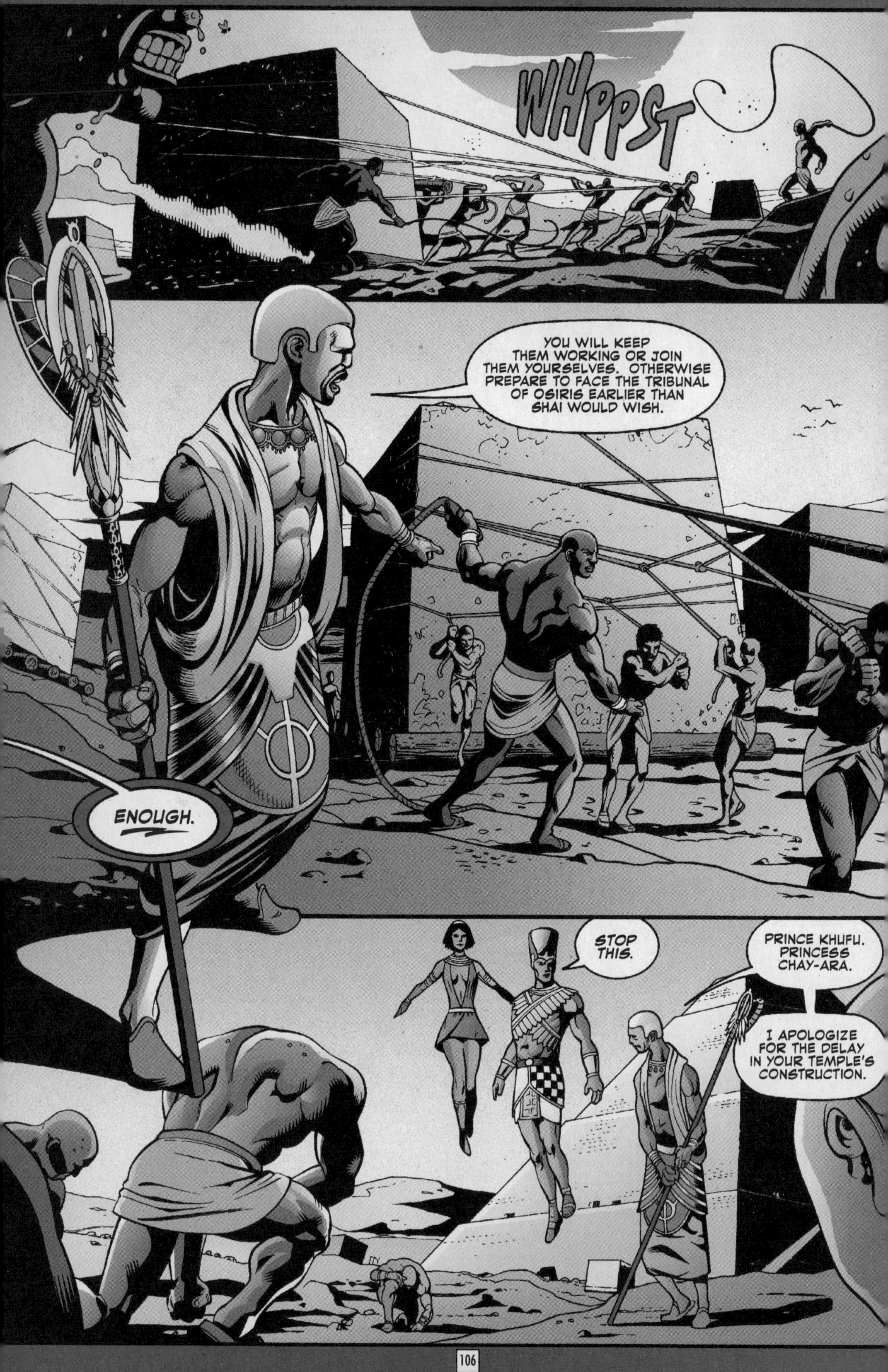
WHPPST
YOU WILL KEEP THEM WORKING OR JOIN THEM YOURSELVES. OTHERWISE PREPARE TO FACE THE TRIBUNAL OF OSIRIS EARLIER THAN SHAI WOULD WISH.
ENOUGH.
STOP THIS.
PRINCE KHUFU. PRINCESS CHAY-ARA.
I APOLOGIZE FOR THE DELAY IN YOUR TEMPLE'S CONSTRUCTION.

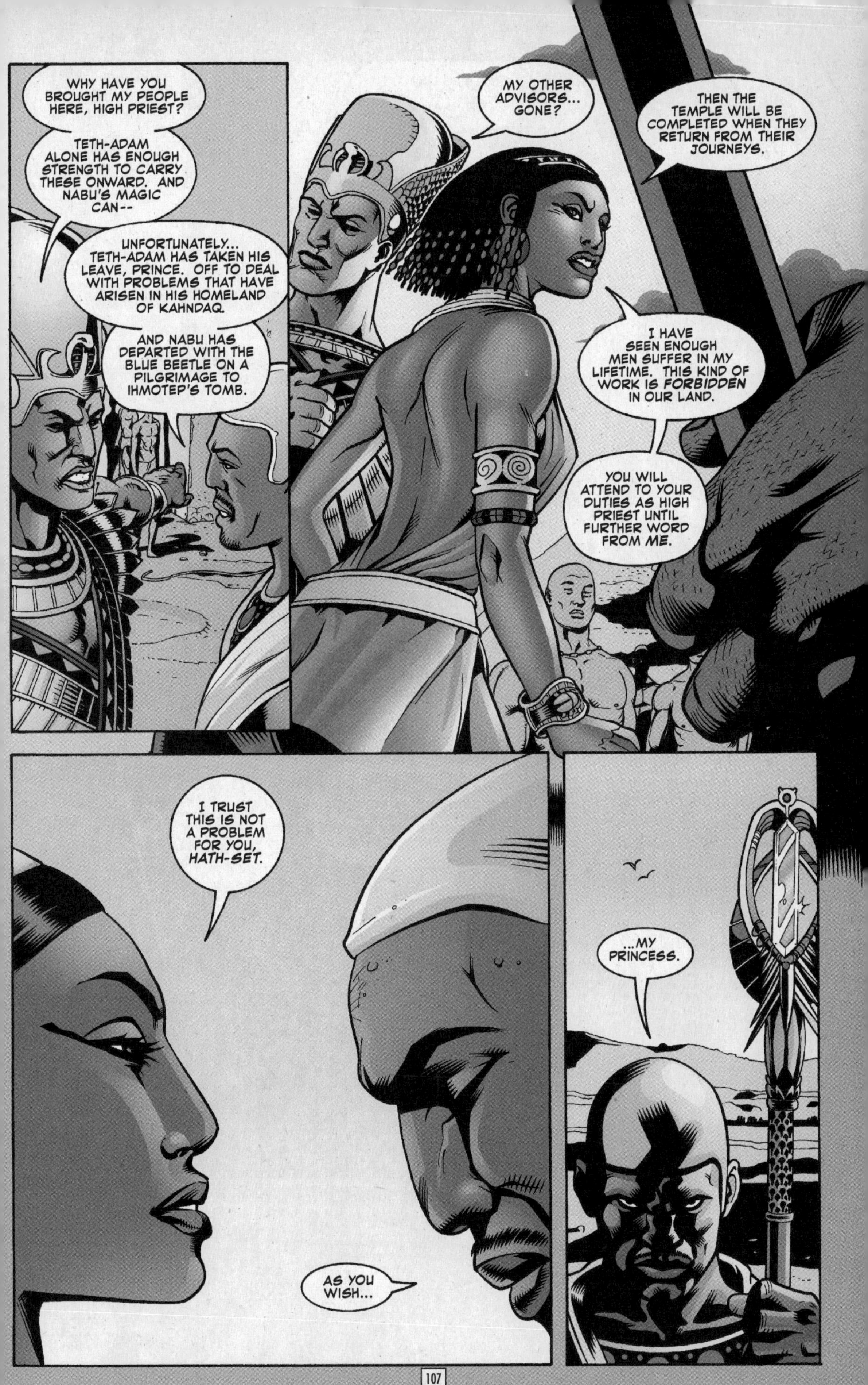
WHY HAVE YOU BROUGHT MY PEOPLE HERE, HIGH PRIEST?
TETH-ADAM ALONE HAS ENOUGH STRENGTH TO CARRY THESE ONWARD. AND NABU'S MAGIC CAN--
UNFORTUNATELY... TETH-ADAM HAS TAKEN HIS LEAVE, PRINCE. OFF TO DEAL WITH PROBLEMS THAT HAVE ARISEN IN HIS HOMELAND OF KAHNDAQ.
AND NABU HAS DEPARTED WITH THE BLUE BEETLE ON A PILGRIMAGE TO IHMOTEP'S TOMB.
MY OTHER ADVISORS... GONE?
THEN THE TEMPLE WILL BE COMPLETED WHEN THEY RETURN FROM THEIR JOURNEYS.
I HAVE SEEN ENOUGH MEN SUFFER IN MY LIFETIME. THIS KIND OF WORK IS *FORBIDDEN* IN OUR LAND.
YOU WILL ATTEND TO YOUR DUTIES AS HIGH PRIEST UNTIL FURTHER WORD FROM *ME*.
I TRUST THIS IS NOT A PROBLEM FOR YOU, *HATH-SET*.
AS YOU WISH...
...MY PRINCESS.

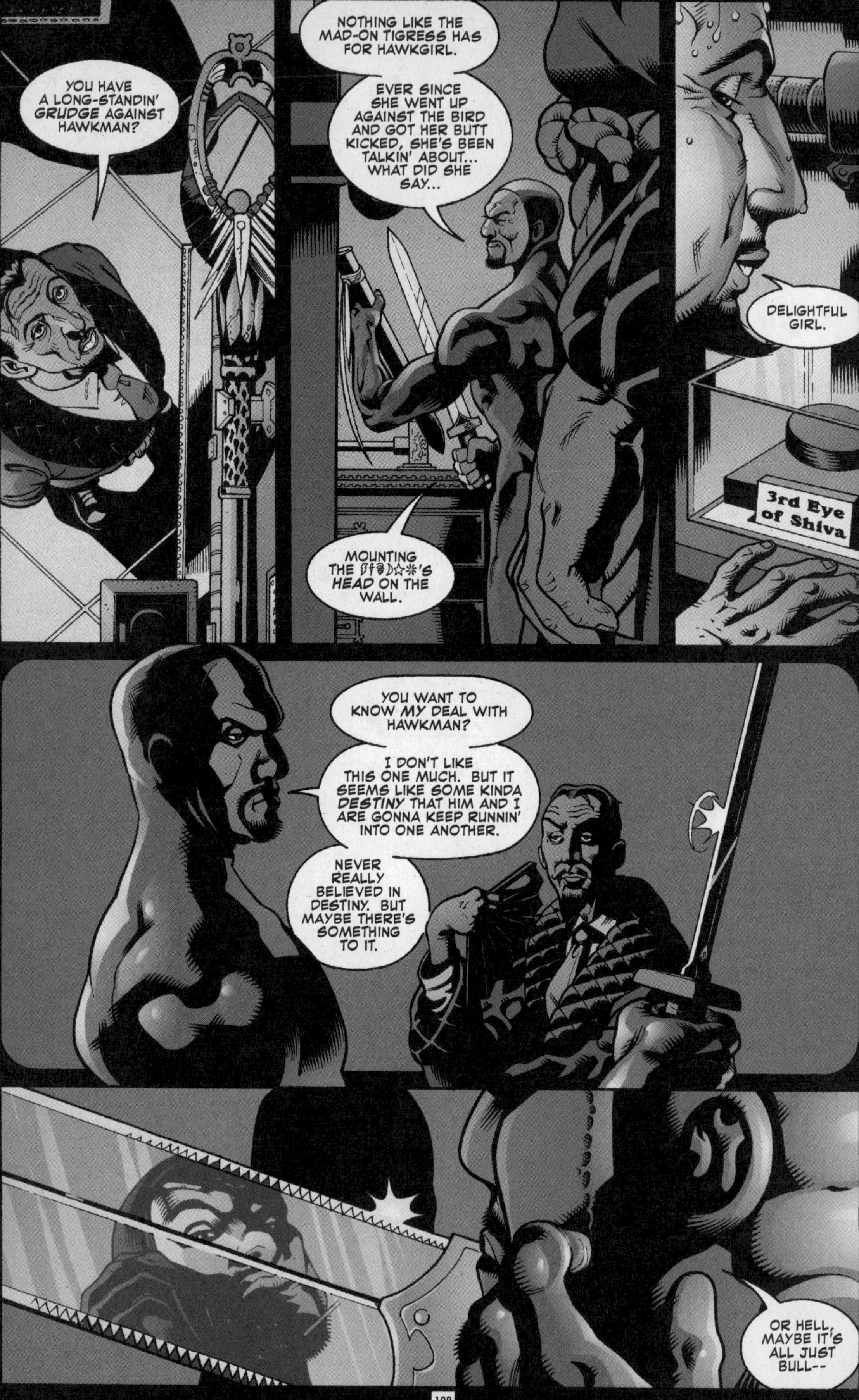
YOU HAVE A LONG-STANDIN' GRUDGE AGAINST HAWKMAN?
NOTHING LIKE THE MAD-ON TIGRESS HAS FOR HAWKGIRL.
EVER SINCE SHE WENT UP AGAINST THE BIRD AND GOT HER BUTT KICKED, SHE'S BEEN TALKIN' ABOUT... WHAT DID SHE SAY...
MOUNTING THE ♯†☻☆✲'S HEAD ON THE WALL.
DELIGHTFUL GIRL.
3rd Eye of Shiva
YOU WANT TO KNOW MY DEAL WITH HAWKMAN?
I DON'T LIKE THIS ONE MUCH. BUT IT SEEMS LIKE SOME KINDA DESTINY THAT HIM AND I ARE GONNA KEEP RUNNIN' INTO ONE ANOTHER.
NEVER REALLY BELIEVED IN DESTINY. BUT MAYBE THERE'S SOMETHING TO IT.
OR HELL, MAYBE IT'S ALL JUST BULL--

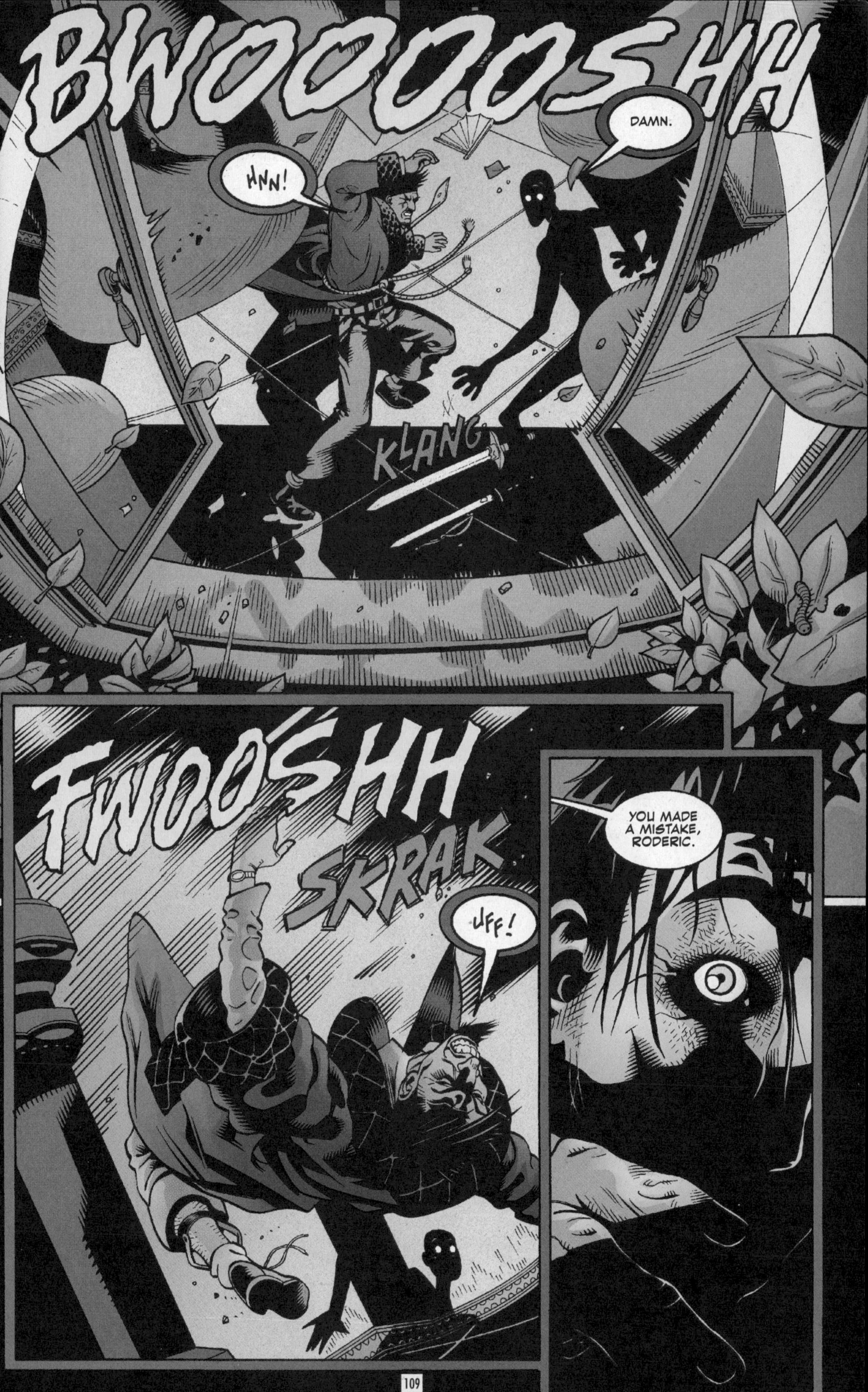
BWOOOOSHH
DAMN.
HNN!
KLANG
FWOOSHH
SKRAK
UFF!
YOU MADE A MISTAKE, RODERIC.

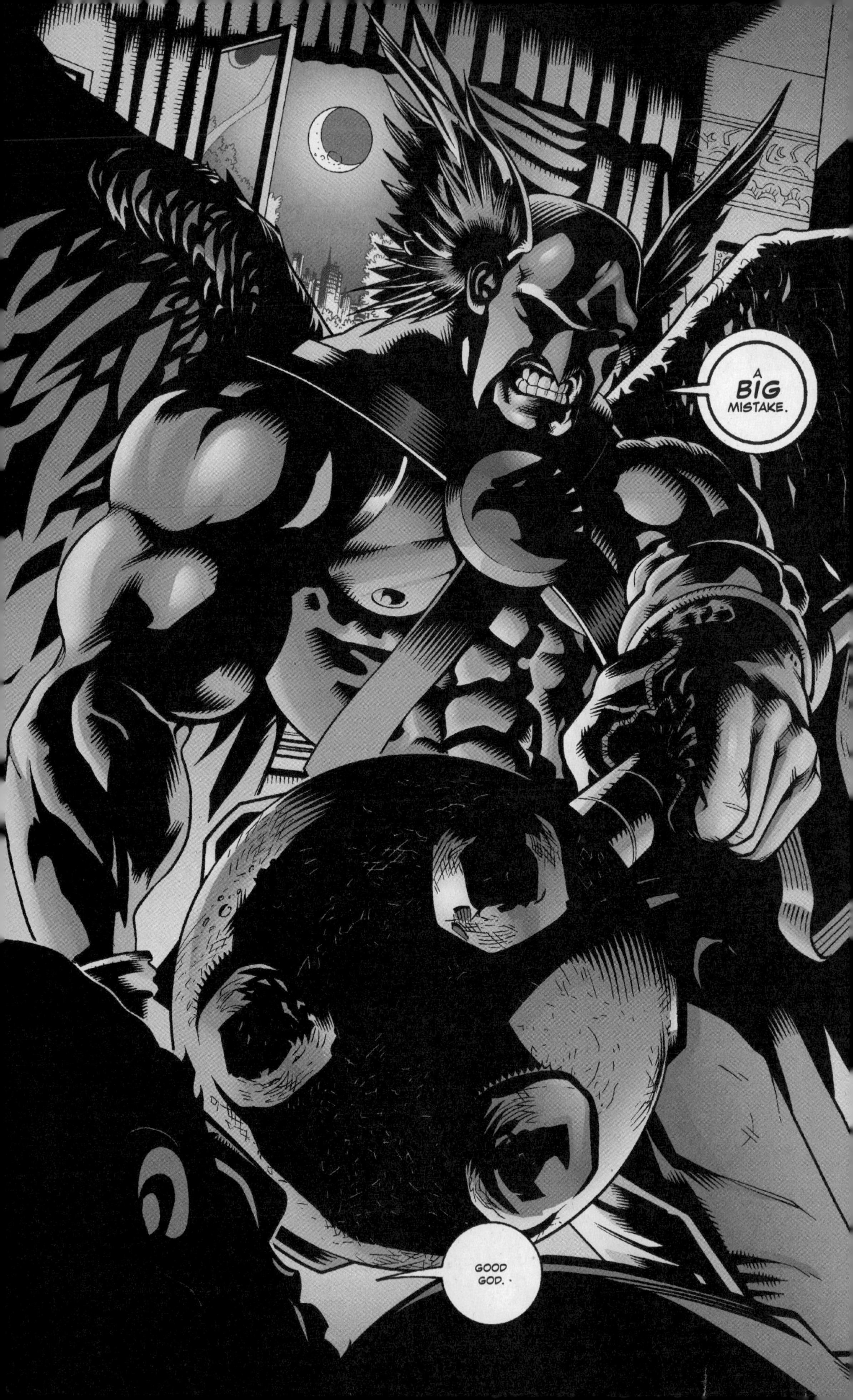
A BIG MISTAKE.
GOOD GOD. .

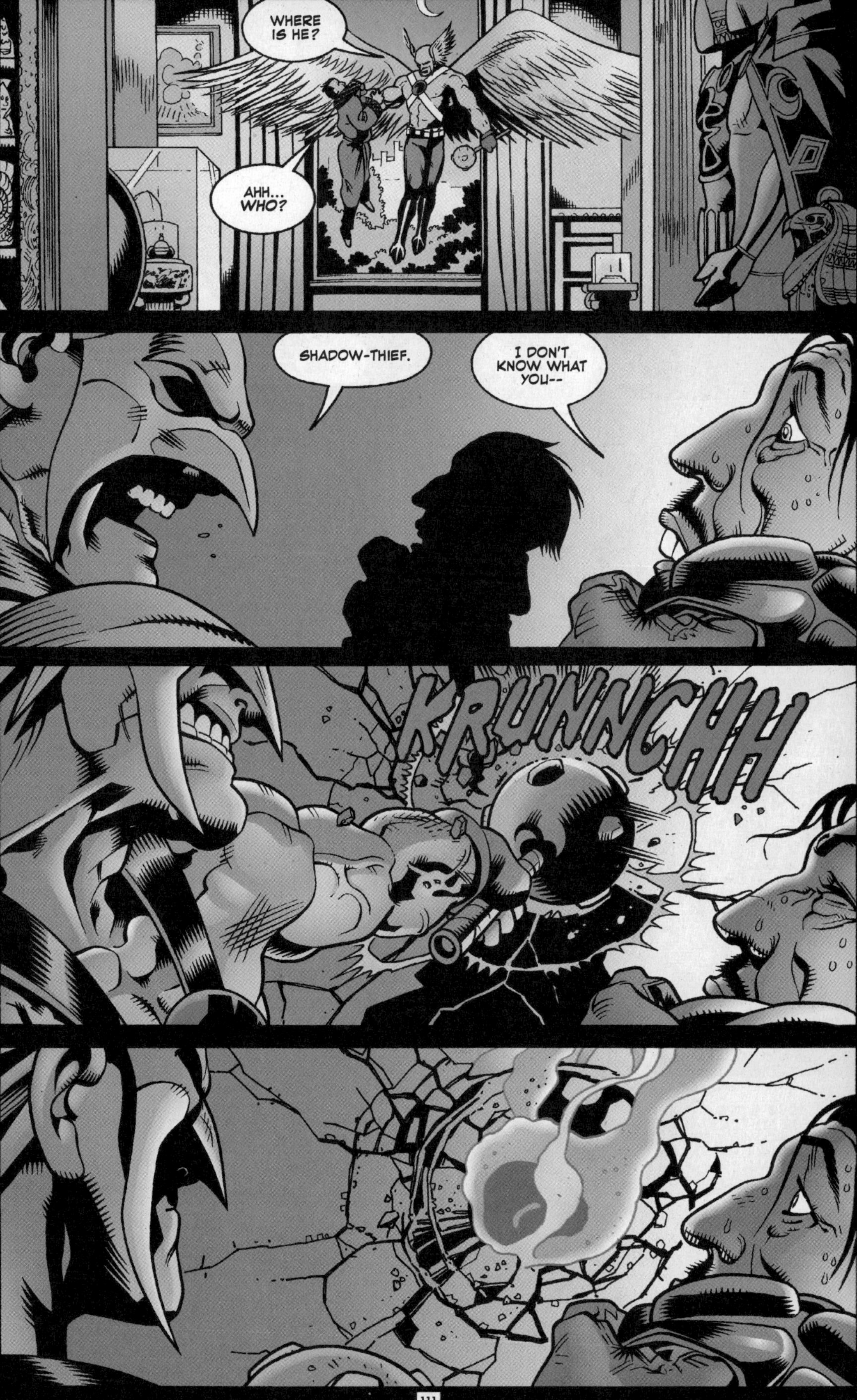
WHERE IS HE?
AHH... WHO?
SHADOW-THIEF.
I DON'T KNOW WHAT YOU--
KRUNNCHH

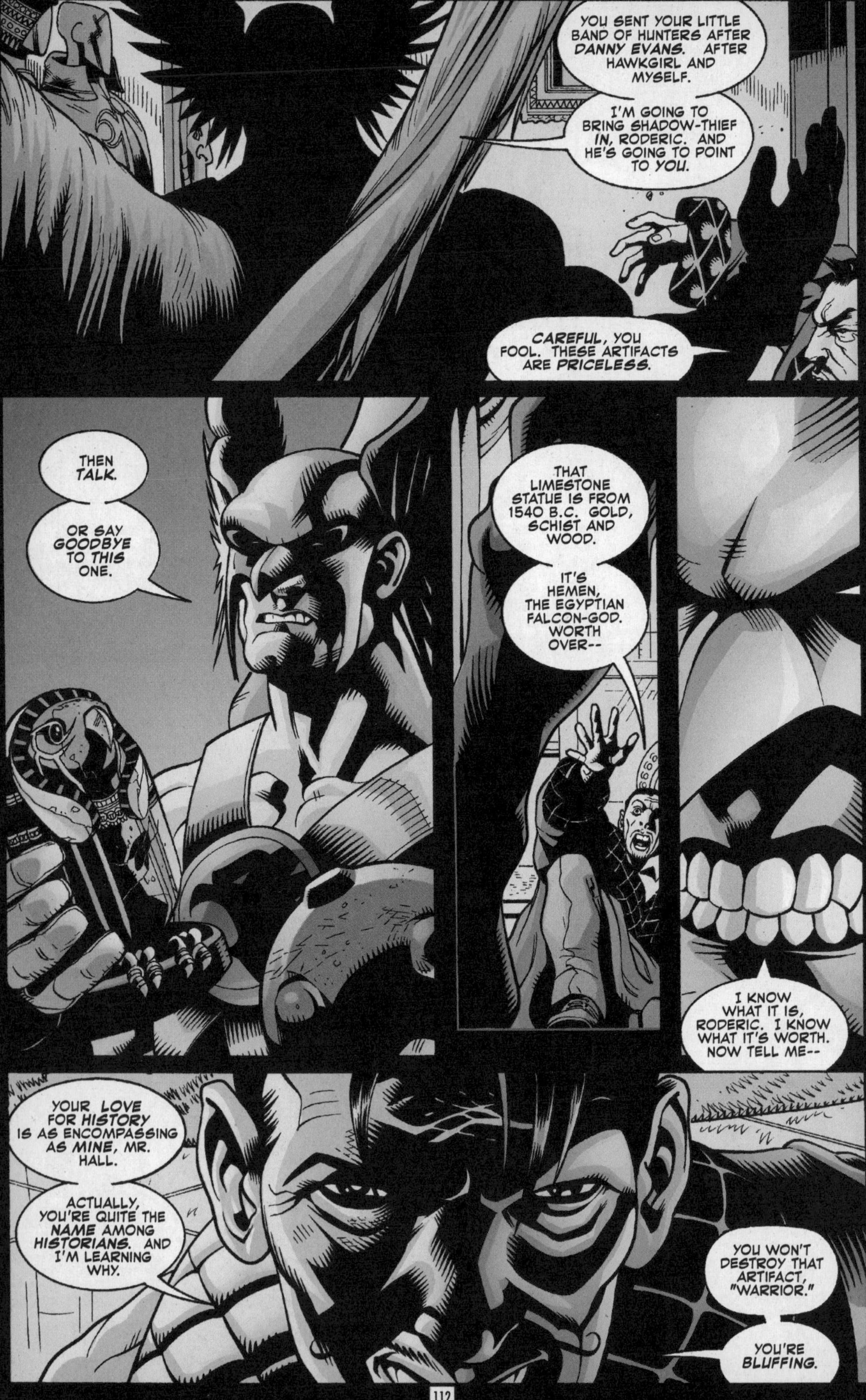
YOU SENT YOUR LITTLE BAND OF HUNTERS AFTER DANNY EVANS. AFTER HAWKGIRL AND MYSELF.
I'M GOING TO BRING SHADOW-THIEF IN, RODERIC. AND HE'S GOING TO POINT TO YOU.
CAREFUL, YOU FOOL. THESE ARTIFACTS ARE PRICELESS.
THEN TALK.
OR SAY GOODBYE TO THIS ONE.
THAT LIMESTONE STATUE IS FROM 1540 B.C. GOLD, SCHIST AND WOOD.
IT'S HEMEN, THE EGYPTIAN FALCON-GOD. WORTH OVER--
I KNOW WHAT IT IS, RODERIC. I KNOW WHAT IT'S WORTH. NOW TELL ME--
YOUR LOVE FOR HISTORY IS AS ENCOMPASSING AS MINE, MR. HALL.
ACTUALLY, YOU'RE QUITE THE NAME AMONG HISTORIANS. AND I'M LEARNING WHY.
YOU WON'T DESTROY THAT ARTIFACT, "WARRIOR."
YOU'RE BLUFFING.

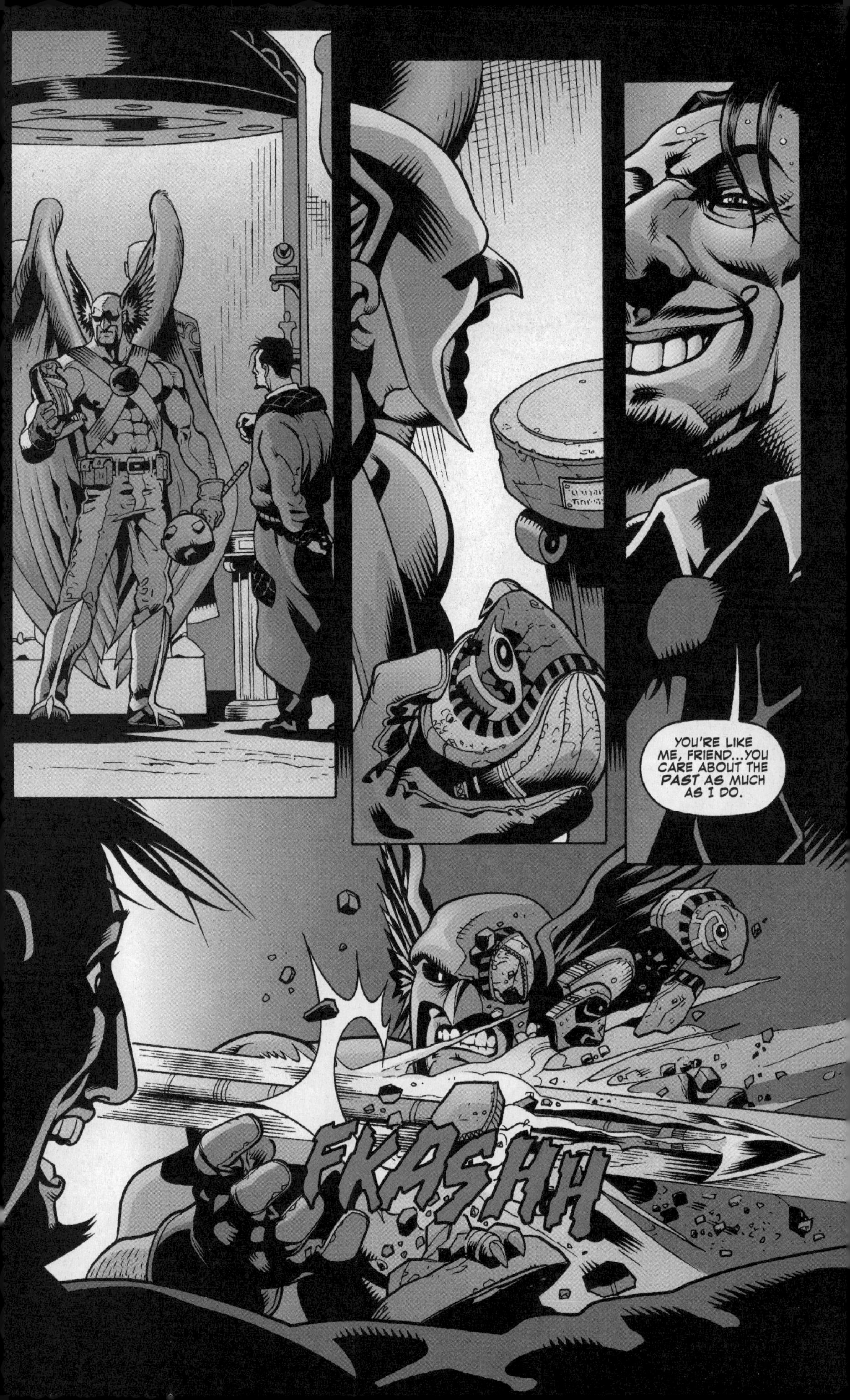
YOU'RE LIKE ME, FRIEND...YOU CARE ABOUT THE PAST AS MUCH AS I DO.
FKASHH

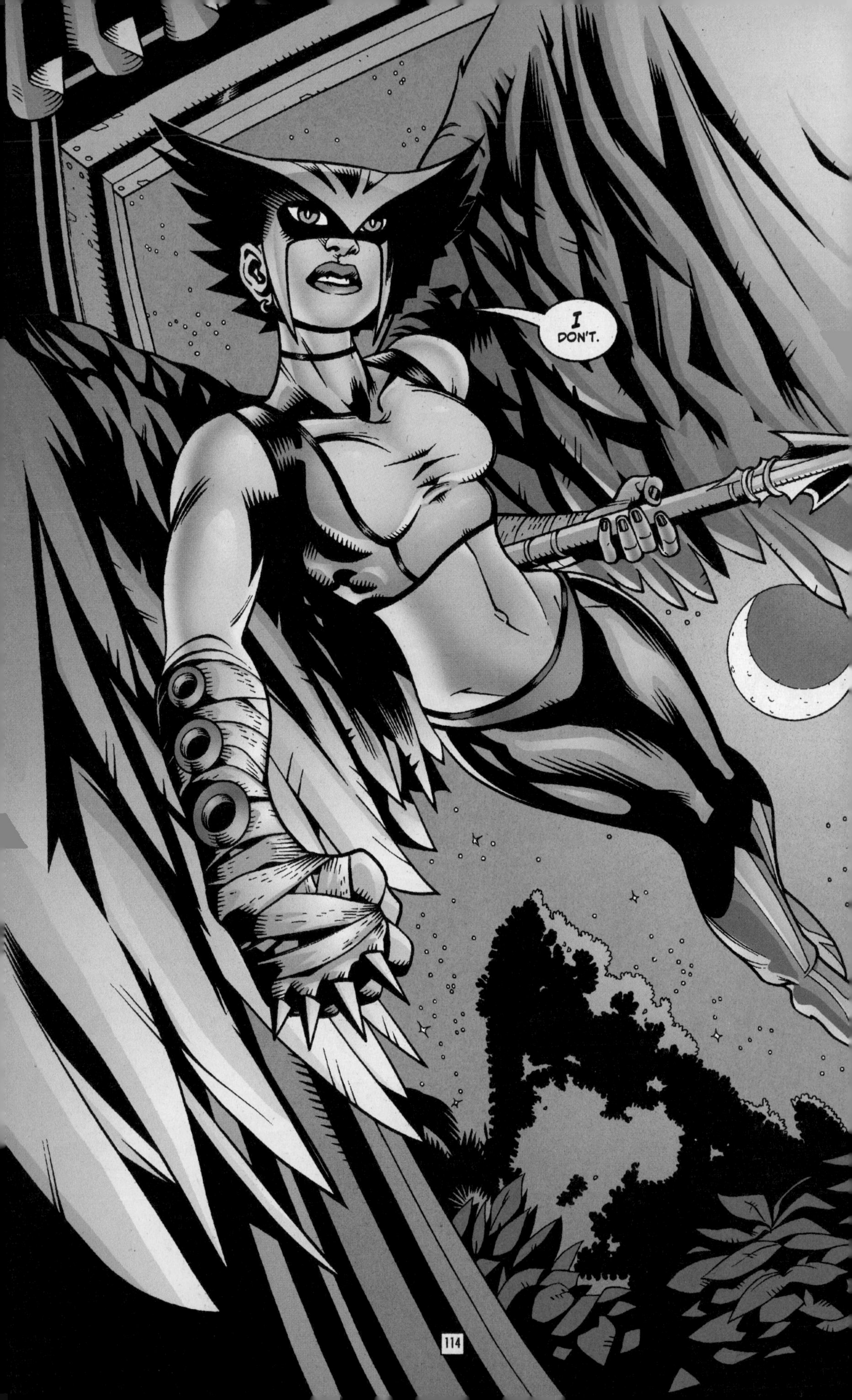
I DON'T.

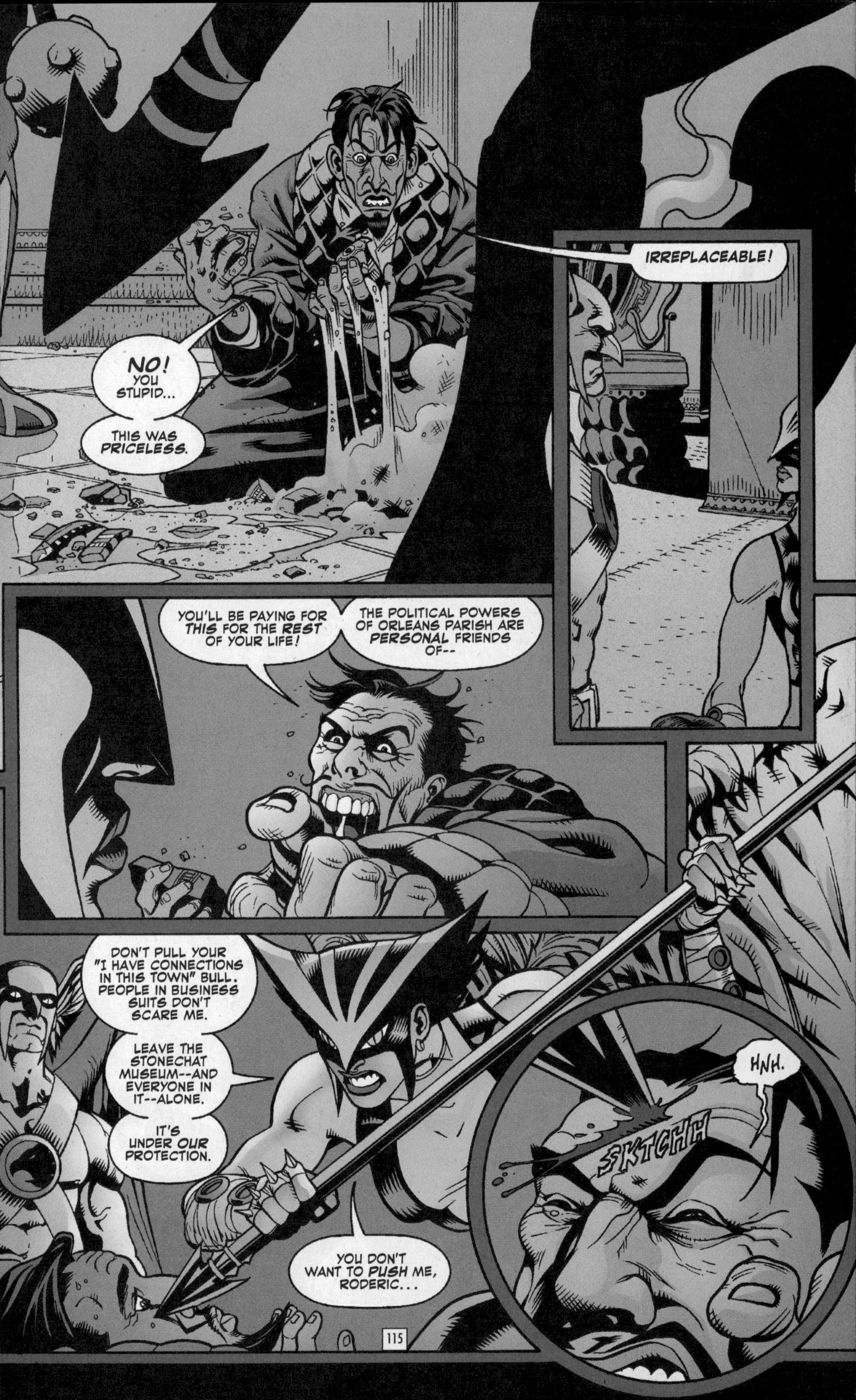
NO! YOU STUPID...
THIS WAS PRICELESS.
IRREPLACEABLE!
YOU'LL BE PAYING FOR THIS FOR THE REST OF YOUR LIFE!
THE POLITICAL POWERS OF ORLEANS PARISH ARE PERSONAL FRIENDS OF--
DON'T PULL YOUR "I HAVE CONNECTIONS IN THIS TOWN" BULL. PEOPLE IN BUSINESS SUITS DON'T SCARE ME.
LEAVE THE STONECHAT MUSEUM--AND EVERYONE IN IT--ALONE.
IT'S UNDER OUR PROTECTION.
SKTCHH
HNH.
YOU DON'T WANT TO PUSH ME, RODERIC...

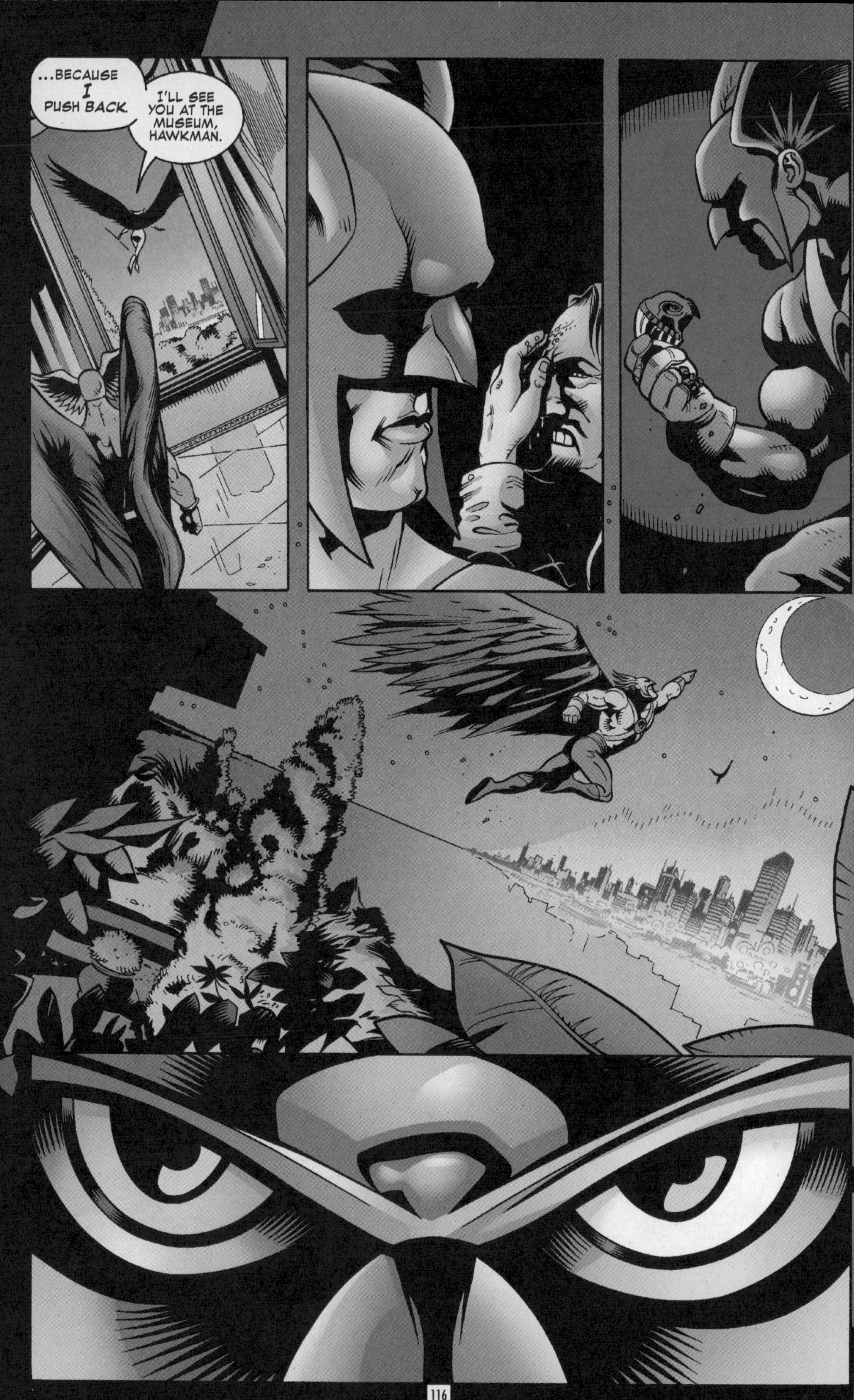
...BECAUSE I PUSH BACK.
I'LL SEE YOU AT THE MUSEUM, HAWKMAN.

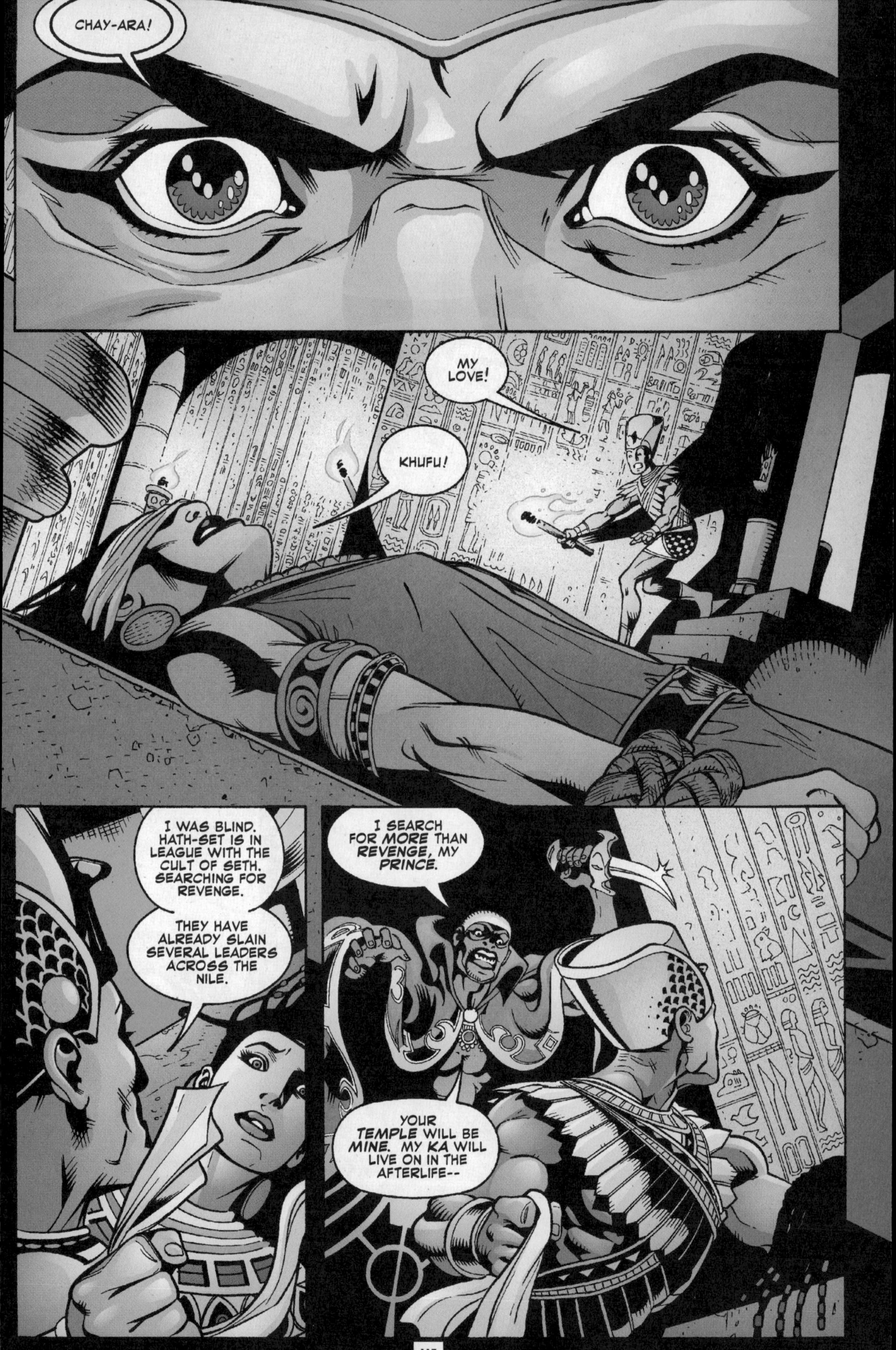
CHAY-ARA!
MY LOVE!
KHUFU!
I WAS BLIND. HATH-SET IS IN LEAGUE WITH THE CULT OF SETH. SEARCHING FOR REVENGE.
THEY HAVE ALREADY SLAIN SEVERAL LEADERS ACROSS THE NILE.
I SEARCH FOR MORE THAN REVENGE, MY PRINCE.
YOUR TEMPLE WILL BE MINE. MY KA WILL LIVE ON IN THE AFTERLIFE--

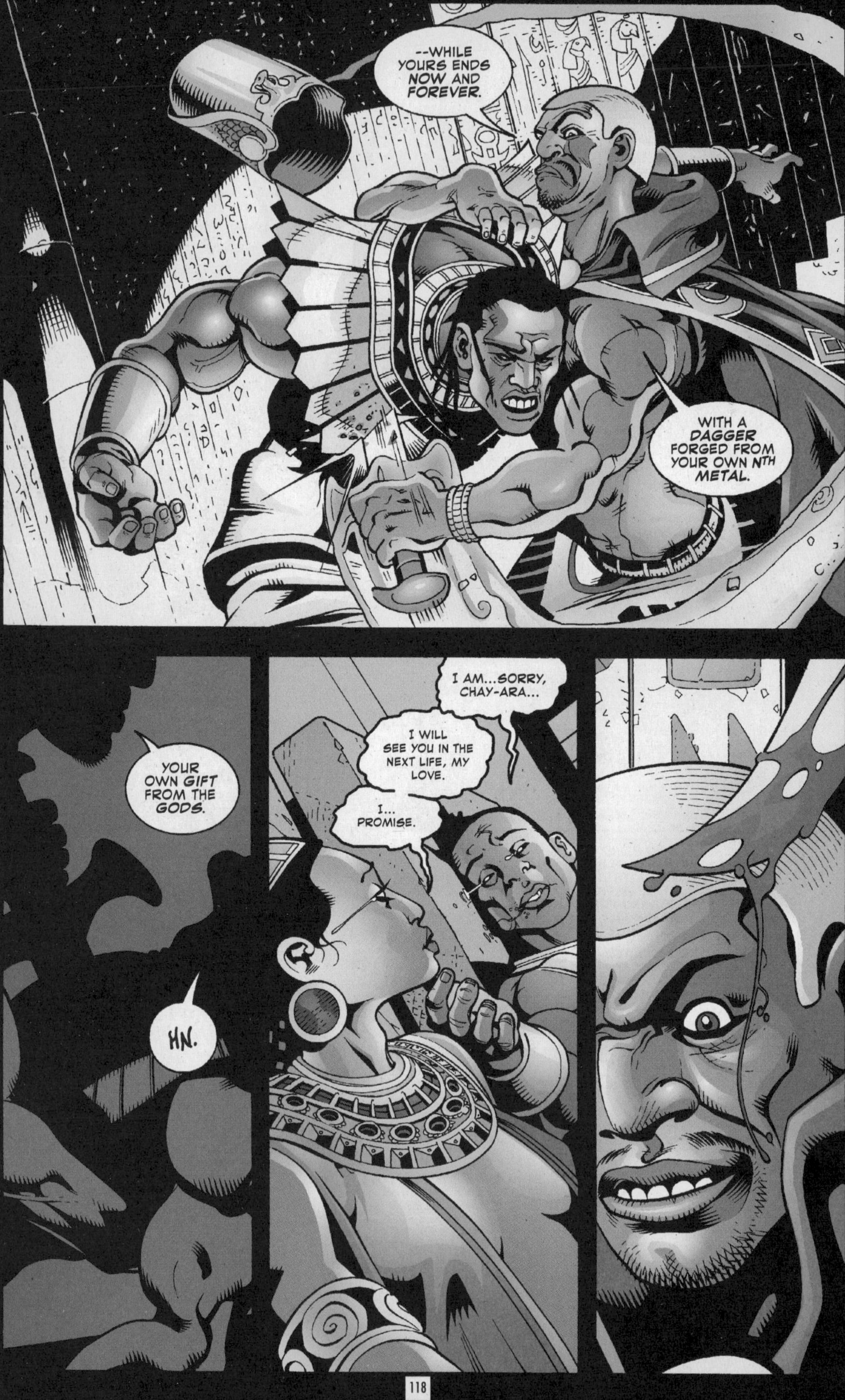
--WHILE YOURS ENDS NOW AND FOREVER.
WITH A DAGGER FORGED FROM YOUR OWN NTH METAL.
YOUR OWN GIFT FROM THE GODS.
HN.
I AM...SORRY, CHAY-ARA...
I WILL SEE YOU IN THE NEXT LIFE, MY LOVE.
I... PROMISE.

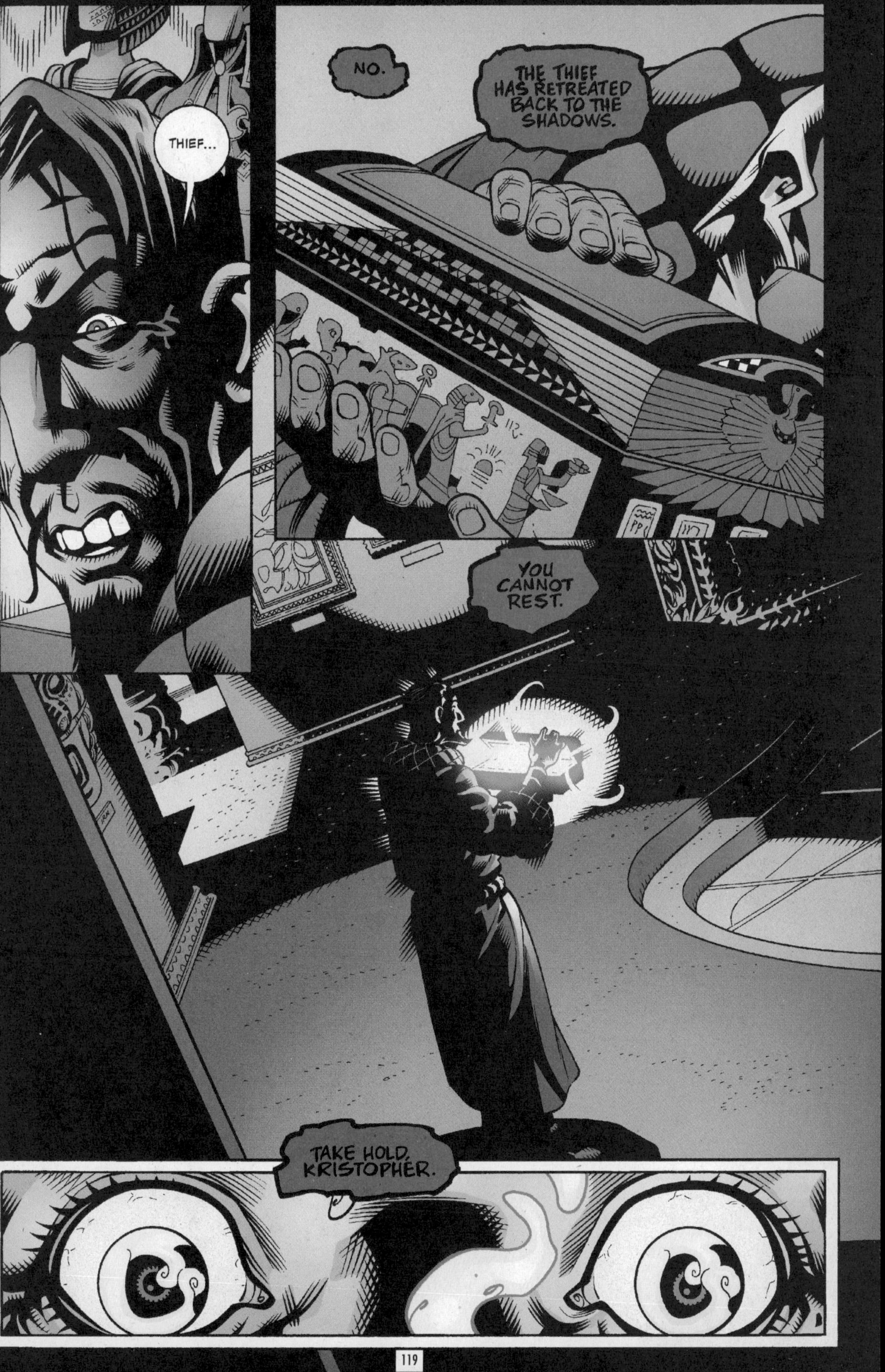
THIEF...
NO.
THE THIEF HAS RETREATED BACK TO THE SHADOWS.
YOU CANNOT REST.
TAKE HOLD, KRISTOPHER.

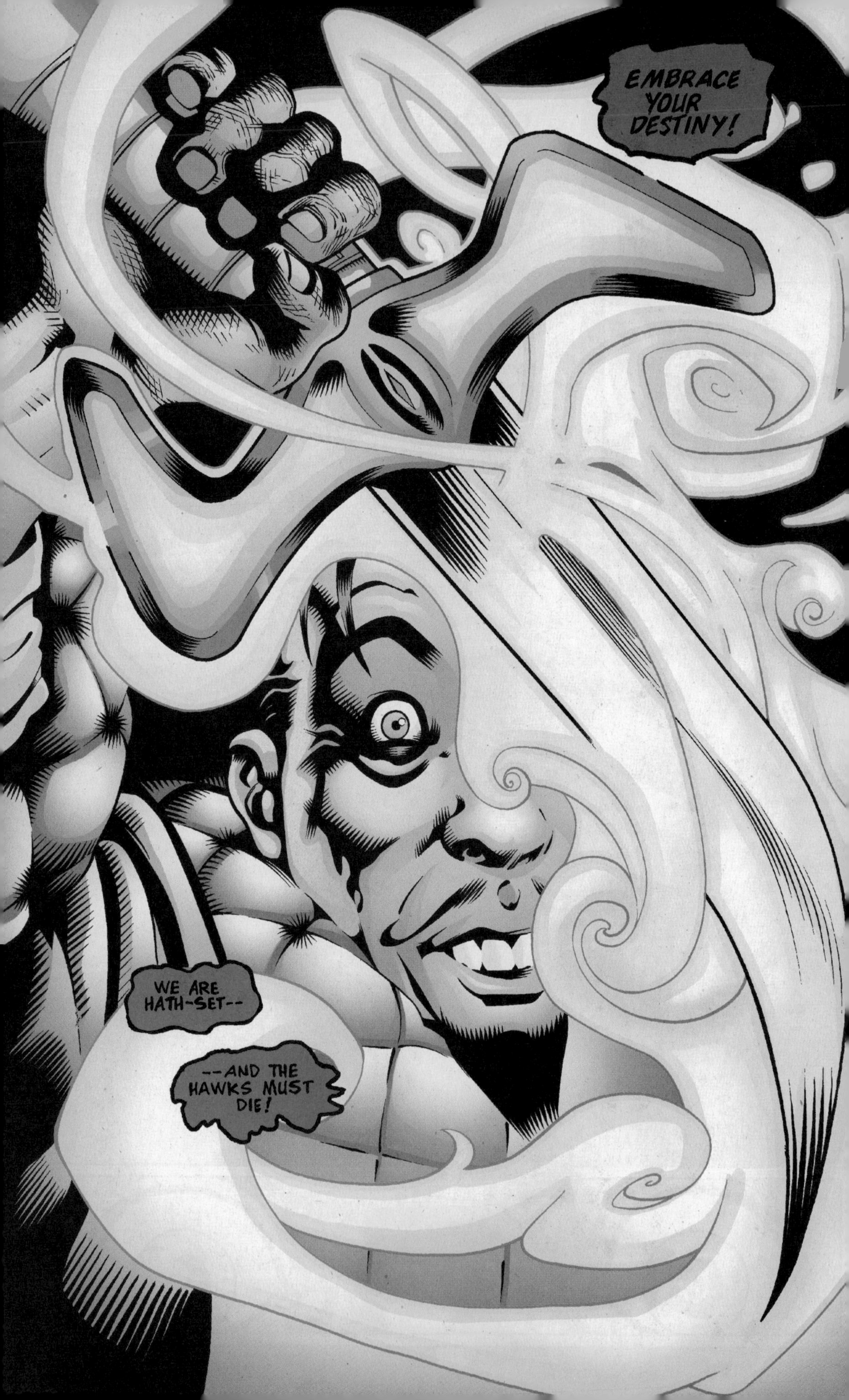
EMBRACE YOUR DESTINY!
WE ARE HATH-SET--
--AND THE HAWKS MUST DIE!

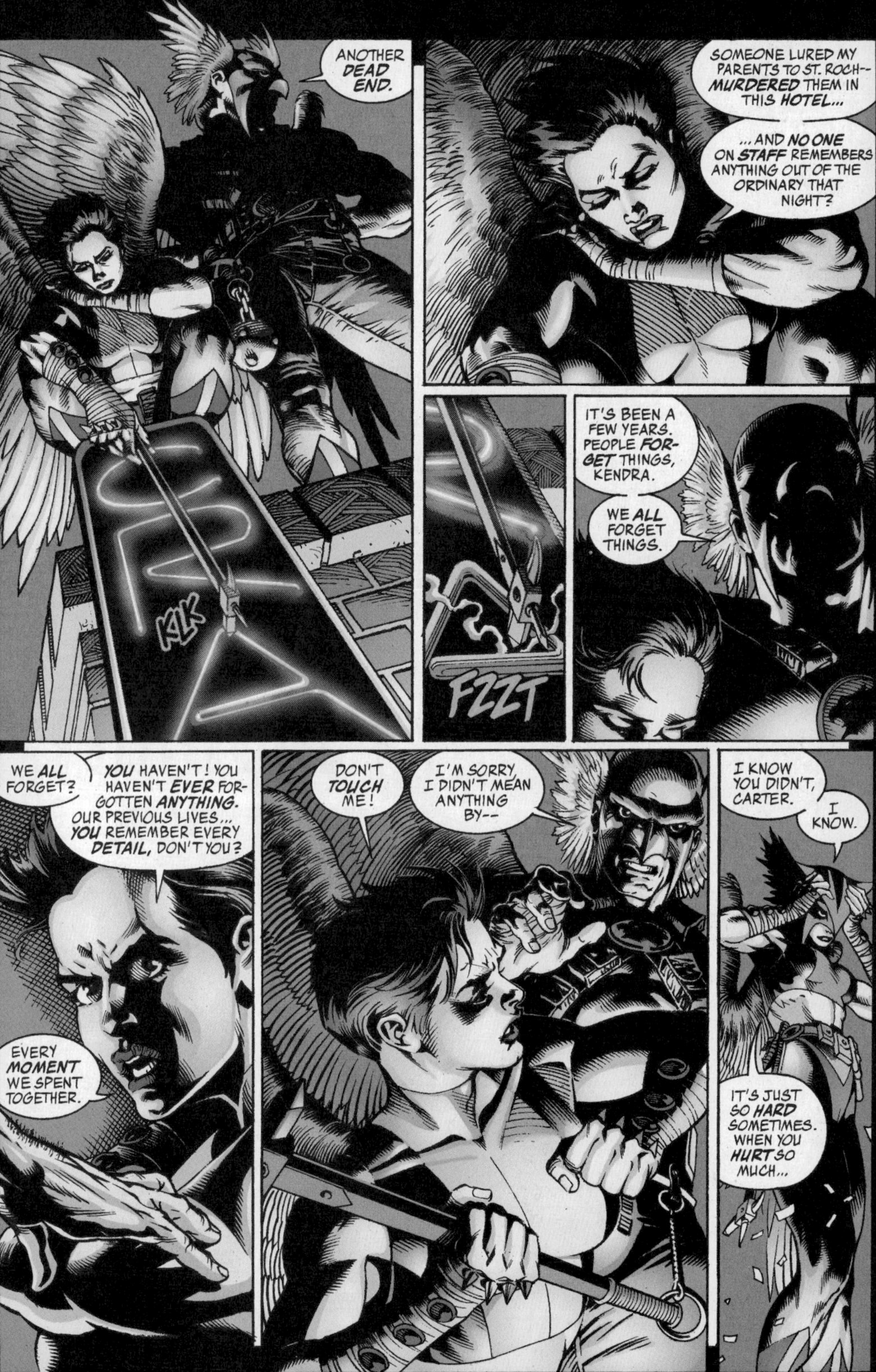
ANOTHER DEAD END.
KLK
SOMEONE LURED MY PARENTS TO ST. ROCH-- MURDERED THEM IN THIS HOTEL...
...AND NO ONE ON STAFF REMEMBERS ANYTHING OUT OF THE ORDINARY THAT NIGHT?
FZZT
IT'S BEEN A FEW YEARS. PEOPLE FORGET THINGS, KENDRA.
WE ALL FORGET THINGS.
WE ALL FORGET?
YOU HAVEN'T! YOU HAVEN'T EVER FORGOTTEN ANYTHING. OUR PREVIOUS LIVES... YOU REMEMBER EVERY DETAIL, DON'T YOU?
EVERY MOMENT WE SPENT TOGETHER.
DON'T TOUCH ME!
I'M SORRY, I DIDN'T MEAN ANYTHING BY--
I KNOW YOU DIDN'T, CARTER.
I KNOW.
IT'S JUST SO HARD SOMETIMES. WHEN YOU HURT SO MUCH...

# SLINGS and ARROWS

**PART ONE**

...AND EVERYONE ELSE IS SMILING.

GEOFF JOHNS & JAMES ROBINSON *story* | GEOFF JOHNS *words* | RAGS MORALES *penciller* | MICHAEL BAIR *inker* | JOHN KALISZ *colorist* | HEROIC AGE *seps* | BILL OAKLEY *letterer* | STEVE WACKER *associate editor* | PETER TOMASI *editor*

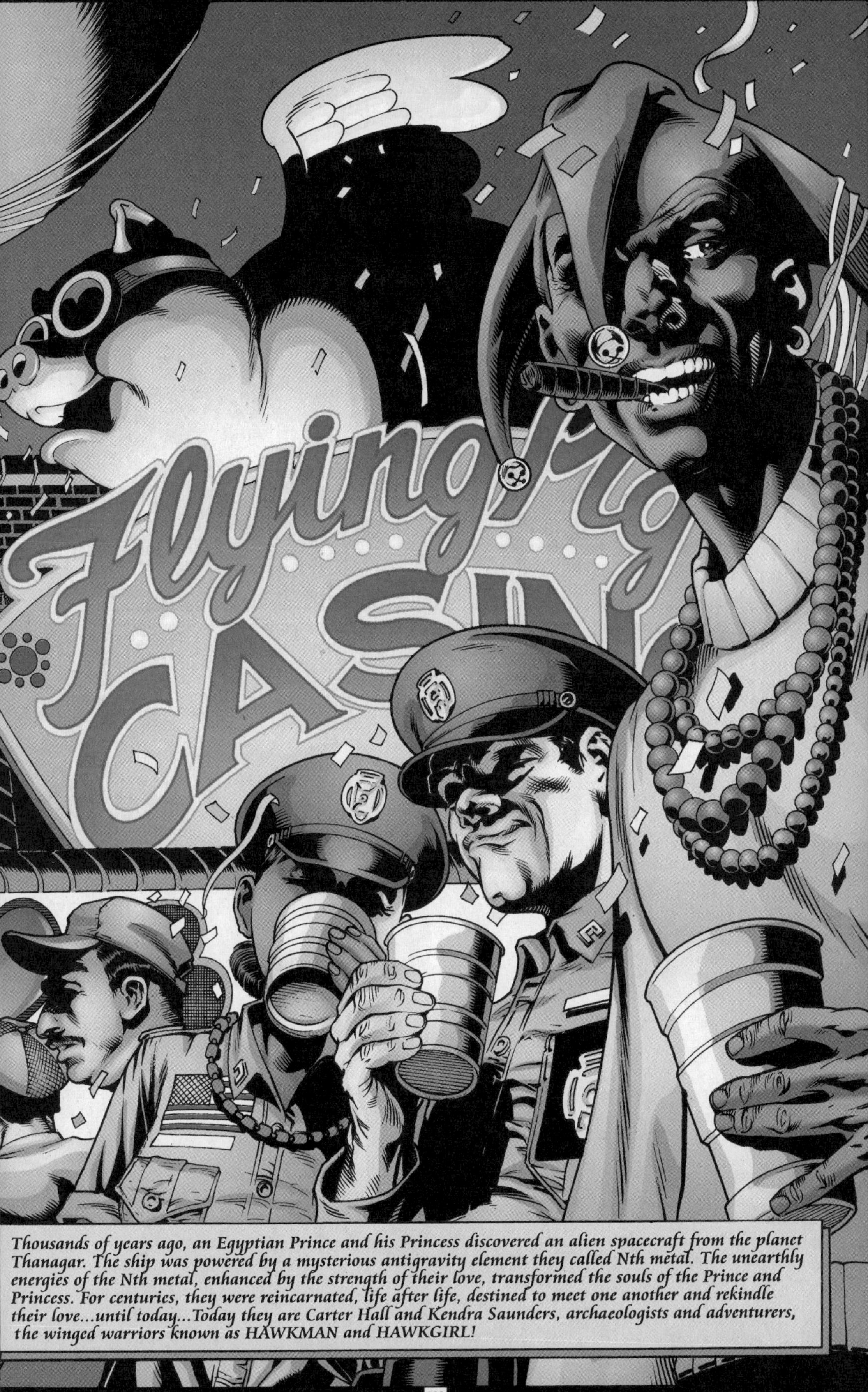
Flying Pig
CASINO
Thousands of years ago, an Egyptian Prince and his Princess discovered an alien spacecraft from the planet Thanagar. The ship was powered by a mysterious antigravity element they called Nth metal. The unearthly energies of the Nth metal, enhanced by the strength of their love, transformed the souls of the Prince and Princess. For centuries, they were reincarnated, life after life, destined to meet one another and rekindle their love...until today...Today they are Carter Hall and Kendra Saunders, archaeologists and adventurers, the winged warriors known as HAWKMAN and HAWKGIRL!

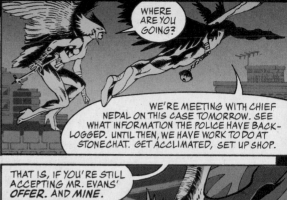

--HE COMES! OUR "LA NUIT DE TOUS SAINTS" KING THIS YEAR!

LUNDI GRAS KING

HE MAY BE ONE'A TH' BIGGEST CULINARY STARS IN AMERICA, BUT HE WAS *BORN* AND *BRED* RIGHT HERE IN THE CITY THE SAINTS FORGOT. ST. ROCH!

GIVE CHRISTOPHER COOK A WELCOME!

GOOD TO BE BACK! EH, DARLIN'?

WHERE ARE YOU GOING?

WE'RE MEETING WITH CHIEF NEDAL ON THIS CASE TOMORROW. SEE WHAT INFORMATION THE POLICE HAVE BACKLOGGED. UNTIL THEN, WE HAVE WORK TO DO AT STONECHAT. GET ACCLIMATED, SET UP SHOP.

THAT IS, IF YOU'RE STILL ACCEPTING MR. EVANS' *OFFER.* AND MINE.

I *HATE* THE HUMIDITY HERE. I LIKE *HOT,* BUT *DRY HOT.* TEXAS HOT.

WHAT--

I'LL BE A FIELD AGENT FOR THE MUSEUM, CARTER--

--BUT I'M DONE WORKING TONIGHT.

I WANT TO GET TO KNOW ST. ROCH IF I'M GOING TO *STAY* HERE.

...BUY ME A PO' BOY?

THUK

MY GOD!

124

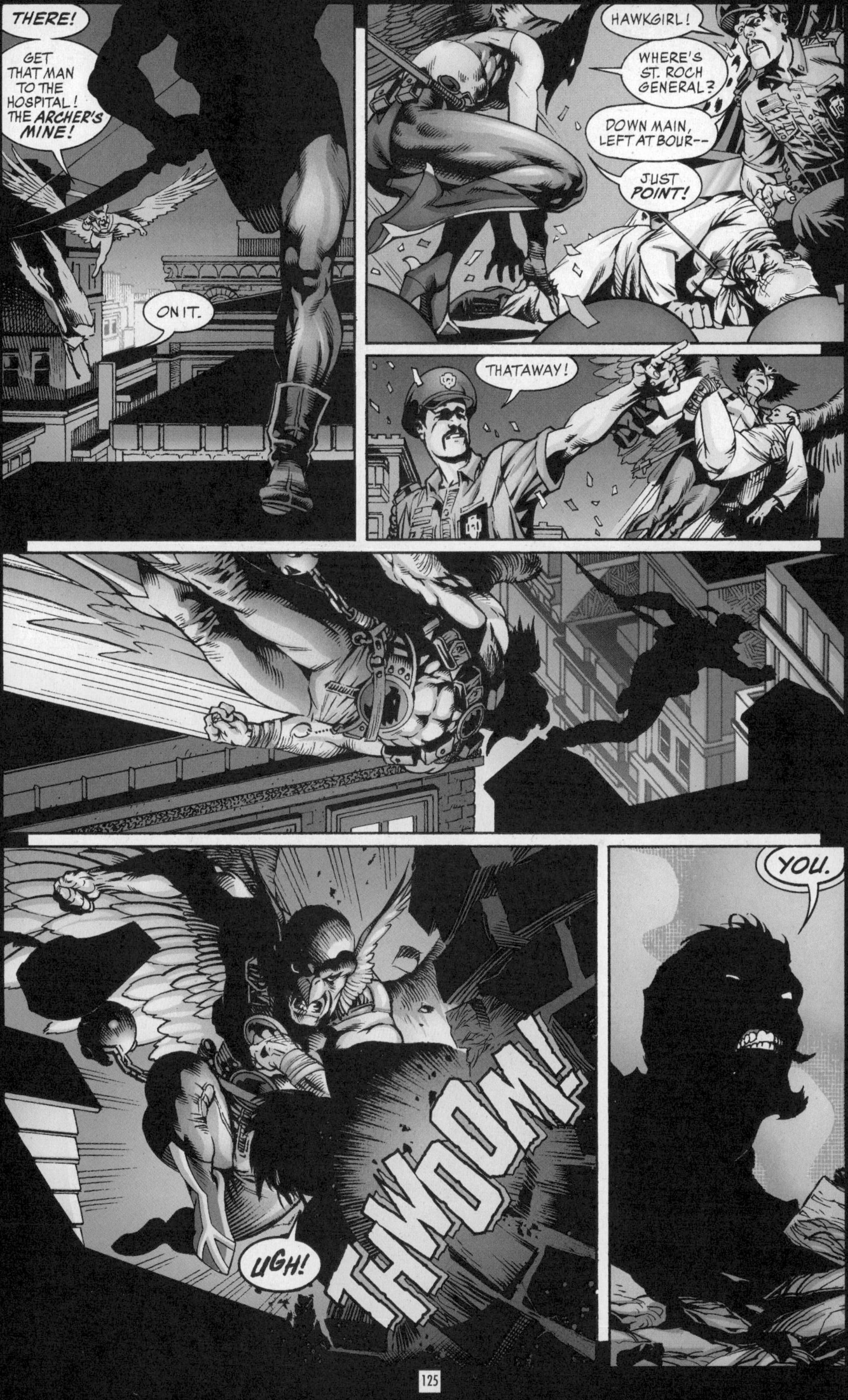
THERE!
GET THAT MAN TO THE HOSPITAL! THE ARCHER'S MINE!
ON IT.
HAWKGIRL!
WHERE'S ST. ROCH GENERAL?
DOWN MAIN, LEFT AT BOUR--
JUST POINT!
THATAWAY!
UGH!
THWOOM!
YOU.

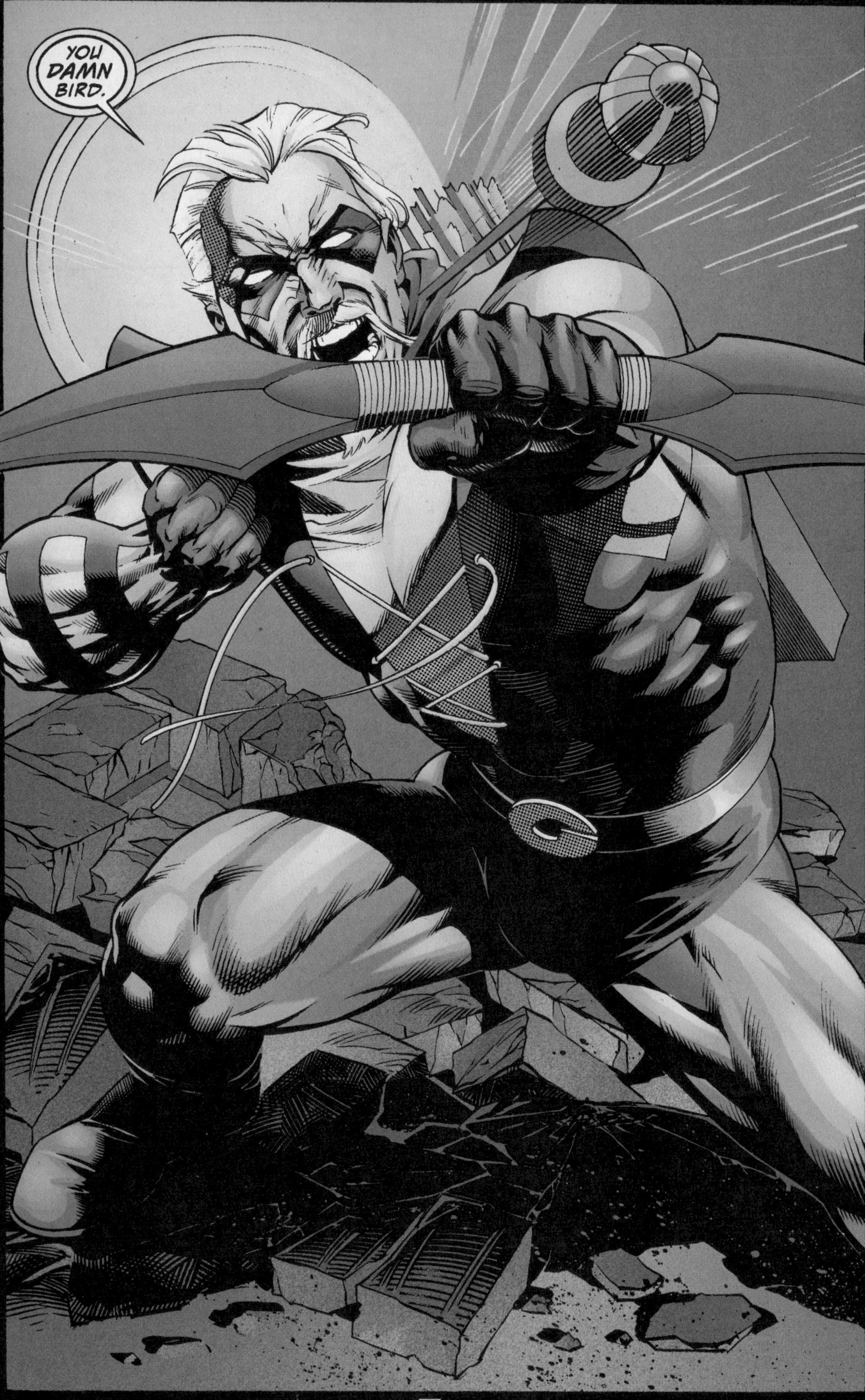
YOU DAMN BIRD.

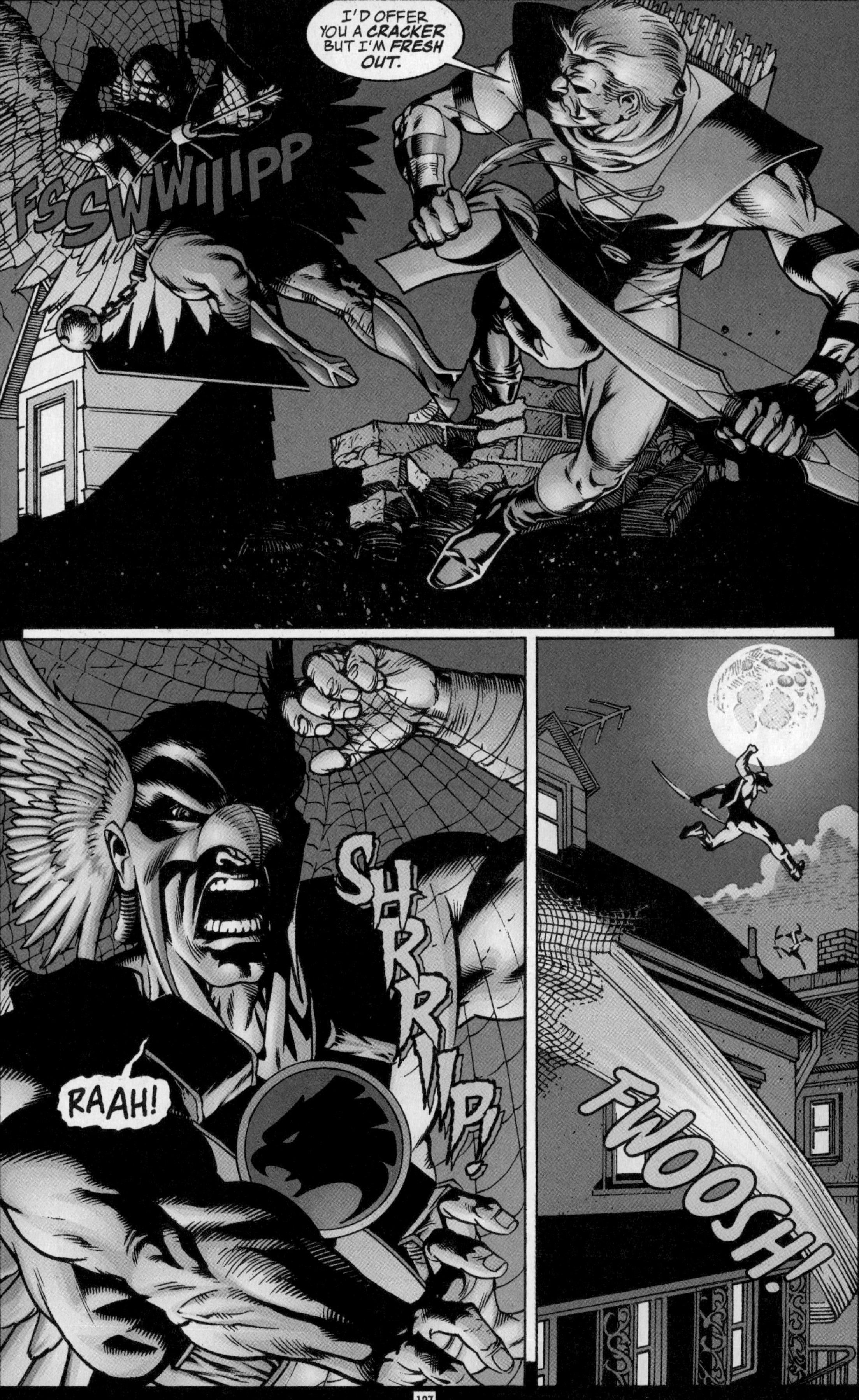
I'D OFFER YOU A CRACKER BUT I'M FRESH OUT.
FSSWWIIIPP
SHRRIP!
RAAH!
FWOOSH!

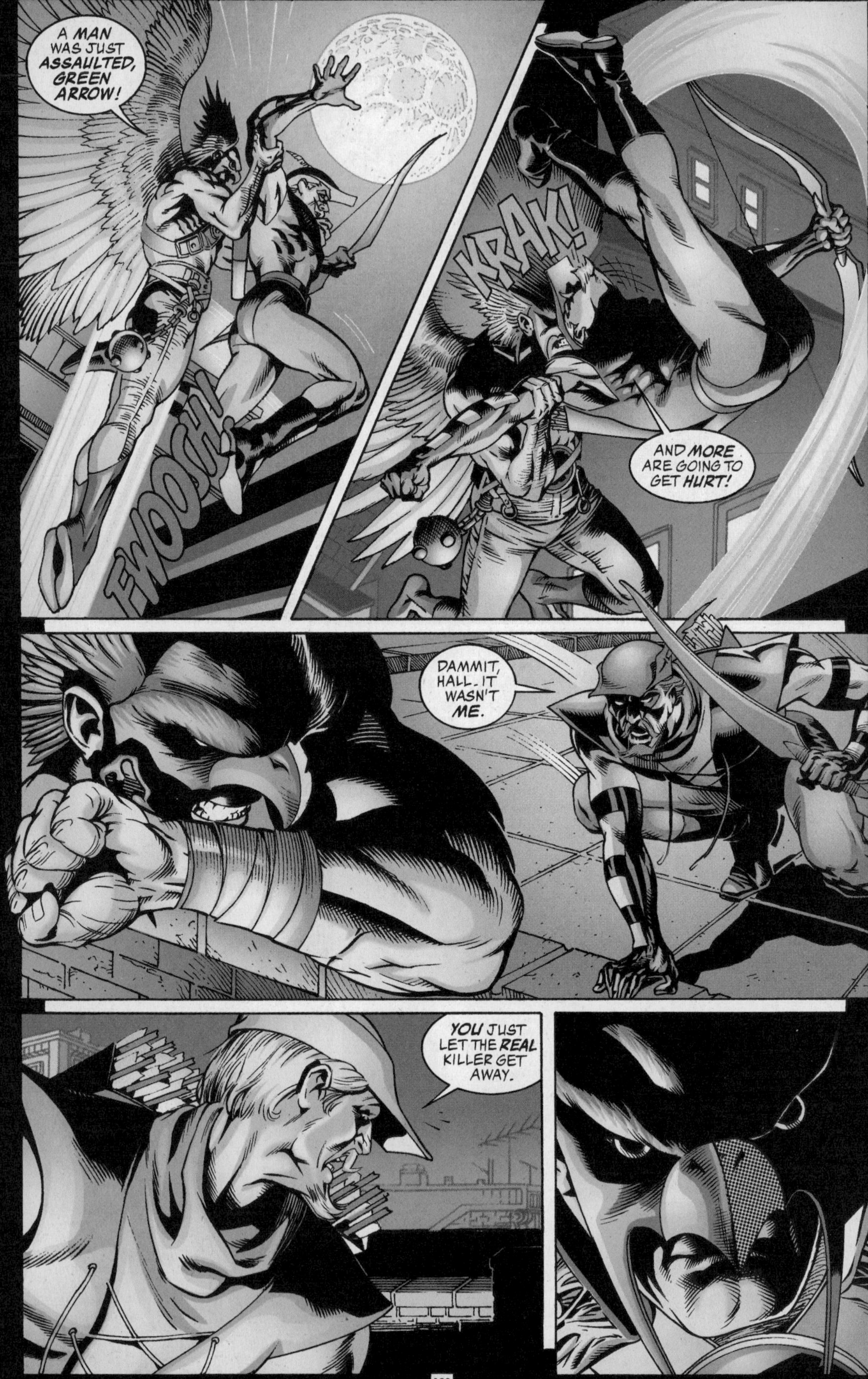
A MAN WAS JUST ASSAULTED, GREEN ARROW!
FWOOSH!
KRAK!
AND MORE ARE GOING TO GET HURT!
DAMMIT, HALL. IT WASN'T ME.
YOU JUST LET THE REAL KILLER GET AWAY.

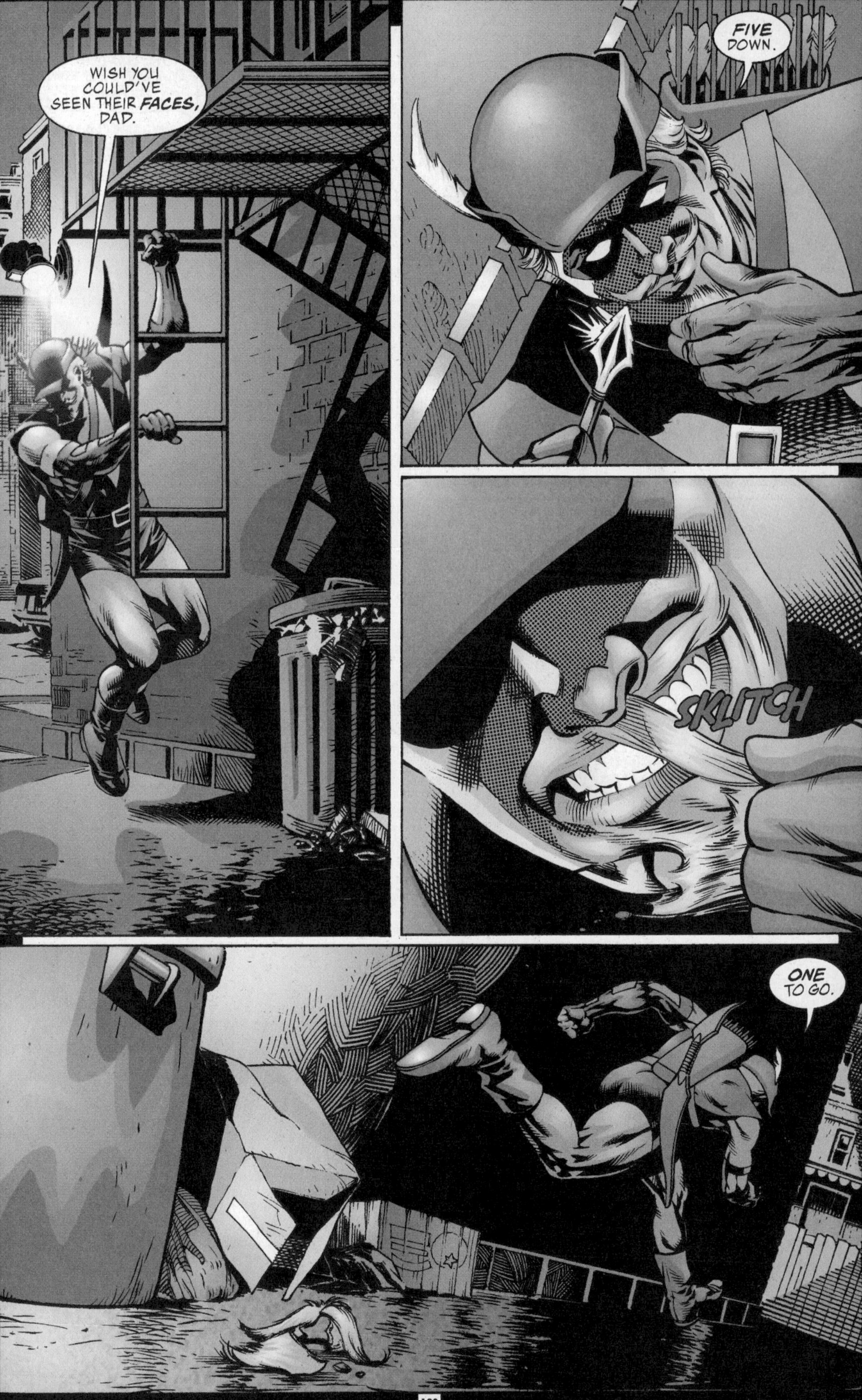
WISH YOU COULD'VE SEEN THEIR FACES, DAD.
FIVE DOWN.
SKLITCH
ONE TO GO.

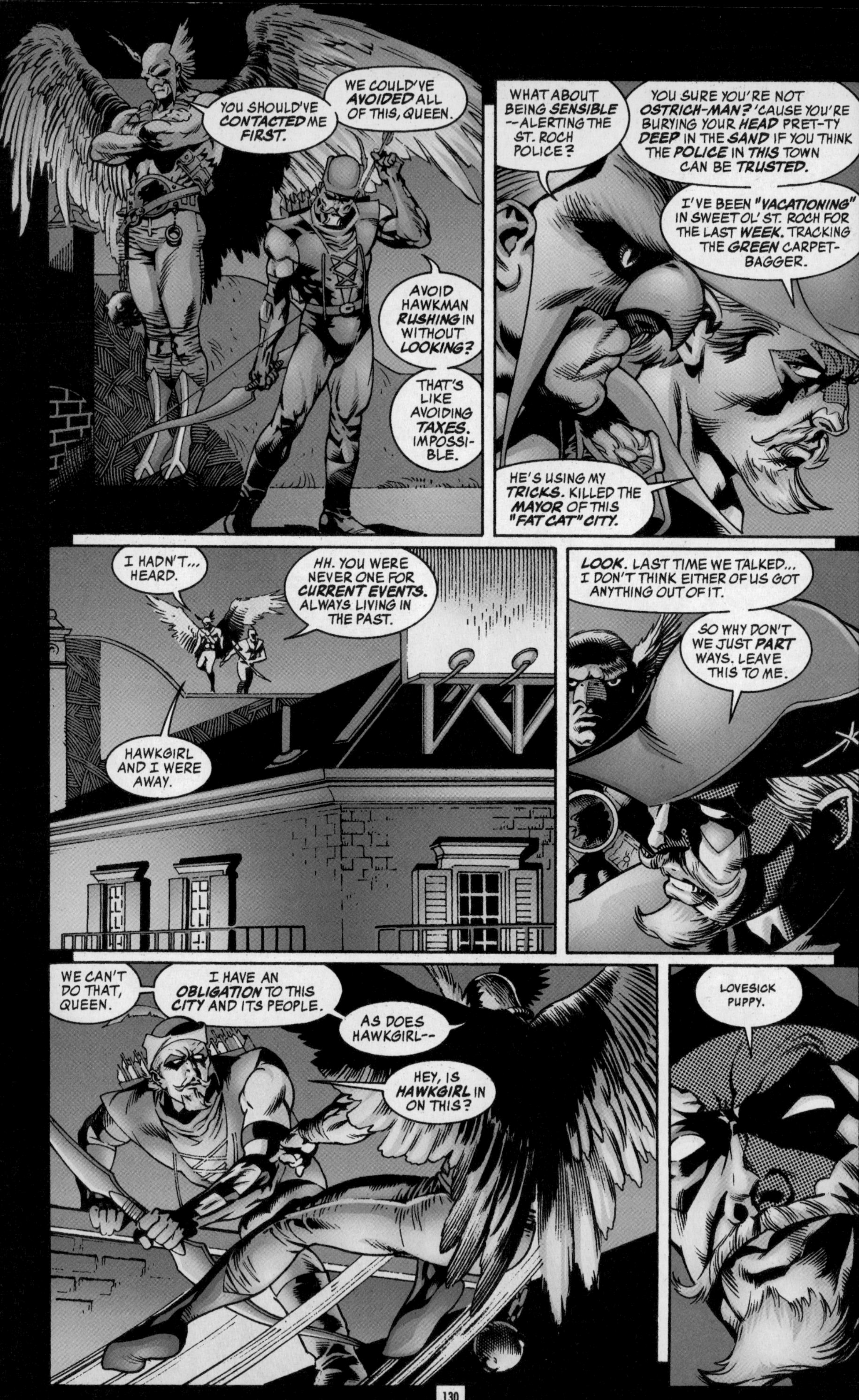

YOU SHOULD'VE CONTACTED ME FIRST.
WE COULD'VE AVOIDED ALL OF THIS, QUEEN.
AVOID HAWKMAN RUSHING IN WITHOUT LOOKING?
THAT'S LIKE AVOIDING TAXES. IMPOSSI-BLE.
WHAT ABOUT BEING SENSIBLE --ALERTING THE ST. ROCH POLICE?
YOU SURE YOU'RE NOT OSTRICH-MAN? 'CAUSE YOU'RE BURYING YOUR HEAD PRET-TY DEEP IN THE SAND IF YOU THINK THE POLICE IN THIS TOWN CAN BE TRUSTED.
I'VE BEEN "VACATIONING" IN SWEET OL' ST. ROCH FOR THE LAST WEEK. TRACKING THE GREEN CARPET-BAGGER.
HE'S USING MY TRICKS. KILLED THE MAYOR OF THIS "FAT CAT" CITY.
I HADN'T... HEARD.
HH. YOU WERE NEVER ONE FOR CURRENT EVENTS. ALWAYS LIVING IN THE PAST.
HAWKGIRL AND I WERE AWAY.
LOOK. LAST TIME WE TALKED... I DON'T THINK EITHER OF US GOT ANYTHING OUT OF IT.
SO WHY DON'T WE JUST PART WAYS. LEAVE THIS TO ME.
WE CAN'T DO THAT, QUEEN.
I HAVE AN OBLIGATION TO THIS CITY AND ITS PEOPLE.
AS DOES HAWKGIRL--
HEY, IS HAWKGIRL IN ON THIS?
LOVESICK PUPPY.

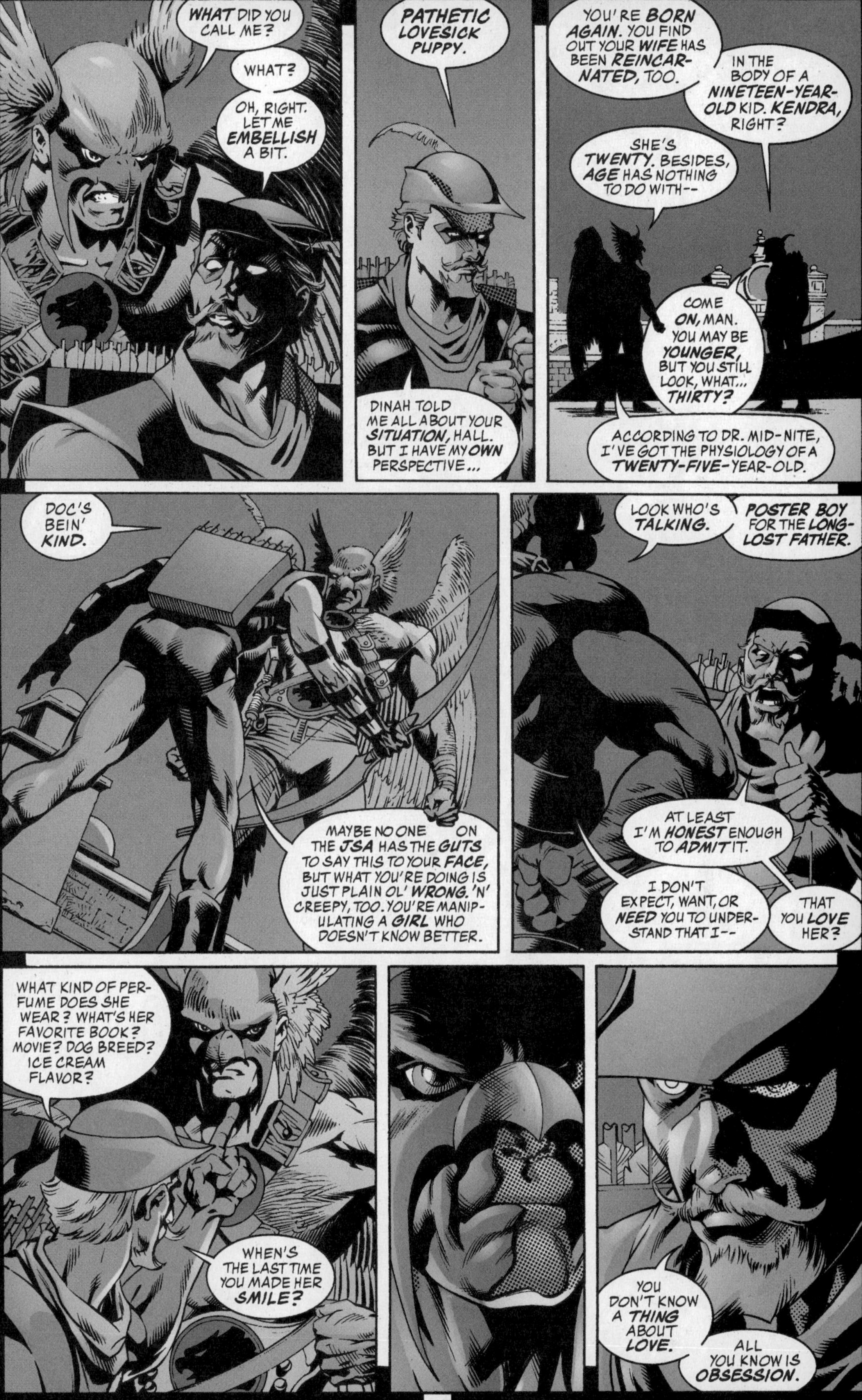
WHAT DID YOU CALL ME?
WHAT?
OH, RIGHT. LET ME EMBELLISH A BIT.
PATHETIC LOVESICK PUPPY.
DINAH TOLD ME ALL ABOUT YOUR SITUATION, HALL. BUT I HAVE MY OWN PERSPECTIVE...
YOU'RE BORN AGAIN. YOU FIND OUT YOUR WIFE HAS BEEN REINCARNATED, TOO.
IN THE BODY OF A NINETEEN-YEAR-OLD KID. KENDRA, RIGHT?
SHE'S TWENTY. BESIDES, AGE HAS NOTHING TO DO WITH--
COME ON, MAN. YOU MAY BE YOUNGER, BUT YOU STILL LOOK, WHAT... THIRTY?
ACCORDING TO DR. MID-NITE, I'VE GOT THE PHYSIOLOGY OF A TWENTY-FIVE-YEAR-OLD.
DOC'S BEIN' KIND.
MAYBE NO ONE ON THE JSA HAS THE GUTS TO SAY THIS TO YOUR FACE, BUT WHAT YOU'RE DOING IS JUST PLAIN OL' WRONG. 'N' CREEPY, TOO. YOU'RE MANIPULATING A GIRL WHO DOESN'T KNOW BETTER.
LOOK WHO'S TALKING.
POSTER BOY FOR THE LONG-LOST FATHER.
AT LEAST I'M HONEST ENOUGH TO ADMIT IT.
I DON'T EXPECT, WANT, OR NEED YOU TO UNDERSTAND THAT I--
THAT YOU LOVE HER?
WHAT KIND OF PERFUME DOES SHE WEAR? WHAT'S HER FAVORITE BOOK? MOVIE? DOG BREED? ICE CREAM FLAVOR?
WHEN'S THE LAST TIME YOU MADE HER SMILE?
YOU DON'T KNOW A THING ABOUT LOVE.
ALL YOU KNOW IS OBSESSION.

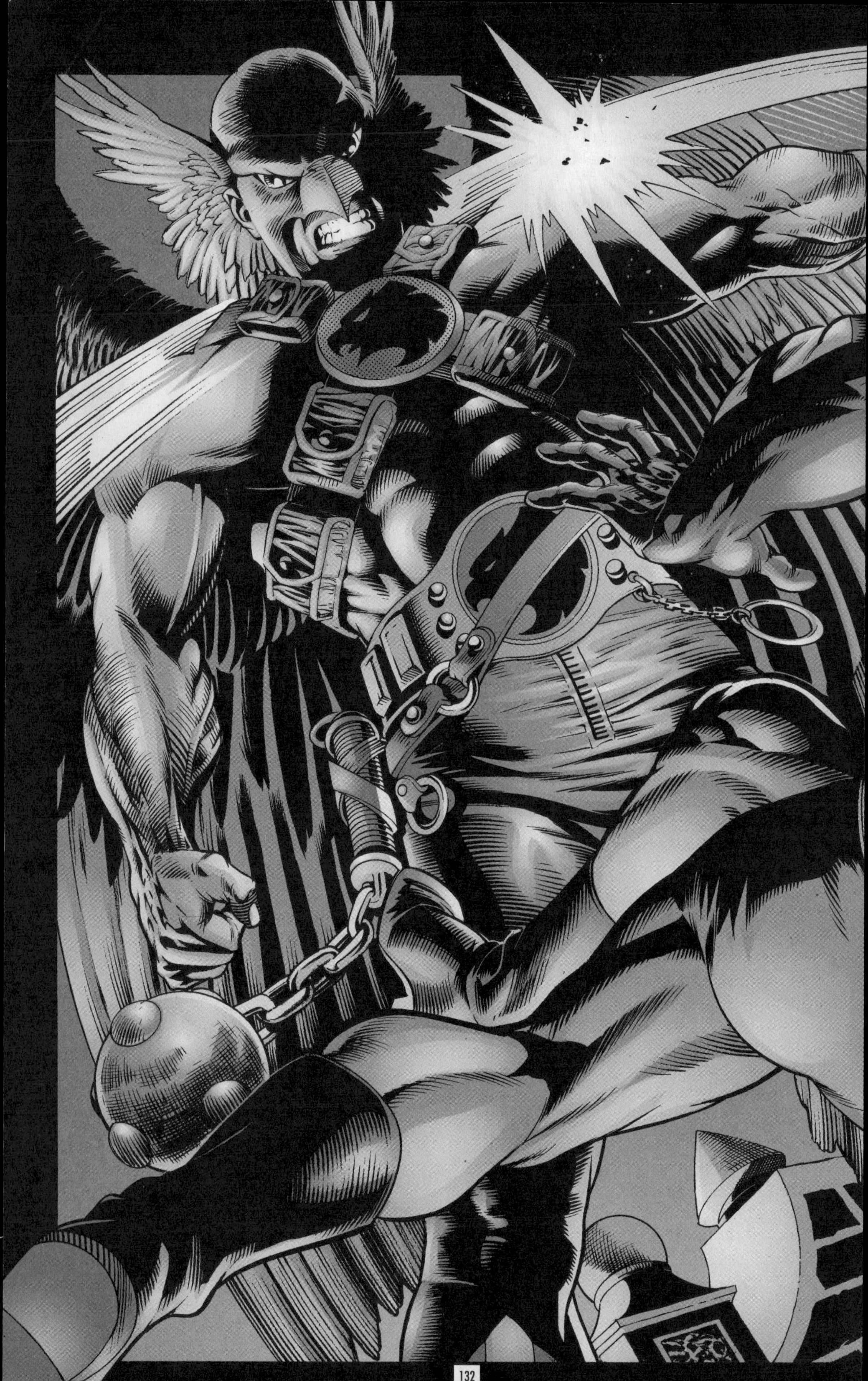

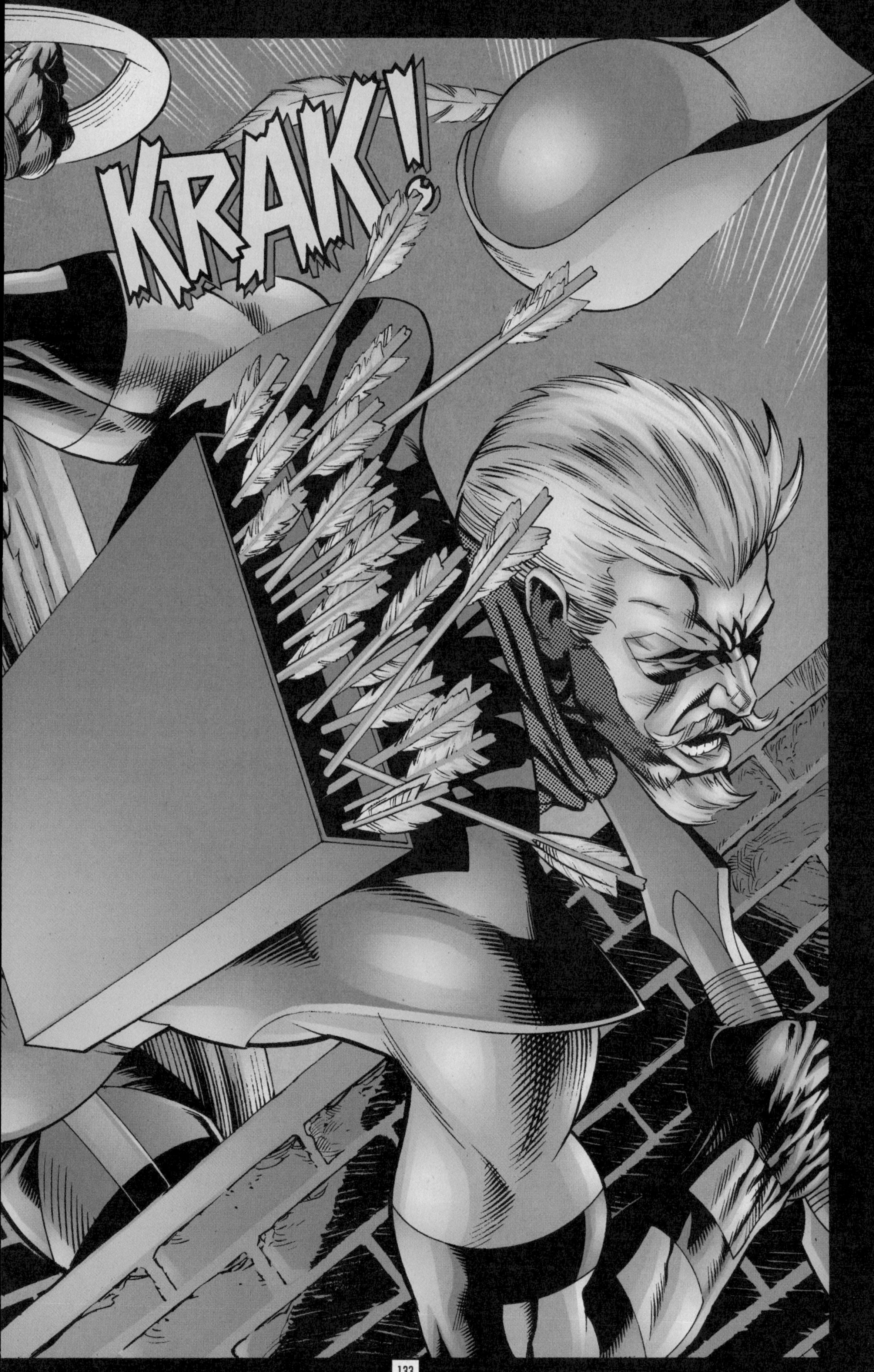
KRAK!

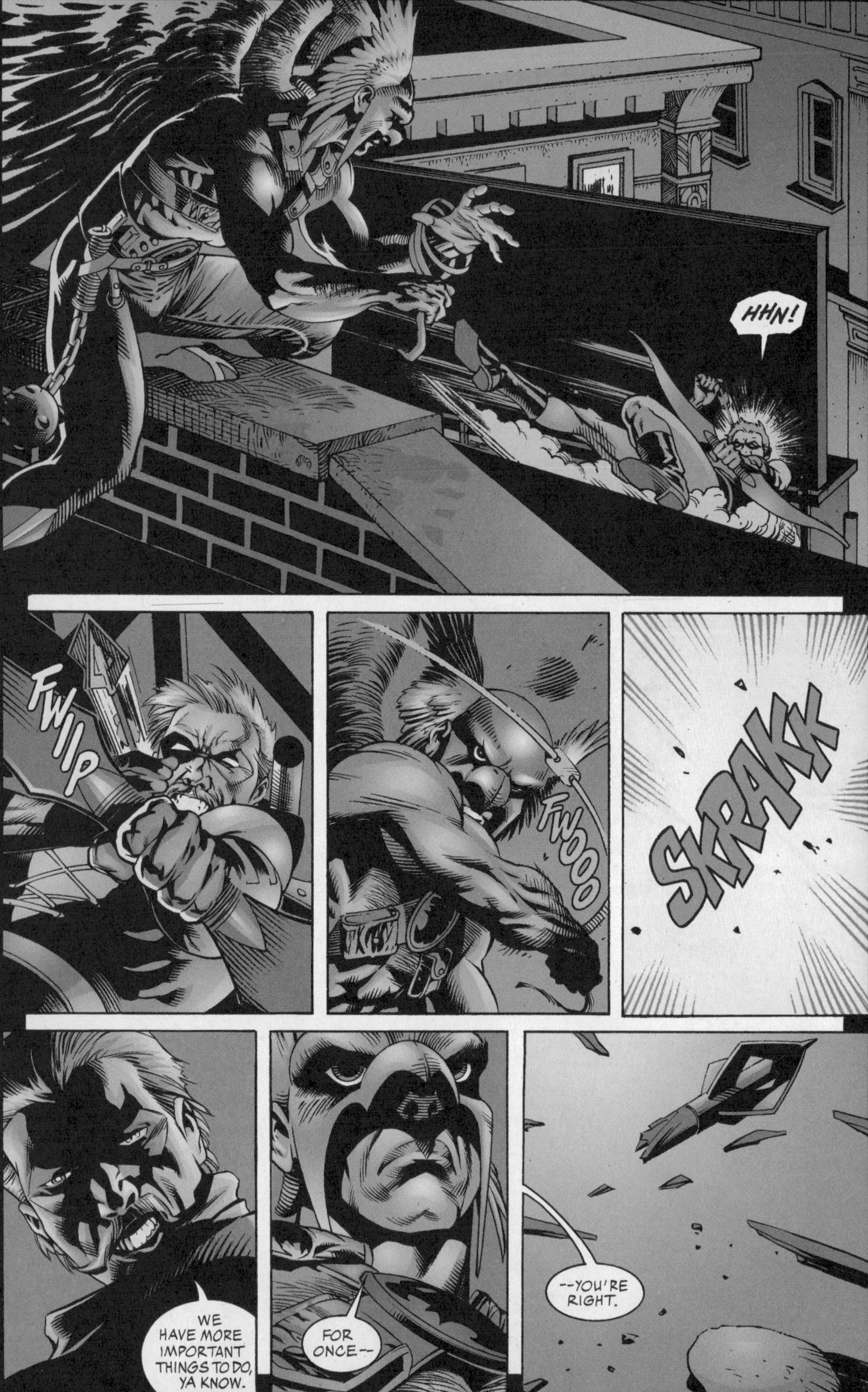
HHN!
FWIIP
FWOOO
SKRAKK
WE HAVE MORE IMPORTANT THINGS TO DO, YA KNOW.
FOR ONCE--
--YOU'RE RIGHT.

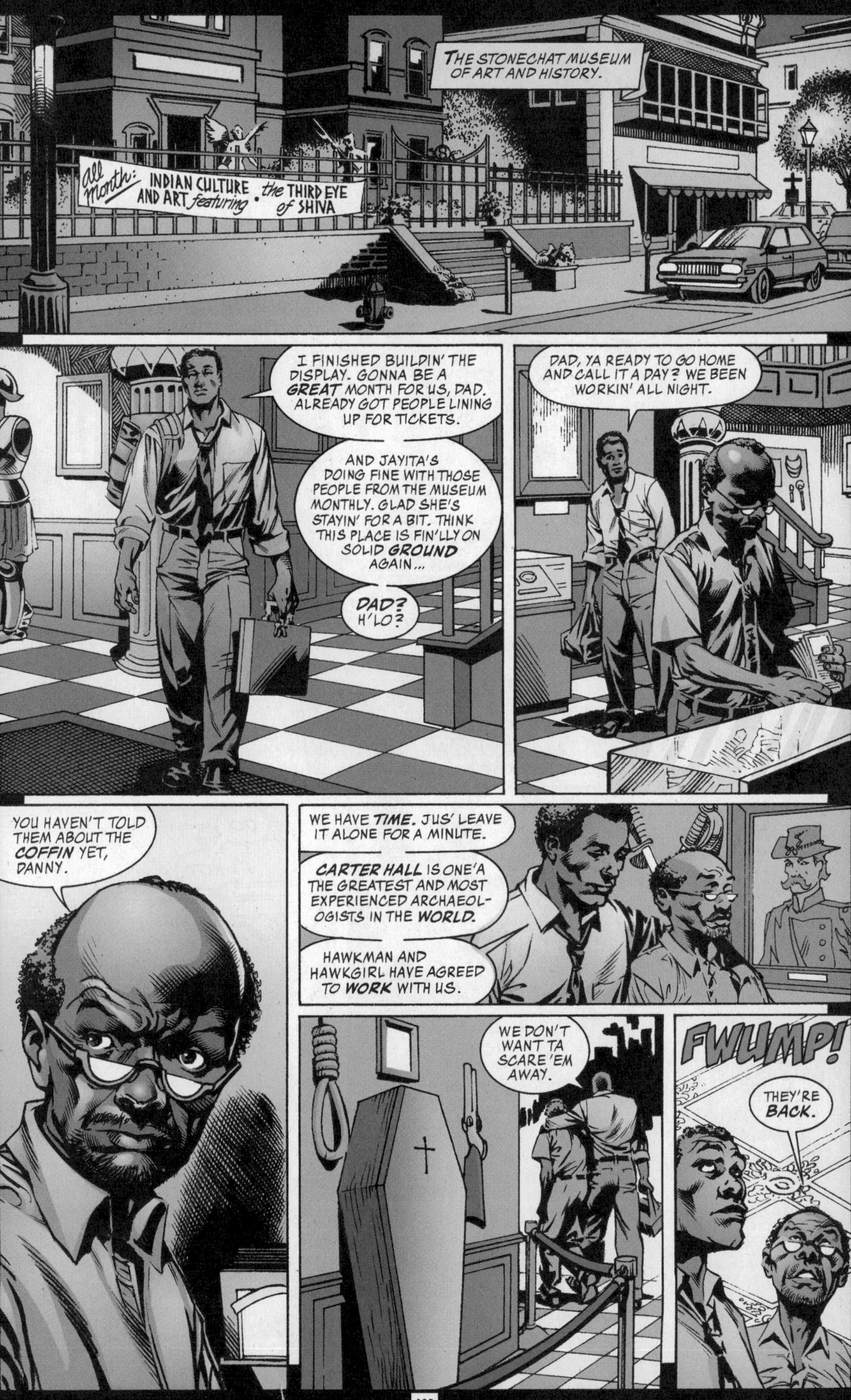
THE STONECHAT MUSEUM OF ART AND HISTORY.
All month: INDIAN CULTURE AND ART featuring • the THIRD EYE of SHIVA
I FINISHED BUILDIN' THE DISPLAY. GONNA BE A GREAT MONTH FOR US, DAD. ALREADY GOT PEOPLE LINING UP FOR TICKETS.
AND JAYITA'S DOING FINE WITH THOSE PEOPLE FROM THE MUSEUM MONTHLY. GLAD SHE'S STAYIN' FOR A BIT. THINK THIS PLACE IS FIN'LLY ON SOLID GROUND AGAIN...
DAD? H'LO?
DAD, YA READY TO GO HOME AND CALL IT A DAY? WE BEEN WORKIN' ALL NIGHT.
YOU HAVEN'T TOLD THEM ABOUT THE COFFIN YET, DANNY.
WE HAVE TIME. JUS' LEAVE IT ALONE FOR A MINUTE.
CARTER HALL IS ONE'A THE GREATEST AND MOST EXPERIENCED ARCHAEOL-OGISTS IN THE WORLD.
HAWKMAN AND HAWKGIRL HAVE AGREED TO WORK WITH US.
WE DON'T WANT TA SCARE 'EM AWAY.
FWUMP!
THEY'RE BACK.

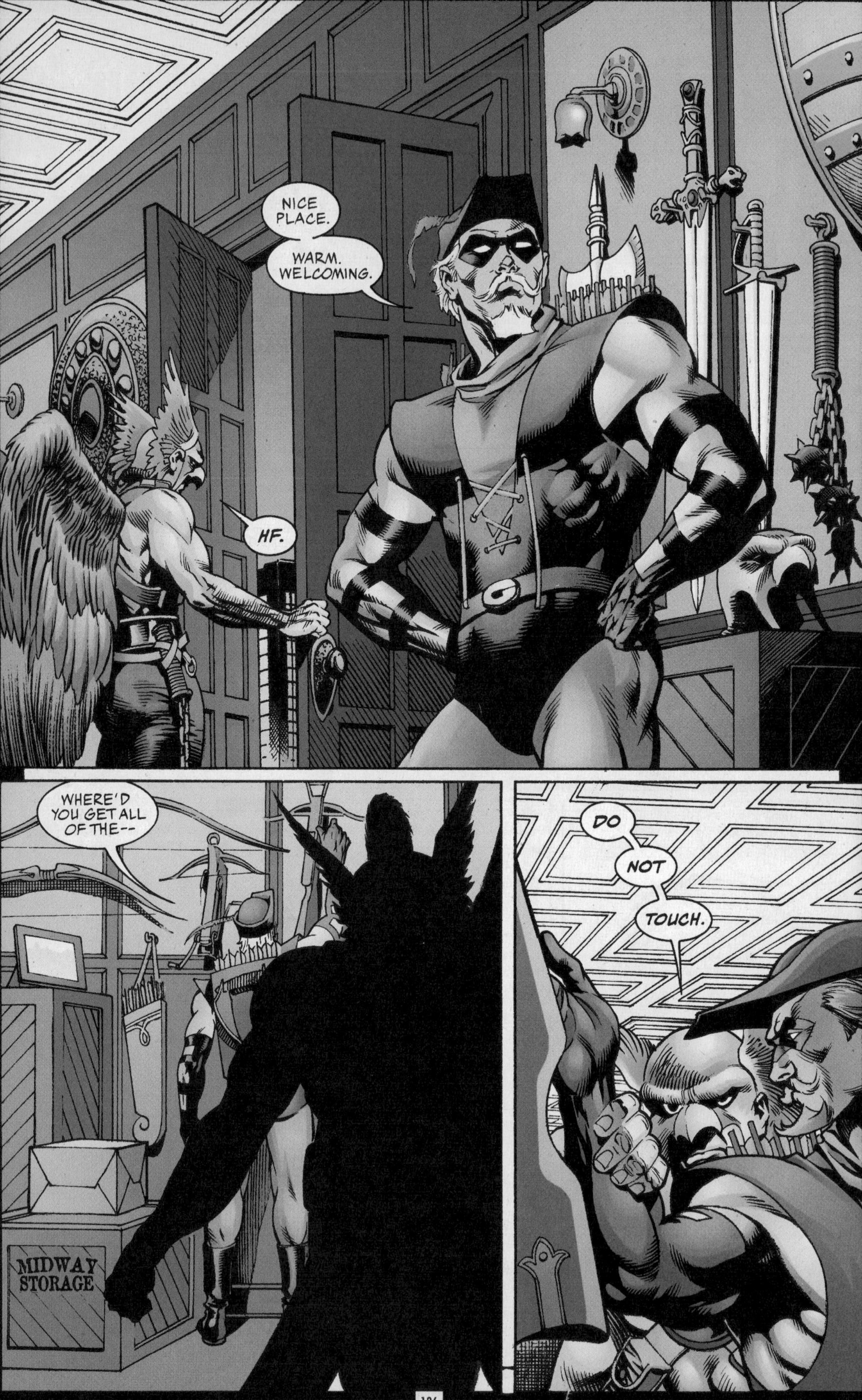
NICE PLACE.
WARM. WELCOMING.
HF.
WHERE'D YOU GET ALL OF THE--
MIDWAY STORAGE
DO
NOT
TOUCH.

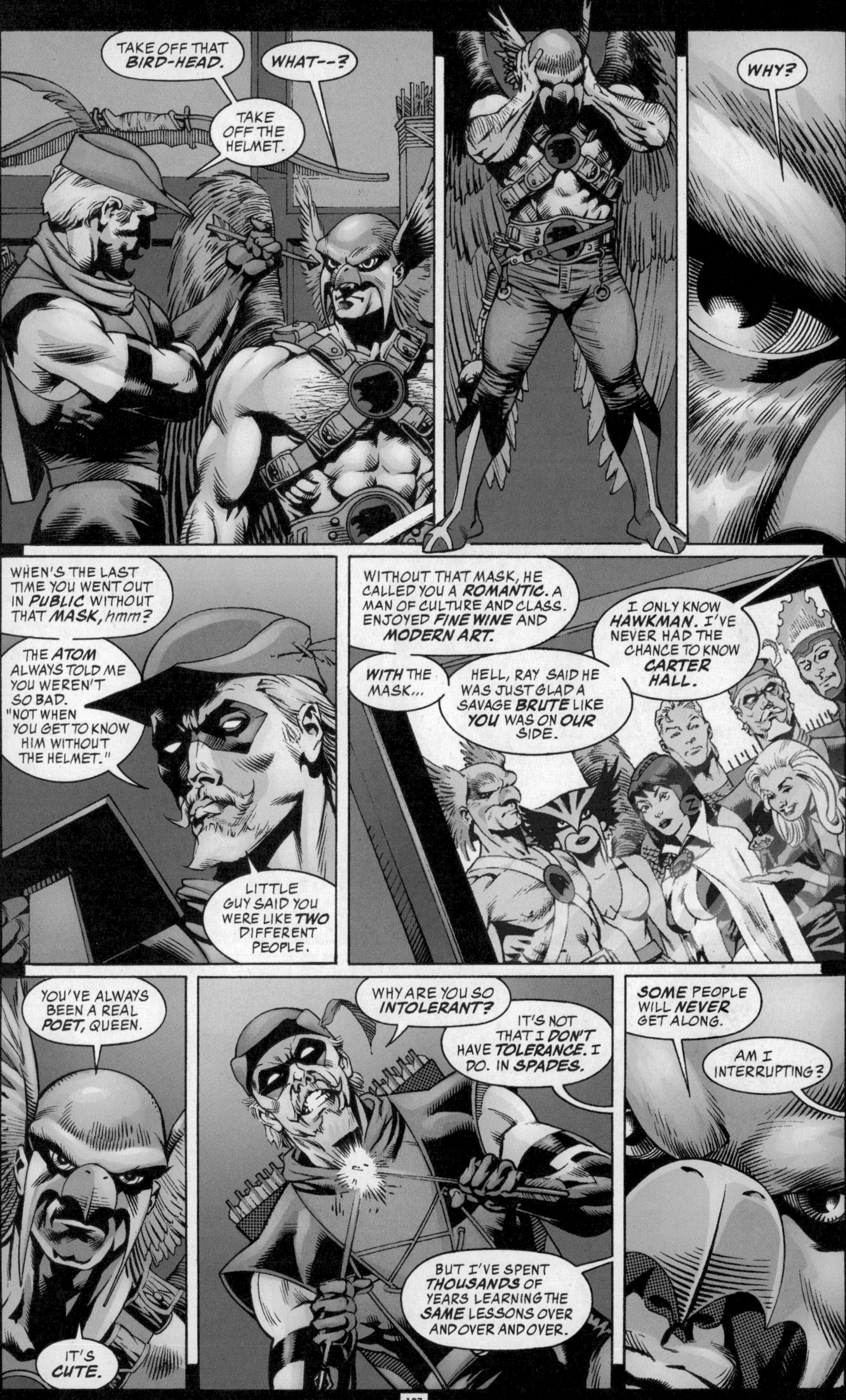
TAKE OFF THAT BIRD-HEAD.
WHAT--?
TAKE OFF THE HELMET.
WHY?
WHEN'S THE LAST TIME YOU WENT OUT IN PUBLIC WITHOUT THAT MASK, hmm?
THE ATOM ALWAYS TOLD ME YOU WEREN'T SO BAD. "NOT WHEN YOU GET TO KNOW HIM WITHOUT THE HELMET."
LITTLE GUY SAID YOU WERE LIKE TWO DIFFERENT PEOPLE.
WITHOUT THAT MASK, HE CALLED YOU A ROMANTIC. A MAN OF CULTURE AND CLASS. ENJOYED FINE WINE AND MODERN ART.
WITH THE MASK...
HELL, RAY SAID HE WAS JUST GLAD A SAVAGE BRUTE LIKE YOU WAS ON OUR SIDE.
I ONLY KNOW HAWKMAN. I'VE NEVER HAD THE CHANCE TO KNOW CARTER HALL.
YOU'VE ALWAYS BEEN A REAL POET, QUEEN.
IT'S CUTE.
WHY ARE YOU SO INTOLERANT?
IT'S NOT THAT I DON'T HAVE TOLERANCE. I DO. IN SPADES.
BUT I'VE SPENT THOUSANDS OF YEARS LEARNING THE SAME LESSONS OVER AND OVER AND OVER.
SOME PEOPLE WILL NEVER GET ALONG.
AM I INTERRUPTING?

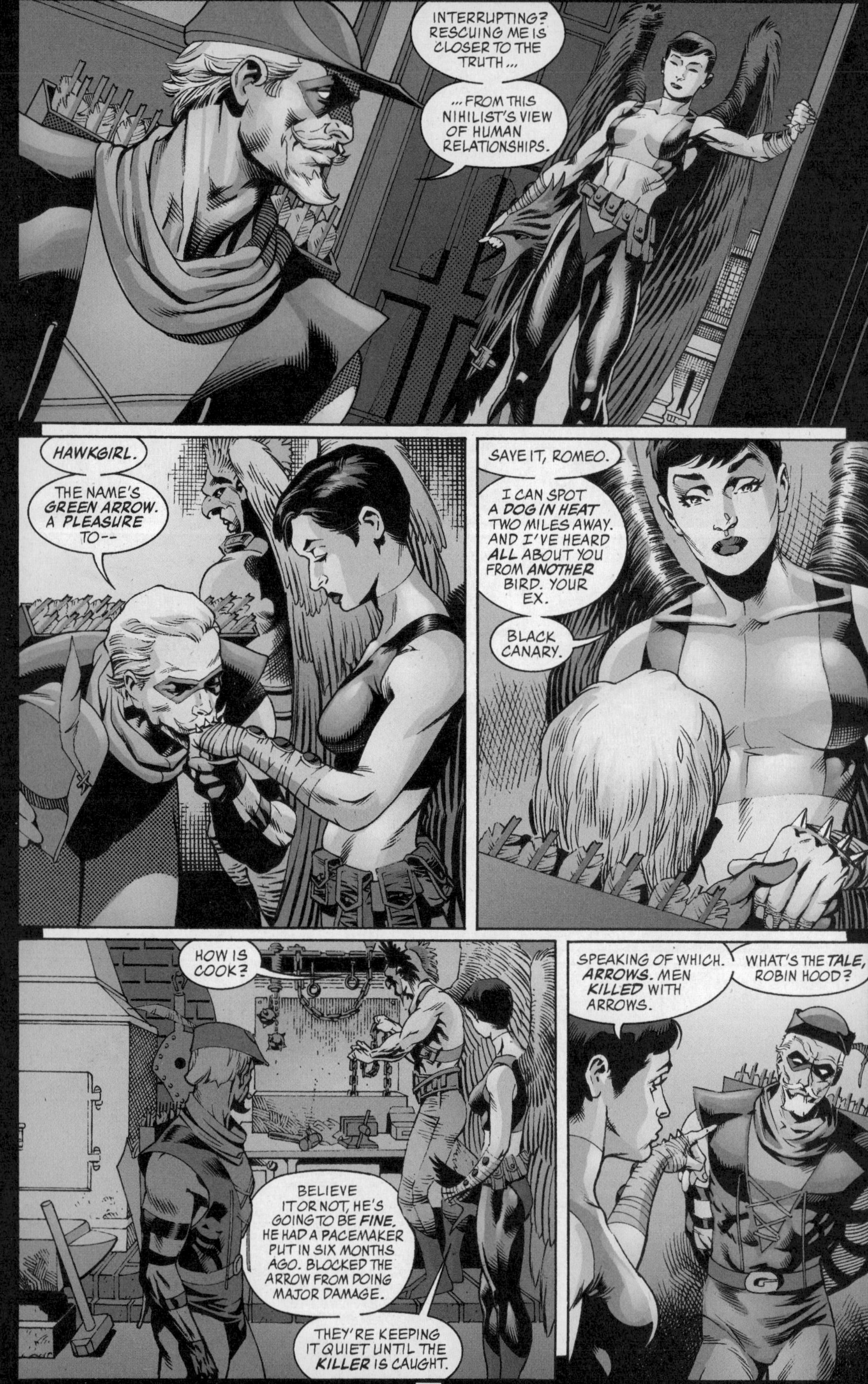
INTERRUPTING? RESCUING ME IS CLOSER TO THE TRUTH...
...FROM THIS NIHILIST'S VIEW OF HUMAN RELATIONSHIPS.
HAWKGIRL.
THE NAME'S GREEN ARROW. A PLEASURE TO--
SAVE IT, ROMEO.
I CAN SPOT A DOG IN HEAT TWO MILES AWAY. AND I'VE HEARD ALL ABOUT YOU FROM ANOTHER BIRD. YOUR EX.
BLACK CANARY.
HOW IS COOK?
BELIEVE IT OR NOT, HE'S GOING TO BE FINE. HE HAD A PACEMAKER PUT IN SIX MONTHS AGO. BLOCKED THE ARROW FROM DOING MAJOR DAMAGE.
THEY'RE KEEPING IT QUIET UNTIL THE KILLER IS CAUGHT.
SPEAKING OF WHICH. ARROWS. MEN KILLED WITH ARROWS.
WHAT'S THE TALE, ROBIN HOOD?

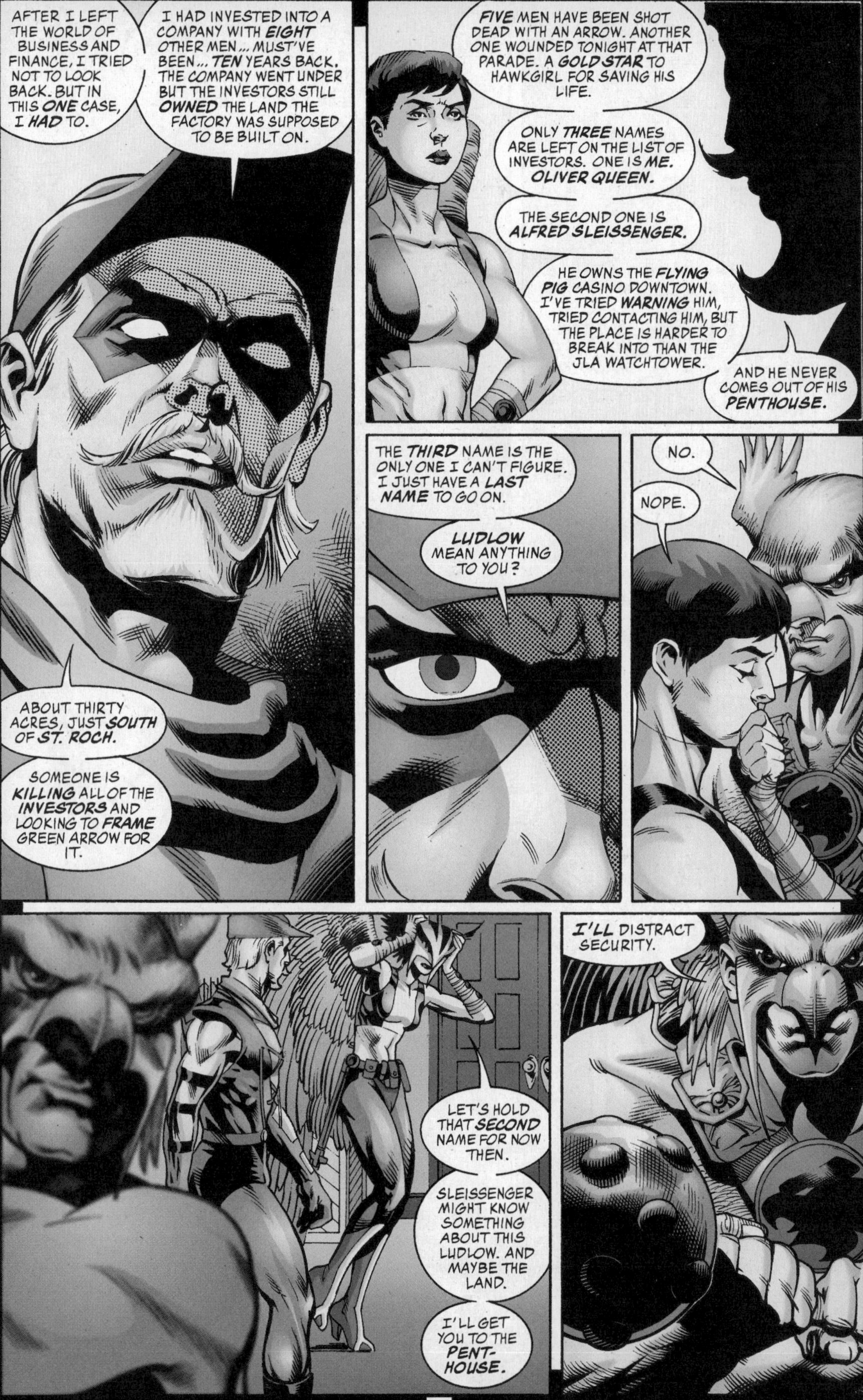

AFTER I LEFT THE WORLD OF BUSINESS AND FINANCE, I TRIED NOT TO LOOK BACK. BUT IN THIS ONE CASE, I HAD TO.
I HAD INVESTED INTO A COMPANY WITH EIGHT OTHER MEN... MUST'VE BEEN... TEN YEARS BACK. THE COMPANY WENT UNDER BUT THE INVESTORS STILL OWNED THE LAND THE FACTORY WAS SUPPOSED TO BE BUILT ON.
ABOUT THIRTY ACRES, JUST SOUTH OF ST. ROCH.
SOMEONE IS KILLING ALL OF THE INVESTORS AND LOOKING TO FRAME GREEN ARROW FOR IT.
FIVE MEN HAVE BEEN SHOT DEAD WITH AN ARROW. ANOTHER ONE WOUNDED TONIGHT AT THAT PARADE. A GOLD STAR TO HAWKGIRL FOR SAVING HIS LIFE.
ONLY THREE NAMES ARE LEFT ON THE LIST OF INVESTORS. ONE IS ME. OLIVER QUEEN.
THE SECOND ONE IS ALFRED SLEISSENGER.
HE OWNS THE FLYING PIG CASINO DOWNTOWN. I'VE TRIED WARNING HIM, TRIED CONTACTING HIM, BUT THE PLACE IS HARDER TO BREAK INTO THAN THE JLA WATCHTOWER.
AND HE NEVER COMES OUT OF HIS PENTHOUSE.
THE THIRD NAME IS THE ONLY ONE I CAN'T FIGURE. I JUST HAVE A LAST NAME TO GO ON.
LUDLOW MEAN ANYTHING TO YOU?
NO.
NOPE.
LET'S HOLD THAT SECOND NAME FOR NOW THEN.
SLEISSENGER MIGHT KNOW SOMETHING ABOUT THIS LUDLOW. AND MAYBE THE LAND.
I'LL GET YOU TO THE PENT-HOUSE.
I'LL DISTRACT SECURITY.

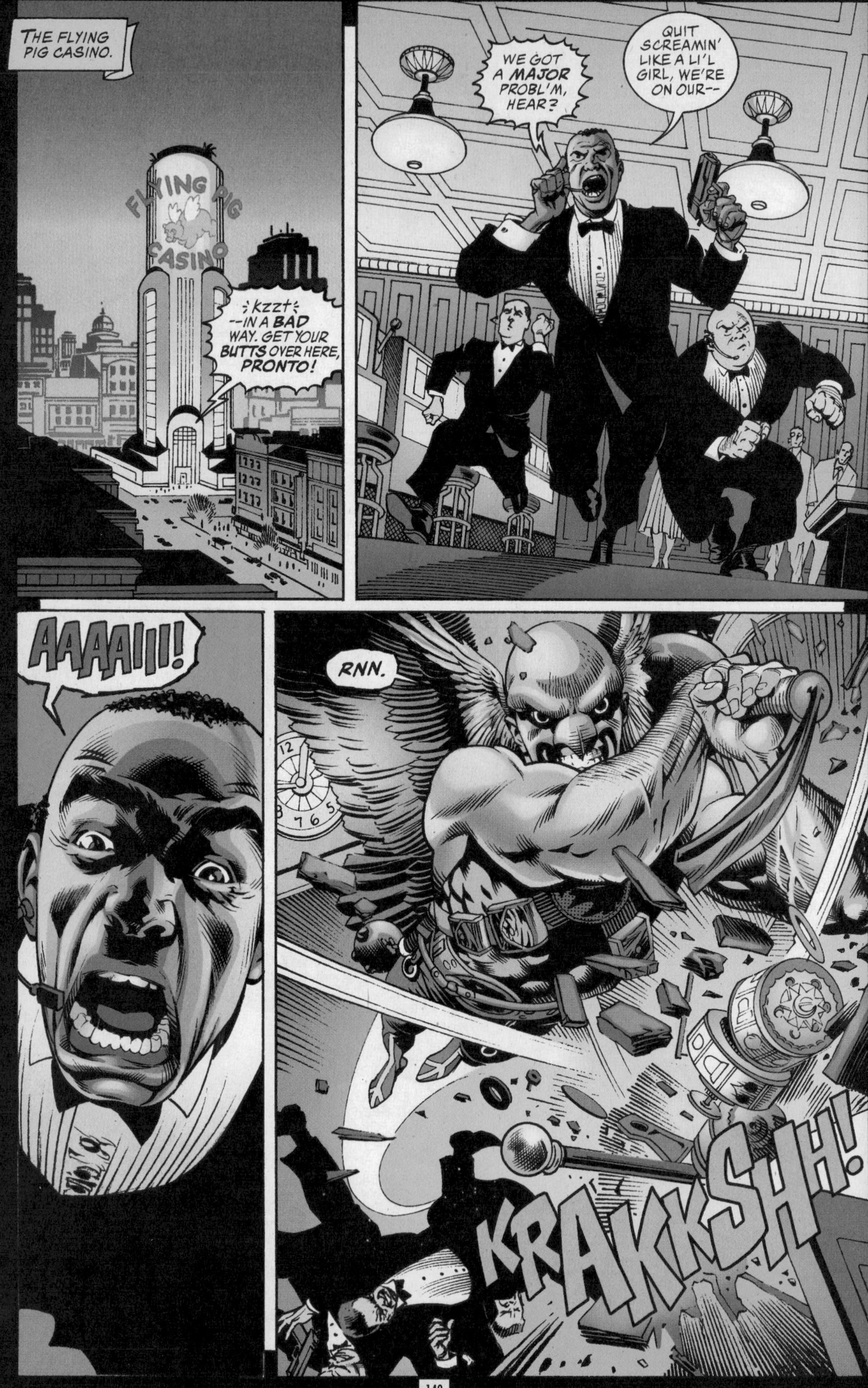
THE FLYING PIG CASINO.
FLYING PIG CASINO
⁘kzzt⁘ --IN A BAD WAY. GET YOUR BUTTS OVER HERE, PRONTO!
WE GOT A MAJOR PROBL'M, HEAR?
QUIT SCREAMIN' LIKE A LI'L GIRL, WE'RE ON OUR--
AAAAIIII!
RNN.
KRAKKSH!

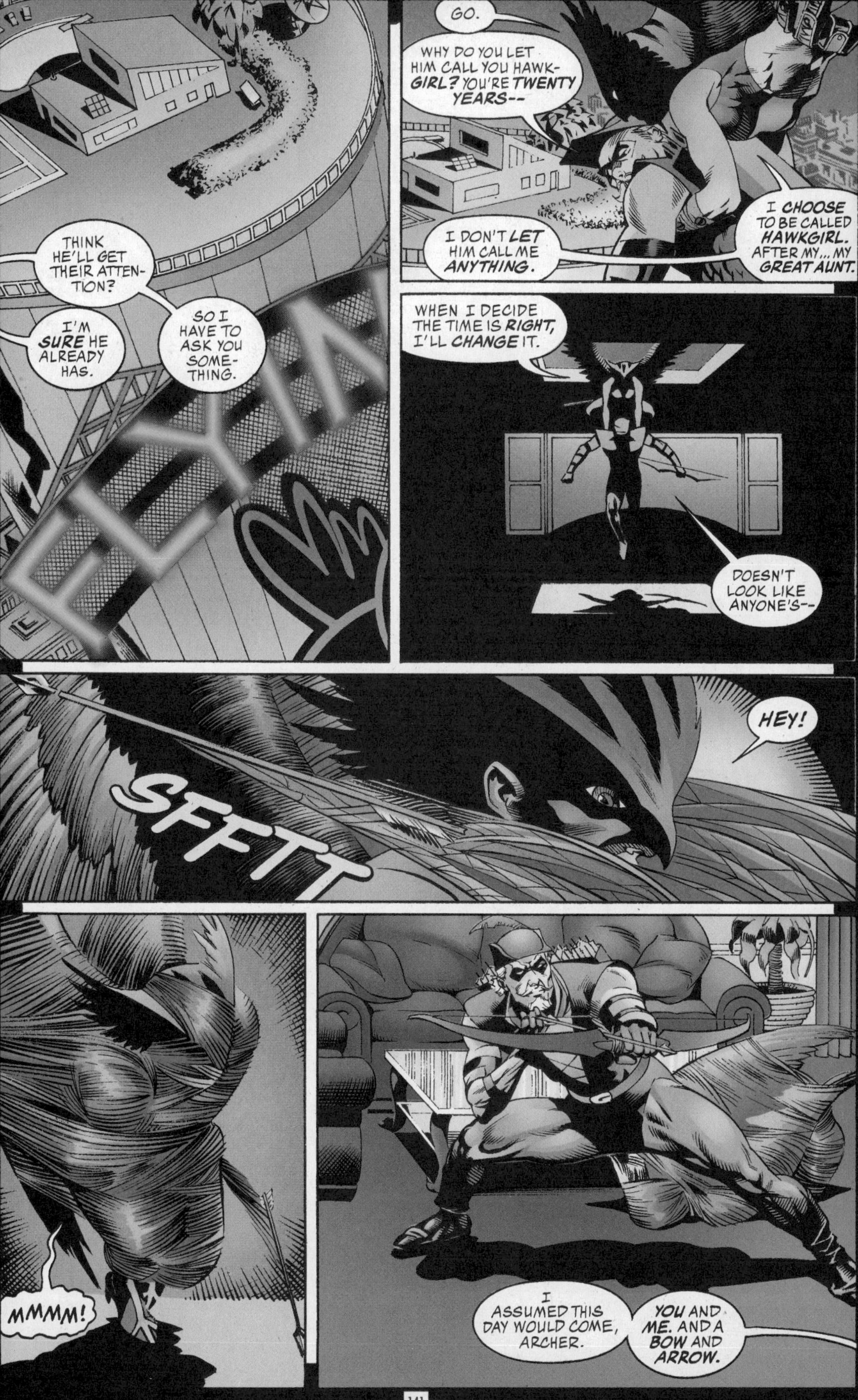
THINK HE'LL GET THEIR ATTENTION?
I'M SURE HE ALREADY HAS.
SO I HAVE TO ASK YOU SOMETHING.
FLYIN
GO.
WHY DO YOU LET HIM CALL YOU HAWKGIRL? YOU'RE TWENTY YEARS--
I DON'T LET HIM CALL ME ANYTHING.
I CHOOSE TO BE CALLED HAWKGIRL. AFTER MY... MY GREAT AUNT.
WHEN I DECIDE THE TIME IS RIGHT, I'LL CHANGE IT.
DOESN'T LOOK LIKE ANYONE'S--
SFFTT
HEY!
MMMM!
I ASSUMED THIS DAY WOULD COME, ARCHER.
YOU AND ME. AND A BOW AND ARROW.

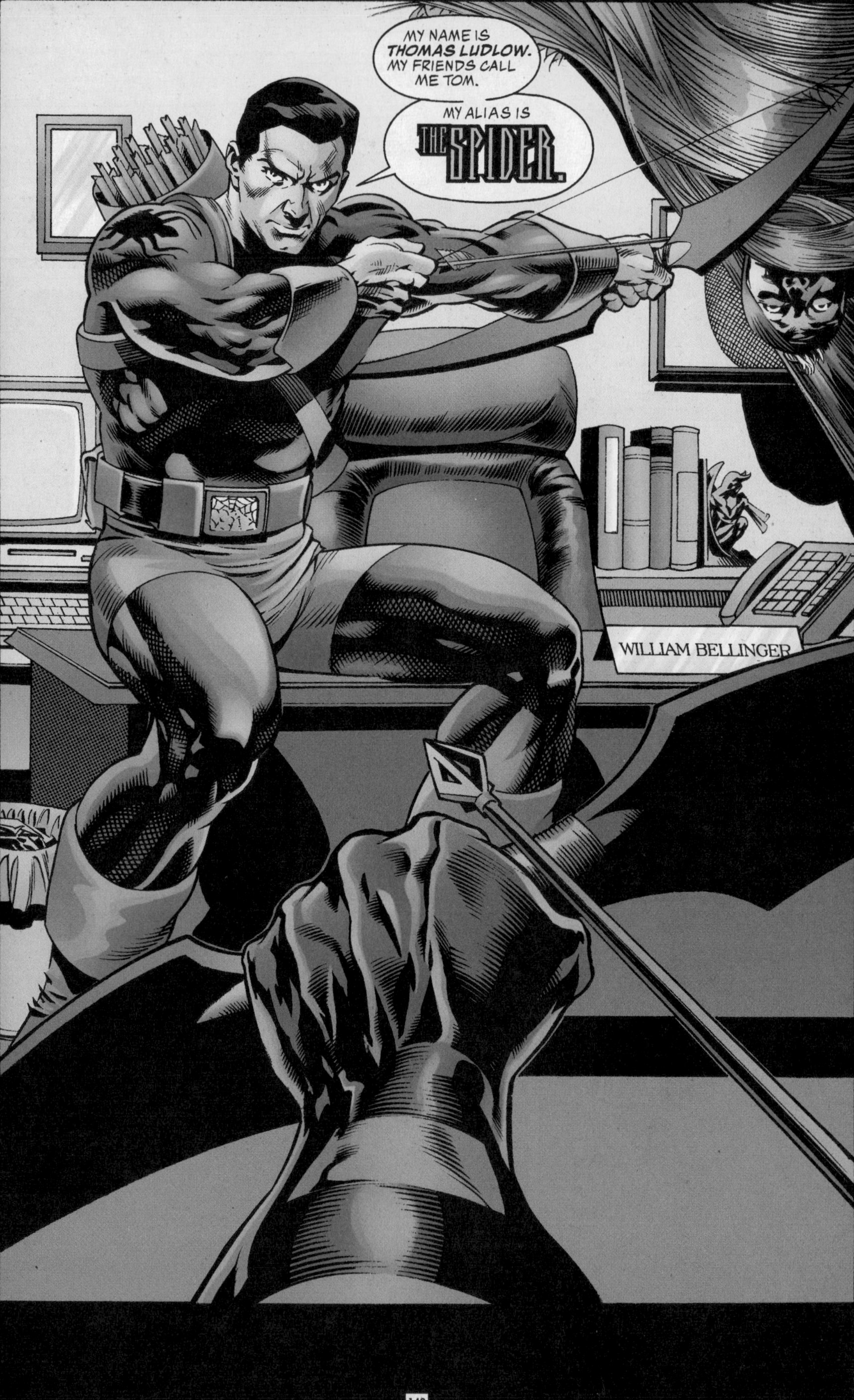

MY NAME IS THOMAS LUDLOW. MY FRIENDS CALL ME TOM.
MY ALIAS IS THE SPIDER.
WILLIAM BELLINGER

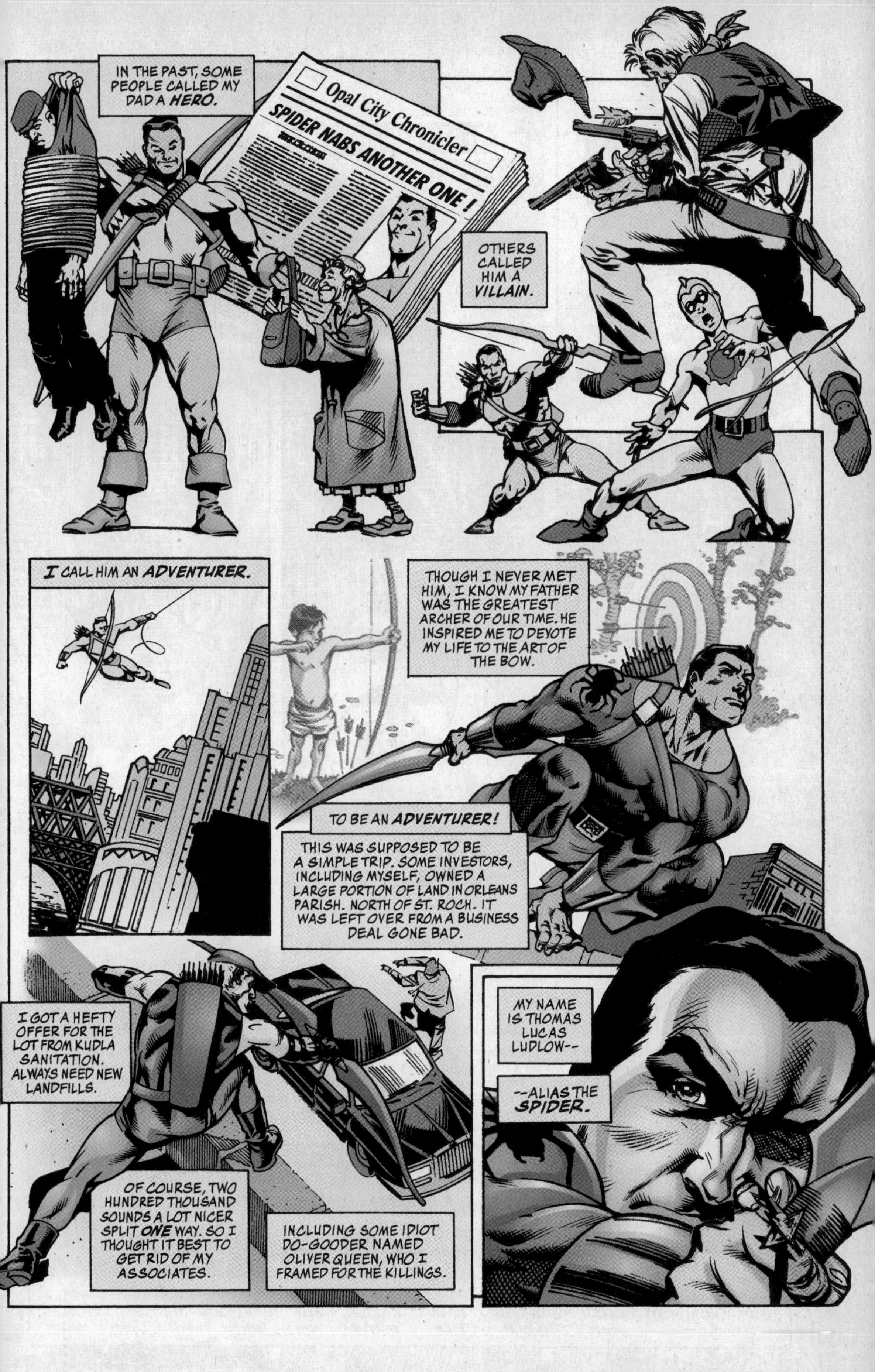
IN THE PAST, SOME PEOPLE CALLED MY DAD A HERO.
Opal City Chronicler
SPIDER NABS ANOTHER ONE!
OTHERS CALLED HIM A VILLAIN.
I CALL HIM AN ADVENTURER.
THOUGH I NEVER MET HIM, I KNOW MY FATHER WAS THE GREATEST ARCHER OF OUR TIME. HE INSPIRED ME TO DEVOTE MY LIFE TO THE ART OF THE BOW.
TO BE AN ADVENTURER!
THIS WAS SUPPOSED TO BE A SIMPLE TRIP. SOME INVESTORS, INCLUDING MYSELF, OWNED A LARGE PORTION OF LAND IN ORLEANS PARISH. NORTH OF ST. ROCH. IT WAS LEFT OVER FROM A BUSINESS DEAL GONE BAD.
I GOT A HEFTY OFFER FOR THE LOT FROM KUDLA SANITATION. ALWAYS NEED NEW LANDFILLS.
OF COURSE, TWO HUNDRED THOUSAND SOUNDS A LOT NICER SPLIT ONE WAY. SO I THOUGHT IT BEST TO GET RID OF MY ASSOCIATES.
INCLUDING SOME IDIOT DO-GOODER NAMED OLIVER QUEEN, WHO I FRAMED FOR THE KILLINGS.
MY NAME IS THOMAS LUCAS LUDLOW--
--ALIAS THE SPIDER.

AND UNFORTUNATELY, TODAY'S *ADVENTURE* HAS JUST GONE *SOUTH.*

**GREEN ARROW**

**HAWKGIRL**

**HAWKMAN**

Thousands of years ago, an Egyptian Prince and his Princess discovered an alien spacecraft from the planet Thanagar. The ship was powered by a mysterious antigravity element they called Nth metal. The unearthly energies of the Nth metal, enhanced by the strength of their love, transformed the souls of the Prince and Princess. For centuries, they were reincarnated, life after life, destined to meet one another and rekindle their love...until today...Today they are Carter Hall and Kendra Saunders, archaeologists and adventurers. The winged warriors known as HAWKMAN and HAWKGIRL!

# SLINGS *and* ARROWS PART TWO

| GEOFF JOHNS & JAMES ROBINSON | GEOFF JOHNS | RAGS MORALES | MICHAEL BAIR | JOHN KALISZ | HEROIC AGE | BILL OAKLEY | STEPHEN WACKER | PETER TOMASI |
|---|---|---|---|---|---|---|---|---|
| story | words | penciller | inker | colorist | seps | letterer | associate editor | editor |

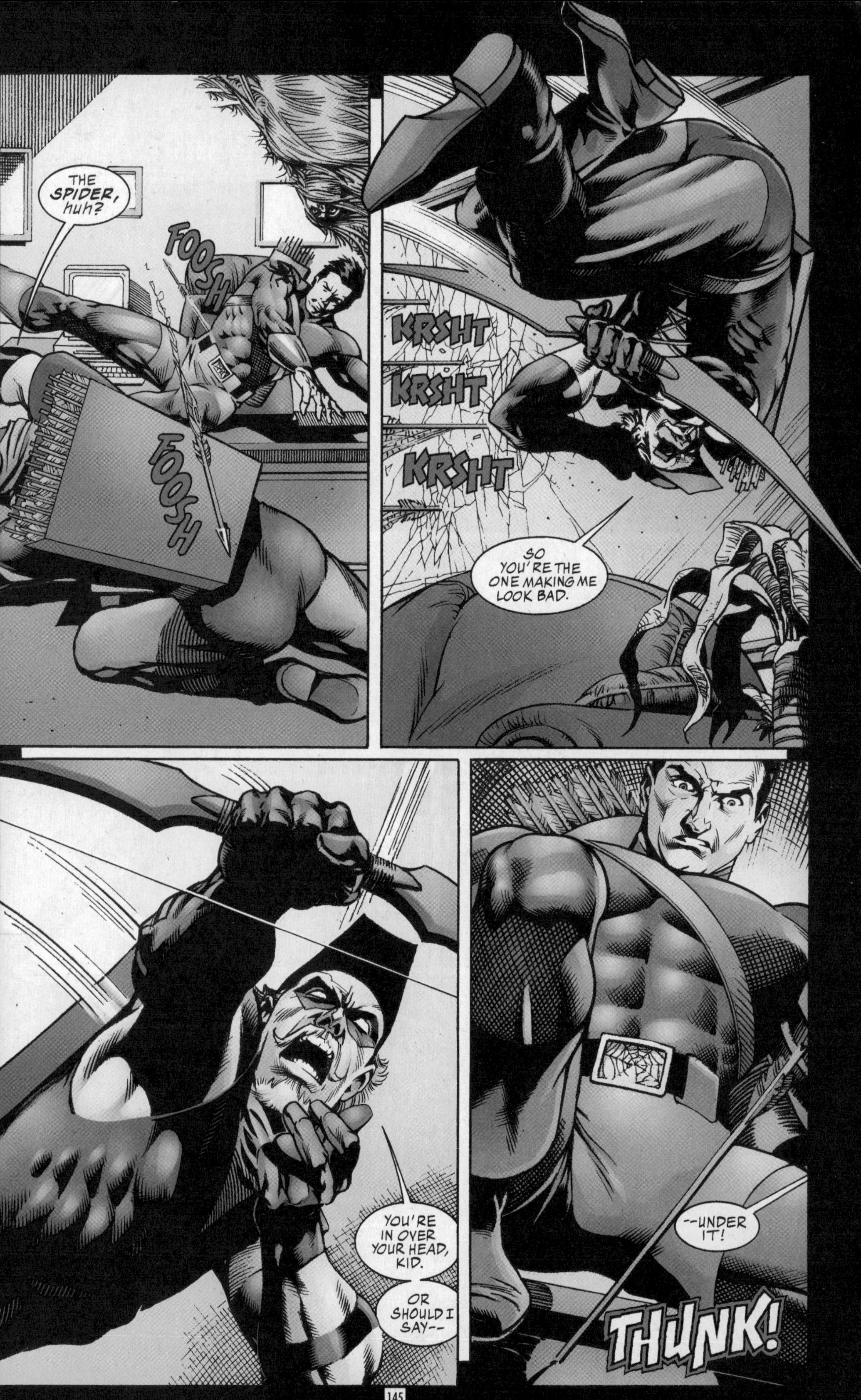
THE SPIDER, huh?
FOOSH
FOOSH
KRSHT
KRSHT
KRSHT
SO YOU'RE THE ONE MAKING ME LOOK BAD.
YOU'RE IN OVER YOUR HEAD, KID.
OR SHOULD I SAY--
--UNDER IT!
THUNK!

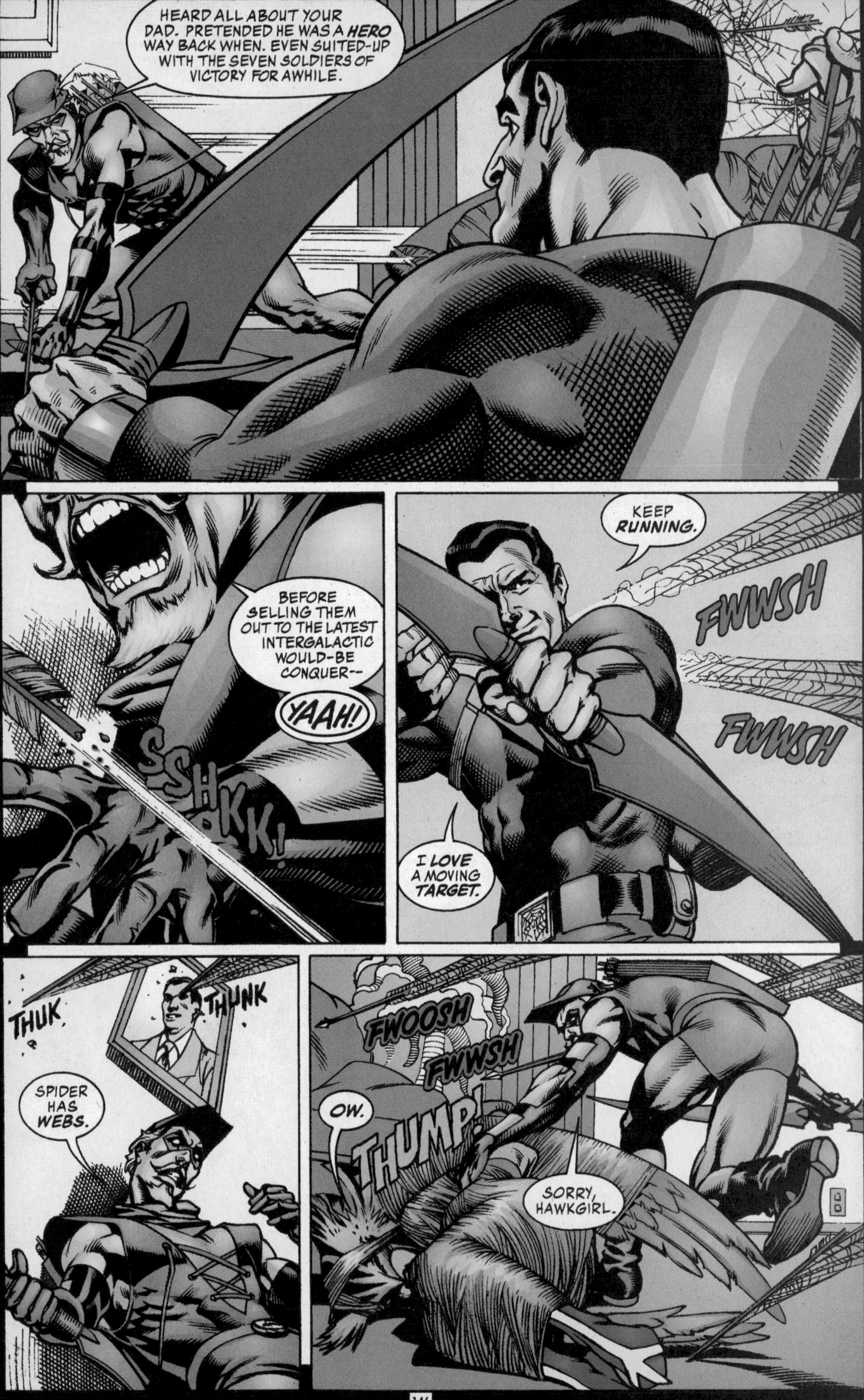
HEARD ALL ABOUT YOUR DAD. PRETENDED HE WAS A HERO WAY BACK WHEN. EVEN SUITED-UP WITH THE SEVEN SOLDIERS OF VICTORY FOR AWHILE.
BEFORE SELLING THEM OUT TO THE LATEST INTERGALACTIC WOULD-BE CONQUER--
YAAH!
SSHKK!
KEEP RUNNING.
FWWSH
FWWSH
I LOVE A MOVING TARGET.
THUK
THUNK
SPIDER HAS WEBS.
FWOOSH
FWWSH
OW.
THUMP!
SORRY, HAWKGIRL.

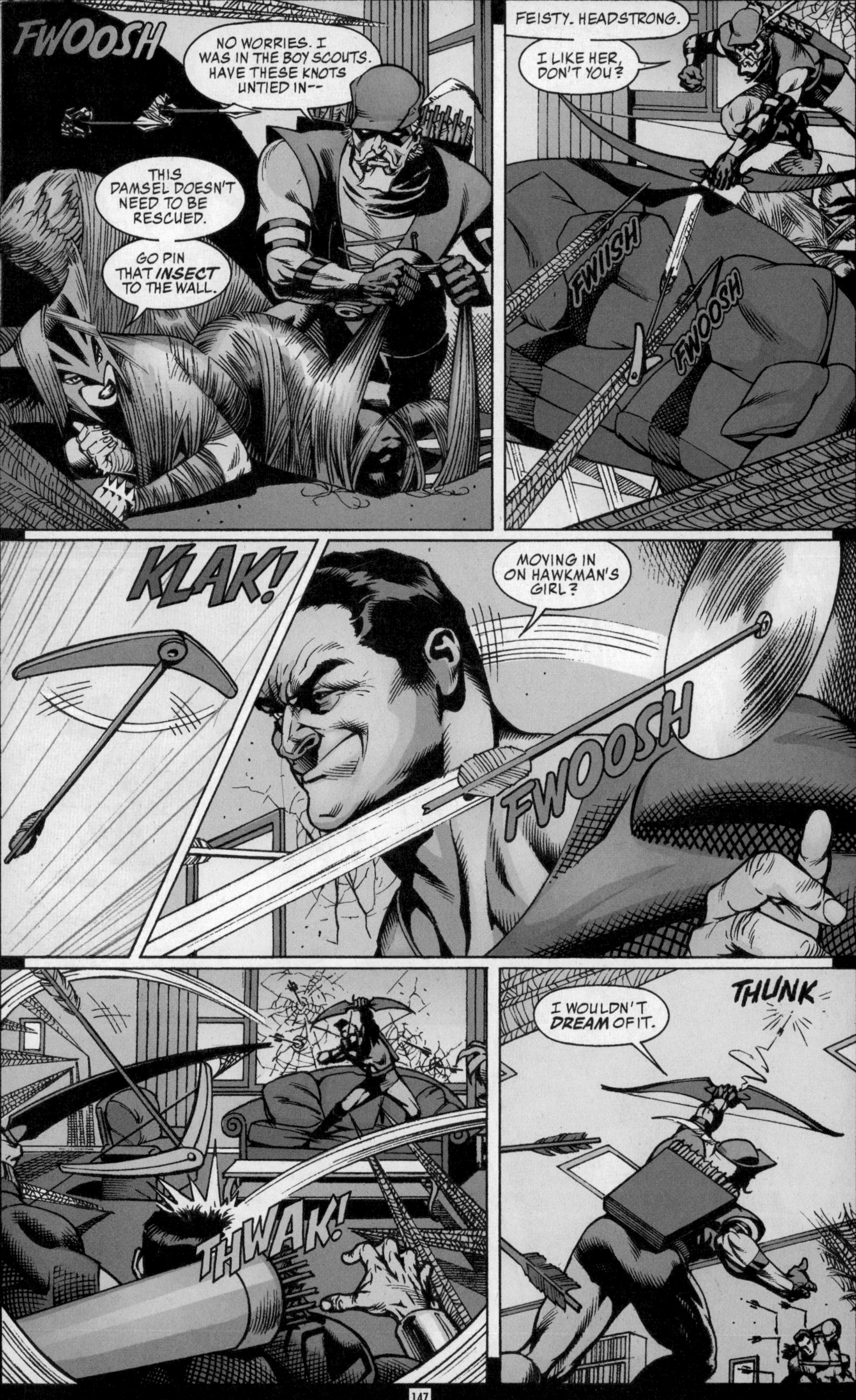

FWOOSH
NO WORRIES. I WAS IN THE BOY SCOUTS. HAVE THESE KNOTS UNTIED IN--
THIS DAMSEL DOESN'T NEED TO BE RESCUED.
GO PIN THAT *INSECT* TO THE WALL.
FEISTY. HEADSTRONG.
I LIKE HER, DON'T YOU?
FWIISH
FWOOSH
KLAK!
MOVING IN ON HAWKMAN'S GIRL?
FWOOSH
THWAK!
THUNK
I WOULDN'T **DREAM** OF IT.

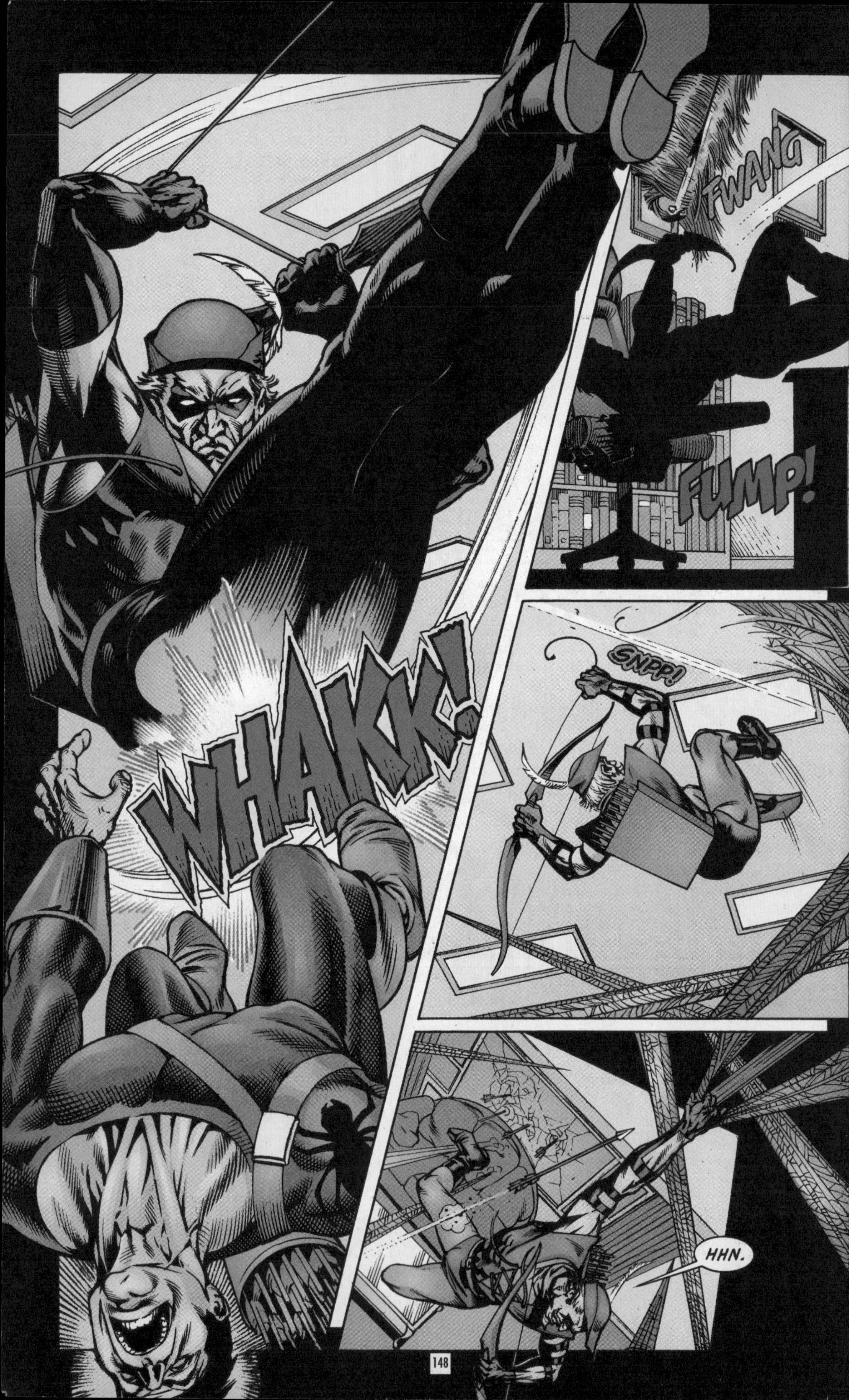
FWANG
FUMP!
WHAKK!
SNPP!
HHN.

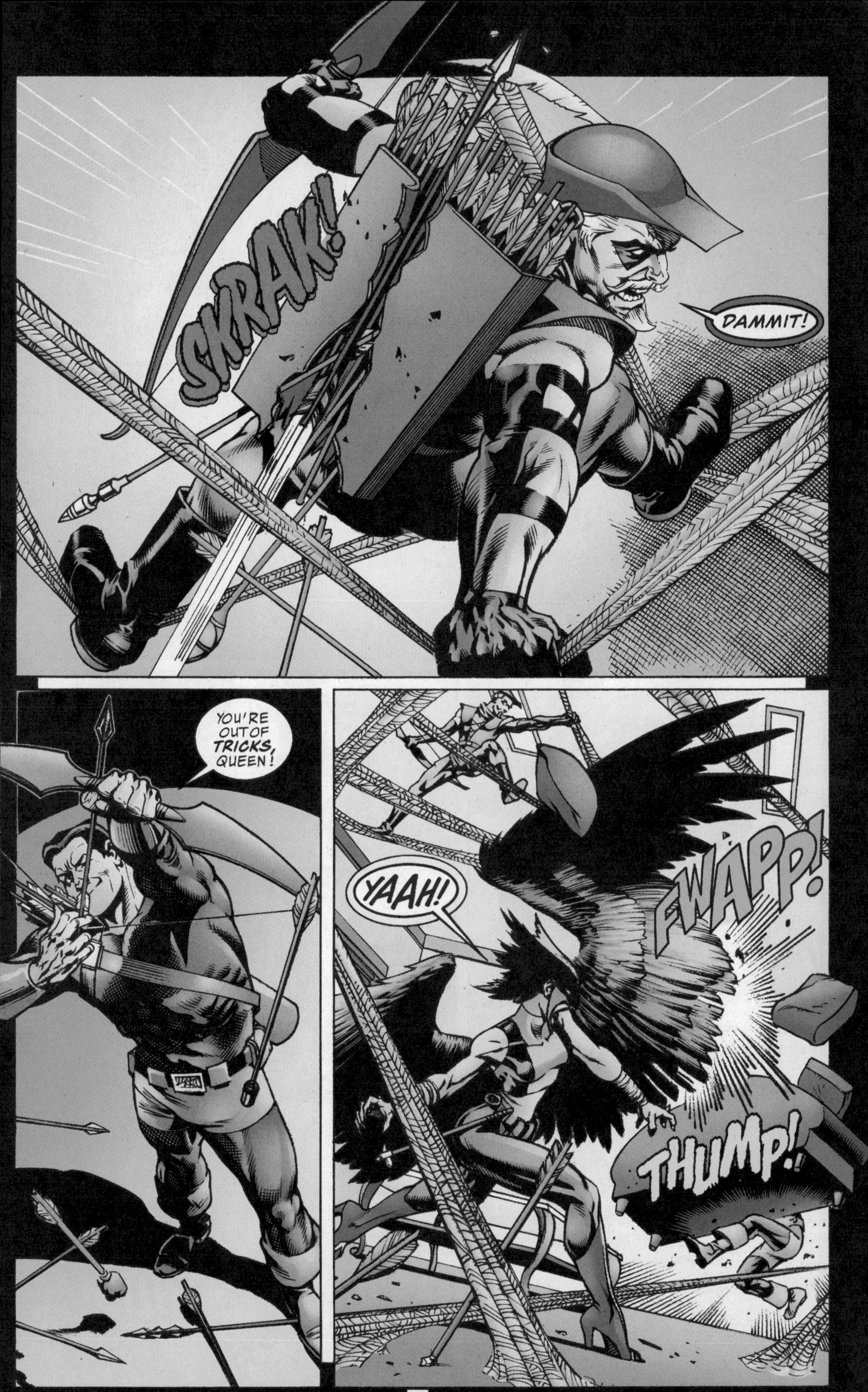
SKRAK!
DAMMIT!
YOU'RE OUT OF TRICKS, QUEEN!
YAAH!
FWAPP!
THUMP!

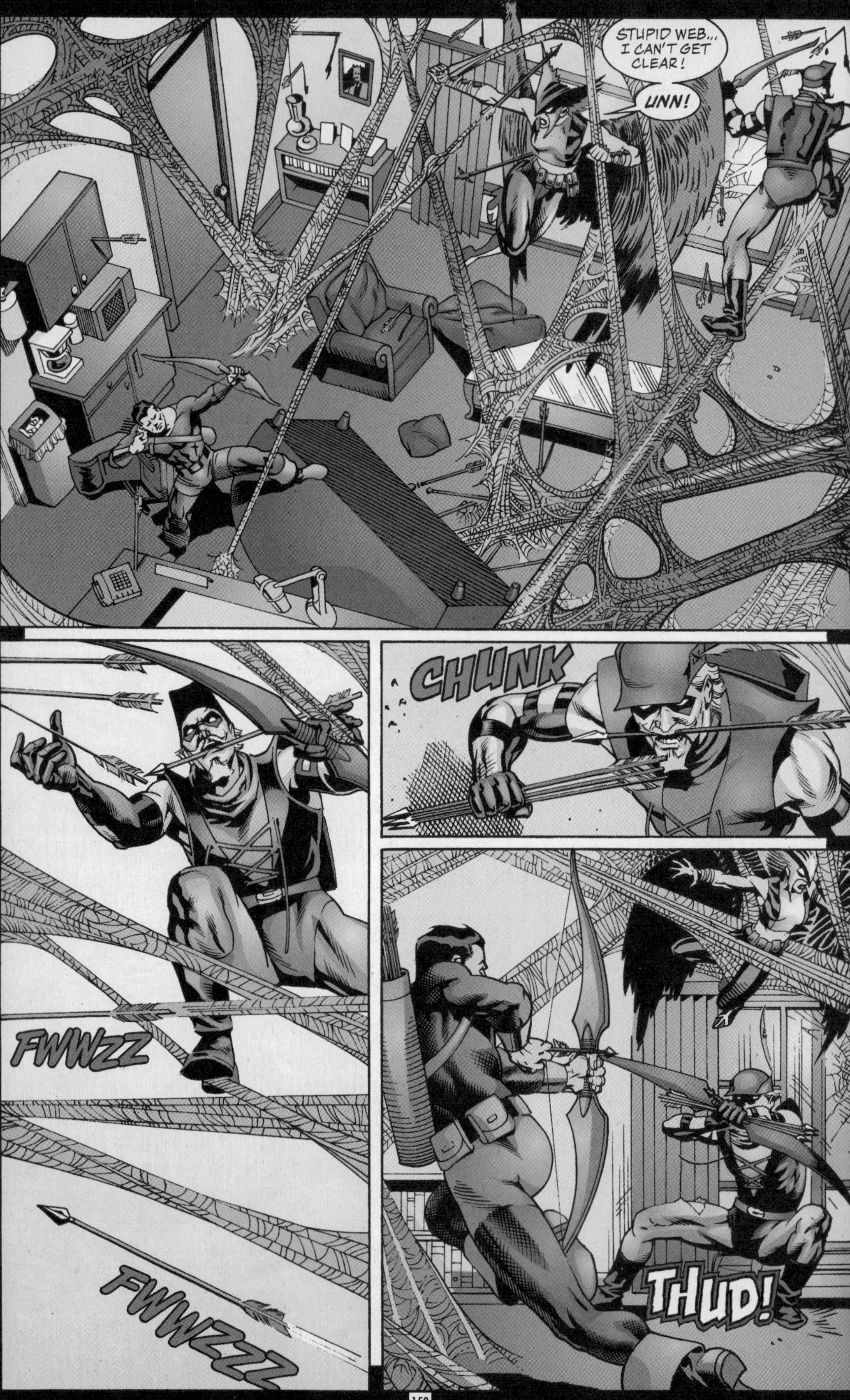
STUPID WEB... I CAN'T GET CLEAR!
UNN!
CHUNK
FWWZZ
FWWZZZ
THUD!

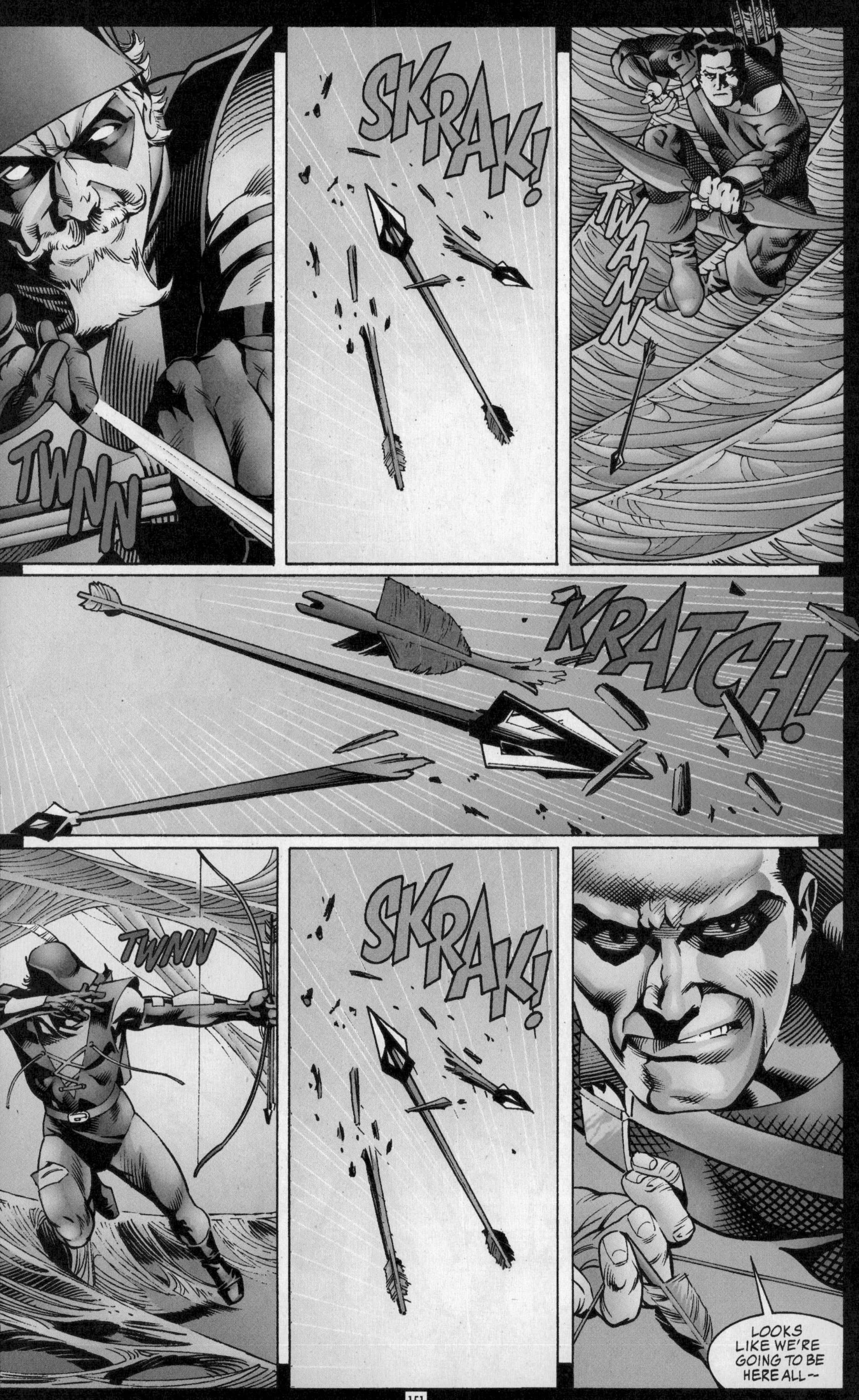
TWNN
SKRAK!
TWANN
KRATCH!
TWNN
SKRAK!
LOOKS LIKE WE'RE GOING TO BE HERE ALL--

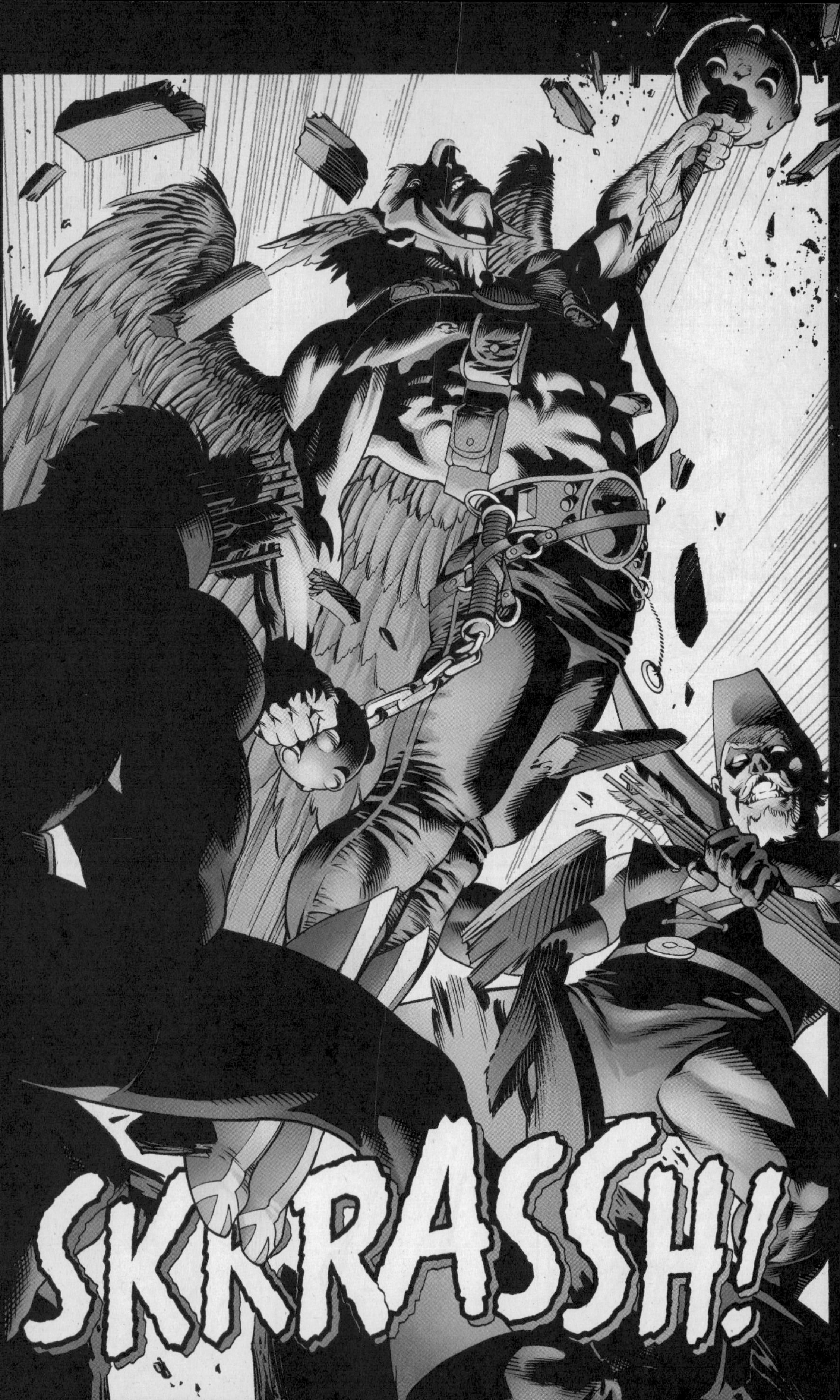
SKKRASSH!

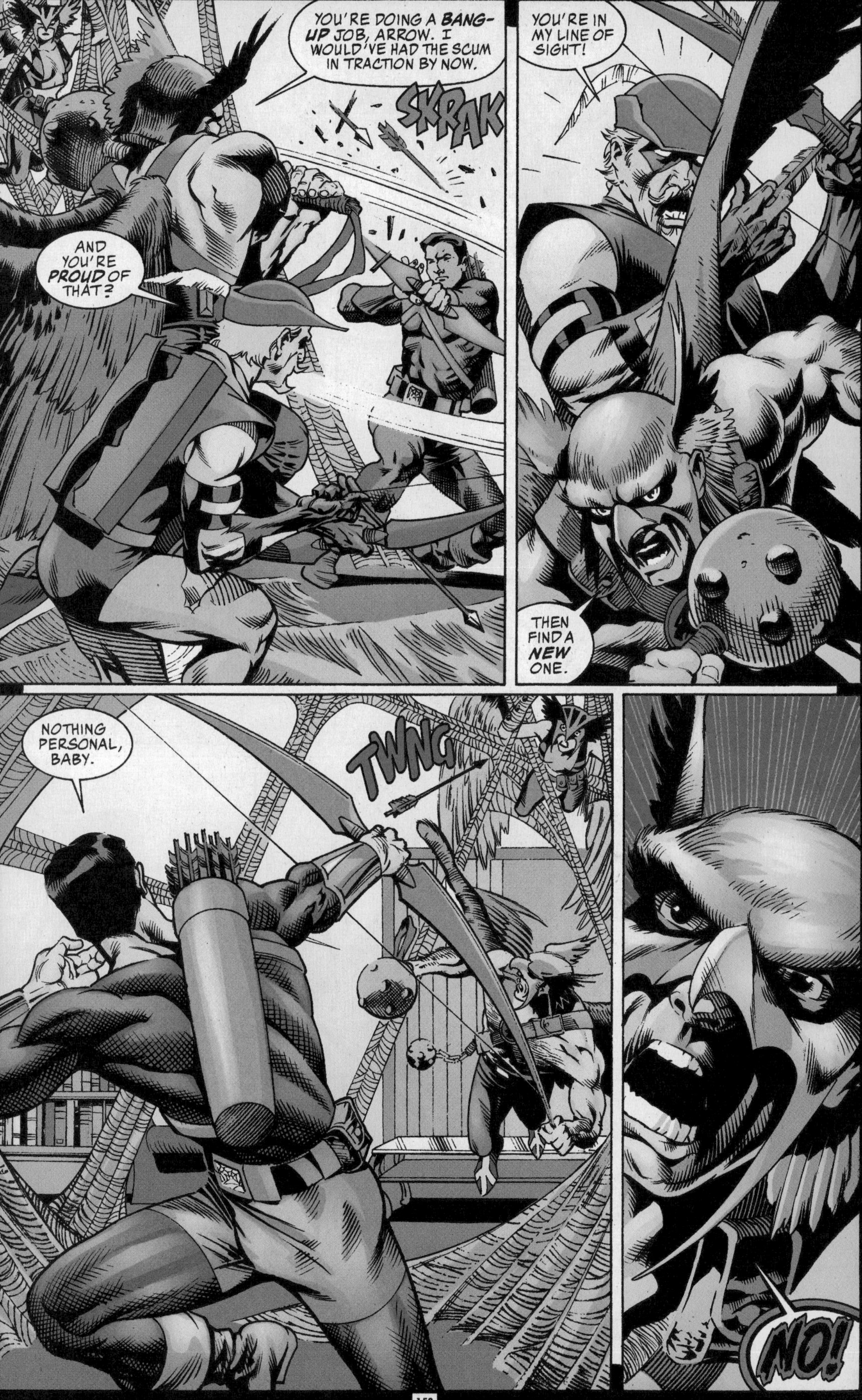
YOU'RE DOING A BANG-UP JOB, ARROW. I WOULD'VE HAD THE SCUM IN TRACTION BY NOW.
SKRAK
AND YOU'RE PROUD OF THAT?
YOU'RE IN MY LINE OF SIGHT!
THEN FIND A NEW ONE.
NOTHING PERSONAL, BABY.
TWNG
NO!

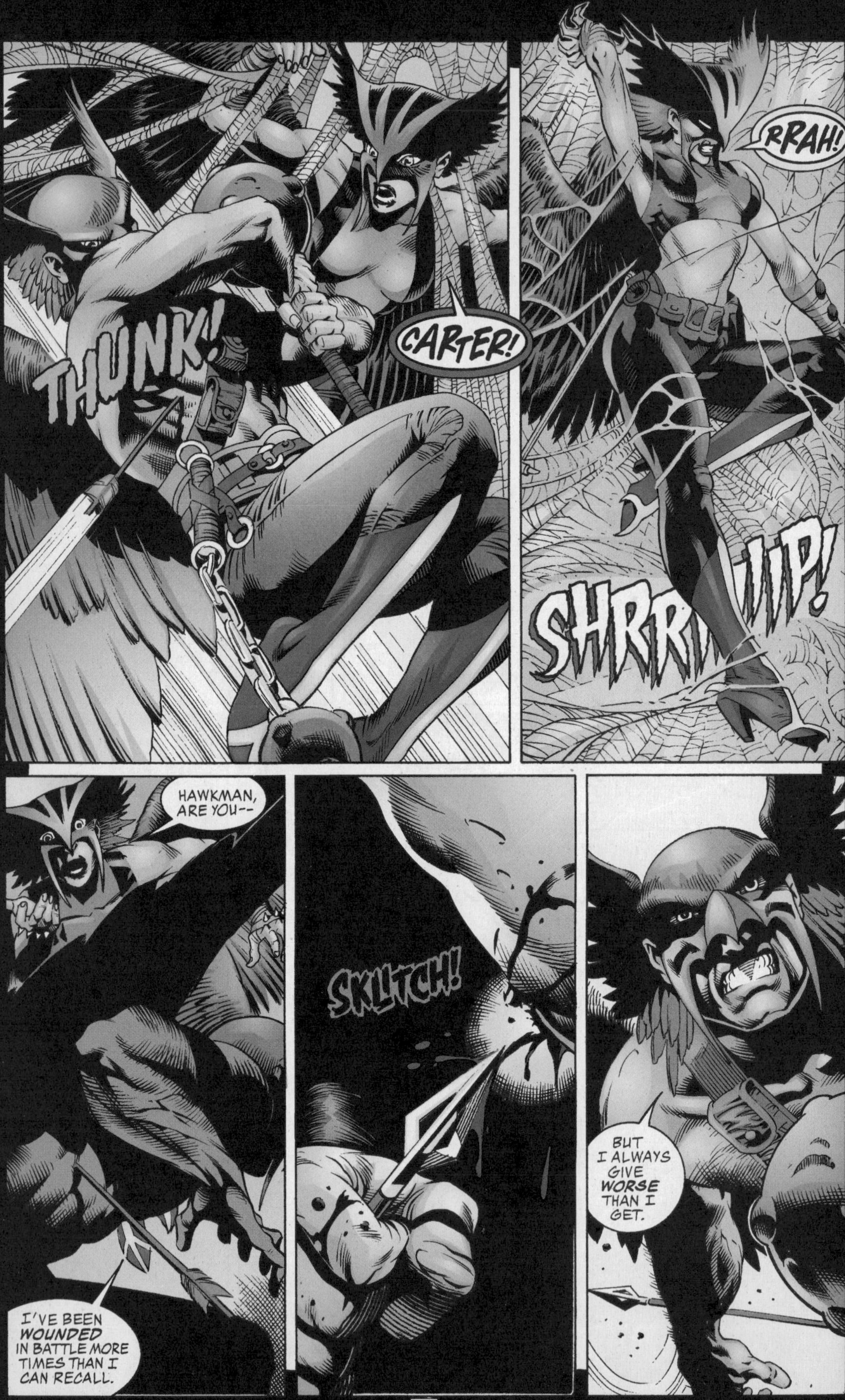
THUNK!
CARTER!
RRAH!
SHRRIIIP!
HAWKMAN, ARE YOU--
I'VE BEEN WOUNDED IN BATTLE MORE TIMES THAN I CAN RECALL.
SKLITCH!
BUT I ALWAYS GIVE WORSE THAN I GET.

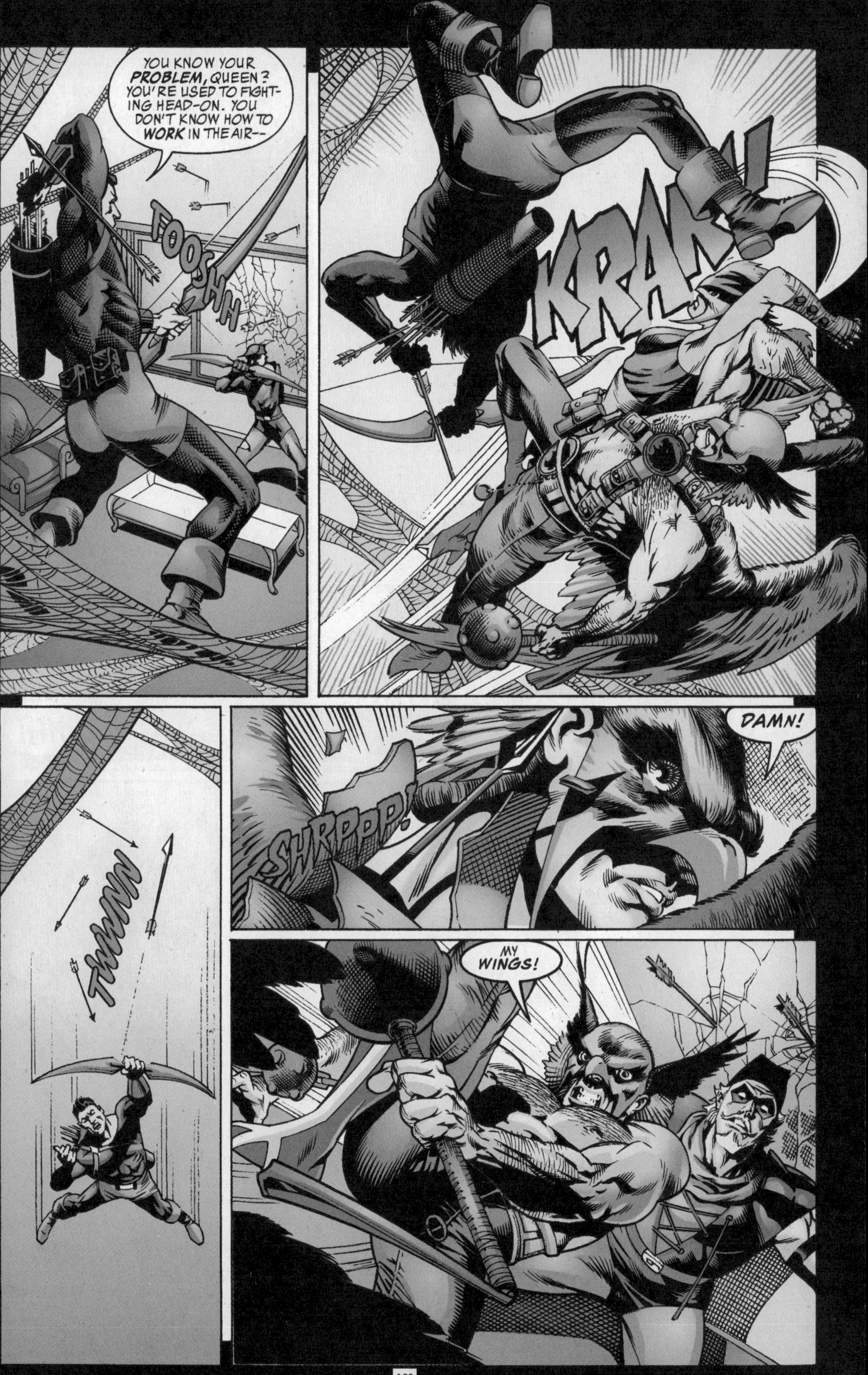

YOU KNOW YOUR PROBLEM, QUEEN? YOU'RE USED TO FIGHTING HEAD-ON. YOU DON'T KNOW HOW TO WORK IN THE AIR--
FOOSHH
KRAM!
THWWN
DAMN!
SHRPPP!
MY WINGS!

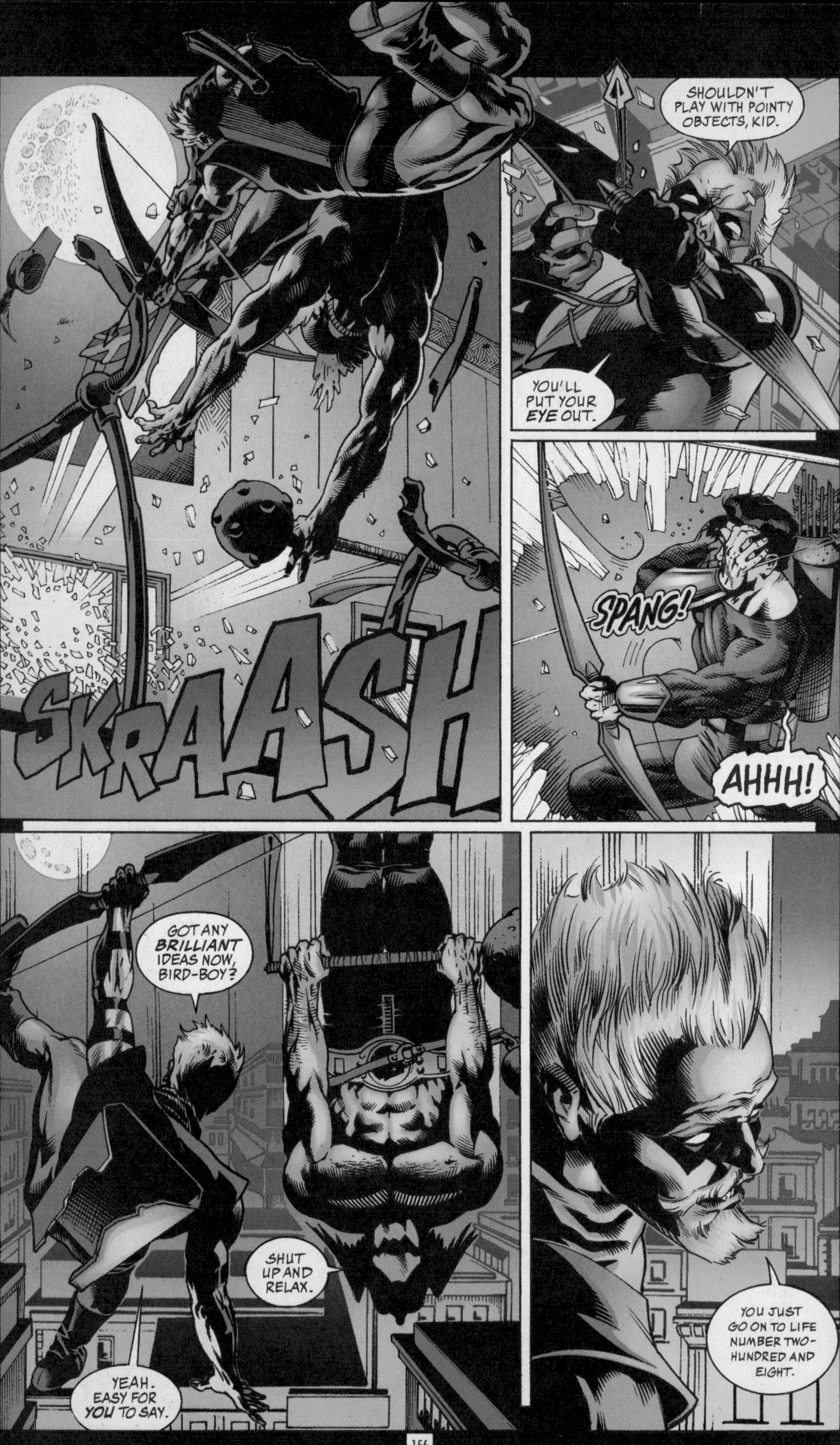

SHOULDN'T PLAY WITH POINTY OBJECTS, KID.
YOU'LL PUT YOUR EYE OUT.
SKRAASH
SPANG!
AHHH!
GOT ANY BRILLIANT IDEAS NOW, BIRD-BOY?
SHUT UP AND RELAX.
YEAH. EASY FOR YOU TO SAY.
YOU JUST GO ON TO LIFE NUMBER TWO-HUNDRED AND EIGHT.

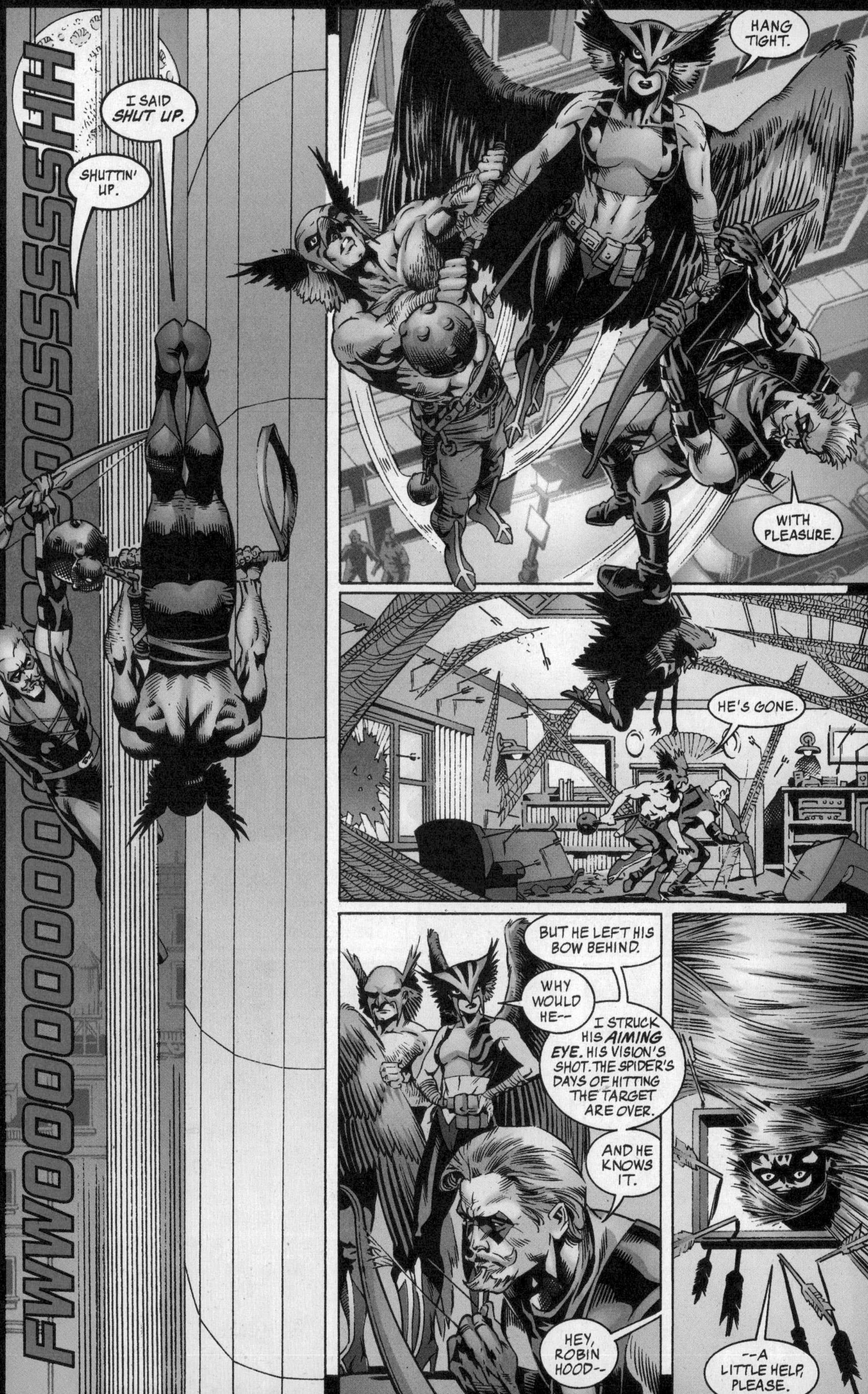

FWWOOOOOOOOOOSSSSSHH
I SAID SHUT UP.
SHUTTIN' UP.
HANG TIGHT.
WITH PLEASURE.
HE'S GONE.
BUT HE LEFT HIS BOW BEHIND.
WHY WOULD HE--
I STRUCK HIS AIMING EYE. HIS VISION'S SHOT. THE SPIDER'S DAYS OF HITTING THE TARGET ARE OVER.
AND HE KNOWS IT.
HEY, ROBIN HOOD--
--A LITTLE HELP, PLEASE.

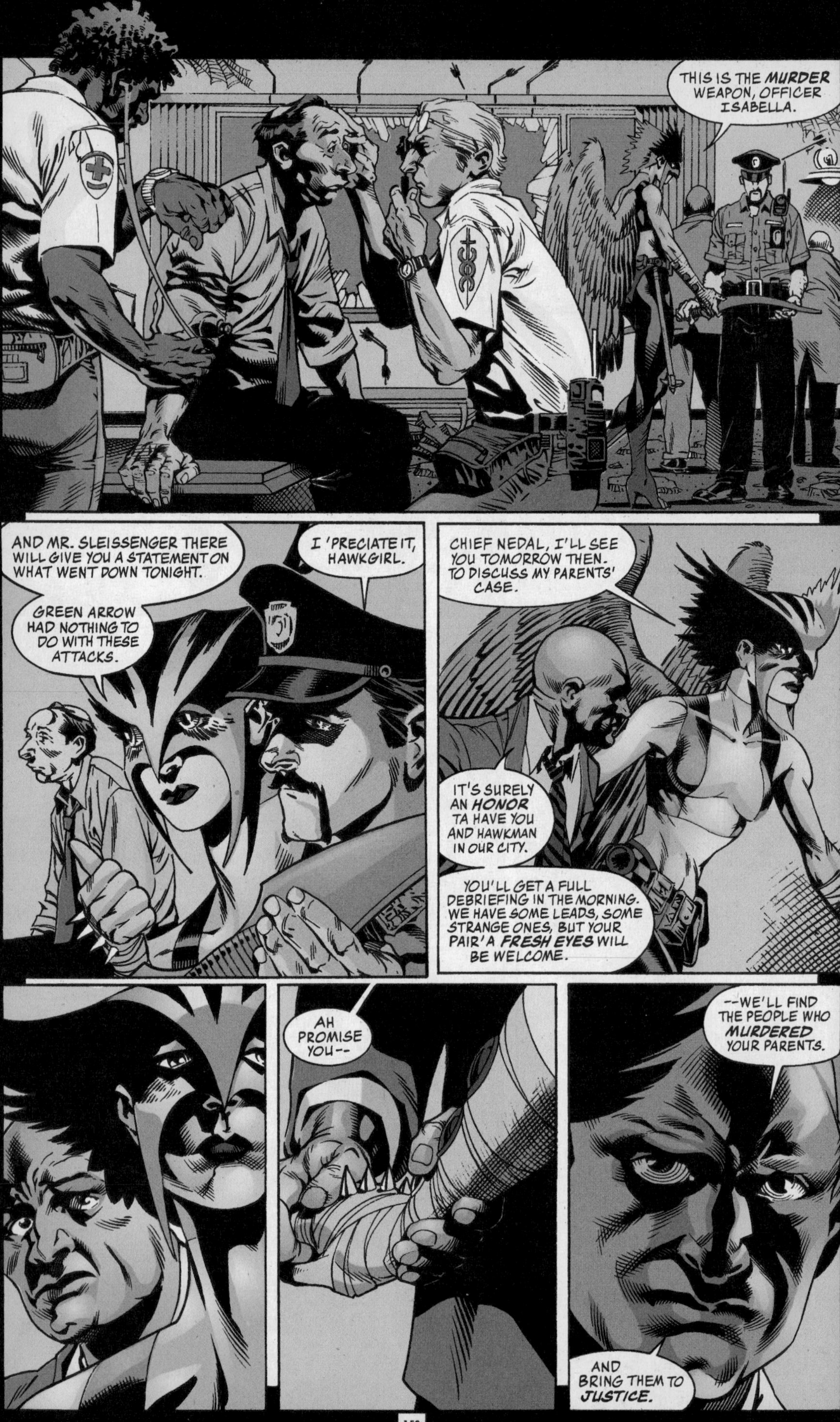
THIS IS THE MURDER WEAPON, OFFICER ISABELLA.
AND MR. SLEISSENGER THERE WILL GIVE YOU A STATEMENT ON WHAT WENT DOWN TONIGHT.
GREEN ARROW HAD NOTHING TO DO WITH THESE ATTACKS.
I 'PRECIATE IT, HAWKGIRL.
CHIEF NEDAL, I'LL SEE YOU TOMORROW THEN. TO DISCUSS MY PARENTS' CASE.
IT'S SURELY AN HONOR TA HAVE YOU AND HAWKMAN IN OUR CITY.
YOU'LL GET A FULL DEBRIEFING IN THE MORNING. WE HAVE SOME LEADS, SOME STRANGE ONES, BUT YOUR PAIR' A FRESH EYES WILL BE WELCOME.
AH PROMISE YOU--
--WE'LL FIND THE PEOPLE WHO MURDERED YOUR PARENTS.
AND BRING THEM TO JUSTICE.

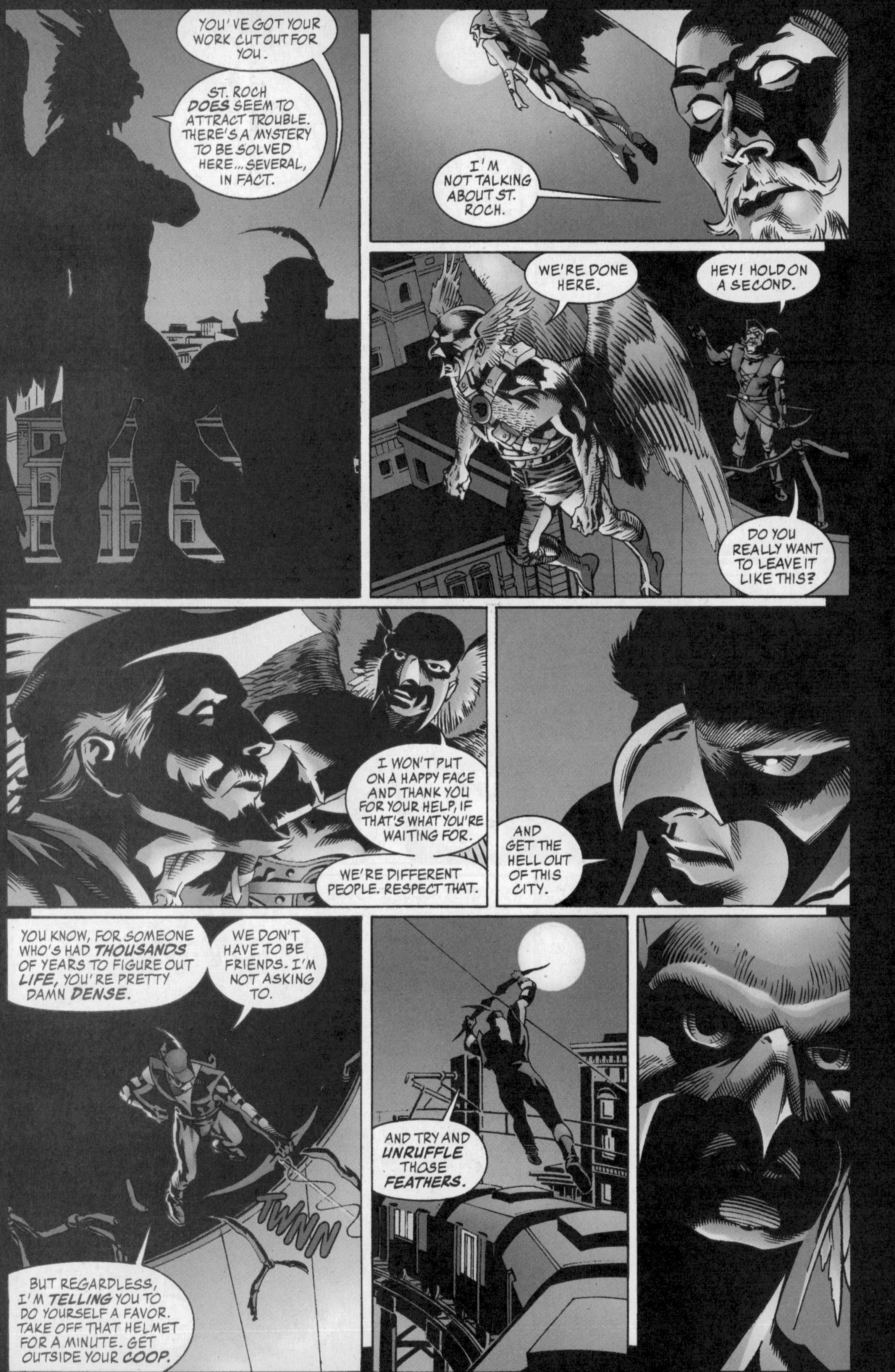
YOU'VE GOT YOUR WORK CUT OUT FOR YOU.
ST. ROCH DOES SEEM TO ATTRACT TROUBLE. THERE'S A MYSTERY TO BE SOLVED HERE...SEVERAL, IN FACT.
I'M NOT TALKING ABOUT ST. ROCH.
WE'RE DONE HERE.
HEY! HOLD ON A SECOND.
DO YOU REALLY WANT TO LEAVE IT LIKE THIS?
I WON'T PUT ON A HAPPY FACE AND THANK YOU FOR YOUR HELP, IF THAT'S WHAT YOU'RE WAITING FOR.
WE'RE DIFFERENT PEOPLE. RESPECT THAT.
AND GET THE HELL OUT OF THIS CITY.
YOU KNOW, FOR SOMEONE WHO'S HAD THOUSANDS OF YEARS TO FIGURE OUT LIFE, YOU'RE PRETTY DAMN DENSE.
WE DON'T HAVE TO BE FRIENDS. I'M NOT ASKING TO.
TWNN
BUT REGARDLESS, I'M TELLING YOU TO DO YOURSELF A FAVOR. TAKE OFF THAT HELMET FOR A MINUTE. GET OUTSIDE YOUR COOP.
AND TRY AND UNRUFFLE THOSE FEATHERS.

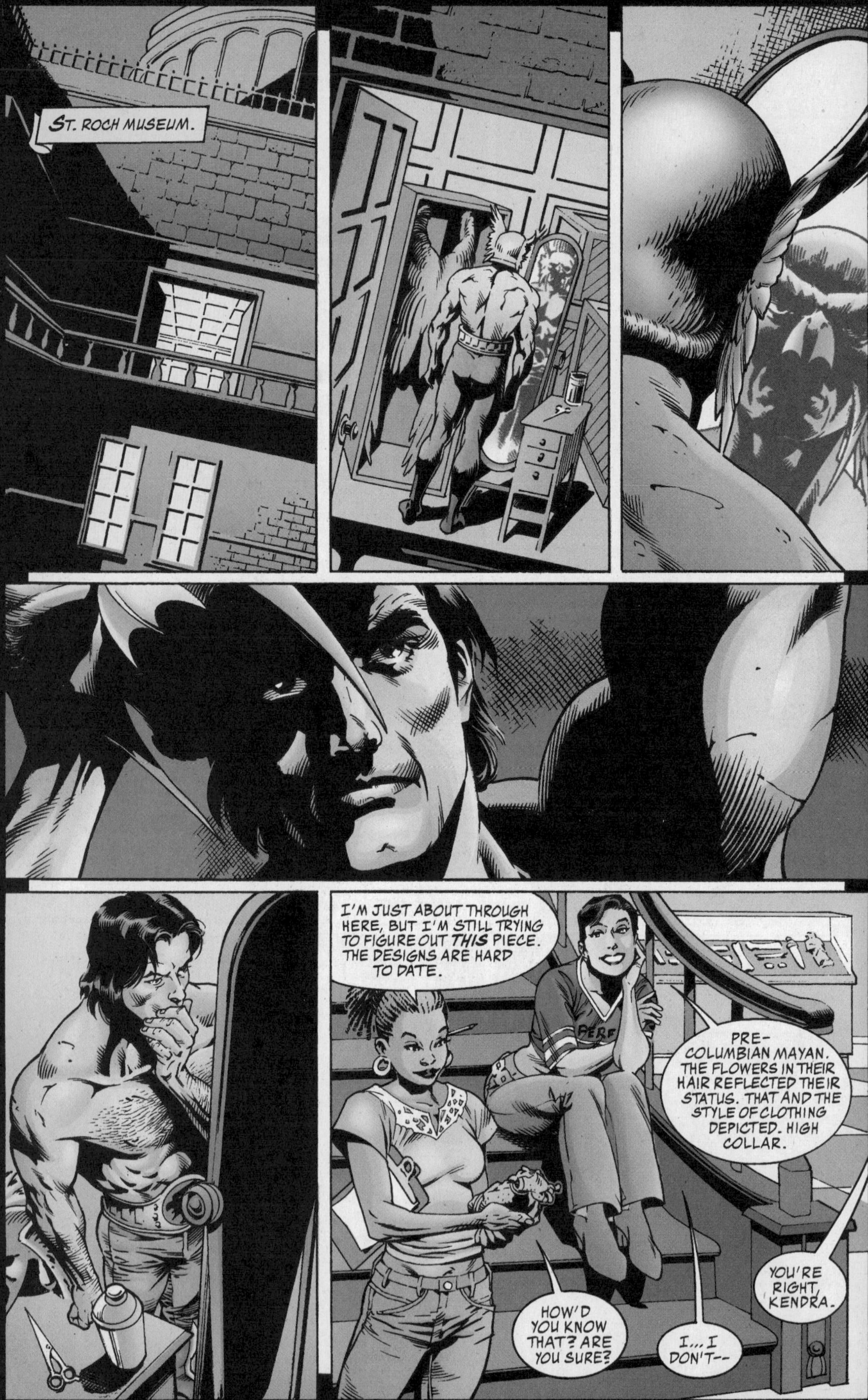
ST. ROCH MUSEUM.
I'M JUST ABOUT THROUGH HERE, BUT I'M STILL TRYING TO FIGURE OUT THIS PIECE. THE DESIGNS ARE HARD TO DATE.
PRE-COLUMBIAN MAYAN. THE FLOWERS IN THEIR HAIR REFLECTED THEIR STATUS. THAT AND THE STYLE OF CLOTHING DEPICTED. HIGH COLLAR.
HOW'D YOU KNOW THAT? ARE YOU SURE?
I... I DON'T--
YOU'RE RIGHT, KENDRA.

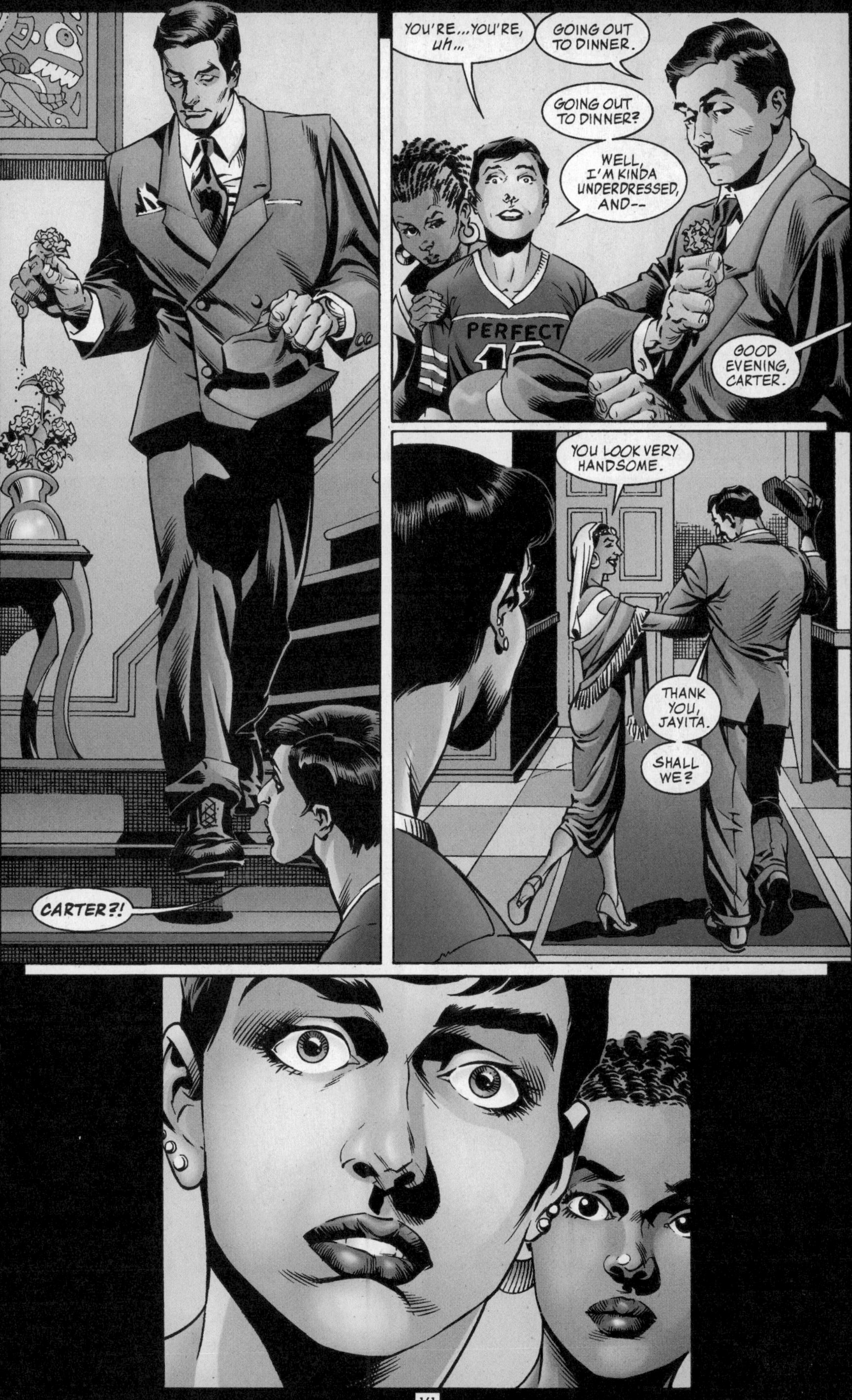
CARTER?!
YOU'RE...YOU'RE, UH...
GOING OUT TO DINNER.
GOING OUT TO DINNER?
WELL, I'M KINDA UNDERDRESSED, AND--
GOOD EVENING, CARTER.
PERFECT
YOU LOOK VERY HANDSOME.
THANK YOU, JAYITA.
SHALL WE?

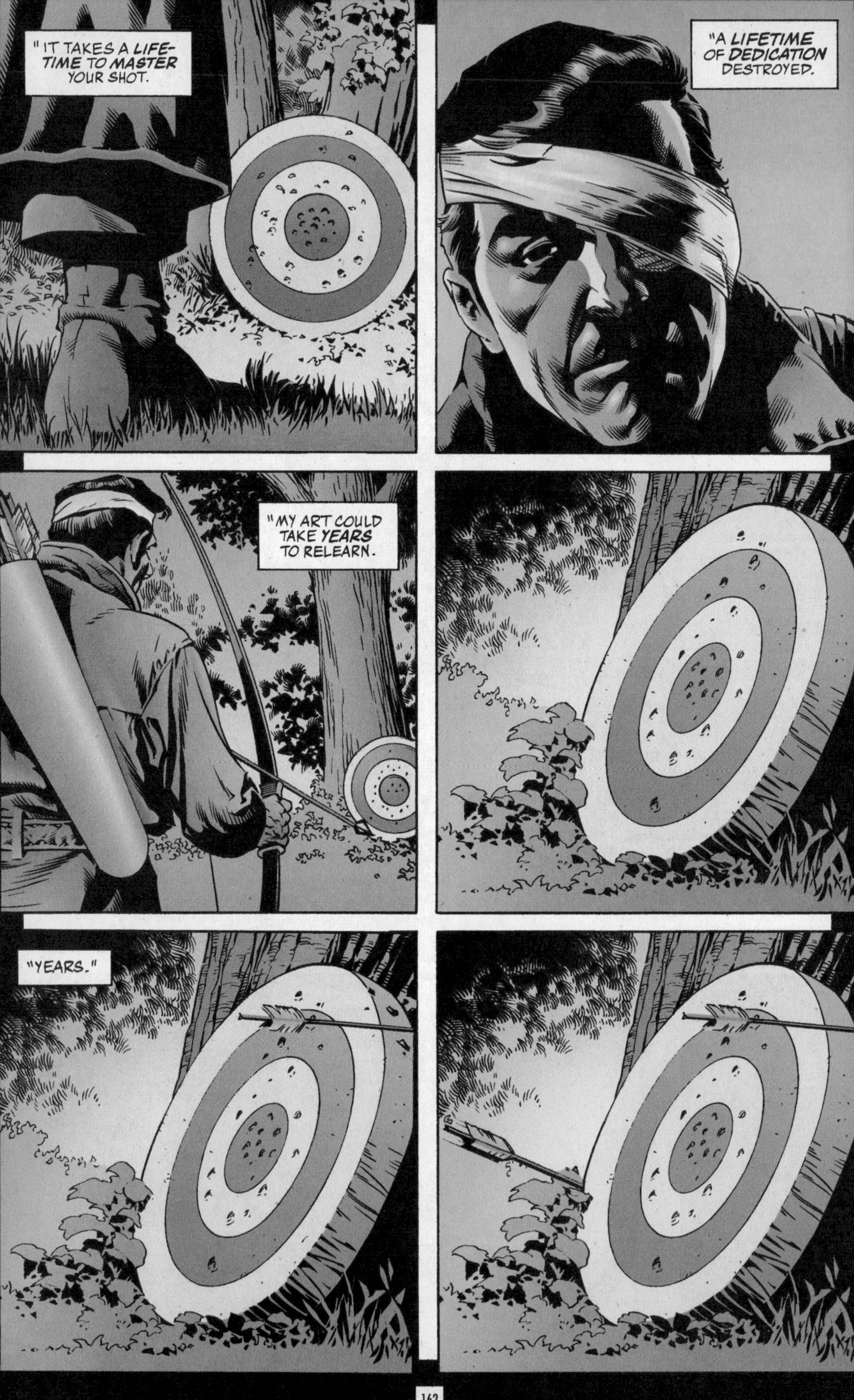

"IT TAKES A LIFETIME TO MASTER YOUR SHOT.
"A LIFETIME OF DEDICATION DESTROYED.
"MY ART COULD TAKE YEARS TO RELEARN.
"YEARS."

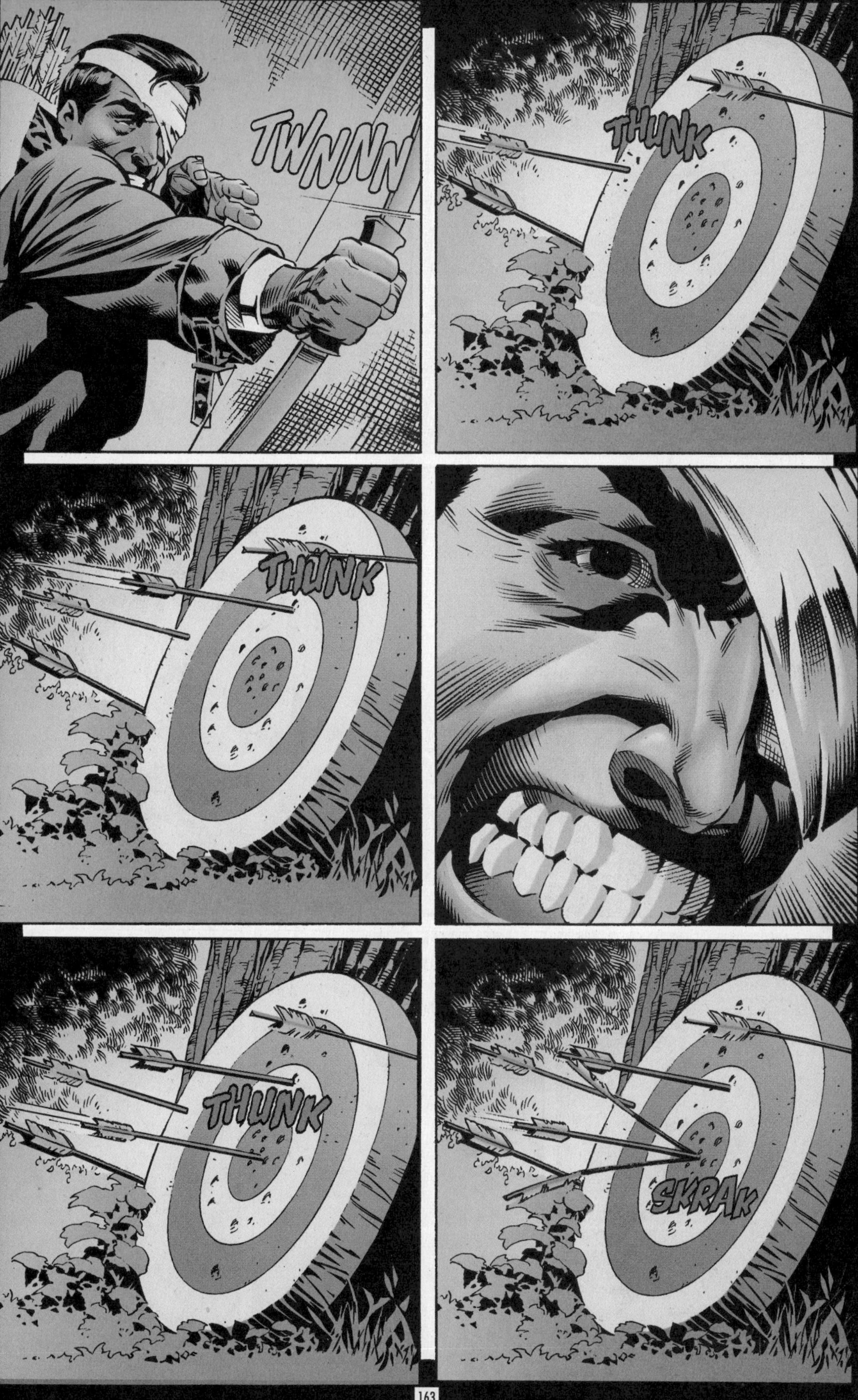
TWNNN
THUNK
THUNK
THUNK
SKRAK

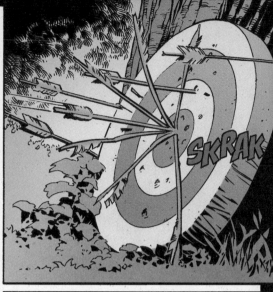

SKRAK

SKRAK

TWNN

FUMP!

END

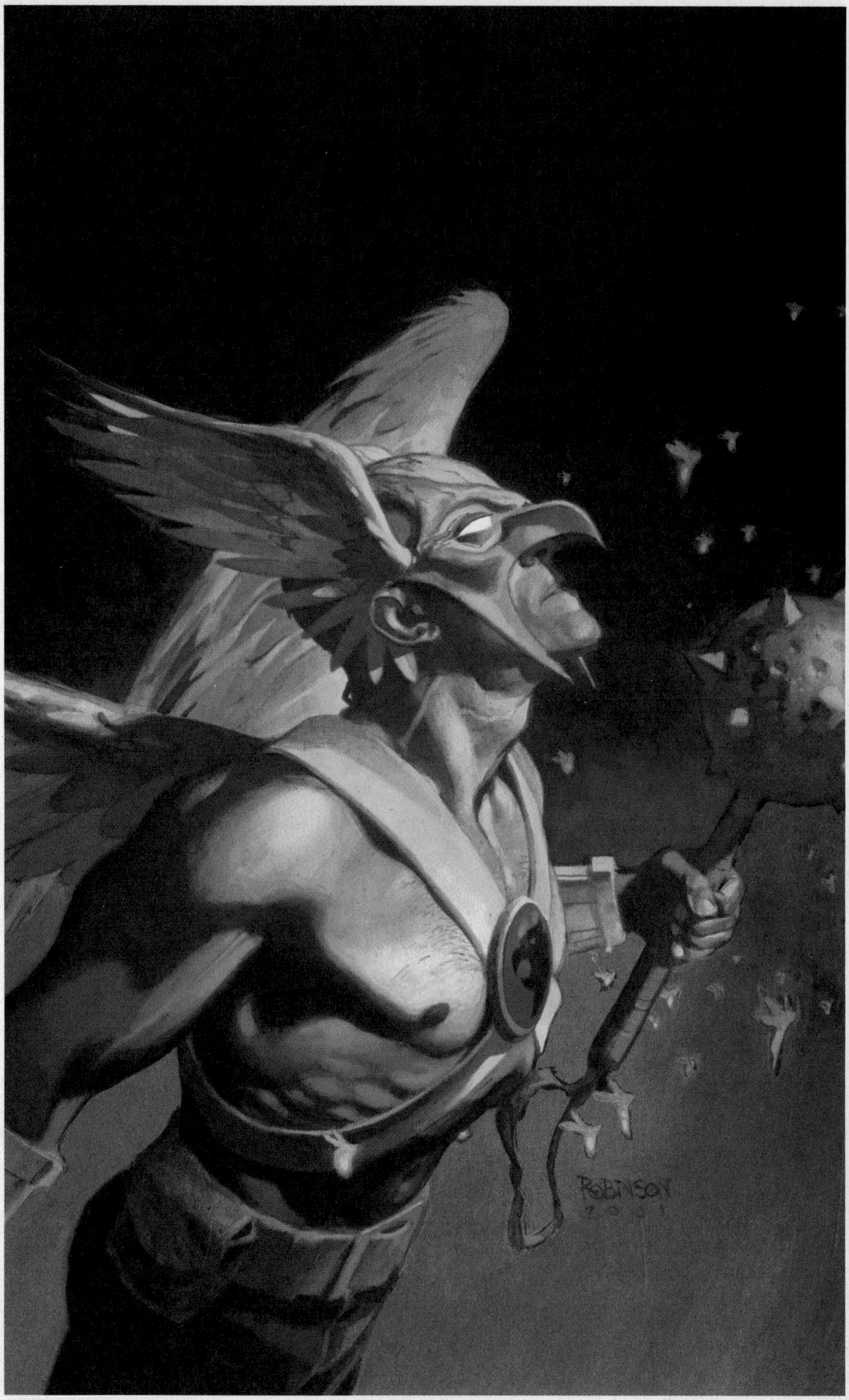
ROBINSON

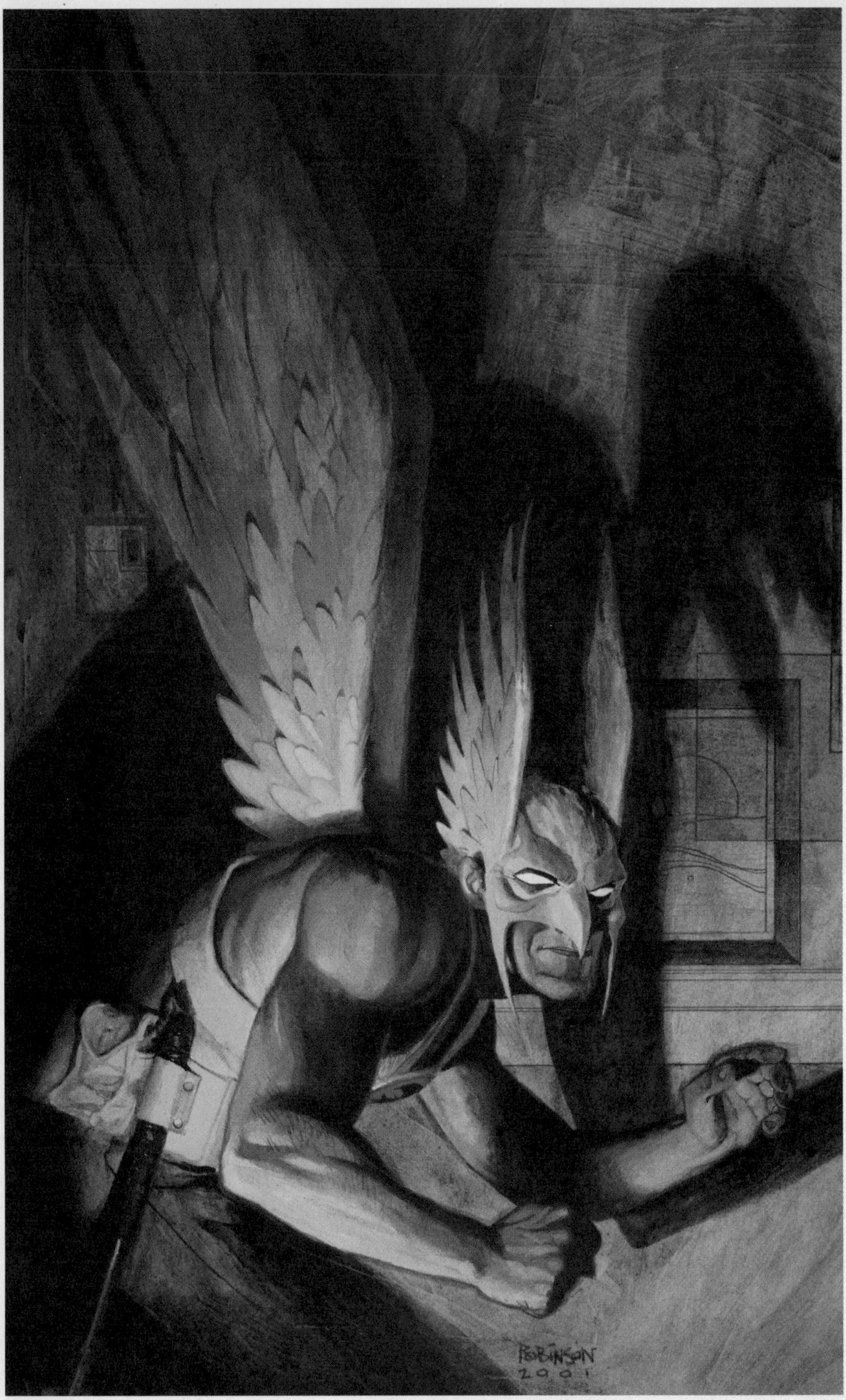
ROBINSON
2001

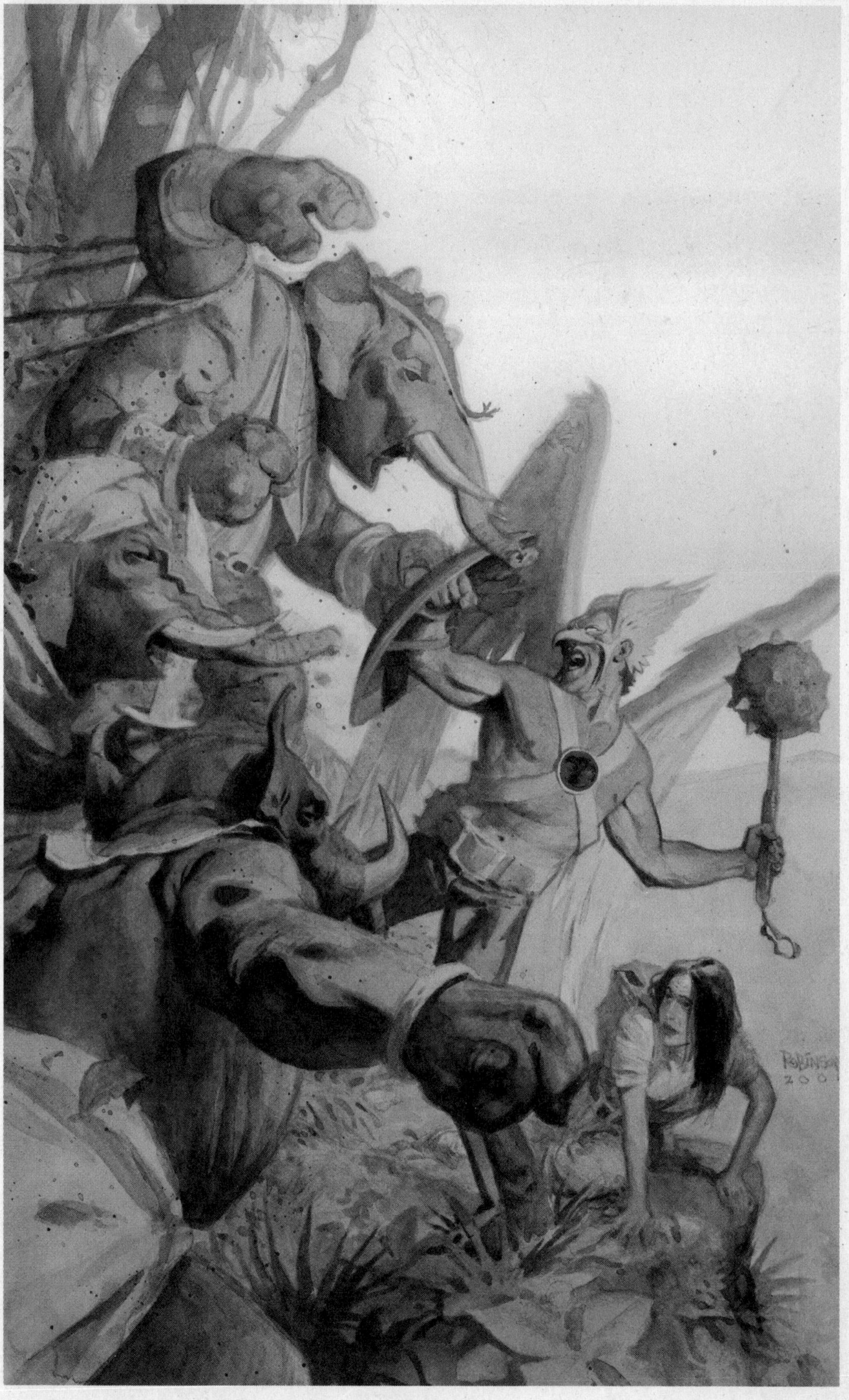

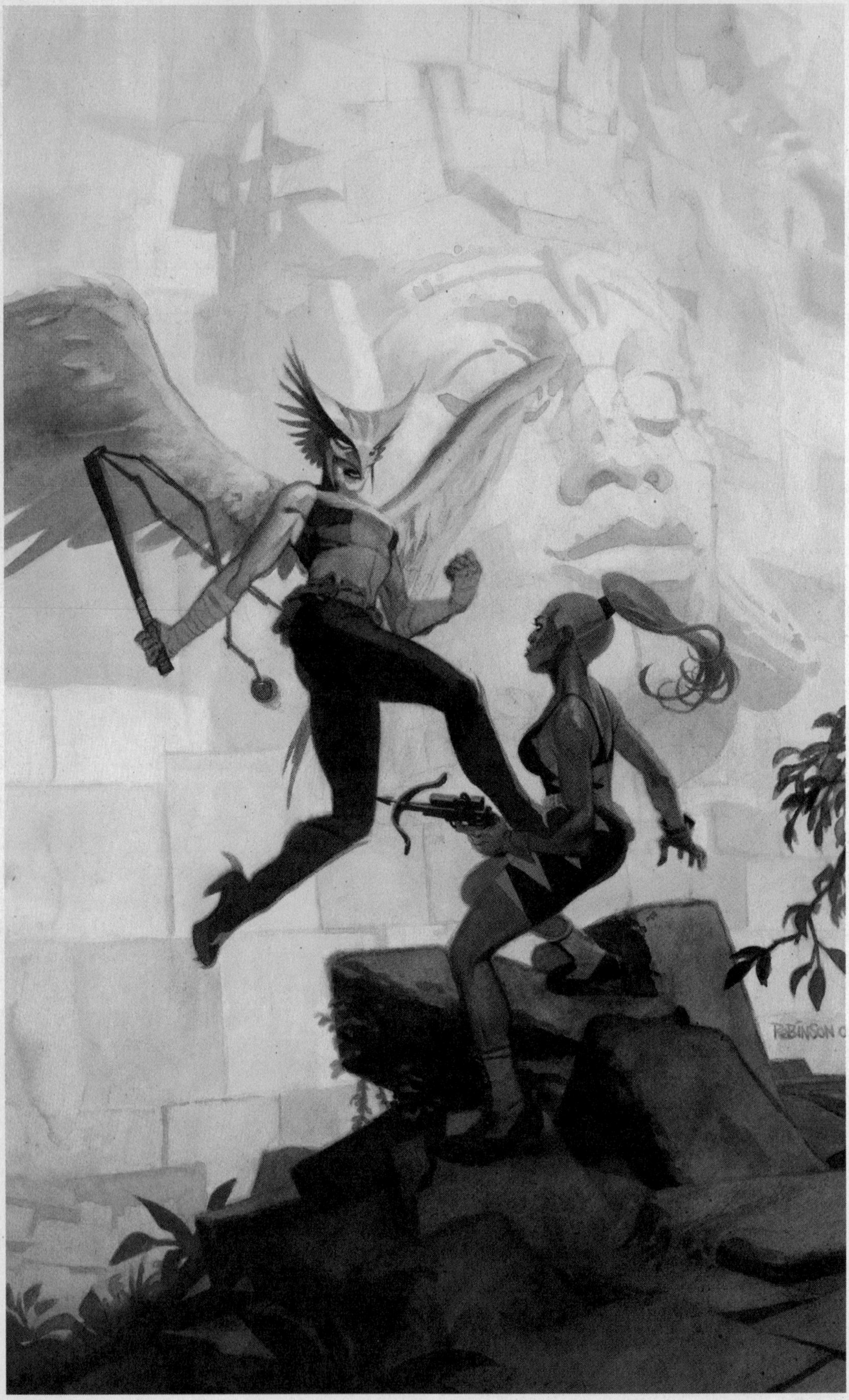
ROBINSON

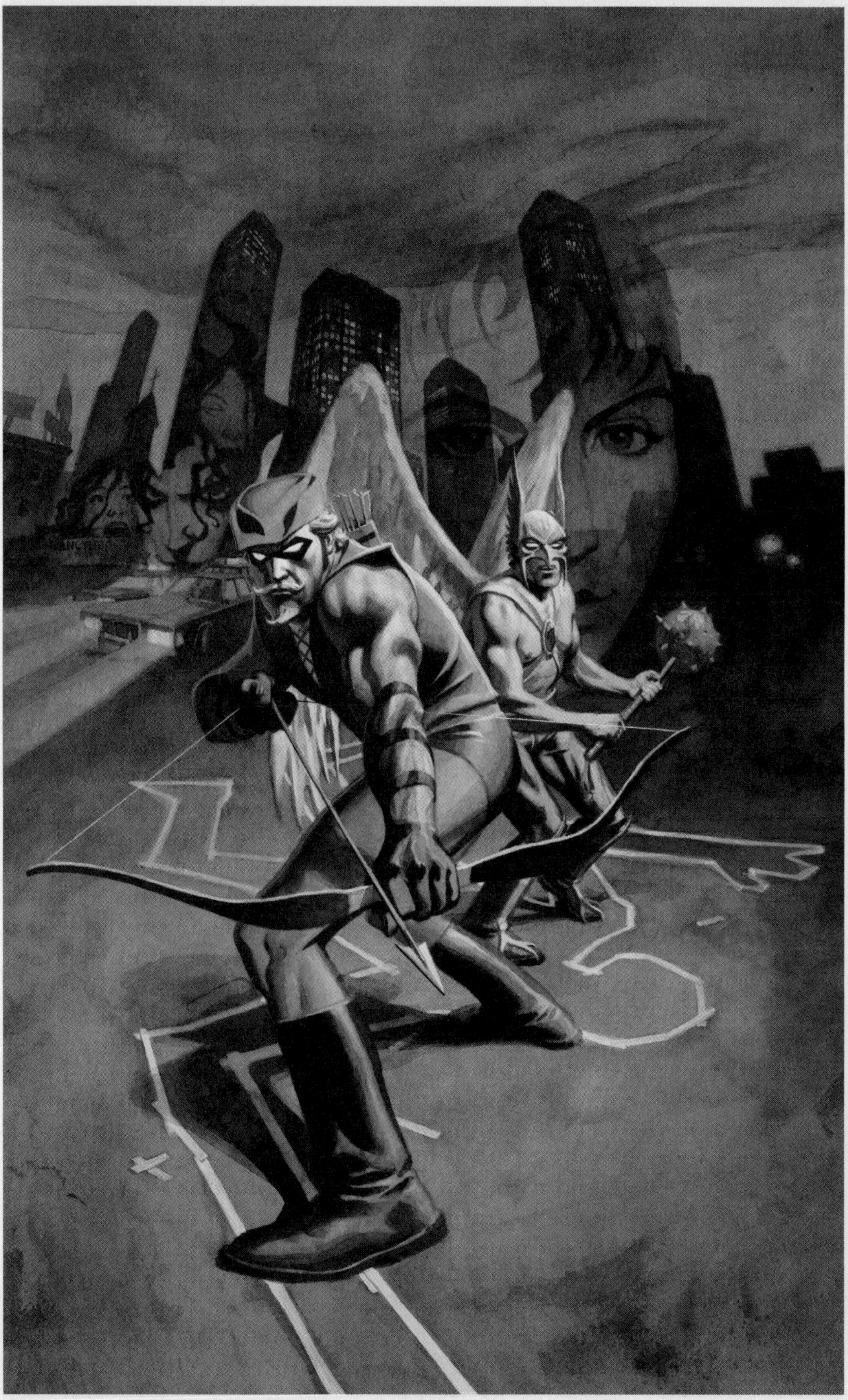

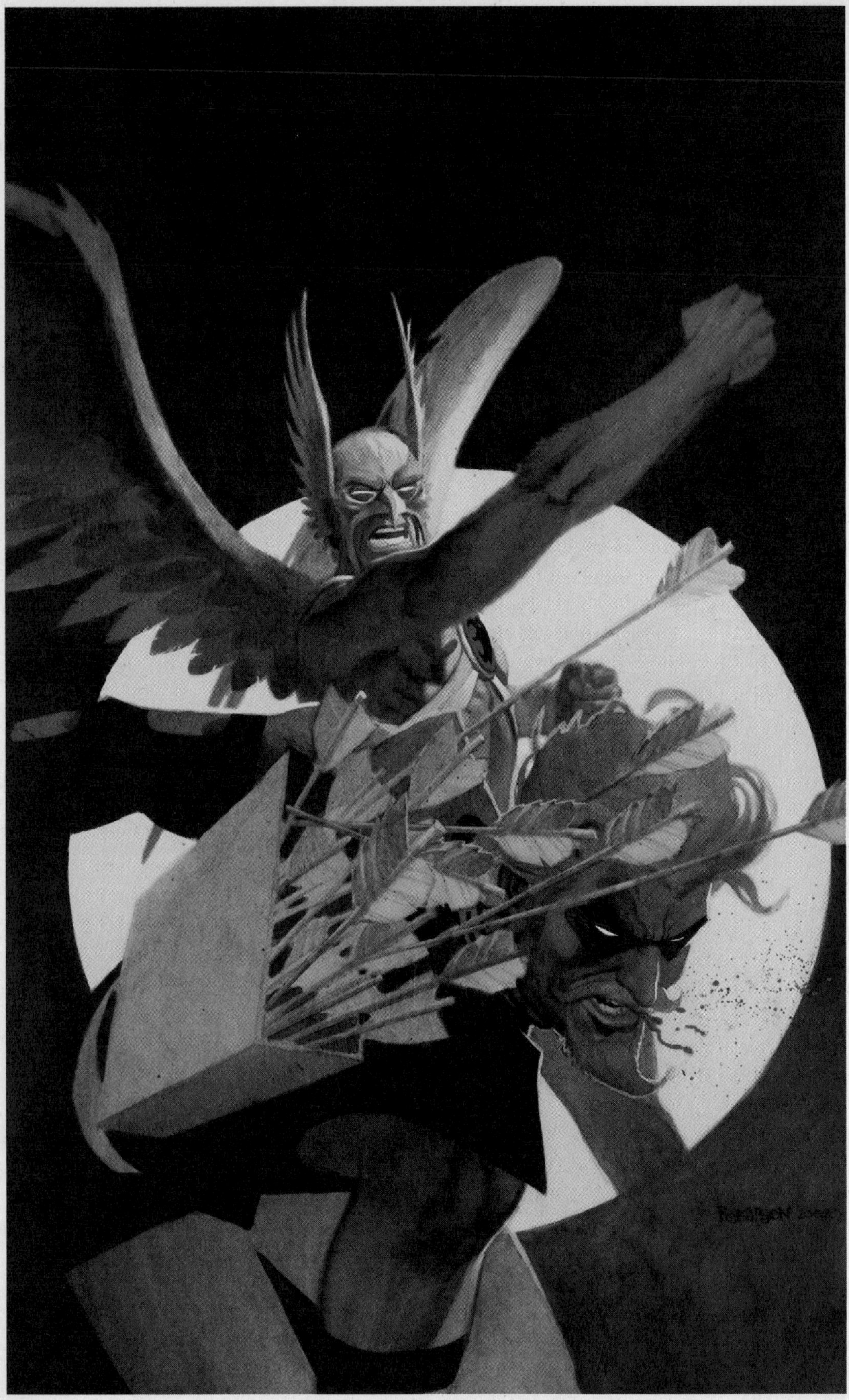

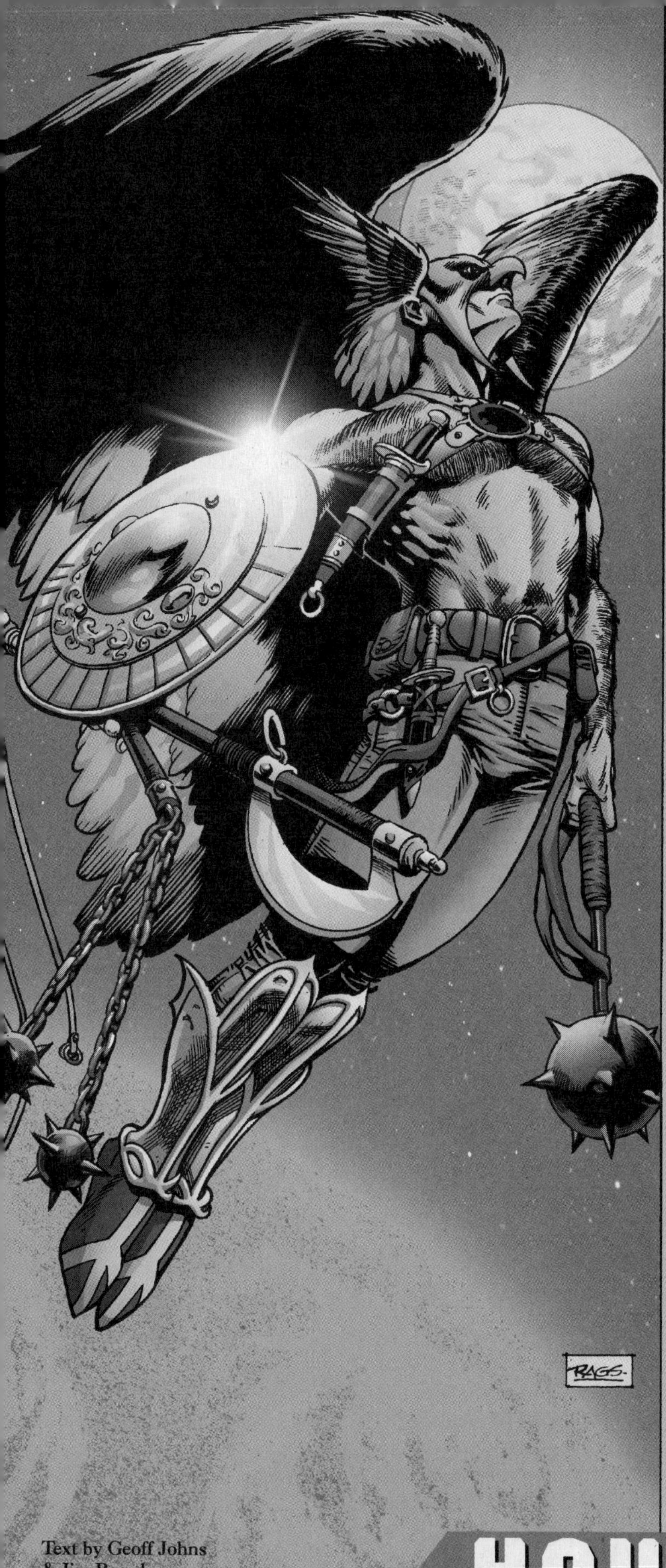
RAGS

Real Name: Carter Hall
Occupation: Adventurer
Base of Operations: St. Roch, Louisiana
Marital Status: Single
Ht: 6' 1"    Wt: 195 lbs.
Eyes: Blue    Hair: Brown
First Appearance: FLASH COMICS #1 (January, 1940)

Hawkman has lived a thousand lives, and in each one has waged a battle against evil. His soul began its journey in Ancient Egypt as Prince Khufu of the 15th Dynasty. Too early in their lives, Khufu and his great love, Chay-Ara, were murdered by a sorcerer named Hath-Set. Due to his exposure to a strange golden element (Thanagarian Nth metal) that he discovered in the wreckage of an alien spacecraft, Khufu and Chay-Ara were reincarnated again and again, each time unaware of their previous lives.

In the 1940s, Khufu lived as Carter Hall. It was here that he first adopted the guise of Hawkman, a founding member of the legendary Justice Society of America. This career continued for decades, until he and his partner Hawkgirl (a reborn Chay-Ara) were swept up in a temporal anomaly and seemingly vanished from existence. Carter's soul answered to a higher calling, and he freed himself from the anomaly, reclaiming his heroic identity as Hawkman. He now possesses the memories of all his previous incarnations.

Hawkman utilizes Nth metal as a component of his wings and boots, which enable him to fly at terrific speeds and with great agility. The metal also allows its user to lift incredible weights and to withstand temperature extremes. The Nth metal has several other properties that Carter has yet to tap into.

Carter Hall is striving to balance his innate warrior's anger with the princely wisdom of his ancient beginnings. He is blinded by his love for Kendra Saunders, the most recent incarnation of his beloved Chay-Ara, and will soon learn the consequences of this blindness.

Text by Geoff Johns
& Jim Beard
Art by Rags Morales

# HAWKMAN

# HAWKGIRL



Real Name: Kendra Saunders
Occupation: Adventurer
Base of Operations: St. Roch, Louisiana
Marital Status: Single
Ht: 5' 6"   Wt: 120 lbs.
Eyes: Green   Hair: Black
First Appearance: JSA SECRET FILES & ORIGINS #1 (August, 1999)

Kendra Saunders is not who she thinks she is. A frightening event in Austin, Texas, led Kendra to attempt suicide, but in the aftermath, her body was inhabited by the soul of an ancient Egyptian princess (who was one of Kendra's ancestors). Mid-life reincarnation is a rare occurrence, and little of Princess Chay-Ara's life and memories have surfaced since the event. This has left Kendra in an even more troubled and unbalanced state.

Plagued by nightmares and reeling from her parents' mysterious and untimely deaths, Kendra left her home in Austin and went to live with her grandfather, Speed Saunders. He began training her for an incredible destiny: to become the new Hawkgirl. Kendra'a trust in her grandfather overcame her initial reluctance to take on the role, and she now wears the wings and raiment of her great-aunt Shiera Sanders, the original Hawkgirl, as her own. Kendra has also joined the latest incarnation of the Justice Society of America.

Recently, a bold new personality has entered Kendra's life in the form of the newly reincarnated Hawkman. Originally Khufu, Chay-Ara's lover in ancient Egypt, Hawkman looks to Kendra for any sign of their fated romance, a romance that has transcended the centuries until now. Hawkman's attentions have confused and angered Kendra, who only desires to sort through her jumbled memories.

Hawkgirl is determined to find and hunt down the person who murdered her parents. The city of St. Roch, Louisiana, has become the starting point for her quest.

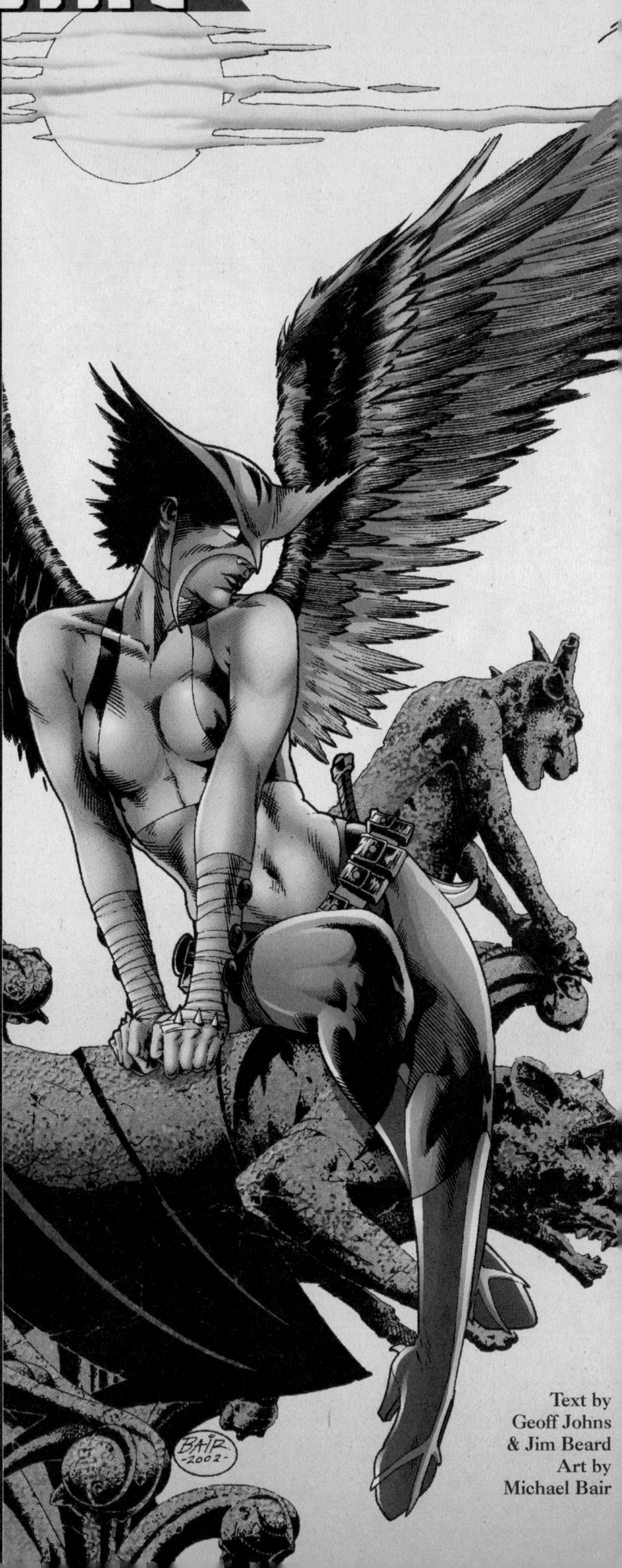
BAIR
2002

Text by
Geoff Johns
& Jim Beard
Art by
Michael Bair

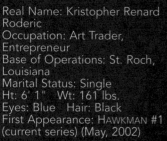

Real Name: Kristopher Renard Roderic
Occupation: Art Trader, Entrepreneur
Base of Operations: St. Roch, Louisiana
Marital Status: Single
Ht: 6' 1"   Wt: 161 lbs.
Eyes: Blue   Hair: Black
First Appearance: HAWKMAN #1 (current series) (May, 2002)

Reclusive and secretive, Kristopher Roderic is one of the world's foremost dealers in art and antiquities. Known for his ruthless acquisition of entire art collections, Roderic is arrogant enough to believe that, given enough time and money, he can claim any historical treasure that he sets his eye on. He has also angered many a museum curator for forever locking beautiful and invaluable works out of public view.

Roderic's exact net worth has not been determined, as it is tied to a multitude of different holdings, many of them illegal. His influence extends internationally, and he maintains many criminal contacts. He also retains numerous covert operatives, all of whom stand ready to accept his money and do his bidding.

Roderic has recently acquired something beyond earthly value: the memories of a previous life as Hath-Set, an ancient Egyptian sorcerer. How and why remains to be seen, as it was thought that Hath-Set inhabited the body of an Egyptian woman named Dr. Helene Astar. Along with these memories, Roderic also gained a deep-rooted hatred for Hawkman and Hawkgirl, the reincarnated souls of royalty from Hath-Set's era. Roderic now knows that he has killed the two in many of their earlier lives, and he has set about reclaiming certain weapons of Hath-Set, with which he intends to murder them again.

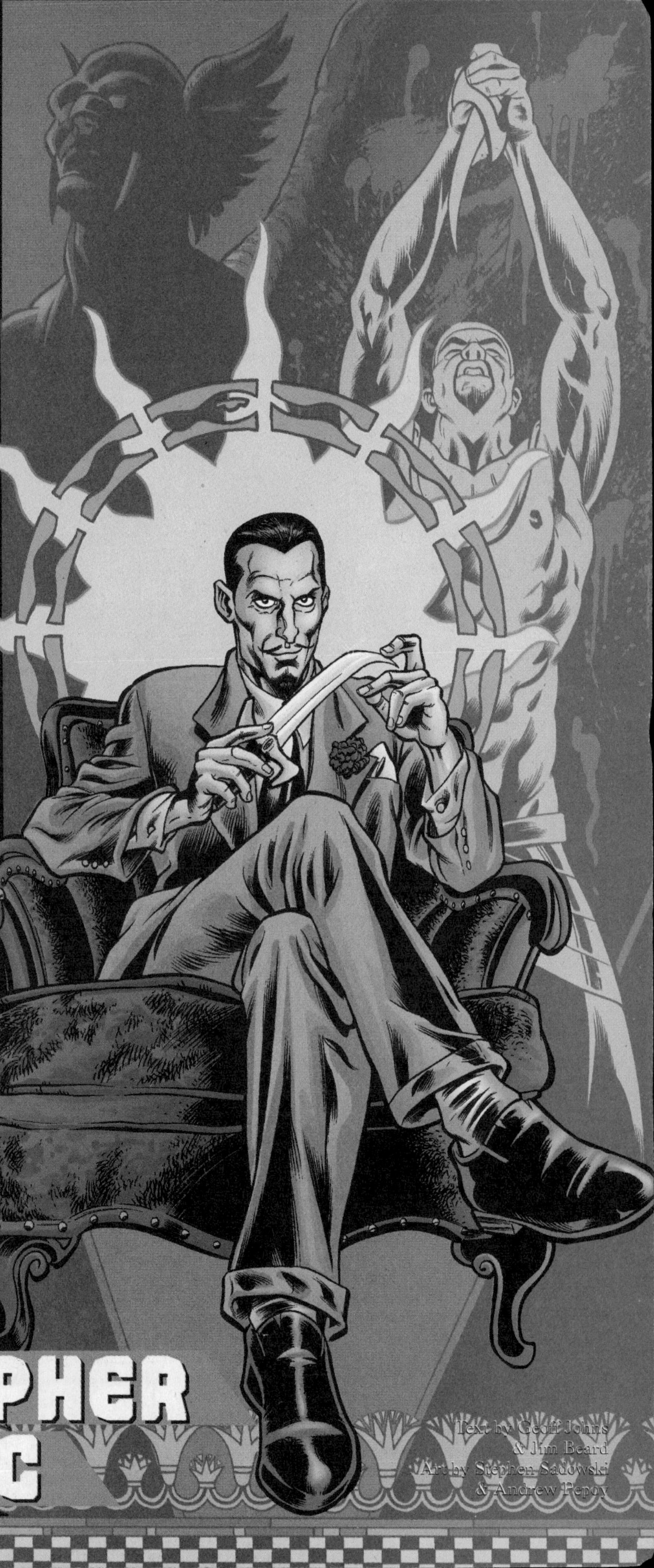

# KRISTOPHER RODERIC

Text by Geoff Johns & Jim Beard
Art by Stephen Sadowski & Andrew Pepoy

# THE STONECHAT MUSEUM

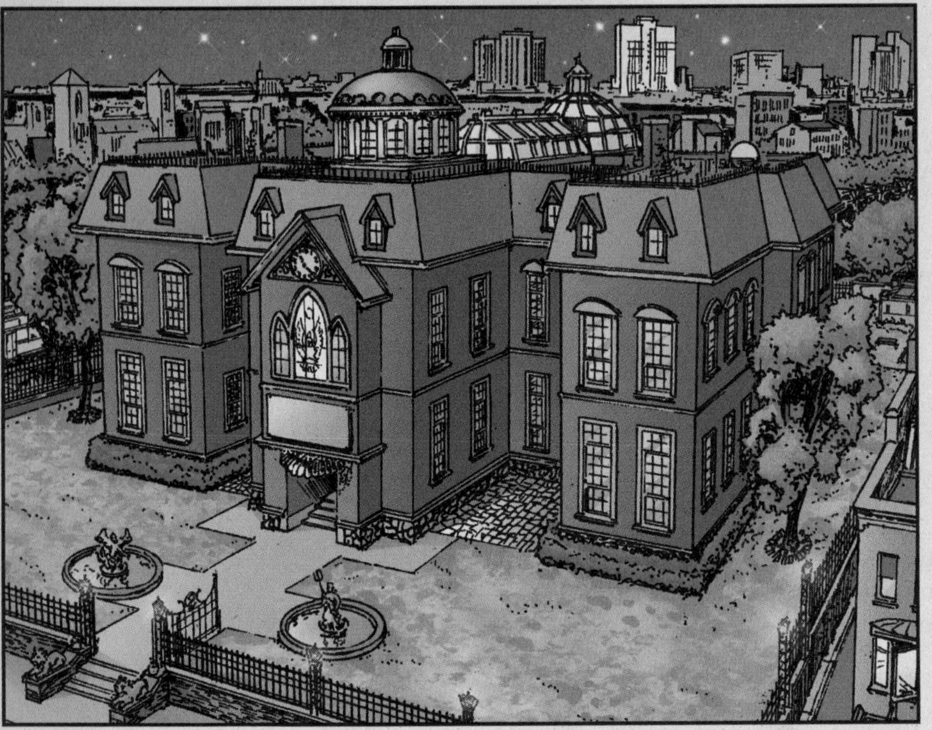

First Appearance:
HAWKMAN #1 (current series) (May, 2002)

The Stonechat Museum of Art & History has seen years of both feast and famine since its founding in 1859 as part of the antebellum expansion of the old city of St. Roch. Originally the Algier Mansion, located in the picturesque Lagnappe District of St. Roch, now it is a state-of-the-art information center and archive. Its primary focus has been Southern American History, but decades of reckless acquisition by past curators have led the Museum's collection down eclectic and spectacular avenues. The culmination of their work is a cornucopia of art and artifacts that has caught the eye and imagination of collectors across the globe.

Stonechat has recently struggled for its very existence, but now that the institution is seemingly under the protection of the heroes known as Hawkman and Hawkgirl, there has been a much more positive atmosphere around the venerable old building. With the heroes now part of the staff, visitor attendance, the lifeblood of any museum, has begun to increase. There are weekly children's hours as well as monthly soirees to encourage familiarity with the museum among the city's people.

**Text by Geoff Johns, Jim Beard and Eliot Brown**
**Art by Eliot Brown**

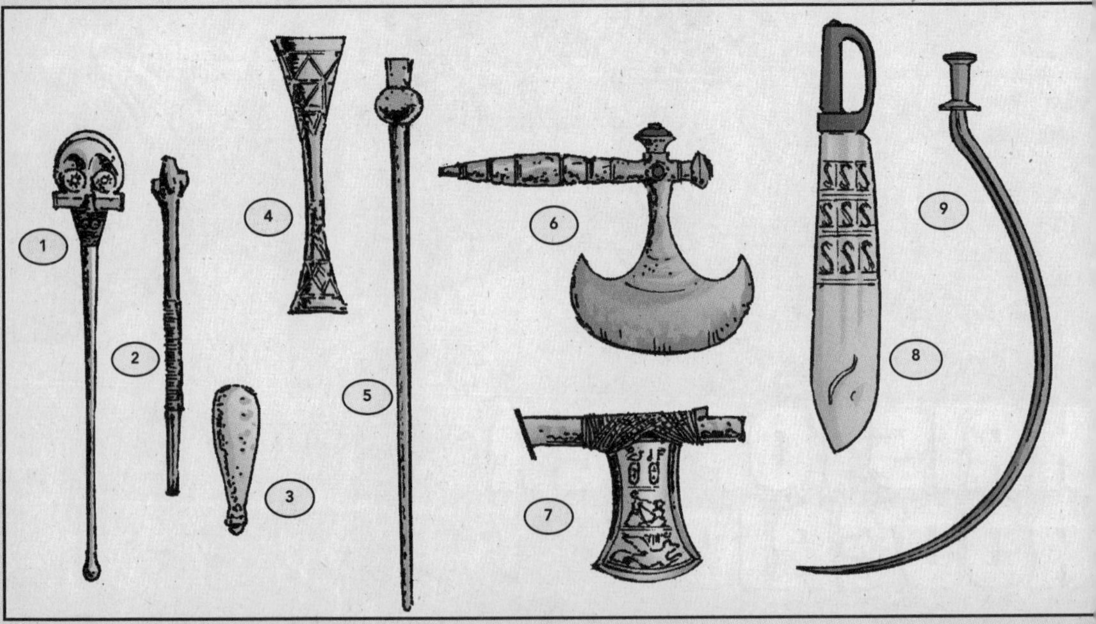
1
2
3
4
5
6
7
8
9

## THE ARMORY
### Second Floor

The Second Floor Grand Salon. Currently showing an overview of the world's hand weapons. Arranged in rough chronological order, from 2,000 B.C. to present day.

## STAFF PORTRAIT

While many museums are defined by their collections, the Stonechat is also defined by its employees (left to right): Research Archaeologist Jayita Andu is one of the world's most promising young experts on the Indian sub-continent. Dr. Oliver Evans has held the position of Museum Director for less than a year but has made an immediate impact on the Stonechat's organization and staff. He brings many years of art and art education experience to the museum. His son, resident field archaeologist Dr. Danny Evans, has toiled for the past ten years to make the museum one of the most distinctive in the world. A graduate student in Art History, Susan Morrison is a passionate young sculptor, so passionate, in fact, that she has placed her own work into the museum displays without the Director's advance knowledge or consent. Fresh out of the St. Roch College of Arts & Sciences, Jeremy Barlow's focus is History and Anthropology — his focus, that is, *when* he can focus, as his eye can be caught and swayed by a new subject, or person, on any given day.

1. Wooden club from Marquesas Islands, Central Pacific.
2. Fijian Wooden club, grass-bound handle.
3. Maori club of jade, called mere or patu pounamou. New Zealand.
4. Guyana wooden club macana, grass-bound handle.
5. Pierced stone fitted over tapering wood shaft. Papua, New Guinea.
6. Bronze ceremonial axe, 750 B.C., Sweden.
7. Ancient Egyptian war-axe in bronze and gold, shows King Ahmose smiting enemy.
8. New Guinea wooden sword, in imitation of visiting sailor's cutlass.
9. Ethiopian Shotel, two-edged double-curved sword to reach around opponent's shield.
10. Indian fighting pick, "crowbill" type, used against chain mail armor.
11. Katar punching dagger from India with bifid blade as sword-catcher.
12. British 1796 Pattern light cavalry saber used in Napoleonic Wars.
13. Spear with bamboo shaft, Dervish, Sudan 1880.
14. Lead "knuckle duster" found on American Civil War battlefield.
15. British Pattern rifled pistol in .577 caliber, with detachable carbine stock, 1856.
16. Colt 1911 Government Automatic in .45 ACP, semi-automatic, detachable 8-round magazine.
17. Vickers Mark I, water-cooled in .303in British, made in 1912, WWII variant shown.

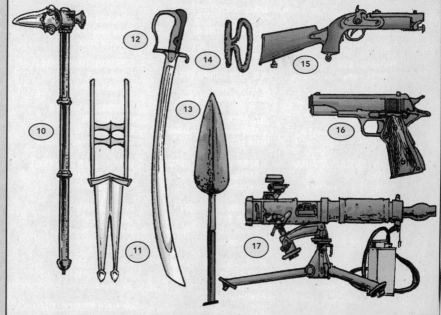

# OF ART & HISTORY

# THE STARS OF THE
# DC UNIVERSE
## CAN ALSO BE FOUND IN THESE BOOKS:

## GRAPHIC NOVELS

**ENEMY ACE: WAR IDYLL**
George Pratt

**THE FLASH: LIFE STORY OF
THE FLASH**
M. Waid/B. Augustyn/G. Kane/
J. Staton/T. Palmer

**GREEN LANTERN: FEAR ITSELF**
Ron Marz/Brad Parker

**THE POWER OF SHAZAM!**
Jerry Ordway

**WONDER WOMAN: AMAZONIA**
William Messner-Loebs/
Phil Winslade

## COLLECTIONS

**THE GREATEST 1950s
STORIES EVER TOLD**
Various writers and artists

**THE GREATEST TEAM-UP
STORIES EVER TOLD**
Various writers and artists

**AQUAMAN: TIME AND TIDE**
Peter David/Kirk Jarvinen/
Brad Vancata

**DC ONE MILLION**
Various writers and artists

**THE FINAL NIGHT**
K. Kesel/S. Immonen/
J. Marzan/various

**THE FLASH: BORN TO RUN**
M. Waid/T. Peyer/G. LaRocque/
J. Ramos/various

**GREEN LANTERN:
NEW DAWN**
R. Marz/D. Banks/R. Tanghal/
various

**GREEN LANTERN: BAPTISM
OF FIRE**
Ron Marz/Darryl Banks/
various

**GREEN LANTERN: EMERALD
LIGHTS**
R. Marz/Darryl Banks/
various

**HAWK & DOVE**
Karl and Barbara Kesel/
Rob Liefeld

**HITMAN**
Garth Ennis/John McCrea

**HITMAN: LOCAL HEROES**
G. Ennis/J. McCrea/
C. Ezquerra/S. Pugh

**HITMAN: TEN THOUSAND
BULLETS**
Garth Ennis/John McCrea

**IMPULSE: RECKLESS YOUTH**
Mark Waid/various

**JACK KIRBY'S FOREVER PEOPLE**
Jack Kirby/various

**JACK KIRBY'S NEW GODS**
Jack Kirby/various

**JACK KIRBY'S MISTER MIRACLE**
Jack Kirby/various

**JUSTICE LEAGUE: A NEW
BEGINNING**
K. Giffen/J.M. DeMatteis/
K. Maguire/various

**JUSTICE LEAGUE:
A MIDSUMMER'S NIGHTMARE**
M. Waid/F. Nicieza/J. Johnson/
D. Robertson/various

**JLA: AMERICAN DREAMS**
G. Morrison/H. Porter/J. Dell/
various

**JLA: JUSTICE FOR ALL**
G. Morrison/M. Waid/H. Porter/
J. Dell/various

**JUSTICE LEAGUE OF AMERICA:
THE NAIL**
Alan Davis/Mark Farmer

**JLA: NEW WORLD ORDER**
Grant Morrison/
Howard Porter/John Dell

**JLA: ROCK OF AGES**
G. Morrison/H. Porter/J. Dell/
various

**JLA: STRENGTH IN NUMBERS**
G. Morrison/M. Waid/H. Porter/
J. Dell/various

**JLA: WORLD WITHOUT
GROWN-UPS**
T. Dezago/T. Nauck/H. Ramos/
M. McKone/various

**JLA/TITANS: THE TECHNIS
IMPERATIVE**
D. Grayson/P. Jimenez/
P. Pelletier/various

**JLA: YEAR ONE**
M. Waid/B. Augustyn/
B. Kitson/various

**KINGDOM COME**
Mark Waid/Alex Ross

**LEGENDS: THE COLLECTED
EDITION**
J. Ostrander/L. Wein/J. Byrne/
K. Kesel

**LOBO'S GREATEST HITS**
Various writers and artists

**LOBO: THE LAST CZARNIAN**
Keith Giffen/Alan Grant/
Simon Bisley

**LOBO'S BACK'S BACK**
K. Giffen/A. Grant/S. Bisley/
C. Alamy

**MANHUNTER: THE SPECIAL
EDITION**
Archie Goodwin/Walter Simonson

**THE RAY: IN A BLAZE OF
POWER**
Jack C. Harris/Joe Quesada/
Art Nichols

**THE SPECTRE: CRIMES AND
PUNISHMENTS**
John Ostrander/Tom Mandrake

**STARMAN: SINS OF THE
FATHER**
James Robinson/Tony Harris/
Wade von Grawbadger

**STARMAN: NIGHT AND DAY**
James Robinson/Tony Harris/
Wade von Grawbadger

**STARMAN: TIMES PAST**
J. Robinson/O. Jimenez/
L. Weeks/various

**STARMAN: A WICKED
INCLINATION...**
J. Robinson/T. Harris/
W. von Grawbadger/various

**UNDERWORLD UNLEASHED**
M. Waid/H. Porter/
P. Jimenez/various

**WONDER WOMAN:
THE CONTEST**
William Messner-Loebs/
Mike Deodato, Jr.

**WONDER WOMAN:
SECOND GENESIS**
John Byrne

**WONDER WOMAN: LIFELINES**
John Byrne

**DC/MARVEL: CROSSOVER
CLASSICS II**
Various writers and artists

**DC VERSUS MARVEL/
MARVEL VERSUS DC**
R. Marz/P. David/D. Jurgens/
C. Castellini/various

**THE AMALGAM AGE
OF COMICS:
THE DC COMICS COLLECTION**
Various writers and artists

**RETURN TO THE AMALGAM
AGE OF COMICS:
THE DC COMICS COLLECTION**
Various writers and artists

## OTHER COLLECTIONS
## OF INTEREST

**CAMELOT 3000**
Mike W. Barr/Brian Bolland/
various

**RONIN**
Frank Miller

**WATCHMEN**
Alan Moore/Dave Gibbons

## ARCHIVE EDITIONS

**THE FLASH ARCHIVES
Volume 1**
(FLASH COMICS 104, SHOWCASE
4, 8, 13, 14, THE FLASH 105-108)
J. Broome/C. Infantino/J. Giella/
various

**THE FLASH ARCHIVES
Volume 2**
(THE FLASH 109-116)
J. Broome/C. Infantino/J. Giella/
various

**GREEN LANTERN ARCHIVES
Volume 1**
(SHOWCASE 22-23,
GREEN LANTERN 1-5)

**GREEN LANTERN ARCHIVES
Volume 2**
(GREEN LANTERN 6-13)
All by J. Broome/G. Kane/
J. Giella/various

**SHAZAM ARCHIVES Volume 1**
(WHIZ COMICS 2-15)

**SHAZAM ARCHIVES Volume 2**
(SPECIAL EDITION COMICS 1,
CAPTAIN MARVEL ADVENTURES 1,
WHIZ COMICS 15-20)
All by B. Parker/C.C. Beck/
J. Simon/J. Kirby/various

**THE NEW TEEN TITANS
Volume 1**
(DC COMICS PRESENTS 26,
THE NEW TITANS 1-8)
Marv Wolfman/George Pérez/
various

**TO FIND MORE COLLECTED EDITIONS AND MONTHLY COMIC BOOKS FROM DC COMICS,
CALL 1-888-COMIC BOOK FOR THE NEAREST COMICS SHOP OR GO TO YOUR LOCAL BOOK STORE.**

Visit us at www.dccomics.com

DCU0011